Taxing Choices

Taxing Choices
The Politics of Tax Reform

Timothy J. Conlan
George Mason University

Margaret T. Wrightson
Georgetown University

David R. Beam
Illinois Institute of Technology

CQ
PRESS

A Division of Congressional Quarterly Inc.
1414 22nd Street, N.W., Washington, D.C. 20037

Printed in the United States of America

Library of Congress Cataloging-in-Publication Data

Conlan, Timothy J.
    Taxing choices : the politics of tax reform / Timothy J. Conlan, Margaret T. Wrightson, David R. Beam.
        p. cm.
    ISBN 0-87187-480-6
    1. United States. Tax Reform Act of 1986. 2. Taxation--Law and legislation--United States. 3. Income tax--Law and legislation--United States. 4. Legislation--United States. I. Wrightson, Margaret Tucker, 1950- . II. Beam, David R. III. Title.
KF6276.558.A16C66   1989
343.7304--dc20
[347.3034]   89-17353
                                                                      CIP

For Our Children

Robert

Catherine

Scott

and

Elizabeth

Contents

Tables and Figures

TABLES

FIGURES

Preface

When we began work on this study in the summer of 1986, we had three different goals and audiences in mind. First, as instructors of courses in the legislative process, public policy, and American government, we wanted to enliven and inform textbook descriptions of the congressional process and public policy making with a case study detailing the passage of a particular bill. The struggle to pass the Tax Reform Act of 1986 (TRA) seemed attractive because it raised significant political, economic, and theoretical issues; involved most of the key actors and institutions in the political process; and addressed a problem that students, and everyone else, could readily identify with. From our own involvement in the TRA, we knew that the tax-reform story dramatically conveyed the dynamics of the legislative process. (At the time this project was initiated, Margaret Wrightson and Timothy Conlan were the staff director and assistant staff director respectively of the Senate Subcommittee on Intergovernmental Relations, from which vantage point they participated in Finance Committee and Senate floor deliberations over intergovernmental aspects of H.R. 3838.)

Our second goal was to focus the attention of policy analysts in academia and government—as well as political scientists, economists, and other informed observers—on important but frequently overlooked aspects of the policy process. We believe that a good case study must do more than tell an engaging story: it should inform and instruct the reader about the nature and dynamics of the governmental process. As staff members of the U.S. Advisory Commission on Intergovernmental Relations, all three of us had studied the political evolution of federal legislation in such diverse fields as education, environmental protection, civil rights, public assistance, and government management. These studies, together with our subsequent research, suggested that conventional interpretations of the policy process too often neglected the consequences of recent institutional changes in Congress, in party politics, and in the techniques of political communication and coalition building. In particular, we noted the often surprising ability of individual congressional entrepreneurs to initiate and shape key policies. From prior studies of environmental politics, we recognized that under certain circumstances divided party government could promote as well as hinder legislative enactments. Finally, we had seen that ideas as well as interests could have a powerful independent influence on policy making, both in the form of compelling, professionally tailored policy prescriptions and in the guise of vague but emotionally charged policy symbols. On both first impression and detailed investigation, we found each of these themes in the tax-reform story. Consequently, the TRA was an ideal vehicle to illuminate what we call the "new politics of reform."

Third, in undertaking this task, we hoped to satisfy the need among legal, historical, economic, and political scholars for an accurate and balanced treatment of the development and passage of the Tax Reform Act itself. In so doing, we enjoyed excellent cooperation from decision makers, congressional and executive branch staff, and outside lobbyists and experts who helped develop and shape the legislation. In all, we were able to gain interviews and assistance from more than seventy participants, including James Baker III, Steve Bailey, Stephanie Becker, Rick Belas, Sen. Bill Bradley, Dave Brockway, Don Carlson, George Carlson, Buck Chapoton, John Colvin, Ray Conkling, Mitch Daniels, Thomas Dawson, Gina Despres, Douglas Dillon, Joe Dowley, Rep. Tom Downey, Amy Dunbar, Rep. John Duncan, Sen. Dave Durenberger, Tom Dwyer, Mike Evans, Rep. Bill Frenzel, Joe Gale, Harvey Galper, Rep. Dick Gephardt, Pete Glavas, Rep. Bill Gradison, Ed Greelegs, Ben Hartley, Ted Hester, Manuel Johnson, Rep. Jim Jones, Ken Kies, Rob Leonard, Rep. Robert Matsui, Mary McAuliffe, Rep. Ray McGrath, Charles McLure, Roger Mentz, Joe Minarik, Sen. George Mitchell, Sen. Pat Moynihan, Speaker Tip O'Neill, Sen. Bob Packwood, Ron Pearlman, Rep. Don Pease, Jim Perkins, Karen Phillips, Alexander Polinsky, Rep. Charles Rangel, Mary Beth Riordan, Rep. Dan Rostenkowski, Bob Rozen, Rep. Marty Russo, John Scheiner, Bernie Schmidt, Beryl Sprinkel, Gene Steuerle, Flora Sullivan, Frank Toohey, Randy Weiss, Bill Wilkins, and Anne Zeppenfeld. To each we owe a considerable debt.

Our joint effort on this volume demonstrates the truth of the maxim of triple authorship, that "three heads are better than one." Despite the tensions that inevitably accompany collaboration on a complex and lengthy project, the result is a much better developed study than any of us could or would have produced alone. Nearly every chapter reflects the expertise, skill, and effort of at least two, and more often three, writers.

This project was conceived and planned by Timothy Conlan, who also assumed responsibility for the book's organization and publication arrangements. Margaret Wrightson was involved from a very early stage, and she and Conlan together conducted the interviews and wrote the narrative based upon them that appears in Chapters 3 through 8. Although it is difficult to distinguish their contributions, Conlan was the main researcher and initial author of the chapters on the administration and the House of Representatives and Wrightson on the Senate and the conference committee. David Beam contributed many of the themes that are prominent in our conclusion—which was a joint effort by all three authors—as well as the text of Chapter 2 and major portions of Chapter 1.

We would like to acknowledge the helpful comments of those who read all or part of the manuscript, including John Colvin, Gina Despres, Barbara Ferman, Rob Leonard, Jane Mansbridge, Walt Oleszek, Ron Pearlman, Alexander Polinsky, Paul Quirk, Bob Rozen, Irene Rubin, Jim Verdier, Joe White, Aaron Wildavsky, and John Witte. We are especially indebted to several individuals who provided detailed commentaries on all or several chapters, including R. Douglas Arnold, Charles McLure, Joe Minarik, Gene Steuerle, John Tierney, and an anonymous reviewer for CQ Press. We are deeply grateful to Michael Thomas, who conducted several of the interviews that contributed to Chapter 3, and to Elliot Rosen, who made many of the resources of *Tax Notes* available to us. Lynn Schwalje and Declan Cashman transcribed many of the interviews we conducted, and Lynn Schwalje also compiled our index. We would also like to thank two graduate assistants at Georgetown University, Greg Birkenstock and Ben Everidge, for their assistance in data collection and analysis.

Finally, we are grateful to the fine staff at CQ Press for their helpful and professional assistance at every step along the way. Special thanks go to Joanne Daniels, who endorsed this project so enthusiastically; to Nancy Lammers, who managed the process of editing and producing the book; to Janet Schilling, who edited the manuscript; and to Ann O'Malley, who skillfully handled the numerous production tasks. This book is dedicated to our families, who found the many days, evenings, and weekends to be as "taxing" as the authors did.

Timothy J. Conlan
George Mason University

Margaret T. Wrightson
Georgetown University

David R. Beam
Illinois Institute of Technology

1   Introducing a New Order: The Tax Reform Act of 1986

There is nothing more difficult to take in hand, more perilous to conduct, or more uncertain of success, than to take the lead in the introduction of a new order of things.

—Machiavelli, *The Prince*

"I feel like we've just played the World Series of tax reform—and the American people won." So declared President Ronald Reagan on Wednesday, October 22, 1986, as he signed into law the principal domestic initiative of his second term.[1] He went on to describe the new tax act as "the best antipoverty bill, the best profamily measure, and the best job-creation program to come out of the Congress" as well as a "sweeping victory for fairness" that would "take us into a future of technological invention and economic achievement" and "keep America competitive and growing into the 21st century."

In truth, P.L. 99-514, the Tax Reform Act of 1986 (TRA), may not have warranted all the accolades the president heaped upon it. Many commentators were more reserved. For example, economist Henry J. Aaron later warned that, although the TRA was an "important improvement," it was *not* a real "revolution" in policy (as the president had stated), did *not* inaugurate a new era of tax simplicity, did *not* launch the economy into a new era of growth, and did *not* "purge the tax system of distortions or illogic." Some critics, like Chevron's chief executive George M. Keller, even branded it "tax *de*form . . . a terrible step backwards."[2]

Yet all observers agree that something remarkable happened in 1986. No previous income-tax statute approached the TRA in scope or depth. The 900-page document altered most provisions of U.S. tax law, creating what is now rightly named the Internal Revenue Code of 1986.

Especially in political terms, the TRA was little less than a modern miracle. The cause of tax reform has long been viewed as the most quixotic of political quests. Although there was dissatisfaction with many aspects of the tax system—among experts inside and outside government, among the public, and, indeed, within the halls of Congress—few policy makers wished to undertake the Herculean task of devising an alternative system and gaining consensus behind it. This was true even for many who became the cause's principal proponents: in this drama, even good guys wore gray hats.

Thus, at its inception, tax reform was the unlikeliest of long shots; at

1

several interim points, it appeared to be the deadest of ducks. Nonetheless, the TRA rose from the grave to which press accounts, informed observers, and the participants themselves repeatedly consigned it. Over a twenty-three-month period (beginning in November 1984 with the Treasury Department's utopian draft proposal, dubbed Treasury I), the "immovable" became the "unstoppable" in the words of Sen. Robert Packwood, R-Ore. Initially reluctant leaders in both the House and Senate pressed comprehensive tax reform forward against implacable foes to the muffled cheers of a largely indifferent public. Hearts and minds were changed as key legislators turned their backs on organized political constituents and historic personal commitments to embrace a new cause.

The legislation that they adopted altered so many provisions of the U.S. tax code as to stagger the imagination and vocabulary. As one leading accounting firm later cautioned its clients: "Describing [the TRA] and suggesting ways to tackle and master its stunning breadth and depth are tasks that will challenge the taxpayer and tax adviser. The legislation begs for superlatives and epithets. . . . The magnitude of change cannot be overstated." [3]

Nonetheless, the statute's major provisions (as summarized in Table 1−1) created not a patchwork but a tapestry. Underlying Congress's actions is a new tax philosophy—or at least an intermeshing of several clear philosophical thrusts. Although America's traditional tax values and practices were not wholly discarded, the TRA was greatly influenced by more recent theories and goals, especially the "flat tax" archetype: a low, single-rate tax on all income. As adopted, tax reform departed from that Platonic ideal but nonetheless approached it with fewer brackets, lower rates, and a broader base of taxable income. It also reversed a post−World War II trend by increasing the share of taxes borne by private corporations.

Fewer Brackets.   Under the TRA, the number of tax brackets (which had ranged from 11 percent to 50 percent) was reduced from fifteen in 1986 to five in 1987 (a transition year) and then down to just two (15 percent and 28 percent) in 1988 and thereafter.[4] The TRA marked a near abandonment of the graduated rate structure that had characterized the income-tax system from its inception in 1913. No longer did "the rich" face sharply higher tax rates than did the bulk of the middle and upper middle class. On the corporate side as well, the number of rate brackets was reduced from five to three.

To the president, this change was one of the TRA's proudest features. On signing it into law, he warned that "the steeply progressive nature" of the income tax had "struck at the heart of the economic life of the individual, punishing the special effort and extra hard work that had always been the driving force of our economy." Such "oppressive" taxation, he added, could never have been imagined by the Founding

Fathers, as it violated the "freedom of expression" of the economic entrepreneur, who deserves protection from government quite as much as writers and speakers.

In truth, tax progressivity was abandoned more in principle than in practice. The TRA was designed to be "distributionally neutral" among income groups and, according to some studies, it actually shifted some of the tax burden from lower- and middle- to upper-income taxpayers.[5] Because various breaks, incentives, and loopholes had eroded the base of taxable income, few well-to-do individuals had actually paid taxes at the highest legislated rate, which stood as high as 70 to 91 percent during the 1960s and 1970s. The TRA also benefited low-income people because a rise in the standard deduction and personal exemption, as well as liberalization of the earned income tax credit, removed some six million poor from the tax rolls. Nonetheless, the 1986 TRA marked a historic change in U.S. policy by taxing families with incomes of $300,000 at the same marginal rate as those receiving one-tenth that amount.

Lower Rates. Replacing the idol of structural progressivity was a new economic deity: lower rates. Washington's policy makers danced the tax-reform limbo—"How low can you go?"—as they jettisoned a variety of prior economic and social objectives. Top "marginal" rates—that is, the amount owed to government for each additional dollar a taxpayer earns—were cut from a maximum of 50 percent in 1986 to 28 percent at the top of the income scale, down from 70 percent when Ronald Reagan took office in 1981. Corporate tax rates were reduced as well, with the maximum falling from 46 percent to 34 percent. Though not originally designed to be a tax cut, the TRA was expected to produce somewhat lower personal tax bills for about two-thirds of all individual taxpayers.

Again, the president saluted these accomplishments. With the new act, he boasted, "America will have the lowest marginal rates . . . among the major industrialized nations." Indeed, top rates abroad ranged from 56 percent in West Germany to 70 percent in Japan. The new top American rate was actually lower than the minimum rate of 29 percent in Britain.[6]

A Broader Base. Tax reform also "broadened the base" by eliminating many of the exemptions, credits, and deductions that had traditionally marked tax policy, while reducing or limiting still more. As Table 1−1 shows, these included provisions of interest to many "average" citizens, like deductions for consumer interest, state sales taxes, individual retirement accounts (IRAs), medical expenses, and two-earner families. Others, like the favorable tax treatment of capital gains and the investment tax credit (ITC), had principally benefited business or the well-to-do. Only a few personal deductions and exemptions—including those for state and local income and property taxes, home mortgage interest on a primary residence, and employer-provided fringe benefits—emerged unscathed by

Table 1—1   Key Provisions of the Tax Reform Act of 1986

The 1986 TRA:

Reduced

the number of individual tax rate brackets from fourteen to two

individual tax rates from a maximum marginal rate of 50% to 28%

corporate income taxes from a maximum rate of 34% from 46%, with lower brackets at 15% and 25%

Increased

the standard deduction (or old "zero bracket" amount) from $2,480 to $3,000 for single taxpayers and from $3,670 to $5,000 for married couples

personal and dependency exemptions from $1,080 to $2,000 in 1989 and after

and liberalized the earned income tax credit for low-income families with children

taxes on unearned income in excess of $1,000 by children under age 14 by applying the parents' top rate

the alternative individual minimum tax (AMT) by adding preference and adjustment items and raising the rate to 21%

corporate minimum taxes by creating an alternative minimum tax of 20%, with a $40,000 exemption, to replace the previous add-on minimum tax

penalties for tax negligence and fraud

Repealed

deductions for state and local sales taxes

deductions for consumer interest (like credit card, auto, and student loans), with a phase-out through 1990

the "marriage penalty" deduction for two-earner households

the $50 tax credit for political contributions

the exclusion of $100 of dividend income

income exemptions for many "private activity" municipal bonds

provisions for income-averaging

the 60% deduction for long-term capital gains, treating all capital gains (short- or long-term) as ordinary income

the exclusion of income from unemployment compensation benefits

deductions for expenses of adopting a child

the exclusion for most prizes and awards

deductions for charitable contributions by non-itemizers

deductions for educational travel

extra personal exemptions for the elderly and blind

deductions for the land-clearing expenses of farmers

lower rates on the capital gains of corporations

the investment tax credit (ITC) for business expenditures on machinery, automobiles, and other property placed into service after December 31, 1985

(Table 1—1 continued)

Limited or Modified

deductions for medical and dental care to expenses over a 7.5% income floor, up from 5% under previous law

deductions for contributions to individual retirement accounts (IRAs) and 401(K) plans

deductions for business meals and entertainment to 80% of expenses

deductions for mortgage interest to qualified first or second homes

the exclusion of scholarship and fellowship grants

deductions for home office expenses

personal exemptions, as well as the lower 15% tax rate, for upper-income taxpayers

reporting requirements for municipal bonds

the deductibility of losses from "passive" economic activities to income gained only from other "passive" activities, rather than salary or dividend income

foreign tax credits

many miscellaneous individual and employee business expense deductions (included among them employment-related education, professional and union dues, work-related tools and supplies, tax and investment counseling, and job-search costs) by imposing a 2% income floor

deductions for business cruise travel

credits for the rehabilitation of historic buildings and the provision of low-income housing

credits for research and development

depreciation rules for business property under the accelerated cost recovery system (ACRS)

Retained

deductions for state and local income, real estate, and personal property taxes

deductions for mortgage interest on a primary residence and a second or vacation home

exemptions for income from "public activity" municipal bonds

tax deferral on the proceeds from the sale of a personal residence

credit for child and dependent care expenses

credit for the elderly and the permanently and totally disabled

deductions for alimony, business gifts, and gambling losses

the exclusion of employer-provided fringe benefits, life insurance proceeds, workers' compensation payments, and veterans' disability benefits

tax incentives for natural resources (including oil and gas drilling, timber growing, and solar and geothermal energy)

Congress's fiscal sword. And because of lower tax rates, even the worth of those was diminished by up to 44 percent.

These changes and others, including a tougher alternative minimum tax, closed the most egregious loopholes and severely curtailed opportunities for the "tax sheltering" of income. Together, they led the president to stress that "everybody . . . [would] pay their fair share." Broadening the tax base in this manner was the pain that paid for the anticipated pleasure of lower rates. The lower rates were possible without an enormous loss of federal revenue only because the TRA made more income subject to taxation.

Higher Corporate Costs.   Finally, the TRA marked a sharp departure from another trend in tax policy making, one that had been encouraged earlier in Reagan's presidency: the shift from business to individual taxation. Instead, corporate America took a tax "hit" estimated at $120 billion through 1991, while individual taxes fell by the same amount. Elimination of the ITC was the most prominent single factor, but changes in accounting rules and a tough new corporate minimum tax also added significantly to business's burden. Consequently, within a year of the TRA's enactment, the once prolific breed of large corporations that had gotten by with paying little or no federal taxes became "a vanishing species." [7]

Within the corporate sector, however, the effects of the TRA differed considerably, depending upon prior tax levels. Indeed, one of its most important effects was to "level out" the effective tax rates borne by different industries. In general, for example, the new tax package hurt manufacturing more than services.

This aspect of the change was perhaps the most remarkable politically. The Reagan administration and its Republican congressional allies were rightly regarded as friends of business, which has strong lobbies on Capitol Hill. During his first year in office, the president initiated tax cuts offering business a cornucopia of special benefits, justified largely as tools for stimulating investment and economic growth. The TRA, in contrast, moved in the opposite direction by raising business taxes and eliminating special investment incentives.

On this subject the president said nothing.

The Riddle of Tax Reform

The successful enactment of such costly and sweeping changes to the tax code caught virtually everyone by surprise. Dramatic breakthroughs in public policy are considered rare in American politics and, for both political and institutional reasons, are rarer still in the field of taxation. In 1985—the year the TRA was introduced in Congress and passed by the

House of Representatives—political scientist John Witte concluded an authoritative study of the politics of federal income taxation with this bold and confident prediction: "There is nothing, absolutely nothing in the history or politics of the income tax that indicates that any of these [contemporary tax reform] schemes has the slightest hope of being enacted in the forms proposed." [8] Indeed, in 1986—the year the TRA was enacted—economist David G. Davies concurred with Witte's assertion, writing, "Meaningful reform . . . under present political institutions is essentially doomed to failure." [9]

Those two somber appraisals were not the isolated naysayings of ivory tower skeptics. Virtually every participant in the tax-reform process— from legislators to lobbyists—concurred at almost every step along the way that the effort was futile. Secretary of State George Shultz, who is credited by some with helping to sell President Reagan on the cause, concluded from his experience as Treasury secretary in the Nixon administration that: "Despite the popularity of tax reform as a political slogan, the elimination of many large tax preferences would be so unpopular that it is almost inconceivable that congressional enactment would follow any presidential proposal." [10] And House Ways and Means Committee chairman Dan Rostenkowski, D-Ill., later said, "I don't believe the members ever felt that we were going to see the final product." [11] Sen. Packwood admitted to Sen. Bill Bradley, D-N.J., after the conference report was finally agreed to, "I never believed it would really happen."

Why such universal pessimism? After all, for years economic experts had recommended tax reform as a way to promote greater fairness and economic growth. Opinion polls indicated that the general public was critical of the status quo. And in 1985 the issue was put forward by a popular president who had just achieved a smashing landslide reelection victory. The powerful skepticism seemed to reflect a combination of bitter historical experience, daunting institutional obstacles, and the persuasive logic of the most influential theories of political behavior.

A Tradition of Incrementalism

History certainly offered little cause for optimism about the prospects for enacting comprehensive tax reform. Over many years the federal income-tax system had earned a well-deserved reputation for resisting fundamental change. Taxation was instead a preeminent example of "incremental" policy making in which legislative changes consist of marginal adjustments to existing tax policy. As Witte explains:

> Legislative changes in tax policy usually begin as marginal adjustments
> to the existing structure. Simple changes in parameters account for most
> of the modifications and most of the revenue effects. Applicable rates,
> bracket changes, exemption levels, standard deductions, depreciation

percentages, investment credits, depletion allowances—the list of changes that can be accomplished by simply altering a number is very long. . . . Tax laws can also be easily and marginally altered by expanding or contracting eligible groups, actions, industries, commodities, or financial circumstances.

In fact, the sizable accumulation of such small changes in the tax code over time has mainly been in a direction opposite to fundamental tax reform (see Chapter 2). A dominant tendency has been the proliferation of special tax benefits known as "tax expenditures." It is true that reform measures had often been advanced. But as Witte adds:

Most proposals that would have produced major changes either in revenues or in the structure of tax laws were never seriously considered. Large-scale overhauls . . . remained essentially academic exercises and never got more than a perfunctory examination by Congress. Even more modest recommendations to begin to move toward such a goal . . . were summarily dropped.[12]

For this reason, even the most dedicated advocates of comprehensive tax reform were forced by the record of experience to wonder if their quest, like Don Quixote's, was not an "impossible dream."

The Madisonian Frustration

This pattern is by no means unique to tax issues. "Our political system is built to block dramatic change," political scientist Norman Ornstein has observed. "Every element of the system is designed to look skeptically at something that will turn the world upside down."[13]

In large part, this institutionalized hesitancy reflects the nation's constitutional heritage. When the framers drafted the basic law of the United States some two hundred years ago, the protection of liberty was their first concern. They constructed a form of government that would cool the passions of the populace as well as impose restraints on those who achieved positions of authority. Power was divided, decentralized, and thus restrained. Although this system of checks and balances proved generally successful in ensuring a free, stable, democratic government, it also often seemed "the most successful contrivance the world has ever known for preventing things from being done."[14]

In the United States, and in contrast to the parliamentary systems found in most of the world's democracies, there is no direct link between the executive and legislative branches. A president is not assured that his party will hold a majority in Congress or even that his partisans at the other end of Pennsylvania Avenue will support his initiatives. Instead, all bills must run what is aptly described as the "obstacle course on Capitol Hill"[15] past the committees, leadership, and duly elected members of two separate and distinctive chambers. Those adopted in somewhat different form must somehow be reconciled and reaccepted by both bodies. Finally, all legislation must be signed by the president himself, who represents a third set of political and institutional constituents. Thus it is not surprising that to bill signings (as to the biblical wedding feast) "many are called but few are chosen."

Over two centuries, many of the structural details of the American system have been altered. Yet the federal government remains indicted as slow to respond, hesitant to act. A tendency toward political delay and deadlock has been a source of frustration for reformers of every ideological persuasion. In the 1950s and 1960s, it was liberal Democrats who most often chafed at the restraining bit of institutionalized inertia. But in the 1980s, it was the activist conservatives of the Reagan right who echoed the lament of previous generations of young turks. David Stockman, the brash, bright ideologue who served as Ronald Reagan's first budget director, protested:

> Our Madisonian government of checks and balances, three branches, two legislative houses, and infinitely splintered power is conservative, not radical. It hugs powerfully to the history behind it. It shuffles into the future one step at a time. It cannot leap into revolutions without falling flat on its face.[16]

Trends during the 1970s actually reinforced the diffusion of power, both for the government in general and for tax policy in particular. Early in the decade, Congress challenged the misuse of presidential authority during Vietnam and Watergate by asserting for itself a stronger role in budget making, foreign affairs, and other policy areas. Equally important, a young generation of legislators revolted against their own institutional leaders and procedures. Seniority rules were relaxed, as was the oligarchic rule of committee chairmen, with power dispersed and decentralized to both subcommittees and individual members. At the same time, new procedures governing committee activities and voting processes opened up to closer public scrutiny activities that had previously been conducted in private.

One of the principal targets—and victims—of congressional reform was Wilbur D. Mills, D-Ark., who from 1959 through 1974 ruled the House Ways and Means Committee, historically the single most influential committee on tax policy issues. Anarchy replaced autocracy, however. Later Ways and Means chairmen—Al Ullman, D-Ore., and initially Dan Rostenkowski—were far less effective, and the status of the committee plummeted. Indeed, in 1980 one tax expert warned that "the consideration of tax legislation has completely disintegrated. The picture has become one of almost utter chaos without responsible control residing anywhere." Another analyst went so far as to recommend that responsibility for developing tax proposals be taken away from Congress entirely and given to a politically independent federal revenue board. Only such sweeping changes, he argued, could remedy the failure of existing institutions and processes.[17]

Special Interest Politics

The pessimism generated by the clear historical and institutional obstacles to tax reform was reinforced by prevailing notions of political and economic behavior. Whether intuitively perceived by politicians or elegantly espoused by academicians, the consensus was that the opponents of reform were likely to be the most influential.

An important, even determinative, role in fixing policy outcomes has long been attributed to organizational interests. Indeed, one prominent group theorist, Arthur Bentley, regarded society itself as nothing more than a complex of such groups. When its groups are fully analyzed, he wrote, "everything is stated," adding, "when I say everything, I mean everything." [18]

Two related developments in the 1970s and 1980s bolstered that traditional perspective. First, thousands of new Washington lobbies and political action committees (PACs) were created. What Madison deplored as the "spirit of faction" was clearly ascendant. By one count, 25 percent of all the organizations represented in Washington were founded after 1970. The influence of business was especially strong, as corporations and trade associations comprised about three-quarters of all the groups with a lobbying presence. The number of PACs grew even more rapidly, up 559 percent between 1974 and 1984, while corporate PACs exploded from 89 to 1,682.[19] By 1984 there were seven political action committees for every member of Congress.

When it came to tax reform, the vast majority of these business groups had something to lose, as journalist William Greider notes:

> Every lobbyist understands [that if] . . . individuals pay less taxes, hundreds of corporate loopholes must be closed. . . . Every economic interest—from tobacco to insurance to labor to banks—is present to defend itself. . . . Tax reform is boom time for Washington's 15,000 lobbyists.[20]

The importance of this trend was underscored by theories probing the economic foundations of political behavior. According to analysts from this "rational choice" perspective, effective control of the political process by organized economic interests is the norm. They argued that an average, presumably rational citizen would not invest the time and energy needed to influence the government on his or her own behalf because the costs of obtaining information and organizing for action would almost certainly outweigh any benefits. Moreover, citizen reformers would have to overcome the "free rider" problem: the benefits of reform could be expected to accrue to many—including the most passive onlookers—while activists alone would bear the costs of obtaining them.

Thus, rational choice analysts expect tax policy to be dominated by those organized interests able to secure tax advantages large enough, and narrowly defined enough, to benefit them disproportionately. And indeed, the vast and multifaceted system of special benefits and tax breaks that reformers sought to abolish seemed to exemplify this pattern of what Wilson describes as "client politics." [21] Once having obtained such benefits, of course, organized groups also are likely to lobby vigorously against change. This logic was used to predict the failure of tax reform. Economist David Davies argued that the great bulk of "taxpayers remain rationally ignorant of tax matters" while the "congressional tax and finance committees are at present virtual prisoners of highly organized, well financed, single issue, special interest groups. . . . These powerful organizations exert influence on tax laws far in excess of their small size." [22]

Conclusion

Taken together, the political process seemed stacked against tax reform in the 99th Congress. Disinterested doubters and outright opponents greatly outnumbered the advocates of reform. Across Washington, lobbyists and legislators bet their reputations—and occasionally their careers—on the failure of the TRA.

Yet tax reform *was* enacted by Congress and signed by the president thirteen months after the first legislative "markup," or drafting session. Its enactment reflected an unanticipated political dynamic, for few of the presumed preconditions for reform had been met. Key obstacles were simply vanquished by "the bill that would not die."

A probe of this dynamic not only clarifies the passage of tax reform but also offers insights into recent changes in the political system that make such nonincremental policy leaps easier than is generally recognized. Tax reform was not a typical case of legislative enactment, but it was a "hard" case—an archetype of the institutionalized barriers to fundamental policy change. Its adoption suggests that American government has become less rigid and less prone to the Madisonian stalemate that has long worried political commentators. Neither institutional fragmentation, nor partisan division, nor the pressures of organized interests, nor the lack of strong public support necessarily prevents the translation of innovative policy ideas into law.

Consequently, the tax reform story has important implications for each of three theories that structure our understanding of political behavior and policy making: (1) the "pluralist/incrementalist" school; (2) the "presidential/majoritarian" model; and (3) the "ideational/entrepreneurial" perspective. In sum,

- Acceptance of this far-reaching legislation in the face of powerful organized opposition—and without the backing of strong organized support—clearly contradicts the pluralist/incrementalist view that policy making is chiefly a process of adjustment among contending groups. Tax reform did not reflect the balancing of group pressures nor did it demonstrate the cautious, incremental changes of law that normally accompany this kind of pluralist politics.
- The adoption of tax reform also was inconsistent with important aspects of the presidential/majoritarian paradigm of many political reformers, which does account for some other nonincremental policies. In particular, tax reform did not result from presidential mobilization of a partisan majority on behalf of a popular cause.
- Only part of tax reform's passage reveals the influence of experts and policy entrepreneurs armed, not with the traditional weapons of influence, but with the power of ideas. Though the role of such individuals, stressed recently in the literature of policy studies, is evident, they alone did not and could not have made tax reform law.

For these reasons, the TRA's enactment is significant, not only for its immediate effects on the economy, the federal budget, and the take-home pay of millions of Americans, but for lessons it offers about the policy process, the motivations of policy makers, and the sometimes unexpected effects of institutional arrangements on legislative outcomes.

The remainder of this book probes the TRA's development and adoption. Chapter 2 examines the historical context of reform, including both the status of the U.S. tax code and of ideas about appropriate tax policy. Chapters 3 through 8 explore the process that led to policy change, detailing the interaction of key administrative officials, legislators, experts, interests, and staff from President Reagan's first order to the Treasury Department to the signing of the legislation in October 1986. Finally, Chapter 9 examines the politics of tax reform in light of both traditional and contemporary policy models. It also offers our conclusions about the changing nature of the American political process.

Notes

1. This and other quotations of the president's remarks are from "Tax Reform Act of 1986: Remarks on Signing H.R. 3838 into Law, October 22, 1986," *Weekly Compilation of Presidential Documents* 22 (October 27, 1986): 1423–25.
2. Henry J. Aaron, "The Impossible Dream Comes True," in *Tax Reform and the U.S. Economy,* ed. Joseph A. Pechman (Washington: Brookings Institution, 1987), 10; and Kenneth Labich, "Tough Times Living with Tax Reform," *Fortune,* November 9, 1987, 113.
3. Arthur Andersen & Co., *Tax Reform 1986: Analysis and Planning* (Chicago:

Arthur Andersen, 1986), 3—4.

4. The combination of a phase-out of the 15 percent rate and a surcharge creates a third "hidden" bracket of 33 percent. For individuals, this rate applies to those with taxable incomes of $43,150—$100,480. Income above that level for individuals (and over $192,930 for a family of four) is taxed at the lower 28 percent rate. Thus, those in the highest income bracket actually have *lower* rates than those with upper-middle incomes.

5. A slightly progressive pattern in effective, as opposed to statutory, tax burdens results once the TRA's corporate tax increases are distributed to the mostly upper-income owners of capital. See Aaron, "The Impossible Dream Comes True," 13—14.

6. Richard I. Kirkland, Jr., "U.S. Tax Cuts Now Go Global," *Fortune*, November 24, 1986, 131—32.

7. Anne Swardson, "Big Firms Return to Tax Rolls: Era of Nonpaying Corporations Fading, New Survey Finds," *Washington Post*, September 23, 1988, F1.

8. John F. Witte, *The Politics and Development of the Federal Income Tax* (Madison: University of Wisconsin Press, 1985), 380.

9. David G. Davies, *United States Taxes and Tax Policy* (New York: Cambridge University Press, 1986), 287.

10. George P. Shultz and Kenneth W. Dam, *Economic Policy beyond the Headlines* (Stanford, Calif.: Stanford University Alumni Association, 1977), 54.

11. Interview with Rep. Dan Rostenkowski, March 12, 1987. This and approximately seventy other interviews were conducted as part of research for this book. Unattributed quotations were obtained from these sources.

12. Witte, *Politics and Development*, 244—45.

13. Norman Ornstein, quoted in "Stumbling Blocks Await Reagan's Tax Package," *Journal of Commerce*, May 31, 1985, 15A.

14. Charles Evans Hughes, quoted in Thomas K. McCraw, "The Historical Background," in *American Society: Public and Private Responsibilities*, ed. Winthrop Knowlton and Richard Zeckhauser (Cambridge, Mass.: Ballinger, 1986), 18.

15. This phrase is from Robert Bendiner, *Obstacle Course on Capitol Hill* (New York: McGraw-Hill, 1964).

16. On hesitancy in government, see James MacGregor Burns, *The Deadlock of Democracy* (Englewood Cliffs, N.J.: Prentice-Hall, 1963); James L. Sundquist, *Constitutional Reform and Effective Government* (Washington: Brookings Institution, 1986); and David A. Stockman, *The Triumph of Politics: The Inside Story of the Reagan Revolution* (New York: Avon Books, 1987), 9.

17. Stanley S. Surrey, "Our Troubled Tax Policy: False Routes and Proper Paths to Change," *Tax Notes*, February 2, 1981, 185; and John F. Witte, "The Income Tax Mess: Deviant Process or Institutional Failure?" (Paper delivered at the annual meeting of the American Political Science Association, New Orleans, August 29—September 1, 1985), 19.

18. Arthur Bentley, *The Process of Government*, quoted in James Q. Wilson, *Political Organizations* (New York: Basic Books, 1973), 5—6.

19. Kay Lehman Schlozman and John T. Tierney, *Organized Interests and American Democracy* (New York: Harper and Row, 1986), 75—77; and Harold W. Stanley and Richard G. Niemi, *Vital Statistics on American Politics* (Washington: CQ Press, 1988), 143.

20. William Greider, "Taxes behind Closed Doors," *Frontline* #411 (Boston: WGBH Transcripts, 1986), 5.

21. James Q. Wilson, *The Politics of Regulation* (New York: Basic Books, 1980), 369.
22. Davies, *United States Taxes*, 285—86.

2 Something Old, Something New: Tax Reform in Historical Context

Comprehensive income taxation seems to make so much sense, one wonders why there has been so little progress in reforming tax systems along these lines.

—Joseph A. Pechman

One expert has described the Tax Reform Act as "apparently coming from nowhere to become the law of the land."[1] This characterization reflects the astonishment of nearly all observers at tax reform's sudden emergence at the top of Congress's political agenda and, even more so, at its legislative acceptance in the face of seemingly overwhelming political obstacles. Still, the substance of tax reform did not come from nowhere. The opposite claim can be made: the legislation contained almost nothing truly original or innovative. Instead the 1986 TRA offered long-recognized solutions to often-considered problems. Though the act departed from the anticipated course of history, it was erected on a firm historical foundation. This chapter traces those origins.

According to contemporary political analysts, the rise to prominence of a major policy issue typically results from the timely convergence of three streams of events—problems, solutions, and political opportunities.[2] So it was in this case. The federal income tax—itself a product of reformers' efforts a century earlier—had by the late 1970s become a widely recognized problem. It had fallen in esteem among experts, political leaders, and the public. For its ills, good doctors offered several remedies, drawing on the storehouse of knowledge and opinion patiently built up over several decades. During the mid-1980s, these centered on a specific cure: base broadening and rate reduction. Together, these developments created circumstances that made tax reform possible—implausible, but still possible, as later actions demonstrated.

Constitutional Foundations of the Income Tax

The first statement of U.S. policy on the income tax, according to the Supreme Court, was contained in the Constitution itself. It was a prohibition. Although Article I, Section 8, stipulated, "Congress shall have Power To lay and collect Taxes, Duties, Imposts and Excises, to pay the Debts and provide for the Common Defense and general Welfare of the

United States," there also were fiscal restrictions. All duties, imposts, and excises were to be uniform throughout the United States, while Article I, Section 9, added, "No capitation, or other direct, Tax shall be laid, unless in Proportion to the Census or Enumeration herein before directed to be taken."

The meaning of this restriction was not altogether clear because the delegates to the Constitutional Convention had failed to distinguish precisely between acceptable "indirect" and impermissible "direct" forms of taxation. Nevertheless, direct taxes were generally understood to include both head (or capitation) and land taxes, neither of which was employed. Instead, the federal government relied on import duties and occasional excises, which were long adequate for its very limited needs, at least during peacetime.

Income taxes were not explicitly barred, however, and seemed far more fair when large amounts of revenue were needed. Average citizens bore the brunt of tariffs and excises, permitting the rich to meet their obligations with disproportionately low payments. Consequently, income taxes were imposed—with later judicial approval—during and immediately after the American Civil War. Though they were modest in coverage (affecting only the wealthiest, with rates up to 10 percent), these wartime levies were attacked as inequitable and socialistic and were permitted to expire after peace was restored. Proponents did not abandon the cause, however, and bills calling for reinstatement were regularly introduced into Congress.

In 1894 a coalition of populists, agrarian radicals, and eastern liberals gained acceptance of income taxation as an alternative to the high federal tariffs burdening farmers and consumers. Yet again, the victory was temporary. Opponents of the new tax challenged its constitutionality, and their arguments found favor in the nation's highest court. In a 5—4 decision, Chief Justice Melville Fuller overturned existing judicial precedent by concluding that an income tax was, after all, a constitutionally proscribed direct tax not apportioned among the states. The nation's movement toward income taxation thus was stalled, and the federal government returned to its traditional revenue sources: customs receipts and duties on alcohol, tobacco, and other goods.

Many legal scholars believe that the Court's decision was unjustifiable, an opinion shared then by the *New York World*, which condemned it as a "victory of greed over need." "Great and rich corporations," the *World* editorialized, "have secured the exemption of wealth from paying its just share towards the support of the Government that protects it." The paper promised, "A way will be found . . . to revoke what Justice Brown well calls this 'surrender of the taxing power to the moneyed class.' " [3]

In fact, a way *was* found to restore income taxation, though not easily or promptly. Nearly two decades' time and a sixteenth amendment to the Constitution were required before income taxation was placed on a sound legal footing. Ironically, it was a staunchly conservative Republican president and Congress that, in 1909, proposed the amendment that made it lawful. During a bitter tariff-reform battle, Democrats and insurgent Republicans proposed adopting a statutory income tax—a measure that, given the Supreme Court's prior ruling seemed unconstitutional. Rather than challenge the judicial branch, President William Howard Taft obtained a compromise including both an immediate tax on corporate profits and the submission of an income-tax amendment for consideration by the states, which might make possible a tax on individual incomes at some future date. Protectionist opponents went along, believing it unlikely that the personal-income-tax measure would ever be ratified.

Under these circumstances, a form of corporate income tax took effect in 1909. Initially it was presented as an excise on the privilege of conducting business, thus avoiding the question of constitutionality. But when the income-tax amendment received unexpected support in industrialized regions, being approved by the necessary thirty-sixth state four years later, President Woodrow Wilson lost little time in moving a bill through Congress, and the personal income tax took effect on March 1, 1913. Cordell Hull, its legislative draftsman, recognized the controversial history of the tax but was also sure that it would exceed "in its justice, flexibility, and productiveness any tax law on the statute books." That opinion was, in fact, long very widely shared.

The Effects of War and Depression

Initially, the individual income tax was but a modest supplement to other federal revenue sources, providing about 6 percent of all federal receipts; the corporate tax provided a like amount. Simple in form (the relevant provisions required only fourteen pages of law) most citizens could ignore it entirely because generous exemptions limited its application to only a small group of the very wealthy, less than 1 percent of the total population. Rates also were very low by later standards, ranging from 1 to 7 percent.

Nonetheless, the adoption of permanent income taxation in 1909 and 1913 opened a new era in the relationship of the national government to its citizens, ultimately permitting a vast expansion in its international and domestic responsibilities. The provision of bountiful revenues, which the income tax ensured, became one of the pillars upon which was erected a very substantial federal establishment, offering services affecting citizens both directly and, even more so, through aid to their state and local governments.

Most of the growth of the income tax resulted from international conflagration and economic calamity—a consequence of the "politics of crisis." During World War I, as during the Civil War, government turned to the income tax to pay the high costs of combat. Rates were temporarily increased to as high as 77 percent, and personal exemptions were cut.[4] During the Great Depression, too, rates were hiked by presidents Herbert Hoover (in 1932) and then Franklin Roosevelt (in 1934 and 1935). Pushed on in part by vigorous social protest movements, Roosevelt rebuked the nation's "economic royalists" and urged a comprehensive overhaul of the tax system "to prevent an unjust concentration of wealth and economic power." Thereafter, the Revenue Act of 1936 increased the maximum rate to 79 percent on income in excess of $5 million, a new high.

It was World War II, however, not the liberal reforms of the New Deal, that transformed the federal income tax from a tax on the "classes" to a tax on the "masses" and made it the real backbone of federal finance. In a brief time, revenues as a percentage of personal income increased from 1.2 percent to 10.2 percent. The number of personal-income-tax returns filed almost doubled between 1940 and 1941, nearly doubled again by 1942, and then again by 1945. Although marginal rates were raised to as much as 94 percent in the highest brackets, people of more modest means bore most of the cost of the new "warfare state." In 1939 taxpayers with incomes under $3,000 had paid just 10 percent of all income tax revenue. By 1948 they were paying half.

The Placid Politics of Post—World War Tax Policy

Although key developments in early U.S. income-tax policy were associated with social protest, war, and domestic crisis, the end of World War II inaugurated a period of continuity and calm. Details, not principles, were the focus of action for the next three decades.

Impenetrably complex and often boring, the making of tax policy became the province of a closed elite of key legislators, executive leaders, and lobbyists whose actions were seldom challenged (or even closely inspected) by the public or its elected representatives. Indeed, for much of the post—World War period—from 1958 through 1974—tax legislation was closely guarded and controlled by a single individual, Wilbur Mills, the powerful chairman of the House Ways and Means Committee.[5] Bills prepared under his oversight were regularly and promptly adopted by the House as a whole. The Senate Finance Committee offered a second review, often functioning as a kind of court of appeals for aggrieved interests, but its role was secondary. The formulation of tax policy, then, was typically a matter of quiet, careful, and expert craftsmanship, with legislation tailored to meet standards of political and professional acceptability, rather than a focus of national political attention. Bipartisan approbation, rather than partisan combat and ideological orations, were the rule, and modest incremental changes were the usual outcome.

Automatic Increases

Nonetheless, despite the substantial continuity, tax policy changed significantly during the decades after World War II. Most notably, the federal personal income tax became an increasingly productive source of revenue; at the same time, the importance of the corporate income tax declined. Setting aside contributions to the social insurance trust funds (for social security, Medicare, unemployment compensation, and the like), revenue from the personal income tax rose from 45 percent of all federal tax receipts in 1950 to 73 percent in 1985. During the same period, the corporate income tax, which in the pre—World War II years often provided more revenue than the individual tax, became steadily less important, with its revenue share declining from 30 percent to 14 percent of the total. Without much national debate, and indeed without widespread awareness, the burden of taxation shifted off of corporations and directly onto an ever-increasing body of individual taxpayers (see Figure 2—1).

In large part, the growing fiscal importance of the personal income tax was a natural consequence of the nation's lasting economic prosperity, coupled with the graduated structure of the tax schedule. Even though Congress sometimes raised the personal exemption, more and more people earned incomes that required them to pay income taxes. Excluding the war years, the population covered by the tax rose from just 5 percent in 1939, to 59 percent in 1950, to 73 percent in 1960, and to 81 percent in 1970.

Steadily rising incomes also moved more individuals and families into the higher tax brackets that once applied only to the well-to-do, a process known as "bracket-creep." In 1965 a family earning the median income was in the 17 percent marginal tax bracket; that is, seventeen cents of every additional dollar it earned was owed to the U.S. government. By 1980 a similarly situated family found itself paying income taxes at the 24 percent rate. For better-off families, those with twice the median income, the increase was even more pronounced. Their tax rate nearly doubled, between 22 to 43 percent from 1965 to 1980.[6]

From the standpoint of the nation's legislators, these automatic escalator effects were a fiscal and political gold mine. They offered politicians pleasure (the opportunity to spend money on popular government services) without pain (the commensurate need to legislate an increase in taxes). Almost never were presidents or legislators forced to read headlines announcing "Congress Enacts Tax Hike" or "President Proposes Higher

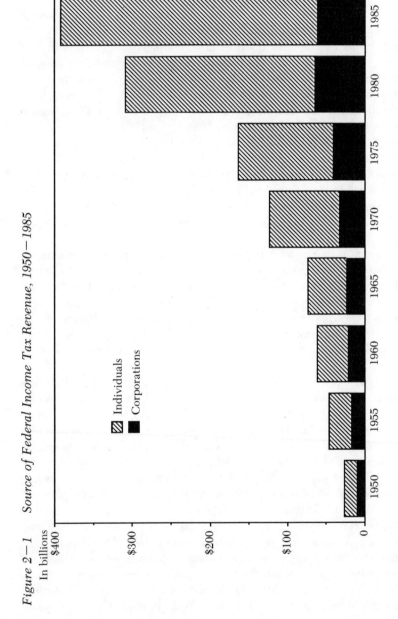

Figure 2—1   *Source of Federal Income Tax Revenue, 1950—1985*

In billions

Individuals
Corporations

Source: Data from U.S. Advisory Commission on Intergovernmental Relations, *Significant Features of Fiscal Federalism, 1987 Edition* (Washington: U.S. Government Printing Office, 1987), 38.

Income Levies." Indeed, before the 1980s, the only legislated tax increases in peacetime occurred during the Great Depression.[7]

Inflation augmented this process, particularly in the 1970s, but also made income taxes more burdensome. Because tax schedules were not "indexed" or adjusted for changes in living costs before 1981, inflation-related growth in one's stated income could spur an upward movement through the tax schedule. Unlike those gains associated with improvements in living standards, however, such artificial tax escalations were not so easy to bear, and they almost certainly contributed to growing popular discontent with the tax system during this period.

The declining importance of the corporate tax reflected a kind of national uncertainty about its proper role. The tax is extremely controversial among economists.[8] First, there is no agreement about its incidence: it is not clear whether the burden of the tax falls ultimately on a corporation's shareholders, on capital investors in general, or is shifted to consumers (in the form of higher prices) or to employees (in the form of reduced wages). Despite this imprecision, the belief that high corporate taxes are bad for business, and consequently slow the nation's economic growth, seems to have won acceptance. Hence, although the corporate rate schedule has not been altered much, measures to liberalize depreciation allowances and encourage investment activity were in place through most of the postwar period. Especially in the late 1970s, when the performance of the U.S. economy faltered, calls for reduced corporate taxes to spur capital formation gained favor and helped shape key features of the dramatic Economic Recovery Tax Act (ERTA) of 1981.

Legislated Reductions

Because revenues rose automatically, the national government has often enacted statutes with the magic phrase "tax reduction" in their titles or adopted net revenue losers that could easily be portrayed that way. Congress, for its part, has regularly adopted bills providing for less revenue than those urged on it by the administration, regardless of which party was in power. "It is," John Witte wrote, "as if there were a continuous force operating much like gravity in the direction of tax reduction." [9]

During the Eisenhower and Kennedy-Johnson administrations, there were actual reductions in marginal tax rates. Between 1965 and 1981, however, tax cuts generally took the form of increases in personal deductions and tax credits, rather than a change in the basic tax-rate schedule. From both an economic and political standpoint, the most impressive cut was the $11.4 billion first-year reduction engineered by President John F. Kennedy at the behest of his economic adviser, Walter W. Heller, in 1964. As finally enacted, the legislation offered a 20 percent tax reduction for individuals and corporations, bringing the top personal income bracket down from 91 percent to 70 percent and lowering the bottom rate from 20 percent to 14 percent. This was not the only such cut, however. Congress adopted fifteen major tax bills between 1954 and 1981. Of these, only three increased governmental revenues, eleven reduced them, and one left revenue unchanged.[10]

Expanding Tax Preferences

Along with such diffuse beneficences, legislators increasingly offered more precisely targeted tax advantages by creating more exemptions, deductions, credits, and exclusions for special purposes, thus aiding specific groups, industries, and even individuals. Such preferences address many kinds of problems. Some are intended to ensure equity in the tax system (for example, by permitting the deduction of expenditures associated with one's business or employment), but many are directed at overtly economic goals, like stimulating investment or industrial research and development, or are designed to advance social aims, like the deductions for child care or charitable contributions and the exclusion of payments into retirement savings accounts.

The growth of these tax breaks or special tax incentives has been the most widely noted, and most frequently criticized, tendency of post—World War II tax policy. Scholarly minded critics, including many in the Treasury Department itself, have protested the steady "erosion" of the tax base and the use of the tax code to foster specific social and economic policies. Many taxpayers and their spokesmen have objected to a system of tax incentives and breaks that creates, at the very least, an appearance of unfairness and enormously complicates both the tax law and the preparation of individual and corporate tax returns. Largely because of such provisions, the income tax statute grew from a model of brevity to more than 2,000 pages by the early 1980s.

Close attention to the number and magnitude of special tax provisions sprang from the efforts of Stanley S. Surrey, who as assistant secretary of the Treasury introduced the concept of "tax expenditures" in 1968.[11] Surrey took the position that special tax provisions are very much the fiscal equivalent of direct spending programs. He also advanced the traditional belief of the Treasury Department that social goals are better pursued through such direct programs than by special tax incentives.

As Figure 2—2 shows, tax expenditures increased rapidly from the late 1960s to early 1980s. This was a result both of newly created provisions and of the expanding scope of older ones. In 1967 some fifty separate tax expenditure "programs" cost the U.S. Treasury about $36.6 billion. By 1984 revenue losses had escalated to $327 billion through more than one hundred separate items. A second tabulation, prepared by John Witte, indicates that Congress adopted almost as many tax expenditure provisions

Figure 2—2   *Tax Expenditures, 1967—1981*

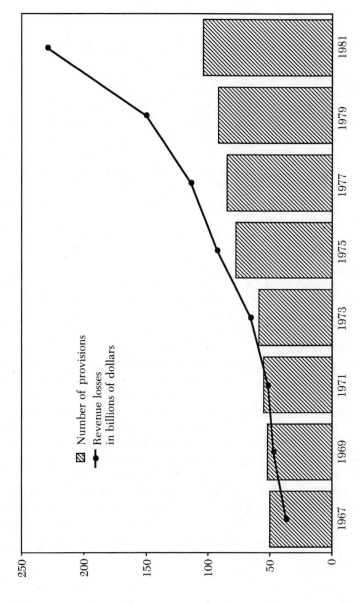

Source: Congressional Budget Office, *Tax Expenditures: Current Issues and Five-Year Budget Projections for Fiscal Years 1982—1986* (Washington: Congressional Budget Office, Congress of the United States, September 1981), 34.

between 1970 and 1982 as during the previous two decades.[12] One particularly sharp increase appeared during the mid-1970s, followed by a second in the early 1980s.

A description of the political dynamics underlying such provisions was provided in a classic article written by Surrey in 1957 when he was a Harvard Law School professor.[13] Tax provisions, Surrey argued, had their roots in the fact that most members of Congress did not really believe in the high rates provided by the tax code. Hence, they were predisposed to grant relief in cases involving any injustice or hardship.

Particular provisions, Surrey suggested, usually begin with a member's being approached by a constituent or other supplicant. Because representatives want to be helpful (helpfulness is, in fact, a key to a successful career in politics), they are likely to draft and introduce remedial legislation. Other legislators, because they need to get along with their colleagues and have favors of their own to request, usually also give such proposals a sympathetic hearing. Since they are not themselves tax experts, Surrey believed, individual representatives may not realize that the concession they are granting could introduce new inequities into the tax system for other taxpayers. The public-at-large is not likely to alert them because it, too, lacks the knowledge to do so. Consequently, Surrey said, "the congressman favoring these special provisions has for the most part no accounting to make to the voters for his action. He is thereby much freer to lend a helping hand here and there to a group which has won his sympathy or which is pressing him for results."[14]

This interpretation, which places organized interests at the origin of most tax provisions, is widely accepted. Political scientists, journalists, and reformers alike often view special interest lobbying as the heart of the policy process. When Surrey wrote, the top tax bracket stood at 91 percent; as a result of cold war pressures for defense spending as well as expanding domestic programs, a major revision of the 1954 tax code had retained World War II's high rate brackets in peacetime. Consequently, upper-income groups had strong incentives to seek tax relief, and perhaps members of Congress had good reasons to grant it.

In stressing the role of lobbyists, however, this classic interpretation may underplay the fact that both the public and political leaders have further reasons for accepting a host of special tax provisions.[15] First, many tax incentives serve purposes whose worth is unchallenged by most taxpayers and benefit broad segments of the population—the deduction for home mortgage interest and exclusion of employer-provided fringe benefits, like health insurance, for example. Second, so-called tax expenditures offer an acceptable method for accomplishing domestic policy goals that cannot be achieved directly in a staunchly free-enterprise political economy. To many Republicans, as well as to some business groups, tax expenditures appear more consistent than other types of national programs with the American ideal of limited government. Sen. Robert Packwood, who in 1986 emerged as an ardent champion of tax reform, was long a leading advocate of tax expenditures for just this reason:

> If the federal government established a grant program for the families of college students, [Packwood] said, it might load the program with so many regulations that students attending only certain kinds of colleges would qualify. On the other hand . . . a tax expenditure would promote a diverse system of higher education.[16]

A variety of factors, then, probably undergirded the steady rise in tax expenditures. Some can be attributed to lobby pressures and the proliferation of interest groups. In addition, legislators—perhaps reacting to what seemed to be the excessive growth and disappointing results of federal domestic programs launched in the 1960s—turned to tax policy as a preferred tool of policy activism. Tax incentives were doubly attractive because they were less subject to legislative scrutiny. Inflation, coupled with the nation's relative economic stagnation, made more taxpayers interested in tax relief in any form. A kind of "if you can't beat them, join them" logic encouraged the proliferation of provisions.

Finally, and ironically, reforms of congressional decision-making procedures made it easier for legislators to be responsive to these popular wishes. The "opening up" of congressional processes and decentralization of authority that began in the early 1970s and that was aimed in part at overthrowing legislative oligarchs like Wilbur Mills, seems in the end to have made tax policy more, not less, susceptible to manipulation serving specialized aims. Witte comments:

> Politicians view tax expenditures as rewards to confer and. . . are eager and willing to associate themselves with the conference of such benefits. Thus, opening up the system and encouraging roll call votes serve to expand, not restrict, the tax expenditure system. . . . By opening up the system to public participation and inspection you simply increase the demand for wider benefits.[17]

Expert Appraisals and Proposals for Reform

At the time of its enactment, the new levy on incomes was pronounced by Congress to be "the fairest and cheapest of all taxes."[18] And so it seemed. Although no tax can be said to be popular, the personal income tax was long regarded as better than the alternatives.[19]

By the late 1970s, however, this supportive appraisal had withered away. What had been the nation's—even the world's—best-regarded source of public revenue was viewed, in the hyperbole of President Jimmy Carter, as a "disgrace to the human race." The 1980s began with the "federal tax structure in disrepute and with almost universal demands for tax revision and tax reduction," as expert and reformer Joseph A. Pechman noted.[20] Indeed, an opinion poll prepared for the U.S. Advisory Commission on Intergovernmental Relations showed that the federal income tax was regularly described as the worst or least fair tax after 1978, taking the place of the local property tax (see Figure 2—3).

Experts directed criticism from two different directions. The larger and more orthodox group of tax economists and attorneys called for the elimination of many special deductions, exemptions, and credits, thus broadening the base. A smaller but quite vocal group believed that income taxation had failed because high marginal rates stamped out individual incentives for economic production. Though both sets of critics believed that thoroughgoing reform was essential, they offered quite different proposals for action. Only in the early 1980s did the possibility of some rapprochement between these two camps appear possible.

Reform I: A Comprehensive Base

Tax equity, as judged by economists, has two dimensions: one "vertical," the other "horizontal." In both, the overarching aim is to ensure that individuals who have the same "ability to pay" are subject to the same taxes. But, according to the former principle, fairness is a matter of progressivity: treating unequals differently; that is, taxing the wealthiest more.[21] In contrast, the notion of horizontal equity stresses that those who receive the same level of total income should also have equal tax bills.

Which standard of fairness is more crucial? For many decades, vertical equity was the principal standard against which a tax was judged. And from the very first, the income tax had a progressive structure, provided through a system of graduated rates and high individual exemptions; later, the degree of progressivity became much more pronounced.

Instituted through political struggle and backed by populist rhetoric, this approach found support from economic scholars, who lent a scientific rationale to what could otherwise be viewed as simply a raid by the masses on the pockets of the "classes." The rich *should* pay relatively more, economists concluded, because they so easily could afford to do so: their ability to pay was greater. According to the principle of the "diminishing utility of income," elaborated in the latter half of the nineteenth century, ten dollars is not as valuable to the millionaire as it is to the pauper. The millionaire's basic needs, after all, are fully satisfied. As his income rises, his need for still more income goes down: that is, the marginal value of every additional dollar diminishes. Thus, it is appropriate that a certain minimum amount of income be free of taxation, as is ensured by personal exemptions, and that income-tax rates increase as one moves toward the upper end of the income scale, as is provided by a progressive rate

Figure 2—3   *Public Opinion on Federal, State, and Local Taxes, 1977—1986*

Question: "Which tax do you think is the worst tax—that is, the least fair?"

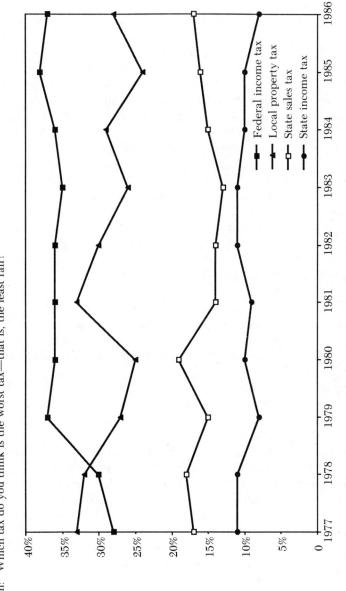

Source: U.S. Advisory Commission on Intergovernmental Relations, *Changing Public Attitudes on Governments and Taxes: 1986* (Washington: U.S. Government Printing Office, 1986), 1.

structure. In some formulations, this theory justifies truly confiscatory rates in the highest income brackets.[22]

But a second view, emphasizing the similar treatment of those similarly situated, gained support throughout the 1960s, 1970s, and 1980s. Indeed, under the TRA, efforts to enhance vertical equity were abandoned in favor of improving horizontal equity and providing lower rates all around.

In U.S. tax literature, the emphasis on horizontal equity derives principally from the writings of Henry C. Simons, a maverick, uncompromising, conservative economic scholar whose works have been termed "the most penetrating and original American contribution to public finance." [23] Simons argued for a truly comprehensive definition of income, including all gains received by a person. More precisely, in Simons's view one's income over any period of time should be defined as the sum of consumption plus any change in economic net worth. Tax equity suffers, Simons believed, unless each individual's full economic gains—and hence, his or her true ability to pay—are measured accurately and completely.[24]

In principle, this aim might seem to be secured by the U.S. tax code. Section 61(a) specifies that "gross income means all income from whatever source derived " (a quotation from the Sixteenth Amendment) "including (but not limited to)" certain items listed, among them compensation for services, rent, dividends, royalties, alimony, pensions, and others. Yet the practice has always been otherwise. From the first, Congress authorized numerous exemptions, deductions, and credits, which have been added to regularly. For example, one's adjusted gross income has not included most social security payments, many prizes and awards, unrealized capital gains, rental allowances for clergy, food stamps, Medicaid, and a variety of other receipts.

To Simons and others of like mind, such special dispensations were suspect because they reduced tax equity. Some also stressed that economic efficiency is undermined when the structure of the tax system encourages or discourages particular types of investment and consumption, thus interfering with the operation of the free market. Consequently, those reformer-critics challenged most departures from their ideal of comprehensive income taxation, including not only the provisions regarded as "abuses" by many, but also those used and accepted by large numbers of taxpayers. Rigid adherence to Simons's definition of income would require including many items that have traditionally been viewed as beyond the ken of the tax code, including gifts, employer-provided fringe benefits, and employee discounts or in-kind reimbursement (like the use of a company car or parking space), as well as the elimination of any special treatment for capital gains or revenues from municipal securities. Indeed, a truly comprehensive income base would give no special treatment to payments of mortgage interest on one's home and also would levy a tax on its imputed rental value. This is the result of what, to any layman, is a most astonishing logic: by purchasing a home and living in it, one has chosen to consume shelter, rather than use the income that could be obtained by renting the property out. Since such rental income would be taxed, so too should be the "imputed rent" one receives by residing in one's own property.[25]

During the 1950s and 1960s, Simons's ideas were kept alive and developed further by a small coterie of tax experts. Perhaps foremost among these was Joseph Pechman, a noted Brookings Institution economist who conducted pioneering empirical research in this area.[26] As a graduate student in the late 1930s and early 1940s, Pechman absorbed the Simons definition of income. In later studies he discovered that the amount of income reported on tax returns fell far short of all personal income as defined by this economic theory. For 1956, he determined, the revenue "leakages" caused by various deductions, exclusions, exemptions, and credits totaled $43 billion, or nearly one-third of the $136 billion tax base.[27] His analyses demonstrated that a move toward truly comprehensive income taxation would permit a dramatic increase in federal revenue—or, alternatively, a reduction in income tax rates by as much as one-third.

Unlike many academic social scientists, Pechman cultivated close contacts throughout the government and sought support for his views in the popular press and through scholarly work. Pechman was an ally of many other expert reformers, among them Stanley Surrey. Testifying before Congress, he offered guidance and support to key legislators (including Hubert Humphrey, Paul Simon, and Paul H. Douglas) over a period of nearly four decades. He also stimulated interest in tax reform in a future president, Jimmy Carter, whom he advised during the 1976 election campaign.

In time, the views of Pechman and his colleagues came to monopolize professional deliberations. Indeed, even in the mid-1960s, a critic protested that the concept of comprehensive income taxation had become "the major organizing concept in most serious discussions of our federal income tax,"[28] both in Congress and among academicians. But whatever their intellectual influence, the comprehensive base reformers enjoyed few policy successes. Twice before Reagan became president—in 1969 and 1976—major legislation was adopted with "tax reform" in its title. Though both bills were signed by Republican presidents, each was primarily the work of a Democrat-controlled Congress. Neither advanced the cause very far, however. The Tax Reform Act of 1969 closed some loopholes and imposed a new minimum tax on certain kinds of previously tax-free income. Yet, the bill also reduced the maximum marginal rate on earned income from 70 percent to 50 percent, while it added so many new tax-relief provisions that reform advocate Rep. Henry S. Reuss, D-Wisc., branded it a fiscal "time bomb" likely to cost the federal government nearly $8 billion a year in lost revenues by 1975.[29] Thus, the bill seemed timid, even to its friends.

In 1976 the tax-reform movement enjoyed a second victory of sorts. Yet again, the gains were just partial. While most acknowledged that it contained some positive measures, one conservative critic still condemned the Tax Reform Act of 1976 as "the worst possible collection of tax preferences for lobbied interests." Some liberals actually sought to have the word "reform" removed from its title.[30] Further, its 413-page text was so complicated that some wags renamed it the "1976 Lawyers' and Accountants' Relief Act."

At other times, the fate of tax reform was even less auspicious. Although President Dwight Eisenhower claimed to have closed "more than 50" tax loopholes with a comprehensive income tax rewrite in 1954, a host of new benefits also was created. When President Kennedy forwarded legislation in 1963 designed to close some of the more glaring loopholes, as well as reduce tax rates, Congress approved the tax cut but rejected most of the reforms. Reform efforts did not even reach Congress during the presidency of Lyndon Johnson.

By the mid-1970s, the lesson seemed clear. As one expert stated, "It appears that there is no grand solution, no simple way to improve the tax system by closing the most criticized 'loopholes.' This has been suggested time and again, in vain." [31] The validity of this assessment was reconfirmed during the Carter administration. Condemnation of the federal income tax and federal bureaucracy was a persistent theme of the former Georgia governor's presidential bid. His proposals ran aground, however, against concerns about the nation's faltering economic performance.[32] What became the Revenue Act of 1978 was loaded down with new tax credits and exemptions, most of them advancing the cause of "capital formation," while traditional reform objectives were wholly abandoned. Though Rep. Fortney "Pete" Stark, D-Calif., chided his colleagues in verse, "With loopholes for dryholes, And tax breaks for wine, The deeds of the lobbyists, Were almost a crime," [33] a chastened Carter signed the bill into law. Thereafter he avoided what had initially been a priority policy objective of his administration.

Reform II: Lower Marginal Rates

The fate of reformers in favor of base broadening and the comprehensive income tax contrasts sharply with that of another reformist cadre, the supply-siders, who gained prominence during the 1970s. Although this latter group never enjoyed the same degree of intellectual acceptability, it gained influence where it matters most: in the Congress and ultimately the White House.

Unlike the base broadeners, supply-side activists were self-styled revolutionaries who challenged the very foundations of the Keynesian economic tradition and the most fundamental precepts of U.S. tax policy.[34] Since the Great Depression and World War II, macroeconomists have been chiefly concerned with the effects of government taxation and spending on the general level of economic activity as regulated by aggregate demand—that is, total private and public spending for goods and services. The adoption of the Employment Act in 1946 made this commitment a foundation of national policy, and successive presidents have sought to moderate recessions and inflation through the adroit use of fiscal policy.

The economic events of the mid-1970s, however, cast doubt on the standard prescriptions. An alternative school of economic thought emerged that considered taxes chiefly in terms of their influence on the supply of labor and capital. Unlike traditional fiscal conservatives, who typically pressed for low corporate taxes and a balanced federal budget, supply-siders emphasized the negative effects of taxation on individual incentives to work, invest, and save. These supply-siders argued that high marginal personal income-tax rates—that is, the high percentage of each additional increment of income earned that was owed to the government—were the main cause of the low productivity growth and relative economic stagnation then troubling the United States.

This point of view was not altogether new, and proponents could trace its lineage from David Hume in the eighteenth century, to Jean-Baptiste Say in the nineteenth, and to Andrew Mellon in the twentieth. Nevertheless, unlike the comprehensive-base approach to taxation, supply-side economics had not been nurtured in the academy for decades. Instead it developed in the early 1970s within a small clique of iconoclastic economists and journalists and interested political sponsors. Only after their views had catapulted into the headlines did they leave a mark in textbooks.

The earliest and most prominent proponent was Rep. Jack Kemp, R-N.Y. A former football player with the Buffalo Bills, Kemp was first elected to Congress in 1970, winning national recognition for his audacious tax-policy proposals. Indeed, he promised "an American renaissance" through lower marginal rates. His book of that title, published in 1979, offered a message "of optimism, of hope, of national renewal" largely through tax relief.[35]

What had poisoned the American dream, according to Kemp's political manifesto, were roadblocks thrown up by government. Of those, high progressive federal taxes seemed the most serious problem. He said:

> The reason I place so much stress on the tax system as the key to spurring real economic growth is that I believe tax rates are so clearly and unnecessarily high . . . that they stifle individual achievement *and*

impoverish the community at large. . . . In taxes, as in all else, there is a
law of diminishing returns. When tax rates increase—as they now do
automatically because of inflation—each increase has the effect of
discouraging one or more individuals. They just give up trying to get
ahead. I once asked a college audience the rhetorical question, "What
would happen if the government took New York Yankee Reggie
Jackson's salary and distributed it equally among all the Yankees?"
From the back of the room came a young voice: "He'd hit singles!"[36]

The heart of Kemp's tax proposal, first introduced in Congress in 1977
with Sen. William Roth, R-Del., was a 10 percent reduction in rates during
each of the three years after its adoption. For example, under Kemp-Roth
I, the highest personal rates were to be cut from 70 percent to 50 percent,
the lowest from 14 percent to 8 percent. Corporate taxes were to be
reduced as well.[37]

Although the Kemp-Roth bill (and its successors) offered tax relief for
all, a principal goal was to provide relief for those in the upper-income
brackets. The reason was that it was this group whose incentives had the
greatest impact on the economy. As George Gilder wrote:

> The key to growth is quite simple: creative men with money. The cause
> of stagnation is similarly simple: depriving creative individuals of
> financial power. To revive the slumping nations of social democracy, the
> prime need is to reverse the policies of entrepreneurial euthanasia.
> Individuals must be allowed to accumulate disposable savings and wield
> them in the economics of the West.[38]

Another leading advocate, Paul Craig Roberts, similarly contended:

> The progressive income tax was implemented to "soak the rich" and
> redistribute income. In practice it works as a barrier to upward mobility
> and discourages people from making their best effort. In pandering to
> envy, the tax system has made it almost impossible for the average
> taxpayer to obtain financial independence.[39]

If narrowly construed, the basic claim of the supply-siders was not
challenged: that tax rates affect economic activity, including the supply of
labor and the channeling of investments. As a consequence, many
economists were concerned that uneven taxation on different industries
might direct the flow of investment funds to inefficient purposes. Thus,
they argued for measures that would create a more "level playing field"
for investors, leaving decisions about the allocation of capital to the
marketplace instead of to tax attorneys.

But some supply-siders believed that the disincentive effect of high tax
rates on the economy was so severe as to significantly reduce federal
revenue collections. As early as 1974, Arthur Laffer, creator of the famed
Laffer Curve, argued that the economic stimulus provided by sharp rate
cuts would make possible the *same* level of governmental services with
lower taxes.

These extreme claims by supply-siders were distinguished more by their audaciousness than by supporting evidence, and they found little favor among the established leadership and mainstream practitioners of the economics profession. Herbert Stein, a former chairman of the Council of Economic Advisers under presidents Richard Nixon and Gerald Ford, observed that supply-siders tended to bolster their position with "isolated anecdotes, post hoc, ergo propter hoc history, and quotations from fourteenth-century Moslem philosophers." [40] The supply-side perspective was so unconventional that it was branded "voodoo economics" by George Bush, who later ended up as Ronald Reagan's running mate and vice president.

Nonetheless, supply-side views won a hearing in the late 1970s that they would not have at other times. The theoretically impossible "stagflation" of the 1970s, with its high unemployment and inflation rates, opened up a search for new ideas, just as the theoretically impossible Great Depression of the 1930s paved the way for the acceptance of the ideas of Lord John Maynard Keynes. Supply-siders moved into this intellectual vacuum.

Second, the supply-side view fixed attention on a source of pain affecting a growing proportion of the public. Because of bracket creep, more and more middle- and upper-middle-income families were moving into the high tax brackets once reserved chiefly for the truly wealthy. In attacking those high marginal rates, supply-siders assumed leadership of an increasingly popular cause.

Finally, from the standpoint of both the public and the politicians, supply-side theories offered something that was almost too good to be true—the theoretical equivalent of the philosopher's stone that transmuted base metals into gold—a denial of the conclusion of most economists that "there's no such thing as a free lunch." Advocates were persuaded, and sought to persuade others, that supply-side policies could give the populace a steady level of public services *and* the benefits of a boom in goods and employment with no inflation while paying *lower* taxes. This optimistic position contrasted sharply with the mood of national malaise and talk of sacrifices and hard trade-offs that had marked the final years of the Carter presidency.

Embraced by candidate and then President Reagan, supply-side theory went from a fringe movement to official government dogma in a short span of time. Indeed, Reagan set in motion a chain of events that produced by far the largest tax reduction in U.S. history—the monumental Economic Recovery Tax Act of 1981.

Viewed in retrospect, the president's initial tax-cut proposal seems comparatively modest: a Kemp-style 10 percent, across-the-board reduction in marginal rates for each of three years. But his initiative sparked a "bidding war" between the White House and Capitol Hill as legislators from both parties sought political favors by offering new tax breaks pleasing to their constituents. Their inability to say "no" to potential beneficiaries escalated the total package far beyond what either Democrats or Republicans would have advanced in sober moments.

As ultimately enacted, ERTA offered a cornucopia of benefits projected to cost the U.S. Treasury $750 billion through fiscal year 1986. For individuals, the benefits included a 23 percent reduction in personal income taxes, including a cut in the top marginal rate from 70 percent to 50 percent. Other "goodies" included liberalized exemptions and deductions for retirement savings, charitable contributions, and estate and gift taxes. For business, the main feature was a wholly arbitrary and extremely generous depreciation schedule for capital equipment. In addition, its "safe harbor leasing" scheme made it possible for tax breaks that were not needed by one corporation to be sold to another. "It would probably be cheaper," Rep. David Obey, D-Wisc., observed, "if we gave everybody in the country three wishes." [41]

Despite these generous economic stimuli, the hoped-for supply-side "miracle" did not come to pass. Unemployment soared to postwar highs in 1981 and 1982, while the stock market plummeted and real interest rates escalated in spite of a reduction in inflation. More troubling still, the federal deficit exploded to levels unimaginable under any of the previous, supposedly freer-spending, administrations. Although the president had promised a return to budgetary balance by 1984, in fact the deficit— stoked by revenue reductions and higher defense outlays—escalated from $79 billion in 1981, to $128 billion in 1982, and up to nearly $208 billion in 1983. David A. Stockman, the Reagan administration's first budget chief, warned that Reagan's successor would inherit a federal debt nearly triple that compiled by all of his thirty-nine predecessors in office.[42]

The consequence was a shift toward new measures for "revenue enhancement" as the scope of the fiscal damage became apparent. In 1982 and again in 1984, Congress took matters into its own hands, striving to recoup, by closing loopholes and increasing excise taxes, some portion of the lost revenues—without directly attacking the president's prized rate reductions. The Tax Equity and Fiscal Responsibility Act of 1982 (TEFRA) and the Deficit Reduction Act of 1984 (DEFRA) restored to the Treasury annual amounts of $27 billion and $23 billion respectively.

In both instances, Congress demonstrated its capacity for independent action, developing legislation without the active support of the president. TEFRA was a historic first, in that the bill was largely crafted by Sen. Robert Dole, R-Kan., chairman of the Senate Finance Committee, despite the constitutional requirement that revenue-raising measures be initiated by the House of Representatives. Furthermore, beginning with the 1982 bill, the House Ways and Means Committee reverted to closed-door sessions to enhance its freedom of action when items of particular sensitivity were put on the chopping block.[43]

In retrospect, some believe that these twin base-broadening measures presaged the ultimate acceptance of the 1986 tax legislation. None were so bold as to draw this hopeful conclusion at the time, however. Instead, most observers stressed the limited and incremental nature of the remedial actions taken in 1982 and 1984. Only the "slowest of the strays" were included in the "cats and dogs" captured by TEFRA and DEFRA, one analyst commented.[44] Any more aggressive steps toward comprehensive income taxation seemed likely to spark much more effective organized resistance, as they always had in the past.

Reform III: The Flat Tax and Beyond

In principle, the aims of both the base broadeners and the supply-siders might be most readily accommodated through a uniform single-rate or flat tax on all income—an approach that would also greatly simplify both the tax code and the preparation of individual and corporate tax returns. This idea gained widespread attention in the early 1980s when two Hoover Institution economists, Robert E. Hall and Alvin Rabushka, recommended a 19-percent levy on all compensation, making payment of taxes so simple and uniform that tax returns might be "printed on a post card." [45] Their concept won a flurry of editorial endorsements, and legislation based upon it was introduced by Sen. Dennis DeConcini, D-Ariz., and others. Sen. Slade Gorton, R-Wash., commented that, when discussing tax issues, his constituents asked most often about the desirability of a flat tax. The idea did have great conceptual appeal: in one survey, 62 percent of those polled said they favored eliminating nearly all deductions and applying a 14 percent tax rate to everyone.[46]

The flat tax had its detractors too. Critics warned that, while offering a reduction at the top end, a considerable tax increase for lower- and middle-income groups would be necessary to make the low, uniform rate possible. Senator Gorton added, "Enthusiasm for [the flat tax] among the average group of Rotarians disappears when they learn that . . . many of them would have to pay more taxes than they do at the present time." [47] The flat tax also jeopardized tax benefits that enjoyed widespread popularity. When respondents to the same poll were shown a list of the tax benefits that might be eliminated to make that low rate possible, they made it clear that they wanted some of the largest and most costly tax expenditures to remain untouched. From a list of fifteen principal deductions and exclusions, most were willing to eliminate only three. For example, 51 percent said the deduction for oil and drilling costs could be terminated. But more than 80 percent wanted to keep the exclusion for social security and veterans' benefits, as well as the deduction for high medical expenses.

Yet, if pure flat-tax proposals seemed unacceptable, the possibility of a move in that direction did not. A combination of intellectual and pragmatic factors led experts and politicians of different ideological persuasions toward a new formula offering somewhat lower rates imposed on a somewhat broader base. By 1985 this seemed to be emerging as a new consensus position. As one review of several books on federal tax issues, all published in that year, noted:

> In broad outline, everyone who writes about tax reform says the same thing. The U.S. personal income tax is unfair, inefficient, and appallingly complicated. To fix the tax, we must sharply curtail tax "loopholes," thereby allowing us to broaden the tax base, reduce tax rates, and achieve substantial improvement in all three major dimensions in one fell swoop.[48]

Historically and conceptually, lower rates and base broadening were not necessarily linked. Most traditional reform proposals had been designed to enhance progressivity by eliminating the tax preferences that particularly benefited the wealthy. Henry Simons supported a progressive tax structure and condemned the Congress of the 1930s for adopting high rates that were not levied in practice—"dipping deeply into great incomes with a sieve," as he phrased it. Stanley Surrey also criticized existing tax expenditures as inconsistent with progressive distributional ideals, pointing out that, in 1977, the top 1.5 percent of taxpayers received over $26 billion in benefits, or 31 percent of the $84 billion total.[49]

These assessments conformed to popular stereotypes as well. The media have periodically charged that some of the very rich, or certain notable corporations, largely escape income taxation by taking advantage of loopholes. During the New Deal, the drive for tax reform was spurred by publicity given to the tools for tax avoidance and evasion available to the wealthy, including the revelation that financier J. P. Morgan had paid no U.S. income tax at all in 1930, 1931, or 1932.[50] A similar outcry appeared in 1968 when, on its last day in office, the outgoing Johnson administration released a study prepared by Assistant Secretary of the Treasury Stanley S. Surrey and Secretary Joseph A. Barr indicating that twenty-one millionaires, and many more individuals with $200,000-plus incomes, had paid no income tax in 1967. These revelations and the taxpayers' revolt they sparked helped shape the Tax Reform Act of 1969. Similarly, in the early 1980s the activist group Citizens for Tax Justice publicized their finding that at least 128 multinational corporations had paid no taxes at all for at least one of the years 1981—1983, despite many billions in combined profits.[51]

The public apparently took these sensational revelations to heart. In 1982 a Lou Harris poll found that 86 percent of the population shared the suspicion that "most higher-income people get out of paying much of their taxes by hiring clever tax accountants and lawyers who show them how to use loopholes in the tax law for tax shelters and other devices."[52] Another survey conducted in the late 1970s revealed a prevailing opinion that more than half of the very wealthy paid no federal income tax at all. This was, of course, a great exaggeration: in fact, according to tax analyst Joseph Minarik, only about 0.6 percent paid no tax.[53]

Despite such convictions, there was always the possibility that revenues gained by eliminating tax loopholes could be used to lower tax rates instead of raising additional revenue by enhancing progressivity. Ideas of this kind had been tossed about for decades. Pechman's early studies suggested that base broadening could permit a reduction in the 1956 rate schedules from 91 percent to 61 percent in the top bracket and from 20 percent to 13 percent for the lowest payers.[54] Two decades later, economist and author Paul Samuelson instructed his thousands of freshman readers that "If loopholes were closed and the erosion of the tax base corrected, rates on all income levels could be cut without revenue loss." [55] And a 1977 report on tax issues observed that representatives of business, labor, and the public, as well as influential members of both political parties, believed "all income should be taxed alike and that the revenue generated by the broader base should be used to lower the tax rates substantially.[56]

Yet, such thought left few marks until several key politicians took up the cause in the early 1980s. Of these, Sen. Bill Bradley, D-N.J., a former Rhodes scholar and—like Representative Kemp—a former professional athlete, fashioned the most influential proposal.[57] Bradley's "Fair Tax" plan, first introduced with cosponsor Sen. Richard Gephardt, D-Mo., in Congress in 1982, called for the simplification of tax laws by eliminating many special provisions, among them the exclusion for employer-paid health and life insurance, the 60-percent exclusion for long-term capital gains, the exclusion of income earned abroad, and benefits to the oil and gas industry. At the same time, Bradley-Gephardt (as the plan was known) continued the movement toward lowered rates that had intensified with ERTA. It combined one basic tax rate with special surcharges to create three rates: 14 percent, 26 percent, and 30 percent, the latter down from 50 percent. Four-fifths of the population, Bradley indicated, would pay the lowest rate, while the top rate was reserved for individuals with adjusted gross incomes over $37,500 and couples making more than $65,000. On the corporate side, too, the Fair Tax plan eliminated most deductions and special depreciation schedules while lowering the rate to 30 percent—exactly equal to the highest proposed individual rate.

The Bradley-Gephardt proposal was not a purist measure; it bowed in the direction of political reality in two respects. First, though a major step toward reform, the Fair Tax fell far short of using a comprehensive definition of income. A number of popular provisions, including deductions for home mortgage interest, charitable contributions, and state and local income taxes, were to be retained for moderate-income taxpayers. Second, the Fair Tax accepted the reality of the so-called Reagan revolution in that it was not designed to draw more money from the rich. "The 1981 tax law demonstrated clearly," Bradley explained, "that many Americans are concerned about the tax treatment of the wealthy—probably because they hope to be wealthy themselves someday." [58] But neither did it offer reductions to the rich and tax increases for the rest. Instead, the Fair Tax aimed to keep the revenue collected from each income group at the same level. Viewed category by category, the bill was "distributionally neutral."

A Republican variant of the Democrat-sponsored Fair Tax was introduced by Senators Kemp and Robert Kasten, R-Wisc., in 1984. Their FAST (for Fair and Simple Tax) also lowered rates and broadened the base, while preserving many of the more widely used deductions. It proposed only a single bracket of 25 percent (later 24 percent), coupled with special deductions for families making less than $40,000 from wages. Thus, its maximum rate was lower than Bradley-Gephardt's. Kemp-Kasten also preserved more special investment incentives, and retained the system of indexation inaugurated in 1981. The result was a proposal that maintained the same distribution of burden for most taxpayers, while offering a rate cut of about 20 percent for those making over $100,000.

In sum, the "lower the rates, broaden the base" approach pioneered by Pechman, advocated by Bradley, and adopted by Kemp seemed by the mid-1980s to hold the middle ground. More complex but more politically feasible than a true flat tax, it offered a compromise of the objectives of the comprehensive income tax reformers on the one hand and supply-side advocates on the other. Still, the real goals of the two main camps of tax reformers remained quite different, even incompatible. Many of the comprehensive income-tax reformers believed that some enhancement in progressivity, or additional revenue to reduce the burgeoning deficit, was essential. Pechman contended that making the personal income tax "a progressive tax in fact as well as name" should be the first order of business.[59] In contrast, lower rates, not base broadening, was the heart of the supply-side agenda. Indeed, George Gilder argued,

> As long as the rates remain so high and progressive, . . . tax "reforms" are futile. . . . A tax code perforated for avoidance is preferable to a system of the same rates without loopholes. . . . The tax reform movement, therefore, would make the system worse. The only desirable reform is reduction in the tax rates.[60]

Conclusion

By 1984 and 1985 a number of elements supportive of tax reform were in place. First and foremost, experts agreed that the income-tax system was seriously flawed. To a considerable degree, there was also consensus on the most appropriate remedy: a combination of base broadening and tax-rate reduction. Leaders in Congress, as well as presidential candidates and presidents, had advocated reform plans. And the public, too, was clearly disenchanted with the status quo.

Still, none of these factors made legislative action on tax reform appear likely. Instead, it was the essentially unanimous opinion of close observers that tax reform was an idea whose time had not yet arrived. The historical record was clearly bleak, and present circumstances seemed little better. By the time Congress addressed the issue, public concern actually seemed to be waning (see Figure 2—4). A Roper poll prepared in April 1986 cautioned, "While tax resentment has not disappeared, it has clearly diminished in intensity, especially in the case of the federal income tax. . . . Fewer people now believe that middle-income families, wage earners and homeowners— the so-called average Americans—pay too much in taxes." Further, popular opinion seemed skeptical of many of the reform proposals being advanced. "Americans want . . . more fairness," the pollsters noted, but "they do not want to make the tax system less progressive, and they do not want to stop using taxes as an instrument of social policy." [61]

Recognizing such constraints, Michael J. Graetz joined John Witte, David Davies, and many others in offering a dismal view. In 1984 he cautioned:

> Prospects for structural tax reform have been dimmed by recent "reforms" in congressional practices; public pressure to enact income tax reforms seems nonexistent; political leadership on tax matters has become increasingly diffuse; committee deliberations are now open to the public and are well-attended by representatives of groups with a special interest in the outcome; and political action committees now have great influence in guiding policy decisions. In short, for those who would urge massive tax reforms, there is more than ample cause for despair.[62]

Few observers dared to be more optimistic, and those that did had reasons that proved to be erroneous—believing, for example, that the magnitude of the deficit and the need to raise taxes might shock the population into accepting a major restructuring of the government's revenue system.[63]

Yet, all these scholarly observers—as well as a host of like-minded politicians and political pundits—were wrong. Between the summer of 1985 and October 22, 1986, when it was signed into law, sweeping tax-reform legislation was moved ahead by a skeptical Congress, in the face of intense interest-group opposition, under the leadership of a sometimes-inattentive president, and to the weak cheers of a largely uninterested public. Further, the bill adopted was intentionally revenue neutral—designed to add no more, but also to provide no less, money to the national coffers. Thus, it nether reduced nor augmented the mounting deficit, which many viewed as the nation's primary economic concern.

As this astonishing outcome suggests, the tax policy-making process was

Figure 2—4   Public Opinion on Income Tax Rates, 1947—1988

Question: "Is Income Tax Too High?"

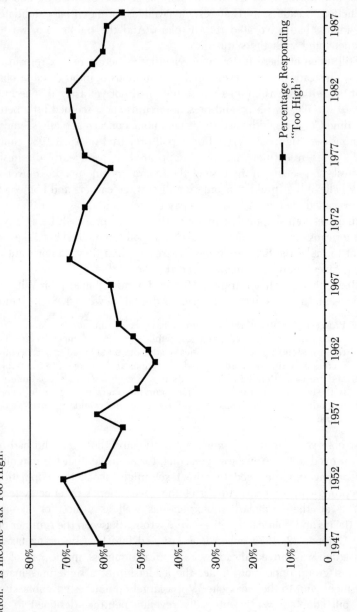

Source: Gallup Poll data, 1947—1973; National Opinion Research Center data, 1976—1988.

in the grip of new political forces. Though those forces were poorly recognized even on the eve of the TRA's enactment, they proved decisive.

Notes

1. Joseph J. Minarik, "How Tax Reform Came About," *Tax Notes*, December 28, 1987, 1359.
2. This conception draws upon John W. Kingdon's informative and insightful *Agendas, Alternatives, and Public Policies* (Boston, Mass.: Little, Brown, 1984). See especially pages 20−21 and 88−94. Kingdon, in turn, was inspired by Michael Cohen, James March, and Johan Olsen, "A Garbage Can Model of Organizational Choice," *Administrative Science Quarterly* 17 (March 1972): 1−25.
3. Quoted in Gerald Carson, *The Golden Egg: The Personal Income Tax: Where It Came From, How It Grew* (Boston, Mass.: Houghton-Mifflin, 1977), 61.
4. The principal, though temporary, respite from these pre−World War II rate increases was offered in the 1920s. President Warren Harding's Treasury secretary, Andrew Mellon, argued for and won a series of five tax reductions slashing top rates from 77 to 25 percent, while also running a budget surplus.
5. The definitive study of Mills's leadership is presented in John F. Manley's "Wilbur D. Mills: A Study in Congressional Influence," *American Political Science Review* 62 (June 1969): 442−64, and in his book, *The Politics of Finance: The House Committee on Ways and Means* (Boston, Mass.: Little, Brown, 1970). See also Catherine E. Rudder, "Tax Policy: Structure and Choice," in *Making Economic Policy in Congress*, ed. Allen Schick (Washington: American Enterprise Institute, 1983), 196−220.
6. See Joseph J. Minarik, *Making Tax Choices* (Washington: Urban Institute, 1985), Table 4, 37.
7. John F. Witte, *The Politics and Development of the Federal Income Tax* (Madison: University of Wisconsin Press, 1985), 249.
8. For a summary discussion, see Joseph A. Pechman, *Federal Tax Policy*, 5th ed. (Washington: Brookings Institution, 1987), chap. 5; and David G. Davies, *United States Taxes and Tax Policy* (New York: Cambridge University Press, 1986), chaps. 6 and 7.
9. Witte, *Politics and Development*, 251, 175.
10. See Pechman, *Federal Tax Policy*, 40−41.
11. See Stanley S. Surrey, *Pathways to Tax Reform* (Cambridge, Mass.: Harvard University Press, 1973). In 1974, his notion was given official standing when the *Congressional Budget Act* required the annual publication of a "tax expenditure budget" including estimates of the revenue lost by each item. Although this effort was mostly cosmetic, as the continuing rise in tax expenditures showed, it did make that growth more apparent, creating a focal point for continuing policy debates.
12. See Witte, *Politics and Development*, 289.
13. Stanley S. Surrey, "The Congress and the Tax Lobbyist: How Special Tax Provisions Get Enacted," *Harvard Law Review* 70 (May 1957): 1145−82.
14. Ibid., 1175.
15. See Ronald F. King, "Tax Expenditures and Systematic Public Policy," *Public Budgeting and Finance* 4 (Spring 1984): 14−31.
16. Robert Havemann, "Tax Expenditures—Spending Money without Expendi-

tures," *National Journal*, December 10, 1977, 1909, quoted in Stanley S. Surrey and Paul R. McDaniel, *Tax Expenditures* (Cambridge, Mass.: Harvard University Press, 1985), 101. Consistent with this philosophy have been proposals to replace environmental regulations with a system of "effluent charges" levied on industrial polluters and the use of an automatic system of "negative income tax" payments to replace the complex welfare grants system. President Reagan himself long urged a program of national support for local "urban enterprise zones" that would offer tax and regulatory relief to struggling neighborhoods.

17. Witte, *Politics and Development*, 330 and 242.

18. H. Rept. 5, 63d Cong., 1st sess., April 22, 1913, quoted in Richard Goode, *The Individual Income Tax* (Washington: Brookings Institution, 1964), 2.

19. Ibid., 11.

20. Joseph A. Pechman, "Tax Policies for the 1980s," in *Economics in the Public Service*, ed. Joseph A. Pechman and N. J. Simler (New York: W.W. Norton, 1982), 145.

21. A progressive tax, in an economic sense, takes a larger fraction of large than of small incomes. In contrast, a regressive (and therefore bad, to most economists) tax does the opposite, taking a larger fraction of lower incomes. A proportional (and simply inadequate) tax takes the same fraction of all incomes. In an income tax, progressivity can be ensured by exempting specific lower incomes from all taxation, or by establishing a system of graduated rates rising toward the upper end of the income scale. In contrast, property taxes, sales taxes, and social security payroll taxes are often judged to be modestly to strongly regressive.

22. A. C. Pigou has written, "It is evident that any transference of income from a relatively rich man to a relatively poor man of similar temperament, since it enables more intense wants to be satisfied at the expense of less intense ones, must increase the aggregate sum of satisfactions." Arthur Cecil Pigou, *The Economics of Welfare*, 4th ed. (London: Macmillan, 1948), 89 (originally published in 1932).

23. Harold M. Groves, *Tax Philosophers: Two Hundred Years of Thought in Great Britain and the United States* (Madison: University of Wisconsin Press, 1974), 85.

24. Henry C. Simons, *Personal Income Taxation: The Definition of Income as a Problem of Fiscal Policy* (Chicago: University of Chicago Press, 1938). See also his *Federal Tax Reform* (Chicago: University of Chicago Press, 1950). Another, earlier contributor to this line of thought was Robert M. Haig. See his edited collection, *The Federal Income Tax* (New York: Columbia University Press, 1921).

25. The same reasoning implies that one should pay a federal income tax on the value of farm or garden vegetables grown and eaten (rather than sold), on clothing knitted and worn, or on housework performed for one's family, rather than on a wage-basis for others. Although few proposals went so far as to call for taxing the preparation of meals, and the administrative obstacles to doing so are obvious, those economist-reformers with a puristic bent *do* regard the failure to do so as a departure from an economically precise comprehensive definition of income.

26. Pechman's intellectual autobiography is presented in Bernard Barber, *Effective Social Science: Eight Cases in Economics, Political Science, and Sociology* (New York: Russell Sage Foundation, 1987), 77—91, upon which the following description is based.

27. Joseph A. Pechman, "Erosion of the Individual Income Tax," *National Tax Journal* 10 (March 1957): 24. See also Joseph A. Pechman, "What Would a Comprehensive Individual Income Tax Yield?" in *Tax Revision Compendium*, submitted to the House Committee on Ways and Means (Washington: U.S. Government Printing Office, 1959).

28. Boris I. Bittker, "A 'Comprehensive Tax Base' as a Goal of Income Tax Reform," in *A Comprehensive Income Tax Base? A Debate*, ed. Boris I. Bittker, Charles O. Galvin, R. A. Musgrave, and Joseph A. Pechman (Branford, Conn.: Federal Tax Press, 1968), 1.

29. Henry S. Reuss, "Foreword" to Joseph A. Ruskay and Richard A. Osserman, *Halfway to Tax Reform* (Bloomington, Ind.: Indiana University Press, 1970), vii. The book offers a full account of the 1969 act.

30. Witte, *Politics and Development*, 194.

31. Roger A. Freeman, *Tax Loopholes: The Legend and the Reality* (Washington: American Enterprise Institute, 1973), 90.

32. A full account of the Carter administration's initiatives is presented in Edward R. Kantowicz, "The Limits of Incrementalism: Carter's Efforts at Tax Reform," *Journal of Policy Analysis and Management* 4, no. 2 (Winter 1985), 217−33.

33. U.S. Congress, House, *Congressional Record*, 95th Cong., 2d sess., October 14, 1978, 38638, quoted in Kantowicz, "The Limits of Incrementalism," 228.

34. Leading supply-side thinkers and activists of the 1970s included George Gilder, Rep. Jack Kemp, Arthur Laffer, Robert Mundell, Paul Craig Roberts, Norman Ture, and Jude Wanniski. Much of their work was publicized through the editorial page of the *Wall Street Journal*. As Kemp notes, these writers, economists, and politicians considered themselves a "movement" advancing a "political and economic revolution." See Kemp's Foreword to Bruce Bartlett, *"Reaganomics": Supply Side Economics in Action* (Westport, Conn.: Arlington House Publishers, 1981), vii.

35. Jack Kemp, *An American Renaissance: A Strategy for the 1980s* (New York: Harper and Row, 1979), 1.

36. Ibid., 36, 46−47.

37. Later versions of Kemp's plan proposed cutting the top rate to 25 percent and added a variety of other embellishments, including a limit on federal spending tied to the gross national product, the elimination of many deductions and credits, indexation, and increased personal exemptions.

38. George Gilder, *The Spirit of Enterprise* (New York: Simon and Schuster, 1984), 144.

39. Paul Craig Roberts, "Supply-Side Economics, Growth, and Liberty," in *To Promote Prosperity: U.S. Domestic Policy in the Mid-1980s*, ed. John H. Moore (Stanford, Calif.: Hoover Institution Press, 1984), 75.

40. Herbert Stein, *Washington Bedtime Stories: The Politics of Money and Jobs* (New York: Free Press, 1986), 123.

41. David A. Stockman, *The Triumph of Politics: The Inside Story of the Reagan Revolution* (New York: Avon Books, 1987), 277.

42. Ibid., 447.

43. This point is noted in Randall Strahan, "Committee Politics and Tax Reform" (Paper prepared for the annual meeting of the American Political Science Association, Chicago, September 1987), 10−12.

44. Minarik, *Making Tax Choices*, 109.

45. See Robert E. Hall and Alvin Rabushka, *Low Tax, Simple Tax, Flat Tax* (New

York: McGraw-Hill, 1983) and *The Flat Tax* (Stanford, Calif.: Stanford University Press, 1985).

46. Lou Harris Poll reported in Timothy B. Clark, "Flat-Rate Income Tax Debate May Spur Attacks on Some Tax Breaks," *National Journal*, November 13, 1982, 1932.

47. Slade Gorton, "Tax Reform and the Legislative Process," in *Options for Tax Reform*, ed. Joseph A. Pechman (Washington: Brookings Institution, 1984), 7.

48. Paul N. Courant, "Book Reviews: Taxes," *Journal of Policy Analysis and Management* 5 (Spring 1986): 598.

49. Simons, *Personal Income Taxation*, 219. On that basis, Simons also argued for less confiscatory rates at the highest levels—"a scale of rates which responsible leaders really approved" and thus would be willing to uphold. See also, Surrey and McDaniel, *Tax Expenditures*, 71−72.

50. Carson, *The Golden Egg*, 118. Tax evasion, involving, for example, the failure to report some income, is illegal. In contrast, tax avoidance simply involves arranging one's financial affairs to take advantage of any possible benefits provided in the law itself.

51. Dale Russakoff, "U.S. Economy Is User and Abuser of Tax Breaks," *Washington Post*, March 17, 1985, A16.

52. Clark, "Flat-Rate Income Tax Debate, 1931.

53. Minarik, *Making Tax Choices*, 7.

54. Pechman, "Erosion of the Individual Income Tax," 25.

55. Paul A. Samuelson, *Economics*, 8th ed. (New York: McGraw-Hill, 1970), 161.

56. Bruce K. MacLaury, "Foreword," in *Comprehensive Income Taxation*, ed. Joseph A. Pechman (Washington: Brookings Institution, 1977), vii−viii.

57. For background on Bradley's thought and initiative, see his book, *The Fair Tax* (New York: Pocket Books, 1984). See also, Joseph A. Pechman, ed., *A Citizen's Guide to the New Tax Reforms: Fair Tax, Simple Tax, Flat Tax* (Totowa, N.J.: Rowman and Allanheld, 1985). This useful volume compares the Bradley-Gephardt, Kemp-Kasten, and Hall-Rabushka proposals, as well as the Aaron-Galper cash-flow tax.

58. Bradley, *The Fair Tax*, 94.

59. Joseph A. Pechman, *The Rich, the Poor, and the Taxes They Pay* (Boulder, Colo.: Westview Press, 1986), 310.

60. Gilder, *Spirit of Enterprise*, 126−27.

61. William Schneider, "Americans Still Wary on Tax Reform," *National Journal*, July 12, 1986, 1740.

62. Michael J. Graetz, "Can the Income Tax Continue to Be the Major Revenue Source?" in *Options for Tax Reform*, ed. Pechman, 42.

63. See, for example, Minarik, *Making Tax Choices*, 157−58, and Henry J. Aaron and Harvey Galper, *Assessing Tax Reform* (Washington: Brookings Institution, 1985), 139.

3 Politics, Professionals, and the President: Developing an Executive Initiative

I am asking Secretary Don Regan for a plan for action to simplify the entire tax code, so all taxpayers, big and small, are treated more fairly. . . . I have asked that specific recommendations, consistent with those objectives, be presented to me by December, 1984.
—Ronald Reagan, January 1984

As the president uttered those words, derisive laughter burst from Democratic legislators gathered to hear his State of the Union Address. Although they were momentarily intrigued, the December deadline suggested Reagan's plan was an inside joke: bureaucratic studies with postelection due dates are a politician's way of avoiding problems, not solving them.

A year later congressional Democrats discovered that the joke was on them. The Treasury Department had taken its mission very seriously, and by the time of the president's next annual message, tax reform had emerged from its bureaucratic burial ground as Reagan's top domestic priority. Coming on the heels of his forty-nine-state electoral sweep in November 1984, the proposal threatened to make a deep imprint on partisan politics as well as tax policy.

This remarkable transformation stemmed in large part from an unexpected confluence of interests among the different groups who served the president. The tax experts in the Treasury Department viewed reform as an opportunity to implement their professional agenda: improving the tax code by promoting equity among individuals with similar incomes and by removing tax preferences that distort the efficient flow of economic capital. Their ultimate success in defining the parameters of reform demonstrates the power of the bureaucracy to mold policy to fit professional norms and to advance institutional missions. The president's own interest in tax reform was always the promise of lower rates. In this he was egged on by "populist conservatives" for whom tax cuts were the raison d'être of reform. They viewed lower taxes in political terms, as a way to cement the "Reagan Revolution" and solidify Republican electoral gains. Decidedly less enthusiastic were the White House pragmatists, whose job was to evaluate the conflicting demands of interest-group and party politics. This last group was small but close to the president.

As a result of these conflicting interests swirling around the Oval Office, the fate of tax reform was often uncertain. Despite his recurring interest in

45

it, Reagan never stepped in to exert strong leadership. In tax reform as throughout his presidency, when it came to concrete policy decisions the president waited for those in his inner circle to make the first move.

Thus it was not until January 1984, when it appeared that Walter Mondale might make tax reform the economic centerpiece of his presidential campaign, that prospects brightened at the White House. Largely as a way to neutralize the Democratic threat, Reagan announced his intention to "study" the problem.

There ensued a two-stage process, beginning at the Treasury Department. Thanks to a calculated decision to insulate candidate Reagan from possible political liabilities, Treasury Secretary Donald Regan was given free reign over tax reform. Pledged to secrecy by the White House and committed to protect his product from the taint of politics, the former Wall Street maverick harnessed the best talent his department had to offer. By the time of Reagan's smashing electoral victory in November, he and a small group of close aides and tax experts had produced a logically coherent and professionally sound reform plan—dubbed Treasury I.

Initially, its contents generated only heartburn among politicos at the White House. "This steps on every Republican toe in the country," said White House Chief of Staff James Baker when he saw Regan's handiwork. Down Pennsylvania Avenue, the screams of agony were louder still, especially from congressional Republicans. Yet the president needed a bold initiative for his second term, and none had been provided during the 1984 campaign. Moreover, Treasury I was being received favorably by some, especially the all-important media. Then, too, what if tax reform did—as some believed it would—realign the political landscape and end the Republicans' minority status? For all of these reasons, tax reform was off and running at the White House.

Thereafter came a game of cabinet-level musical chairs that astonished Washingtonians but advanced the cause of reform. Newly designated Treasury chief James Baker packed the plan back to the Treasury Department for a political tune-up, while Regan stayed behind as White House chief of staff. This switch put a reformer next to the president's ear and launched a thoroughgoing review of tax reform at Treasury, this time through the lens of pure politics. The result was a much modified proposal (Treasury II), unveiled as the president's own and sent to Capitol Hill.

Thus began the perilous journey of tax reform through the political process. Looking back, it must be said that while politics ascended to the top of a long list of concerns during Treasury II—there to stay through the remainder of tax reform—subsequent decisions were constrained or otherwise influenced by what was accomplished in Treasury I. As this chapter shows, professionals gave tax reform its soul while Reagan's political midwives helped give it life.

First Stirrings

Arranging deals over a friendly game of golf has long been a corporate tradition, subsidized by the tax code. Thanks to the TRA, though, which put new limits on business deductions such as country club dues, that tradition has become more costly. Thus, it is ironic that tax reform, in the guise of a flat-rate tax, may have received its initial presidential go-ahead on the links.

In David Stockman's recollection, Reagan was first sold on the notion during an amicable round of golf with Secretary of State George Shultz, a former economics professor, in late 1982. Stockman reported, "By the eighteenth hole the president was convinced that [a flat tax] was a way to reduce the deficit without increasing taxes." Shultz "always carried influence" with Reagan, noted the former assistant secretary for tax policy, John (Buck) Chapoton, and he made the idea seem "realistic." Still, not all observers give so much credit to Shultz. Neither tax reform nor the flat tax was new: the Hall-Rabushka plan had established the idea before that, and the Bradley-Gephardt dual-rate bill had been introduced in Congress. Reagan himself had expressed interest some months earlier.[1]

Whatever the immediate cause, the president was enthusiastic. "It was the kind of simple idea that immediately appealed to the president," observed one White House aide. If a flat tax enhanced economic growth, he thought, it would cut the deficit, foreclosing the need for a dreaded tax increase. Moreover, the notion was in keeping with Reagan's deeply rooted, fiercely held opposition to big government. He often remarked that when success as an actor put him in the top World War II tax bracket of 94 percent, he quit making movies! To the president, the lesson was obvious: high tax rates discouraged individual and corporate initiative. Thus, White House adviser Mitch Daniels insisted that "lower rates were the core" of Reagan's interest in tax reform, especially "getting the top rate down as low as possible." This was, Stockman confirmed, "one of the few things Ronald Reagan deeply wanted."[2]

The idea of flat taxes spun like a top around the corridors of the west wing of the White House in late 1982. "Everyone . . . was talking flat tax," writes the former budget director, "presenting his own version of how it would work."[3] Seeking a bold initiative for 1983, some began drafting language to that effect. The president made mention of the idea for weeks.

In the end, however, a flat-tax proposal was not included in the 1983 State of the Union address. "As [the drafts] came back from the White House . . . the tax-reform paragraphs got watered down step by step," recalled one disappointed Treasury aide. "We were reduced to an afterthought."[4] In part, this was because the necessary consensus on details and definitions never formed. Professionals at Treasury rejected a completely flat-rate tax as regressive and politically unrealistic. Speaking on behalf of his department, Regan objected that, in the aggregate, such a plan would "result in people with annual incomes above $50,000 paying less in taxes, while those with earnings in the middle and lower range would pay $32 billion more! " [5] Treasury wanted tax reform, but according to its own institutional and professional standards, not some ideological icon. Meanwhile, the White House deputy chief of staff, Richard Darman, along with Stockman and Martin Feldstein, the chairman of the president's Council of Economic Advisers, preferred higher taxes, not lower ones. They quietly plotted to turn the president's enthusiasm for flat rates into approval for a "contingency" tax, their not very straightforward plan to solve the deficit problem.

Ultimately, the chief of staff put a stop to it all. A pragmatist, Jim Baker had no special affinity for such reforms, and he worried about the politically dangerous sand traps the golfing twosome had overlooked. As Stockman said: "It meant that we were fixing to cancel the mortgage deduction and tax the welfare checks of blind people. So Shultz' original flat tax idea was packed off to Siberia, in this case a 'deep study mode' at Treasury." [6] Indeed, the study mode was so deep that when the January 1983 address was finally delivered, the president provoked no reaction at all from the Congress. On this occasion, virtually no one outside of Treasury even noticed the one-line request that the department "continue to study ways to simplify the tax code and make it more fair for all Americans."

Treasury Won: An Economist's Dream

Departmental professionals had noticed, of course, and they used the opportunity to keep their own recipes for reform cooking on the back burner. By December 1983 they were searching for ways to get them back on the menu—"to begin exposing the president to various fundamental reform options" in the words of then-Deputy Assistant Secretary Ronald Pearlman—when presidential politics suddenly turned up the heat. As the 1984 primaries approached, the White House learned that Sen. Bill Bradley was working tenaciously to convince Democrats (especially presidential hopeful Walter Mondale) to endorse the Bradley-Gephardt Fair Tax plan. Standing guard over the president's 1984 electoral interests, Baker wanted a plausible comeback. Should Mondale take Bradley's bait, he reasoned, the president must be able to point to his own work on the subject. A full-fledged Treasury study would fit the bill.

Politics thus explained why tax reform was officially turned over to Treasury in 1984. Baker stated unequivocally: "The true reason that we as an administration undertook an examination of this issue was because we were concerned that the other side would be embracing it and using it against us in the 1984 presidential election." In the terms of one analyst, the political stream had (momentarily) merged with the solutions proposed by Treasury tax experts to form a powerful current of support for an administration tax-reform initiative.[7] Needless to say, it was a combination the president—who still hoped reform might provide a further means of cutting taxes—happily endorsed.

A Study Is Born

Although Democrats in Congress laughed off the request as "just another study," Treasury officials were delighted at the chance to rekindle their efforts. Old hands recognized the deck was stacked against them. Yet, as former economic staff coordinator Eugene Steuerle reminisced, it was a chance to "really pull together the theories," and to "explore the frontier."

While the economists' enthusiasm was readily understandable, Secretary Regan's motivations were more complex. As the potential domestic policy highlight of Reagan's second term, tax reform piqued his proprietary interests. Yet its selection was by no means ensured, and Baker's initial reactions suggested that the venture would be fraught with political risks. Even so, the Treasury chief eagerly embraced the challenge.

As an officer of Merrill Lynch before heading to Treasury, Regan had earned a reputation as a maverick, a "corporate populist" on Wall Street. Unlike many businessmen, he embraced the economists' belief that the tax system should be neutral in its effects on different and competing industries:

> For most of my career on Wall Street, I chafed under laws and regulations that gave the banking industry tax breaks that brokerage firms were denied. . . . When the same concept is extended to entire industries, the results range from the absurd to the near piratical.

Regan also had strong negative opinions about the individual side of the tax code, which he deemed "complicated" and "inequitable." To convince the president of this, Regan showed him that General Electric (Reagan's old employer) paid less in taxes than the chief executive's personal secretary. All in all, Regan firmly believed, a tax code that "institutional-ized tax avoidance" was bad for the country. "I wanted to throw it out and start over," he remembers.[8]

On Wall Street, Regan's blustery style and radical ideas had put him at odds with the financial establishment. Those same qualities also put him on the outskirts of Washington's inner circle. On Capitol Hill and among the city's prestigious law firms and lobbies, the new Treasury secretary was discounted as a neophyte with questionable political skills.

Ultimately, this denigration inspired Regan to fight back via tax reform in the same way that he had earlier revolutionized the securities industry.

During the 1984 State of the Union speech, Regan recalled feeling that the Democratic snickering was directed at him as well as at his president. "My anger rose," he later wrote. "I said to myself, just wait. I'll show you guys." [9]

A Revolution Afoot

Two weeks later Regan set out to do just that. As he told the chosen few who had been tapped for the task, the aim was to "revolutionize" the tax code. "Be bold," he instructed. "To think . . . compromise [is] to doom the effort." In Regan's memory his core of professionals had "absolute freedom of thought, speech, and action; political considerations were irrelevant. They were to disregard every factor except fairness, simplicity, and efficiency. 'Nothing is sacred,' I told them." [10]

Regan's own preference for order and hierarchy, reinforced by the professionals' training, meant the Treasury I process pursued a classic path of rational decision making, beginning with a careful diagnosis of the tax code's principal problems. Next, alternative schools of reform were identified and a basic approach was agreed to. Finally, the code was divided into its primary components and an exhaustive list of specific options was examined and debated. Decision-making responsibility was assigned to a select "tax strategy group" comprising the secretary, his business community liaison, key assistant and deputy assistant secretaries with responsibility for economic or tax policy, and the chief of the Internal Revenue Service (IRS).[11] Technical responsibility was shared by the Offices of Tax Policy (dominated by lawyers) and Tax Analysis (staffed by economists).

From start to finish the process took nearly a year as analysts reviewed existing law and crafted the best alternatives their professions had to offer. Early on, when tax theory was the focus of discussion, departmental economists led the process. Later, the lawyers joined in as the group combed through the tax code, zooming in on objectionable provisions, devising substitutes, drafting position papers, and preparing summaries.

Each week the tax strategy group met to discuss, debate, and vote on suggested revisions and proposals. The procedure and organization were deceptively routine. Only Regan's choice of participants, his embargo on outside communication, and his decision to hold political considerations at bay gave away the true dimensions of the revolution afoot.

Predictably, the key to this freedom was Regan's willingness to shelter his forces from the winds of politics and interagency haggling. He forbade all such influences from entering Treasury meeting rooms and took measures to prevent outsiders from listening at the doors. Virtually no one else in the department or outside was privy to the process or materials, including other members of the cabinet and emissaries from Capitol Hill. Even the president and his advisers kept themselves on the other side of Treasury's iron fence. Pearlman recalled:

> The secretary made a decision that we would discuss our recommendations with no one. We'd get a call from a cabinet member saying, "What are you doing to *my* constituency?" And, we'd say, "Sorry, we'll talk to you about the *issues*, but we will not talk about what we're going to do." Members of Congress would also call, and we'd say, "Sorry." I remember going up to the Hill and getting beaten over the head by fairly influential members who said, "This is outrageous. You can't do this."

The Treasury Department is known for secrecy, something one observer attributed to its leakproof organizational culture. Career employees often deal with sensitive financial information and with closely guarded presidential initiatives. Yet the code of silence was extreme even by Treasury standards because it suited White House interests as well as Regan's personal style.

Having moved to capture the popular symbol of tax reform, Reagan's political operatives believed they had much to lose and nothing to gain from the painful specifics of reform. Thus, they kept the White House staff as well as the president uninvolved and unaware of Treasury I throughout the campaign. As Texan Buck Chapoton observed, "They wanted to be able to say, 'Me no Alamo,'" under the obvious assumption that what candidate Reagan (and, it was hoped, the general public) didn't know couldn't hurt him.

Although the secrecy sacrificed a degree of outsider insight, technical advice, and political goodwill, Treasury I would never have emerged as pure without it. In particular, the White House hands-off policy provided freedom to pursue tax reform as the professionals defined it—with far-reaching consequences. Indeed, the president's interest in lower rates *and* no additional taxes was reshaped by experts into the most politically painful and effective discipline in the tax-reform process: revenue neutrality. This tough new standard, which had also been employed in Bradley-Gephardt, said that reform could neither lose nor raise income-tax revenues. Unlike the president, most departmental economists were deeply concerned about enormous federal deficits and were determined not to exacerbate the problem. As Charles McLure put it: "The president said we couldn't raise revenues, and we sure weren't going to lose revenues if I had anything to say about it."

Subsequent to Treasury I—from the preparation of Treasury II to the final passage of H.R. 3838—the contrivance worked to constrain the foes of tax reform and empower its friends. How? By forcing politicians to give up their pet preferences to attain what few of them dared to oppose: lower tax rates. Without the option of raising or losing revenue, base broadening became the principal means to lower rates.

Because base broadening proved to be a highly complex task, policy makers turned to experts and professionals for extra help in crafting proposals. First, politicians had to consider the distributional, sectoral, and revenue implications of their actions, which necessitated reliance on highly skilled revenue estimators and tax economists. Second, when it came to tinkering with details, experts had always been the idea men in tax policy. With so much change in the works, professionals and politicians became locked together as a powerful and ultimately unbeatable duo.

Always the Same. If the White House had no detailed tax-reform ideas, the professionals at Treasury certainly did. As Chapoton observed:

> If you give reform to the tax professionals, you're always going to get the same answers, regardless of political party. You'll be moving toward a pure income tax system . . . [one that only] raises revenue . . . and that influences capital flows to a minimum.

Although such remedies are most commonly identified with economists, they were also shared by departmental lawyers and IRS accountants for reasons of organizational culture and mission, as well as for simplicity in tax administration.

Even so, while experts everywhere agreed that the tax code's problems were severe and that "something" should be done to promote horizontal equity, investment neutrality, and a broad tax base, the larger community of tax professionals and economists argued continuously about what that "something" was. Early Treasury action reflected these debates as the strategy group and its staff of experts defined problems and outlined the broad contours of reform.

Diagnosing the Problem

Looking back, Treasury's assessment of the tax code's principal flaws reflected both its institutional biases and professional assumptions. From a professional perspective, the worst failures were believed to spring from differential treatment of similarly situated individuals and corporations, which produced inequalities, inefficiencies, and lower economic growth. For example, the Office of Tax Analysis estimated that under existing tax law (with a 5 percent rate of inflation) the effective corporate tax rate varied from −8 percent on some kinds of equipment to +40 percent on most structures. Because different businesses invest in different assets, this meant that effective tax rates varied enormously across industries, most notably between capital intensive operations that were highly favored by the tax code and service industries that were not (see Table 3−1).

Treasury experts pointed to similar inequities on the individual side of the code due to special preferences like employee fringe benefits; state and local taxes; business perquisites for meals, entertainment, automobiles, and "working" vacations; and the explosion of tax shelters. A Treasury Department report counted a 400 percent increase in the number of claims for

Table 3–1   *Effective Tax Rates on Investments in Equipment and*
Structures by Selected Industries under Existing Law

Industry	Tax rate (percent)
Agriculture	29
Mining	13
Logging	21
Primary metals	16
Electrical equipment	26
Motor vehicles	8
Food	25
Textiles	19
Pulp and paper	12
Petroleum refining	12
Leather	30
Transport services	9
Service and trade	31

Source: U.S. Department of the Treasury, Office of Tax Analysis, "Tax Reform for Fairness, Simplicity, and Economic Growth: The Treasury Department Report to the President," *Tax Notes,* December 3, 1984, 916.

Note: Assumes equity financing for a corporation in the 46 percent bracket with an inflation rate of 5 percent.

partnership losses—a common shelter—between 1963 and 1982. "Obviously unfair," instructed the authors of the Treasury report. "Even at moderate income levels, taxpayers with similar incomes can incur tax liabilities that differ by thousands of dollars." [12]

From an institutional perspective, Treasury Department professionals worried about two kinds of perverse effects associated with the complexity of the tax code. First, the IRS argued that the labyrinthian tax code with its jumble of contradictory and overlapping policies was a nightmare to administer. Partly because of the rash of major changes in the tax law in 1978, 1981, 1982, and 1984, the IRS was years behind in issuing regulations.

Second, and more troubling still, Treasury officials believed that this jumbled system threatened the department's central mission: raising sufficient revenues to finance government. Quoting Steuerle:

> I felt that if we got out a good study, we could uphold the tradition and reputation of the Treasury Department. The Department's mission is to stand up for the public interest. Congress and taxpayers always bombard the Treasury with requests for special provisions. Recently Treasury had gotten into the political position of never trying to offend anyone and, therefore, not opposing adequately ideas that were clearly bad for the public interest.

The resulting explosion of tax expenditures during the 1970s and early

1980s had dramatically eroded the income-tax base (see Figure 2−2). By 1982 the amount of revenues forgone because of tax expenditures equaled 73 percent of all income taxes collected.[13] Even worse, department officials feared that a "decline in taxpayer morale" could ultimately reduce voluntary compliance and lead to massive tax avoidance. They pointed to evidence that American taxpayers—like their European counterparts—increasingly under-reported income and overstated deductions and expenses. The Office of Tax Analysis estimated that individual taxpayers failed to report $250 billion in 1981, contributing to a total tax loss of $90.5 billion that year.[14] After adjusting for inflation, this loss was 61 percent greater than it had been only five years earlier.

Thus, despite all the subsequent debate over alternative strategies and options, the general goals of reform were hardly questioned around Regan's table. So many assumptions were shared that Treasury's objectives could be spelled out as soon as the president requested the 1984 tax-reform study:

> [We should] simplify the tax code so that the average person can understand it and fewer wasteful efforts will be taken to develop "tax deals" that do not promote economic growth . . . ensure more equal treatment of people and families in equal economic circumstances . . . reduce marginal rates to improve economic incentives without raising middle income families' share of the tax burden . . . remove disincentives to savings . . . [and] provide careful transition rules.[15]

The Limits of Consensus: Choosing a Tax Base

Consensus on goals did not guarantee agreement on means. Economic theory and opinion were divided, and Treasury debates reflected those disagreements. In particular, two different approaches to tax reform existed. One focused on perfecting the existing income-tax system by bringing taxable income into line with true economic income. This could be accomplished with a broad-based, flatter rate income tax indexed to inflation. A single-rate indexed income tax was also an option in deference to the president and other supporters of such an approach. A second approach was to tax consumption instead of income by implementing a national sales or value-added tax (VAT) and a consumed-income tax.

The give-and-take over these options was as stimulating as a civil servant could ask. But although the opportunity to debate truly comprehensive and systematic reform—with a minimum of political interference— was unique, the department's reliance on professional norms and standards to frame the discussion and define policy options was not. As one public administrator has observed, "[professionalism is] the characteristic of public service . . . most significant today."[16]

Neither Flat nor VAT. In February 1985 analysts began sorting through the various alternatives.[17] As the work proceeded, two of the four options were quickly rejected as inappropriate. Experts dismissed a purely flat-rate tax, just as they had when the president first expressed enthusiasm for the idea in 1982, and for the same reason. It was unacceptably regressive. According to the Office of Tax Analysis, in order to be revenue neutral, a single flat rate of 16.8 percent would be required. Even with provisions designed to eliminate taxes on very poor families, such a tax would nearly double the share of federal taxes already paid by families earning less than $20,000 and would decrease the share of taxes paid by those earning over $100,000 by almost half. This was unthinkable.

A VAT and a national sales tax received slightly more consideration, as reflected in volume 3 of Treasury's "Report to the President." As that analysis explained, a national sales tax would impose a percentage tax on most or all retail sales, as is currently done in forty-five states. A value-added tax worked less visibly but toward the same end, by applying a tax to the incremental increase in the value of a product at each stage in its production. In the latter instance, no additional taxes were needed at the point of purchase because they were already embedded in the costs of goods themselves.

From the economists' perspective, such taxes had real advantages: because they are paid only when goods are purchased, they would not discourage saving and investment the way income taxes do, and thus they should ultimately enhance economic growth. But such taxes are regressive, they would impose significant administrative burdens and costs, and they would be inflationary. Conservatives also feared that the public's ready acceptance of such taxes, which are paid out in small increments, might provide a powerful new engine for government spending and growth, as had been the case in many European countries. Ultimately, though, most Treasury officials viewed them only as an alternative to true reform. "Although it made some sense for revenue-raising purposes," Pearlman observed, "we didn't want the VAT to be an excuse for not addressing the [problems of] the income tax."

A Consumed-Income Tax. The rejection of the flat and the value-added taxes left two important alternatives: a comprehensive income and a consumed-income tax. The latter was more radical.

As its name implies, a consumed-income tax uses consumption, not earnings, as a basis for taxation. Under this concept, to the extent that income is saved rather than borrowed or spent, it could be deducted from taxable income. Many economists favored this approach because it encouraged people to save and because it better measured people's ability to pay taxes.[18]

A consumed-income tax would also simplify complexities that stem from attempting to measure income on an annual basis. The existing income tax required highly complex procedures for handling long-term investments.

In contrast, by allowing businesses to immediately write off costs of purchasing capital assets and inventories, the consumed-income tax could eliminate complexities like depreciation and capital gains differentials in one fell swoop.

Not all economists liked the idea, however. Joseph Pechman wrote that it might permit "the accumulation of vast fortunes which would give the owners the ability to exercise great power over the economic and political life of the nation." [19] Others focused on the serious difficulties stemming from the transition to such a system. Since no other countries use a consumed-income tax, would the government have to renegotiate all the nation's tax treaties? Finally, while the consumed-income tax promised to simplify the administration of business taxes, it threatened to complicate personal taxes for anyone borrowing money to make a large capital purchase, most obviously a home or an automobile. [20]

Inside Treasury, resistance came from both the top and the bottom. Although technical problems might have been ironed out, Secretary Regan worried about a greater obstacle—high levels of public confusion and resistance. The specter of widespread public opposition dogged the discussions around the strategy table. Pearlman recalled:

> I remember one Saturday morning when we were talking about this . . . Regan said, "I'll tell you what. The next time you go to a cocktail party, you ask people what they think about a tax system that says borrowings are income and repayments or savings are deductions. They're going to tell you you're crazy!

Although the boss's reluctance might have been enough to block the notion, he was hardly alone. Economist Manuel Johnson recalled widespread rank-and-file resistance to such fundamental change in standard operating procedures and assumptions:

> The tax policy division was institutionally geared to a base-broadening income tax. All the legal expertise in the Tax Policy Division was trained in that direction. . . . IRS was also geared toward that structure. They were intensely concerned about tax shelters and were very strongly in support of broadening the tax base to eliminate all this, what they thought of as useless stuff. That combination was very formidable. If you wanted to move in another direction, you had to resist the whole institutional structure, and they could be extremely stubborn.

Key decision makers ultimately agreed that the consumed-income tax approach was too risky. As McLure recalled, "We could not afford to get to the end of the process and say, 'We tried but couldn't do it.' We couldn't write a law that didn't work." Moreover, no one wanted to be laughed at. "It was such a change," observed Pearlman, "that we weren't sure people would take it seriously."

Still, "a lot of us were disappointed," lamented Johnson. "It made a heck of a lot of sense," agreed Pearlman. In fact, as Pearlman later acknowledged, the abstract lure of the consumed-income tax meant that Treasury officials "probably made the decision to drop [the idea] later than we should have, in terms of devoting resources." While their professional fascination with the notion was understandable, it was also revealing. The very fact that serious and prolonged consideration was given to such a radical change in the tax system—and one very different from what ordinary citizens imagined when asked about tax reform—illustrates the highly rarefied character of Treasury I's decision-making process and the powerful influence of economic ideas and professional norms at that early stage of tax reform.

A Comprehensive Income Tax.   Once the idea of a consumed-income tax was set to rest, the strategy group and its staff of analysts focused on perfecting the existing income tax. The objective was relatively straightforward: to equate *taxable* with *economic* income as fully as possible. For example, if employees received compensation in the form of pension, health, or other fringe benefits rather than wages, the monetary value of these benefits would be taxed. But the legitimate costs of earning income, from the payment of mandatory union dues to the purchase of uniforms, would not. The result would be a broad-based tax with lower, less steeply graduated rates.

Although many thorny technical issues had to be resolved, the task primarily demanded that conventional economic wisdom be distilled into practical proposals. Indeed, Eugene Steuerle, the economist and career bureaucrat who led the economic team charged with generating legislative options, began by compiling and integrating the various ideas and proposals that had accumulated over many years:

> I went through every set of reform proposals that I could find, and I went to every member of the staff, encouraging them to put forward suggestions on how the income tax could be perfected. I wanted to be as comprehensive as possible. In addition, I argued that a general study should be accompanied by a "how to" manual, giving detailed guidance as to how a bill should be drafted. Then members of Congress could vote provisions up or down on a moment's notice—and a moment is often all one gets in the congressional process.

Steuerle's approach had the added advantage of hedging the department's bets on Treasury I. He and others were well aware that the Treasury study's fate was not yet certain and that past reform initiatives had been dismally received in the political arena. He hoped that a catalog of specific, well-crafted proposals could be drawn upon in the future in an incremental fashion if a comprehensive package were not adopted at that time. In his words:

> It wasn't clear that this effort would be anything more than a study. In 1982 and 1984, Bob Dole had been able to achieve some tax reform by simply pulling together a set of proposals that were already well enough

developed that they could be voted up or down quickly. Here was our chance to fill the hopper with good ideas.

Designing a Proposal

Deciding on the basic framework for tax reform had taken five months, from February to June 1984. Yet the group's sojourn ended where it might have begun—in a decision to *improve* rather than *reject* the existing income-tax system. At that point only six months remained until the president's publicly announced due date. Immediately, the tax code was divided into sixteen basic modules, and the economic staff began generating specific reform proposals in each of the areas. The strategy group often began meeting more than once a week.

Just compiling the statistics needed for accurate analysis of the distributional effects of tax law changes was a huge research task.[21] Outside consultants provided some assistance, but the veil of secrecy limited their participation. Even more constraining were the internal limits on staffing and time. Although the tax strategy group devoted unprecedented attention to tax reform, they had competing responsibilities as well—negotiations over DEFRA, the annual economic summit, and the 1984 presidential campaign. Moreover, many of the lawyers in the Office of Tax Policy were occupied with drafting DEFRA and were not readily available to the tax group until August.

Still, it was a hectic and heady experience for all concerned. Regan even compared it to a "dream come true," adding, "The give and take of meetings in which first class minds grappling with a problem that had generally been regarded as insoluble was extremely satisfying. . . . There is no exhilaration like [that] of working all out in the public interest." [22] Others recalled the process in somewhat less idyllic tones: "The tax-policy types went back to all of the ideas they'd ever had in their drawers and presented them in a fairly logical fashion," remarked one. "It was a hell of a lot of work," added economist Beryl Sprinkel. "I never knew the tax code was so vast."

As the exercise progressed, the only major guidelines were that the final product be revenue and distributionally neutral and that it be consistent with the economic logic of a comprehensive income-tax system. Although rate reduction had been the president's primary interest in tax reform from the very beginning, Treasury experts left the issue of tax rates until the very end. Their intention was to expand the tax base as broadly as possible and then reduce tax rates as low as the additional revenues permitted without changing the distribution of the tax burden among different income classes. To be sure, the group believed that cleansing the code would permit a dramatic lowering of the rates, but no one could be certain.[23] "We were flying blind," acknowledged McLure.

Reform for Individuals:
Implementing Conventional Wisdom

On the individual side of the tax code, the Treasury I process focused on three major issues: broadening the individual tax base; simplifying the taxpaying process; and removing the poor from the tax rolls.

Broadening the Base

When Ron Pearlman said that improving the current system "*means* base broadening," he was speaking for most tax experts. For them, ridding the tax code of special incentives and preferences, with their inevitable distortions and inequities, was the penultimate goal of reform. Thus, the Treasury proposal recommended unprecedented base-broadening measures, both by including income that was excluded from taxation and by eliminating costly and widely used deductions that reduced taxable income. Although most of these Treasury proposals became enormously controversial in the political arena, they did not go as far as many Treasury economists would have liked. Nor did they raise sufficient revenues to dramatically lower income-tax rates. Ultimately, individual rate reductions had to be financed in part through additional revenues extracted from corporations.

Excising Exemptions.   Exclusions and exemptions, which allow taxpayers to exclude or subtract money or implicit income before calculating their adjusted gross income (AGI), were one important class of potential base broadeners that Treasury reformers scrutinized in great detail. Some of their resulting recommendations were aimed mainly at the rich, such as tough new restrictions designed to reduce by 80 percent the federal tax revenues lost on interest from tax-exempt municipal bonds.[24] Others directly affected millions of average Americans. Base-broadening reforms hit tax breaks for fringe benefits like life insurance, death benefits, dependent care, education, and legal services. They also targeted special treatment for wage replacements including unemployment, black lung and disability benefits, workmen's compensation, student scholarships, and fellowships. Reformers even played tough with benefits for the nation's war veterans. "Sacred cows were falling like tenpins," commented Don Regan. He recounted the decision to tax the rental value of parsonages provided to clergymen: "The logic of equal treatment that we had imposed on every similar question dictated the answer. 'Tax it as income,' I ruled, adding, 'we've mugged everybody else—why should the clergy escape?' "[25]

Still, as bold as it was, the plan did not eliminate all exclusions from income. While some reformers were willing to ignore politics entirely, others had no intention of winning professional battles only to lose the legislative war. Thus, health insurance—the largest and politically most revered fringe benefit—was only nicked, not bludgeoned. The plan taxed only values exceeding $70 per month for individuals and $175 for families, leaving 70 percent of families unscathed. Social security benefits remained sacrosanct, and individual retirement accounts (which some administration officials touted as advancing family values) were even expanded, allowing new exemptions for full-time homemakers.

Downing Deductions.   Deductions from AGI, which lowered taxable income for itemizing taxpayers, were another class of individual preferences targeted by the tax strategy group. Here, too, the economists' goal of horizontal equity played a strong role in weeding out unacceptable items. Once again, however, the base broadening was uneven, combining dramatic proposals to restrict or eliminate popular deductions with some equally striking omissions.

The most extreme Treasury proposal in this area terminated the deduction for state and local income, property, and sales taxes. This recommendation eliminated the single most generous tax break for millions of Americans, one that had been in the tax code since its inception in 1913. Moreover, because the deduction made state and local taxes less painful to citizens, it was vigorously defended by governors, mayors, and public school officials nationwide.

But to reformers, the state and local deduction was simply too big to ignore. In fiscal year 1985 alone this tax deduction was estimated to cost the federal treasury almost $31 billion in revenues forgone.[26] So large an amount would help to lower tax rates significantly. Equally important to Treasury economists, the subsidy was deemed "inefficient" and "unfair," disproportionately benefiting wealthy individuals and communities. Finally, like the interest exclusion on tax-exempt bonds, tax reformers at Treasury viewed the deduction as just an outmoded vestige of American federalism. As the report declared, "There is no more reason for a federal subsidy for spending by state and local governments than for private spending."[27]

Other less extreme but still controversial decisions involved Treasury I's treatment of charitable contributions and consumer interest. Two of the most important changes were the replacement of the full deduction for charitable contributions with a 2 percent floor (whereby only contributions exceeding 2 percent of AGI could be deducted) and the placement of limitations on large gifts of appreciated property. Although a fully comprehensive income tax would repeal the entire charitable deduction, this idea flew directly in the face of the president's initiatives on volunteerism as an alternative to governmental programs. Expecting the worst, Treasury reformers stopped short of eliminating the deduction except for nonitemizers.

Theory also called for eliminating deductions for consumer interest expenses. Yet these too were saved from extinction. Existing law permitted all interest expenses to be deducted from AGI, from credit cards to home mortgages. Under Treasury I, nonmortgage interest was capped at $5,000 and indexed to inflation—a limitation that would have affected only the wealthiest taxpayers.

Left wholly unscathed was the entire deduction for mortgage interest expenses on primary residences. This was the largest single departure from economic principles in the Treasury recommendations, and it resulted from one of the few occasions when outside politics directly intervened. Recognizing the reverential status accorded homeownership and the monumental clout of the real estate, timber, and homebuilding industries, Treasury economists never considered a full-blown assault on the $25 billion deduction; but they were examining ways to restrict or gradually phase it out. But when the president acknowledged during a meeting with the National Association of Realtors (NAR) in May 1984 that the deduction had not been removed from Treasury's table, the resulting political firestorm forced the White House to publicly declare the deduction off limits. Looking back, a disgruntled McLure called this failure "the achilles heel of tax reform" because the loss made it "impossible to construct a rational and consistent approach to tax treatment of interest." [28]

Simplifying the Code

For millions of Americans who dread their annual encounter with the 1040 form, simplification was a touchstone of tax reform. Politicians accordingly seized on the symbol, and most reformers paid homage to the goal. Yet Treasury I's authors never gave tax simplification the priority that base broadening received (although the two are not incompatible), nor did Congress later. As in the existing code, simplicity was always the first and easiest goal to be sacrificed.

Nevertheless, Treasury estimates did show that raising the income threshold at which tax liability begins (the so-called zero-bracket amount) would reduce the *size* of the taxpaying population. Moreover, base broadening and a larger personal exemption would cut by one-third the number of taxpayers for whom the time and trouble of itemizing deductions would remain worthwhile. If Treasury I's recommendations were implemented, the department estimated that three-quarters of all taxpayers would submit the IRS short form come April 15.[29] Finally, the authors held out the prospect of creating a "filing-free tax system" for those individuals willing to trust the IRS to calculate their taxes on the basis of employer and financial documents filed with the government. Thus, most Americans could anticipate a simpler tax system as well as a fairer, more efficient one if the Treasury recommendations were adopted.

Removing the Poor

One additional tax fairness issue that had raised concerns among tax professionals since the late 1970s was the increasingly large federal tax burden on poor and low-income individuals.[30] Three factors were at work. First, pay increases designed to compensate for high inflation were driving low-income wage earners into higher tax brackets or onto the tax rolls for the first time. Second, recent large increases in social security payroll taxes fell on the nation's work force in a regressive manner. Third, the huge individual and corporate tax cuts adopted as part of ERTA in 1981 had produced disproportionate tax savings for the wealthiest Americans and made the federal tax system more regressive than it had been in the 1970s.

Even before Treasury I, there was growing political and professional consensus that this unfair situation needed correction. Joining liberals on the issue were populist conservatives like Rep. Jack Kemp, R-N.Y., whose Fair and Simple Tax (FAST) bill proposed removing 1.5 million poor from the tax rolls.[31]

Treasury I shared the objective of reducing or eliminating income-tax burdens on the poor—a move that became extremely important in the subsequent politics of tax reform because it bolstered Democratic support for the administration's effort and enhanced its image of fairness. Although the president had given no guidance on this matter, he had accepted conservative arguments that expanding the personal exemption would benefit middle-class families. Steuerle explained, "Since the president and the White House began pushing for an increase in the personal exemption long before tax reform got under way, it was easy to combine the desire of some to reduce taxes for the poor with the desire of others to be 'pro-family.' A more perfect liberal-conservative coalition couldn't have existed." The Treasury plan removed many poor individuals and families from the federal income-tax rolls (and also reduced taxes on many of the nonpoor) by almost doubling the personal exemption, from $1,090 to $2,000 annually. Second, it increased the standard deduction for all filers, especially for heads of households. Third, it expanded and indexed for inflation the earned-income credit. Together, these expensive reforms would have increased by one-third the percentage of taxpayers owing no income taxes. Virtually all families with incomes below the poverty line were dropped from the income-tax rolls. According to Treasury estimates, 37 percent of families with incomes below $15,000 would enjoy lower taxes, while only a tiny fraction would see their liabilities increased.[32]

The Conflict over Corporate Taxation

Having thus applied conventional economic wisdom to the individual side of the tax code, Treasury reformers turned to the more challenging assignment of refashioning corporate taxes. Although the corporate income tax generates a small and declining share of federal revenues, it is far more complex than the individual income tax. Moreover, while economists generally agreed on what a reformed individual income tax should look like, there was far less consensus about the corporate tax. Some proposed the total integration of corporate and individual income taxes, while others favored special treatment for certain forms of investment.

Charles McLure and Eugene Steuerle believed the corporate income tax should tax real economic income from business and capital in a neutral and consistent manner, eliminating the large disparities in effective tax rates between different industries (see Table 3—1). By and large, these differences were caused by the perverse interaction of inflation with different patterns of interest income and expenses; inventory, plant, and equipment investments; and periods of return on investments. To level the corporate playing field, Treasury's economic staff developed innovative proposals to: (1) adjust depreciation allowances, capital gains, the cost of goods sold from inventories, and interest income expense for inflation; (2) replace the existing system of accelerated depreciation (the accelerated cost recovery system—ACRS) with an indexed system of real economic depreciation (a real cost recovery system—RCRS), which would attempt to estimate the actual economic life of different kinds of structures and equipment; (3) eliminate the investment tax credit (ITC); (4) end the preferential treatment for indexed capital gains; (5) eliminate the double taxation of dividend payments; and (6) excise myriad special subsidies for specific industries, from banking and insurance to oil and gas.

Some of these proposals constituted dramatic reversals of prior policies of the Reagan administration. This was especially true of the repeal of the ITC and reforms of ACRS, both of which had been included in ERTA in 1981 as part of the president's strategy for promoting greater economic investment and growth. Even with subsequent "takebacks," these policies reduced corporate taxes by about $46 billion between 1981 and 1984.[33]

Such reversals, when added to the intellectual controversies over corporate taxation, were achieved only after considerable internal debate and disagreement. Among the most outspoken opponents was supply-side economist Manuel Johnson, who favored more generous incentives for capital investment. McLure's real-cost-recovery approach was "too academic," he argued, by seeking "to come up with accurate estimates of the actual economic life of various types of assets." Moreover, it would be politically foolish to "so obviously reject the pattern we set in 1981 [at a time when] trade and competitiveness issues are building." As a result, Johnson favored a consumption-style tax to obviate the need for depreciation. Failing that, he urged the strategy group to adopt the notion of "expensing," allowing immediate write-offs for the costs of capital purchases.

In sharp contrast, McLure argued that ACRS and ITC were best viewed as temporary, ad hoc responses to prevent "confiscatory taxation on income from capital" in a period of rapid inflation.[34] With the beast of inflation tamed, such provisions contributed to unfair variations in effective tax rates. Indeed, studies showed that some corporations even enjoyed negative tax rates. Moreover, without the wasteful and unproductive tax shelters these tax incentives encouraged, capital would more smoothly flow to investments with the greatest economic, not tax, returns.

The McLure-Johnson debates were never fully settled. Indeed, the issue "came up so often we each knew what the other would say before he said it," recalled McLure. Within the rarefied, insulated confines of the tax strategy group, McLure's arguments carried the day and an economic depreciation system was incorporated into Treasury I. A neutral, indexed cost-recovery system corresponded with Secretary Regan's own free-market ideology and with the institutional mission of his department. Once Treasury I was released to the public and James Baker assumed the reins at Treasury, however, outside political factors became far more important, and the matter was reopened and amended.

The Accidental Populists

It was late October 1984 when the tax strategy group sat back to contemplate its accomplishments. Everyone expected to be rewarded for their hard work in the form of lower tax rates. To determine how low, tax reform was handed over to the department's revenue estimators who were reminded of the three ground rules guiding their work. First, the plan should be revenue neutral. There must be no added taxes or revenues forgone. Second, with the exception of the working poor, it should be distributionally neutral across income classes. There must be no windfalls or shortfalls. Third, it should be structurally neutral between individuals and corporations. Such a system of "separate ledgers" meant that final rates for both sides of the tax code would be established independently, according to how broadly the relevant base had been expanded.

The question on everyone's mind was: How low would rates go? Earlier research by Steuerle had shown that marginal income-tax rates during the 1950s and 1960s—before the growth of many of the tax expenditures scheduled for Treasury I's chopping block—had averaged between 20 percent and 22 percent for the vast majority of American taxpayers.[35] McLure and others assumed that the revenue estimators would return with similar figures. But when they reported back with their printouts, the results were far different. As Johnson remembered: "I was apoplectic.

Here it was, October, almost November, and we had done all that work and had brought the [top individual] rate down by only eight points [from 50 to 42 percent]. That was one of the most depressing meetings we had."

Politically, the modest drop in the top rate was disastrous, undermining the entire strategy of building a reform coalition on the appeal of very low, "show-stopper" rates. After all, the Kemp-Kasten proposal offered a flat rate of 24 percent, while the more progressive Bradley-Gephardt proposal's top rate was still only 30 percent. The president would never support such a controversial plan without having more to show for it, nor would supply-siders seeking economic vitality via low tax rates for entrepreneurs. To conventional economists as well, a 42 percent top rate was not low enough to end wealthy taxpayers' craving for tax shelters.

Fortunately, the early estimates were preliminary, and the number crunchers continued working. Distributional neutrality could be defined in somewhat different ways, they found, and this allowed the top rate to come down. Then, too, some additional base broadeners could be added. When these changes were made, the estimators produced a lower three-rate structure of 16-28-37. It was not what economists had hoped for, but it was in the ballpark.

Then a new and equally serious objection reared its head, this time from the department's lawyers. It won't work, they said. Rather than creating a level playing field, the plan would guarantee the creation of a whole new generation of tax shelters. They explained that because there was a nine percentage point difference between the top individual rate of 37 percent and the top corporate rate of 28 percent, partnerships and sole proprietorships (which are taxed as individuals) would be encouraged to convert into corporations. As Pearlman recalled: "When they came back with that rate structure, we *lawyers* said to the secretary, 'We can't have that much disparity. . . . We'll have people deciding whether to go into or stay out of a corporate rate structure based on that rate. We have to reduce the spread.' "

The argument made sense, and Regan listened carefully. Besides he already had a problem with the individual rate structure—16-28-37 had no sex appeal, he complained. It sounded like "a football signal." In the secretary's mind, 15-25-35 was a catchier combination, one with real political potential. And, as he later bragged to the president, 35 percent "exactly halved" the top individual rate in place in 1981. All in all, 15-25-35 was the trio Regan favored, so he turned to his staff and said, in effect, "Do it."

It was easier said than done. Rate reductions of just a few percentage points would cost the treasury tens of billions of dollars once they were applied to tens of millions of taxpayers. But the lawyers provided a solution. To reduce the spread between the top individual and the corporate tax rates, the corporate rate would have to be increased. The resulting revenues could then be used to reduce the highest individual rate and to adjust the lower ones to maintain distributional neutrality. The revenue estimators found that with the proper juggling, a corporate rate of 33 percent, instead of 28 percent, could yield the desired individual rate structure of 15-25-35.

The result satisfied the lawyers and it gave the secretary the marketing edge he desired. But it also did far more. The change in rates altered the very politics of tax reform, converting what had been a modest facade of populism, embodied in the concept of greater tax fairness, into structural pillars that dominated the architecture of reform!

Like the decision on depreciation, the change in rates dramatically reversed past administration policies (which had been championed by Regan) by raising, rather than lowering, taxes on corporations. When combined with corporate base broadening, the decision on rates produced a net corporate tax increase of $165 billion over five years, or an average yearly increase of 30 percent.[36]

To be sure, the resulting increases in corporate taxes were highly relative, exaggerated by the partially unintended generosity of ERTA in 1981. Only the "tyranny of the starting point" made them look so substantial, observed McLure. Moreover, many key policy makers in Congress and the Treasury Department had already concluded that eliminating the costly, on-again off-again ITC was inevitable. Nevertheless, the resulting corporate tax windfall was used to reduce individual tax rates well beyond what could be done on the basis of base broadening alone, adding a populist dimension to the plan that surprised political observers on both the left and the right. Never originally intended, it grew out of professional and technical considerations, reinforced by political insulation. Intended or not, the result dramatically changed the subsequent politics of tax reform by giving a tax cut to millions of Americans. As Pearlman explained:

> Our initial reason for doing this had nothing to do with trying to make this a net tax reduction for individuals. But once the politicians saw this they said, "Aha! This is the way we're going to sell tax reform. It's a tax reduction for individuals." Then it got a life of its own.

To Be or Not to Be

With the tax rates decided, all the major outlines of the Treasury plan were established and the proposal was nearly complete. But it was still just a confidential Treasury proposal. Since the next step belonged to Ronald Reagan, consideration of Treasury I was placed on the president's schedule for November 26, 1984. While the Department hoped for a positive reception, the plan's prospects quickly dimmed when, with the election safely over, news of its contents began to leak from Treasury's high gray walls. Hearing snippets of what they regarded as very bad news, myriad interest groups began to light up the White House switchboards, hoping to head off disaster at the presidential pass. Republican "eagle pins," given in gratitude to wealthy political contributors, began "returning in flocks." Although the president retained his typically detached posture, White House staff, who had not been enthusiastic about tax reform to begin with, sought to insulate him from the negative response as they pondered the fate of Treasury I. Meanwhile, Regan fumed. "Before I briefed the President," he wrote with annoyance, there were news stories of "worried White House aides" who feared "Treasury's tax plan would launch a second term by alienating some of [the president's] staunchest supporters and exciting nobody." [37]

Trying to douse the flames of discontent before they raged out of control, the Treasury chief turned first to reason. Upon releasing the plan, he urged people to evaluate it in its entirety. Lower tax rates for both individuals and corporations, greater fairness, and reduced taxes on the poor were being overshadowed by parochial concerns, he warned. Yet fans of the existing tax code felt no need to read every page of the Treasury manifesto to catch its drift. They knew when their ox was being gored. Nor did most of Washington's political establishment want to be closely associated with it. Indeed, when one congressional wit dubbed it the "biggest trial balloon since the Hindenburg," even the stubborn Regan backtracked. He openly admitted that the plan was "written on a word processor," implying that its provisions could be changed if need be.

Regan's offer notwithstanding, the White House put so much distance between itself and Treasury I during this period that one departmental aide complained, "When [it] was printed up nobody was quite sure where to send it." Indeed, heads were shaking all over the Treasury Department.

The Doomsayers

For weeks a storm of opposition raged relentlessly through the halls of Congress and the corridors of interest-group power in Washington. A lobbyist for real estate developers said the plan would "devastate" the second-home market and "wipe us out," adding, "Usually we exaggerate to get everyone hyped up, but this is no exaggeration." [38] The president of the National Association of Realtors charged that the plan would "drastically increase taxation of homeownership" and immediately joined forces with the powerful National Association of Home Builders and the Mortgage Bankers Association to oppose it.[39] Lobbyists for capital-intensive industries decried the elimination of accelerated depreciation, while a former Treasury official who helped craft ACRS claimed that tax reform would undermine capital investment and "reinstate the declining productivity growth . . . [of] the 1970s." The head of the AFL-CIO said the taxation of fringe benefits would do "serious and unnecessary harm" to the nation's workers. Public officials in New York said that eliminating the state and local tax deduction would be "ruinous to New York's economy" and formed a bipartisan coalition to oppose it. A study conducted for the nonprofit sector estimated that the Treasury plan would reduce charitable contributions by 15 percent. Banks, life insurance companies, chemical companies, oil producers, steel manufacturers, utilities, restaurants, sports and entertainment facilities, credit-card companies, credit unions, colleges, state and local governments, and veterans' groups all expressed immediate opposition to all or portions of the Treasury proposal.[40]

The negative reaction was not lost on members of Congress, and most rushed to defend particular constituencies or supporters. Although the plan was devised at the president's request, the response among congressional Republicans was particularly hostile. Sen. Robert Packwood, R-Ore., who had just been selected chairman of the Senate Finance Committee, promised to "defeat" any legislation that sought to tax employee fringe benefits, a preference he had championed for many years.[41] In the House, an aide to Rep. Bill Archer, R-Texas, the second-ranking Republican on the Ways and Means Committee, recalled that "Republicans were livid over Treasury I—there were just so many unacceptable provisions." Even other members of the Reagan cabinet got into the act, expressing everything from concern to outright opposition.

The Dragon Slayers

In normal times, this chorus of interest-group complaints and congressional reluctance would have been enough to speed Treasury's report to the nearest White House paper shredder. But the postelection period was not a "normal" time at 1600 Pennsylvania Avenue. Reagan's massive forty-nine state sweep on November 6 had elevated the president's "bully pulpit" to an even higher plane. Although no one expected Reagan's second "honeymoon" period to equal his first, the postelection months presented him a golden opportunity to dominate the national agenda with a bold presidential initiative. Yet the vacuous campaign had given the White House nothing suitable to propose. Therefore, when tax-reform proponents spoke up in response to Treasury I critics, White House strategists were more inclined than usual to listen. Here is what they heard.

Academic Wisdom. As could be expected, economists were among the most enthusiastic supporters. After all, Treasury I was an unusually pure statement of economic wisdom. "Ninety percent of Treasury I was what I thought it should have been," declared McLure, and economists from Walter Heller and Joseph Pechman on the left to Milton Friedman and George Stigler on the right lent their applause. Said Alan Blinder: "The fine staff of economists and lawyers at the U.S. Treasury knew what was wrong with the tax code and . . . how to fix it." Alice Rivlin, director of the Congressional Budget Office, called it "an economist's kind of reform." Even consumption-tax champions like Harvey Galper and Henry Aaron endorsed the plan as a substantial improvement over the existing system and the best available hope for comprehensive reform.[42] Only a few dissented—mainly economists with supply-side leanings who advocated greater investment incentives. That group included former administration officials Murray Weidenbaum, Norman Ture, and Martin Feldstein.

Good-Government Groups. Well-known public-interest groups, including Common Cause, Citizens for Tax Justice, and the Tax Foundation, also sang the praises of Treasury I. So did a number of Democratic politicians. "It is a superb proposal," declared Arizona governor Bruce Babbitt. "It is so good that the president will not have the courage to endorse it! "[43] Rep. Charles Rangel, D-N.Y., a liberal from Harlem, praised the plan's reduction of taxes on the poor and introduced a modified version of the bill in Congress, calling it a "giant step forward toward a fair and equitable tax system."

High-Tax Industries. An equally important, if self-interested, element of support came from sectors of corporate America. Because the Treasury proposal redistributed corporate tax burdens (smoothing out the differences between capital-intensive and service industries) Treasury officials always believed retailers and wholesalers would support the reform. For similar reasons, those sectors were joined by high-tech companies and trade associations that received few tax preferences and paid high corporate tax rates. "We have reservations," said the head of one high-tech coalition, "but we think that . . . it will be very beneficial to our firms." Eighteen different firms and associations endorsed the Treasury plan in December, including IBM, General Mills, Bristol Myers, and the National Retail Merchants Association. Ultimately, these organizations formed the Tax Reform Action Coalition (TRAC), which lobbied actively on behalf of tax reform and undermined claims that reform was anti-business.

A Positive Press. To the president's advisers, the most important tax-reform enthusiasts were the journalists and reporters who occupy the front-row seats at all important policy unveilings. They lavished enormous amounts of attention on Treasury I. During the last week of November and the first two weeks of December, the *Washington Post*, the *New York Times*, and the *Wall Street Journal* together carried more than twenty different news articles and fifteen editorials on various aspects of tax reform. Many other stories appeared in regional and local newspapers, on network news broadcasts, in national news weeklies, and in national business magazines.

Better yet for tax reform, media coverage was generally favorable. Taking their cues from the academics and good-government groups, most stories and editorials accepted the basic claim that the plan would make the tax system simpler, fairer, and better, although some raised questions about political feasibility and substantive details. Journalists also picked up on the new math of reform. "Some 56% of the nation's 91.4 million families would get a tax cut," reported *Time*, especially "low and middle income taxpayers." [44] Altogether, the extensive and favorable media reception helped sway White House opinion. In Steuerle's words, "It was the positive press reaction that got people thinking, 'Hey, maybe we *should* make this a political issue.'"

Party Time

As White House aides began to give second thoughts to tax reform, they discovered two further political advantages. One was the siren song of history. Although the president's electoral victory gave him a tremendous opportunity to swing for the fences, only bean balls were being tossed around by White House strategists. Among the options then available, none of Reagan's policy advisers wanted to confront the deficit issue with detailed, substantive proposals. Neither did vague suggestions to tackle crime or foreign trade light up any faces around White House strategy tables. But tax reform, if enacted, promised to be the fiscal grand slam of Reagan's second term.

In addition, some were seduced by the hope that tax reform might trigger voter realignment—a once-in-a-generation opportunity to rewrite the ground rules of party competition in the United States. That prospect tugged especially hard on political strategists in the president's employ, whose business, after all, was electoral politics.

As Republicans were painfully aware, the 1930s witnessed the last such realignment. Then, Democrats had become the majority party and acquired a lasting edge in partisan identification among the voters. By late 1984, however, that edge was disappearing. In November 1984, some opinion polls showed a virtual tie in the percentage of people who identified themselves as Republicans and Democrats. To solidify these gains and perhaps precipitate a realignment, Republicans needed the right set of issues. The process of redefining the parties had begun in Reagan's first term, with its emphasis on lower taxes and less government, but history suggested that a "coincident issue" would be needed to solidify voters' attachment to their new party. [45]

Might tax reform be that issue? In absolute numbers, it created more winners than losers. Moreover, it embodied powerful moral symbols like fairness for the middle class. The president's political allies and advisers—Mitch Daniels in the White House, Frank Fahrenkopf, head of the Republican National Committee, and Richard Wirthlin, the president's chief pollster—believed passage of tax reform would help overcome the image of the Republican party as the defender of the rich and privileged and thus benefit all future Republican candidates. Nor were they alone. As reporter Hedrick Smith writes, "[Jack Kemp's] constant refrain in early 1985 was: 'Tax reform is a realigning issue.'" Democratic worries lent credence to Republican assertions. It is "the stuff of realignment," warned Sen. Bill Bradley in his efforts to gain Democratic support for his version of tax reform. "It's clear what's in it for the Republicans, if they support it and the president pushes for it." [46]

Such arguments eventually made headway among reluctant White House aides. In particular, Richard Darman, the administration's preeminent policy strategist, joined the chorus, predicting that tax reform could tap "legions of quiet populists," including many within the "vast world of the 'white collars,'" who were disillusioned with big government and big business.[47] With this vision uppermost in his mind, Darman set to work to enlist the ever-skeptical James Baker. Eventually, he succeeded.

In contrast to all the political agonizing at the staff level, there were no second thoughts within the Oval Office itself. When the issue was finally recommended as the domestic centerpiece of his second term, the president agreed immediately and enthusiastically. Explaining why, one Treasury insider said, "He wanted it more than his staff realized."

From the very start, Reagan was seduced by the allure of lower taxes, both as a symbol and as a means of implementing his philosophy of limited government. Indeed, the prospect of cutting the top marginal tax rate in half during his presidency, from 70 to 35 percent, was simply irresistible. Finally, it must be said that Regan had a way with Reagan. As the following anecdote illustrates, the Treasury secretary and the president seemed to enjoy an unusual and successful "locker-room" relationship. Given his chance, the boisterous Celt from Wall Street pitched the plan precisely right to appeal to his fellow Irishman, beginning by chastising the amiable Reagan for paying his fair share of taxes: "'Sucker!' I said. 'With the right lawyer and the right accountant and the right tax shelters, you needn't have paid a penny in taxes even if you made more than a million dollars a year—and it would have been perfectly legal.'" [48]

For all his enthusiastic speechmaking and support for the enterprise, by all accounts Reagan was never more than vaguely acquainted with his own proposal. Beyond the basics, Reagan's understanding of the admittedly complex proposal was shallow. For instance, when he was first briefed on the tax plan, despite his obvious enthusiasm, Reagan asked few questions. Out of the entire extraordinary list of far-reaching tax changes, the president focused his concerns on just a few items, such as the proposal to eliminate the business deduction for country club dues.[49]

Reagan's lack of curiosity about the specifics of tax reform was not exceptional. From ERTA to the Iran-contra affair, Reagan rarely did much homework during his two terms as president, and was frequently confused and ill-informed about the policies he advanced. In the case of tax reform, Reagan didn't even wait for his first briefing to claim in a press conference that the Treasury plan "would not result in any individual having his taxes raised." Worse still, even after being briefed about the dramatic corporate tax hike, he told reporters that corporations would not pay more taxes.[50] Both statements were patently untrue, of course, as the storm of protest made clear once the proposal was publicly released. Tax *rates* would be cut for both individuals and corporations, and individuals on average would pay somewhat less, but approximately 10.5 million families, or 22 percent of all households, were scheduled to pay more under Treasury's plan. Corporate taxes as a whole would increase by over 30 percent.[51]

Treasury II: Half a Loaf from the Baker

Transforming Treasury's trial balloon into a presidential proposal required balancing the principled integrity of Treasury I (which gathered support from the media, the academic community, and good-government groups) with the need to mollify interest-group opposition (which could spell dismal death in Congress). Yet, this inevitable political transformation was greatly magnified by a switch that stunned political Washington: the decision by White House Chief of Staff James Baker and Treasury Secretary Donald Regan to exchange jobs.

As Regan describes this event, the decision occurred almost by accident. When leaks began springing up about the hitherto secret tax-reform plan, Regan suspected the White House staff of sabotage, and he threatened to resign. Baker, in turn, sought to soothe Regan's ire by explaining the difficulties of controlling competing agendas and egos in the White House. The Treasury chief recounted his response:

> "You know what the trouble with you is, Baker? You're tired. . . . You know what we should do, Jim? We should swap jobs." Our conversation had been half-serious, half joking. I tossed out these words without thinking. But Baker bobbed his head like a man who had been hit with an idea. "Do you mean that?" he asked. I thought for a moment, "I guess I do."[52]

Although virtually unprecedented, the switch made sense to both men. For Regan, it was a chance to be in charge, to create a more businesslike White House operation. Above all, noted Chapoton, it was a chance to get closer to the president: "He was in awe of the presidency. I can remember meetings when his secretary would buzz and say: Jim Baker's on the line. God, he'd jump up and take it. And I'd think, 'It's only Jimmy. Leave us alone. We're in a meeting.' But Jim was the president to Regan." Baker, in turn, would exchange the grinding pressures of the White House for the second most important and visible cabinet position in government and the challenge of making history by enacting comprehensive tax reform. A savvy politician, Baker knew that winning this one, against long odds, would secure his reputation for years to come. "[T]aking on this challenge," he allowed, "appealed to me." Accordingly, they presented the idea to the president, and on February 4, 1985, Donald Regan became the new presidential chief of staff, bringing along a coterie of aides from the Treasury Department. James Baker III became the new secretary of the Treasury, appointing his trusted assistant and colleague Richard Darman as deputy secretary.

It was an important development in the chronicle of tax reform, something many saw as a key to its success. "The swap was the best thing that could have happened," said Manuel Johnson. "A terrific stroke of genius or luck," concurred Mitch Daniels:

> Jim Baker's as good a congressional handler and negotiator as the administration had, and he was put in a situation of doing that almost full time. And it put down here [in the White House] a person who conceived and believed in tax reform. If you had set out to make second term personnel decisions with only tax reform in mind, you might have decided on that switch.

Not only did Regan's arrival put a strong proponent of reform in the White House, Baker's departure turned a reform skeptic into an advocate. "Until he got involved, I think his influence would have been negative," maintained Pearlman. "When Baker was at the White House, the staff was so hostile to tax reform. All he was hearing was the bad things. Once he got involved, he appreciated the power of the concept." Yet, the switch was not without its substantive consequences.

Seeking the Political Fix

According to Regan, when it came to taxation, "the best politics is no politics." [53] In contrast, one Baker confidante noted that the Texan was "imbued with politics." The significance of this difference was—as one who knew all three men summed it up—that "Baker and Darman were much more interested in a political fix to everything."

This is not to say that the group that designed Treasury I had given no thought to its enactment. They had an overarching political strategy based on their goal of broadening the tax base. It was a "hostage strategy," in McLure's terms: "We thought that if we played no favorites, we could hold all the special interests hostage to each other." That is, in a revenue-neutral context, money to restore one group's preference could come only at the expense of others; barring such changes, all would share in the sacrifice.

Although this general approach clearly contributed to the enactment of tax reform by Congress, Baker scornfully argued that "Treasury I was probably very good tax policy, but it had little if any chance of ever being enacted into law." He believed that a successful legislative game plan had to take account of congressional personalities, procedures, and the intensity of group interests, and that this had to be reflected in the content of a reform plan from the very beginning: "With something this big and comprehensive, it's important from the very start to think about the coalitions that you are going to need to put together in order to pass it." Consequently, Baker and Darman set out to review the entire Treasury proposal "through the prism of politics," taking care to examine how each affected influential interest groups, important voting blocks in Congress, and the personal policy concerns of key individuals on the tax-writing committees.

In keeping with these differences in personal style and approach to policy making, the processes of writing Treasury I and Treasury II differed dramatically. While Treasury I began by defining economic income and expanding the taxable base, Treasury II began, in effect, with dessert. It took as its starting point the low rates that had been developed in the Treasury proposal. Baker and Darman then sweetened the earlier courses as well, making them as politically palatable as possible. Rather than meeting in secret with just a few close aides, Baker flung the doors of the department wide open. Lobbyists for every imaginable interest "wore out his carpet," according to one report.[54] Baker himself went to Capitol Hill to meet with key congressional leaders who would be involved in the legislative process, and he met privately with congressional sponsors of other tax-reform bills, trying to win their endorsement of a common bill.

Building Coalitions.   The result was a series of important changes in the Treasury plan, retaining its broad outlines but substantially altering many of its provisions. Some were done for largely symbolic purposes, to deal with emotional issues where economic reasoning could not be made persuasive to the average American. For example, the floor on charitable contributions was removed. The parsonage allowance for ministers was restored. And the tax-exempt status of veterans' benefits was continued.

Even more common were changes that were carefully tailored to the task of building a stronger political coalition for reform legislation. The most important involved putting back, and even expanding, incentives for capital investment, including restoring the exclusion for long-term capital gains. Treasury I had proposed eliminating the capital-gains exclusion, which was viewed as one of the key components of many tax shelters. Although the effects of this decision had been softened by indexing the basis of assets to inflation, it shocked many Republican legislators and corporate constituents of the administration. Preferential treatment of capital gains had been a feature of the tax code since 1921, and many high-technology firms argued that it was particularly important for attracting capital to new and risky ventures. Baker and Darman believed that they could ill afford to alienate one of the few potential blocks of business support for tax reform, and a capital-gains exclusion of 50 percent, rather than the original 60 percent, was restored in Treasury II. Because the top rate was reduced to 35 percent, however, even this smaller exclusion yielded a lower capital-gains rate of 17.5 percent, rather than the existing rate of 20. (See Appendix.)

More costly were the changes made in Treasury I's capital depreciation provisions. The old arguments between McLure and Johnson over expensing and capital incentives were revisited, but this time Johnson emerged victorious on the heels of vociferous complaints by conservative Republicans and capital-intensive industries. Johnson recalled a dramatic change in attitude: "Business depreciation and taxation blew up [politically] more than anything else. . .from a conservative Republican point of view. [Since] Baker and Darman came over determined to make this thing work [and] their concerns were consistent with mine, I gained a lot more influence on restructuring the business side of reform." Treasury I's real cost recovery system (RCRS) was replaced with a capital cost recovery system (CCRS), which retained the favorable inflation indexing provisions of RCRS but shortened cost recovery periods. The result, according to one business analysis, was a depreciation system "in most cases, more generous than even ACRS." [55]

These changes generally pleased the administration's allies in Congress and solidified a core of business support for tax reform. It is true that most capital-intensive businesses continued to oppose even the revised plan, since it still abolished the ITC and many of the accounting and investment provisions favorable to banks and certain natural resource industries, and it raised overall business taxes by $120 billion over five years. Still, the changes had the intended effect of dividing and to some extent neutralizing business opposition to reform—a key element in Baker's legislative strategy. It was just as one business lobbyist had feared when he warned that "Congress will walk all over us and pick the bones off the carcass," if business failed to provide a united front in opposition to tax reform.[56] High-tech and high-tax industries formed a coalition to support the administration's reform plan, lobbied Congress on its behalf, and prevented consensus-oriented umbrella groups like the Chamber of Commerce from effectively opposing it for many months.

Other changes were aimed directly at the interests of key individuals in

Congress. In an effort to gain the support of Senate Finance Committee Chairman Bob Packwood and to mollify opposition by organized labor, taxation of most fringe benefits was dropped from the plan, and Treasury's proposal to tax health benefits was gutted. In place of the original proposal to tax monthly health insurance benefits in excess of $75 ($175 per family), a provision was added to tax only the first $10 ($25 for families) of free health benefits. In contrast to the Treasury I provision, which was designed to discourage this form of untaxed compensation, the new approach was "devoid of policy rationale" observed Chapoton, and it cut the expected revenue gain in half. Yet Baker's substitute did secure a greater degree of cooperation from Packwood.

Likewise, major changes were made in the proposed tax treatment of oil and natural gas. Treasury I had proposed to eliminate or alter provisions that were enormously favorable to some sectors of the oil and gas industry, such as the oil depletion allowance and expensing of intangible drilling costs, which had long been major targets of tax reformers. The changes were removed from Treasury II, however, in part under the influence of Baker's own policy and political views, stemming from his business and political roots in Texas, as well as the political might of the oil lobby. "The Republican party is going to have to find a new way to finance campaigns in Texas if this goes through," observed one administration official.[57] Such clout gained independent oil producers a meeting with the president himself to discuss their concerns. If anything, though, they were even more strongly represented on the tax-writing committees of Congress, especially the Finance Committee where senators from oil-producing states represented the largest, most senior, and most powerful bloc on the committee. Most observers assumed that any oil and gas reforms left in the president's proposal would be reversed by the Senate. But their deletion from Treasury II reduced expected revenues by $44 billion over five years.[58]

In order to retain Treasury I's rate reductions, not all of its proposed base broadeners could be eliminated. Treasury II recommended many politically daring changes, including repeal of the two-earner deduction (raising $34 billion over five years); taxation of unemployment benefits ($3.8 billion); elimination of the charitable deduction for nonitemizers ($3.1 billion, a less stringent provision than contained in Treasury I); restrictions on business meals and entertainment deductions ($6.9 billion, also less stringent than Treasury I); repeal of income averaging ($18.7 billion); and repeal of the exemption for "private purpose" bonds ($14 billion). Above all, Treasury II continued to call for eliminating the costly investment tax credit ($165 billion), for which there was virtually no support in Treasury, and the equally expensive state and local tax deduction ($149 billion), which was viewed as fiscally unavoidable by Baker, economically inefficient by Treasury staff, and "socialistic" by White House conservatives. Even with the retention of these provisions, however, the costly concessions described above left the plan short of revenues. These were made up in part by revenue-*gaining* changes to Treasury I, including elimination of interest indexing and reduction of the newly proposed deductions for dividends paid from 50 percent in Treasury I to just 10 percent in Treasury II. Both steps would raise tens of billions of dollars over five years. In addition, the minimum tax was strengthened for both corporations and individuals, a step that Treasury economists had earlier said would presage the failure of true reform.

Mixed Reactions

Such changes did not please everyone, particularly the economists who had shaped Treasury I. They objected to many of the changes on both substantive and political grounds. Although economists could and did disagree about the economic merits of different depreciation schedules, they did not disagree about decisions affecting charitable deductions, fringe benefits, or the oil and gas industry. These were viewed as blatantly political decisions lacking any substantive merit.

Economically, when these revisions were combined with the depreciation changes and dilution of indexing, the net result was to substantially erode the vaunted goal of a neutral and consistent tax system. In the view of McLure, Treasury II was only a "dim shadow" of Treasury I.[59] Moreover, some Treasury officials argued that their chances for obtaining truly comprehensive reform in Congress had been seriously weakened because the revised plan began unraveling the "hostage strategy." As Steuerle argued: "Political compromise was inevitable, but the more quickly we moved from being comprehensive, the more difficult it would be to oppose one interest group on the ground that others had not received special treatment." Treasury staff believed strongly that their role was to send the purest possible bill to Congress, in order to minimize the effects of inevitable legislative compromises. The sentiment was echoed on Capitol Hill, as news of one change after another leaked out of Treasury during the spring of 1985. "Members of the committee said, 'What do they think *we're* going to do?'" recalled one House staff member.

Not all of the reaction was negative, however. Baker believed that the changes he made "represented a vast improvement over current tax policy and did indeed have a chance of being enacted." Although most remained no more than lukewarm to reform, House Republicans did agree that the prospects for Treasury II looked better. In the Senate, Packwood retracted his threats to bottle up the legislation. Moreover, pockets of support in the business community were solidified under Treasury II. Indeed, even outside economists remained generally supportive, if somewhat disappointed. Treasury II was an "ugly duckling" compared to Treasury I, concluded Alan Blinder, but "positively winsome" compared to current law.[60] The same conclusion was reached by leading tax professionals who attended the second Ways and Means Committee retreat in the fall of 1985; when pressed for an up-or-down judgment on the revised Treasury proposal, they favored it 10−2 over the existing system.

Inestimable Reforms

In late April 1985, believing that Treasury II was virtually complete, Baker briefed the president. Surprisingly, despite his authorship of Treasury I, Don Regan went along with Baker's judgment that the new plan was more viable politically. "Regan was a delegator," explained his top White House aide, and so he swallowed distasteful changes in the treatment of oil, indexing, depreciation, and foreign taxes. With so much agreement before him, President Reagan easily approved Treasury II.

This, as they say, should have been the last word. But, it was not. After the new plan had been approved by the White House and was being prepared for release, the revenue estimators suddenly declared that the plan was a whopping $50 billion short over five years! It was to be only one in a series of revenue-estimating missteps that would haunt the reform process—and sometimes bring it to the brink of disaster—as harried statisticians sought to model the unpredictable effects of dozens of incompletely drafted, last-minute changes. As Johnson recalled the event: "I just lost it. I felt they couldn't have made [an error] that big. I had stressed to Pearlman over and over that the numbers had to be clean before we went to the Man on this. Fifty billion is a big, big number to make up. We were totally destitute."

Eventually, the shortfall was made up by inserting a "windfall recapture" provision into the new depreciation scheme. This provision was once advocated by Johnson to prevent corporations from benefiting twice from capital incentives, first under existing accelerated depreciation and second under the newly proposed indexed formula. Although the idea plugged the revenue gap temporarily, business opposed it as retroactive taxation and Congress later dropped it.

More important in the long run, this event underscored the enormous difficulty of amending finely balanced, comprehensive tax proposals in a revenue- and distributionally neutral environment. Throughout the Treasury II process, Baker and Darman had encountered unexpected and chronic revenue problems in the process of amending Treasury I. As the $50 billion shortfall illustrated, the expensive additions and subtractions they proposed had been difficult to finance without losing revenues, even with the deletion of interest indexing, large cutbacks in the proposed dividend deduction, and the failure to include funds for costly but unavoidable transition rules. Even so, the problems of maintaining distributional neutrality were often more difficult still. Most of the amendments the duo supported disproportionately aided upper-income individuals, thus distorting the distributional effects of the plan even when revenues were found to cover expenses. "I don't think they understood initially how these constraints were going to interact with what they wanted to do," said one Treasury official. And, in fact, the Treasury II proposal proved to be more generous to the wealthiest taxpayers—those with incomes over $200,000 annually—granting them an average reduction in tax liabilities 22 percent larger than in Treasury I, even though the overall reduction in individual tax liabilities was 18 percent smaller than in Treasury I.

Distributional flaws aside, the computational adventures of Treasury II were still not over. At the very end, after embarrassed Treasury officials had gone back to the White House to gain approval for the windfall recapture provision, and the president's tax-reform blitz was about to begin, a second $10 billion shortfall appeared. "Everybody was so burned out and strung out by that point that we were ready to commit suicide," notes Johnson. "I told Pearlman he was a dead man if he told Baker at that point. I said, you better just go back down and make some adjustments." But Pearlman did tell Baker, advising him that the numbers were tentative and that the estimators were going to "work all night" to double-check them. "The following morning, they said it was OK—no shortfall," he recalled.

In the end, despite Pearlman's labors, the plan the president sent to Congress was not revenue neutral, as congressional aides quickly discovered, and further changes were subsequently demanded to make it so. Despite this and other eleventh-hour corrections in Treasury II, the first of many revenue crises for tax reform had been weathered. The incident became only a footnote in a far larger and more important story.

Going Public

On May 28, 1985, Treasury II was released to the public. The occasion for the unveiling was a prime-time presidential address, followed by two weeks of presidential barnstorming across the country, all designed to grab the nation's attention and establish the tone of the ensuing debate.

To seize the moral and economic high ground, Treasury II was billed as the president's plan for "fairness, growth, and simplicity." Yet these economic principles, while present from the beginning, were now draped in strongly populist rhetoric and sweetened with a powerful political promise: tax reform means a tax cut for average Americans. In the president's words:

> A second American Revolution . . . is gathering force . . . born of popular resentment against a tax system that is unwise, unwanted, and unfair. . . . [Our] proposal . . . will free us from the grip of special interests. . . . It will reduce tax burdens on the working people of this country, close loopholes that benefit a privileged few. . . . We want to cut taxes. . . . The percentage of income tax owed would come down—way down—for [every

income group]. . . . There is one group of losers in our tax plan, those individuals and corporations who are not paying their fair share. . . . These abuses cannot be tolerated. . . . The free rides are over.[61]

If anything, his rhetoric was even more strident in follow-up speeches, which added more explicit attacks on the traditional demons of populist lore: Wall Street scions and Washington bureaucrats.

All of this proved to be too much for some of Treasury I's authors— notably Charles McLure, who had already seen his handiwork twisted and strained in the substance of Treasury II. Rather than a principled defense of economic neutrality, he argued, "the White House tried to sell a thin gruel of pap and crap, in which they misstated a lot of arguments and tried to appeal to the basest instincts of everybody, especially greed." Demonstrating that Washington is not an easy place for policy purists, McLure packed up his bags and returned to Stanford a month after the president's speech, distressed that "for economists, it is troublesome to see how little influence economic arguments exerted once Treasury I went to the White House." [62]

Not all had such exacting standards, however. Other, more favorable reactions were reflected in the press. Thanks to the "great communicator's" active role, Treasury II surpassed Treasury I's impact on the media, receiving enormous amounts of coverage in major newspapers and weekly magazines. There were twelve separate stories and commentaries—for a whopping 524 column inches—in the May 29 New York Times alone. And although Treasury I was preferred in some quarters, Treasury II's coverage was favorable, if not ecstatic. "A vast improvement" said the Chicago Tribune; "Sensible" according to the Atlanta Constitution; "Welcome" (Indianapolis Tribune); "Looks good but needs work" (Philadelphia Inquirer); "He's right" (Denver Post); "Seize this opportunity" (Birmingham News). Even the Washington Post, which was cautious editorially, accompanied its account of Reagan's plan with a front-page story that began: "Tax experts across the political spectrum were almost unanimous yesterday in calling President Reagan's tax-overhaul plan a major improvement." [63]

Despite McLure's disappointment and the partial disaffections of other tax professionals, the president's rhetoric had sold well where it mattered most—in the media. While some old friends were sacrificed in the process, Treasury II's release marked tax reform's coming of age. Throughout the remainder of the tax-reform process, economists as well as other professionals remained integral to reform—both by helping opinion makers and the media define "good" and "bad" and also by providing options, advice, and estimates to the policy makers. But Treasury II signified the passage of tax reform into a very different arena from the one dominated by civil servants and academic experts. It was a domain in which politicians, not professionals, had the upper hand, a place where appearances and symbols often outweighed evidence and substance in decision making.

Notes

1. See David A. Stockman, *The Triumph of Politics: Why the Reagan Revolution Failed* (New York: Harper and Row, 1986), 361−62; and "Reagan 'Tempted' by Flat-Rate Tax," *New York Times*, July 8, 1982, A1.
2. Stockman, *The Triumph of Politics*, 229.
3. Ibid., 363.
4. Quoted in Dale Russakoff, "Tracing the Twisted Path of Reagan's Income Tax Revision Plan," *Washington Post*, September 25, 1985, A4.
5. Donald T. Regan, *For the Record: From Wall Street to Washington* (New York: Harcourt Brace Jovanovich, 1988), 196.
6. Stockman, *The Triumph of Politics*, 364.
7. See John W. Kingdon, *Agendas, Alternatives, and Public Policies* (New York: Harcourt Brace Jovanovich, 1984).
8. Regan, *For the Record*, 207, 193.
9. Ibid., 202−3.
10. Ibid., 206.
11. In addition to Secretary Regan, Pearlman, McLure, and Chapoton, who (until he left the department in mid-1984) was the assistant secretary for taxation, the regular participants included Roscoe Egger, the head of the IRS; Dr. Manuel Johnson, a supply-side economist who was deputy and later assistant treasury secretary for economic policy; Bruce Thompson, assistant secretary for legislative affairs; Thomas Dawson, who was Regan's liaison to the business community; and Albert Kingon, assistant secretary for public affairs. This core group was regularly joined by Dr. Beryl Sprinkel, another economist who was assistant secretary for economic affairs until he became head of the president's Council of Economic Advisers.
12. U.S. Department of the Treasury, Office of Tax Analysis, "Tax Reform for Fairness, Simplicity, and Economic Growth: The Treasury Department Report to the President," *Tax Notes*, December 3, 1984, 882, 884, 910.
13. John F. Witte, *The Politics and Development of the Federal Income Tax* (Madison: University of Wisconsin Press, 1985), 291.
14. Treasury Department, "Report to the President," 884, 911.
15. Regan, *For the Record*, 201.
16. Frederick C. Mosher, *Democracy and Public Service* (New York: Oxford University Press, 1968), 101.
17. Regan, *For the Record*, 206.
18. Henry J. Aaron and Harvey Galper, *Assessing Tax Reform* (Washington: Brookings Institution, 1985).
19. Joseph A. Pechman, *Federal Tax Policy*, 5th ed. (Washington: Brookings Institution, 1987), 211.
20. Treasury Department, "Report to the President," 891.
21. Because existing IRS data compiled from tax returns did not include fringe benefits and other kinds of income that were targeted by reform, a vast new data set was created by merging tax information with census data, and the distribution of existing taxes was recalculated accordingly. See Maureen McCauley, "Treasury Proposal Attempts Improved Definition of Income in Tax Reform Effort," *Tax Notes*, December 24, 1984, 1170−71.
22. Regan, *For the Record*, 209.
23. See Eugene Steuerle and Michael Hartzmark, "Individual Income Taxation, 1947−1979," *National Tax Journal* 34 (1981): 145−66.

24. See Margaret Wrightson, "*The Road to South Carolina: Intergovernmental Tax Immunity and the Constitutional Status of Federalism*," in *Publius: The Journal of Federalism* (Summer 1989).
25. Regan, *For the Record*, 210.
26. U.S. Office of Management and Budget, *Special Analyses: Budget of the United States Government, FY 1987* (Washington: U.S. Government Printing Office, 1987), G-43, 45.
27. Treasury Department, "Report to the President," 893.
28. Charles E. McLure, Jr., "The Tax Treatment of Owner-Occupied Housing: Achilles Heel of Tax Reform?" in *Tax Reform and Real Estate*, ed. James R. Follain (Washington: Urban Institute, 1986), 222, 230.
29. Treasury Department, "Report to the President," 893.
30. See Mary Bourdette and Jim Weill, "The Impact of Federal Taxes on Poor Families," in U.S. Congress, House, Committee on Ways and Means, *Comprehensive Tax Reform, Hearings*, part 4, 99th Cong., 1st sess., 1985, 2940−96.
31. See Jack Kemp, "Fair and Simple Tax (FAST)," in *A Citizen's Guide to the New Income Tax Reforms: FAIR Tax, Flat Tax, Simple Tax*, ed. Joseph Pechman (Totowa, N.J.: Rowman and Allanheld, 1985), 104.
32. Treasury Department, "Report to the President," 879.
33. Perry D. Quick, "Businesses: Reagan's Industrial Policy," in *The Reagan Record*, ed. John Palmer and Isabel Sawhill (Cambridge, Mass.: Ballinger, 1984), 298.
34. Treasury Department, "Report to the President," 916.
35. Steuerle and Hartzmark, "Individual Income Taxation, 1947−79," 156.
36. Calculated from Table 4−2, Treasury Department, "Report to the President," 895.
37. Regan added, "In Wall Street, I had been trained to keep secrets." He was so angered by one White House leak just before the release of Treasury I (which he termed a "treacherous insult") that he attempted to resign from the cabinet. Regan, *For the Record*, 218−19, 251−57.
38. *Tax Notes*, December 3, 1985, 832.
39. Robert Rothman, "Treasury Plan Cuts Real Estate Tax Benefits," *Congressional Quarterly Weekly Report*, December 1, 1984, 3018.
40. See *Tax Notes*, December 17, 1985, 1056, 1154; *Tax Notes*, December 3, 1985, 832.
41. Quoted in Pamela Fessler and Steven Pressman, "Tax Overhaul: The Crucial Lobby Fight of 1985," *Congressional Quarterly Weekly Report*, March 9, 1985, 450.
42. Alan S. Blinder, *Hard Heads, Soft Hearts: Tough-Minded Economics for a Just Society* (Reading, Mass.: Addison Wesley, 1987), 170−71; Alice Rivlin, quoted in "A Forecast of Glad Tidings," *Time*, December 12, 1985, 37; Harvey Galper, "The Tax Proposals of the U.S. Treasury Department," *Australian Tax Forum* (1987): 191−222; and Henry J. Aaron and Harvey Galper, "The Politics of Tax Reform," reprinted in *Tax Notes*, January 6, 1986, 49−53.
43. Bruce Babbitt, quoted in Dan Balz, *Washington Post*, November 29, 1984, A-5. See also Pamela Fessler, "Treasury Tax Overhaul Excites Little Interest," *Congressional Quarterly Weekly Report*, December 1, 1984, 3017; and *Tax Notes*, December 24, 1984, 1186.
44. "Up Go the Trial Balloons," *Time*, December 10, 1984, 22.
45. Everett Carll Ladd, "On Mandates, Realignments, and the 1984 Presidential

Election," *Political Science Quarterly* 100 (Spring 1985): 20, 25; James L. Sundquist, *Dynamics of the Party System* (Washington: Brookings Institution, 1973), chap. 13 and p. 297.

46. Hedrick Smith, "Congress: Will There Be Realignment? " in *Beyond Reagan: The Politics of Upheaval*, ed. Paul Duke (New York: Warner Books, 1986), 146; Bill Bradley, quoted in Anne Swardson and Dan Balz, "Simplification Campaign Taxes Public's Interest," *Washington Post*, April 15, 1985, A3.

47. Richard Darman, quoted in Dale Russakoff, "In Taxes, the Impossible Became the Inevitable," *Washington Post*, June 29, 1986, A12.

48. Regan, *For the Record*, 212−13.

49. Paul Blustein, "Tax Plan's Political Growing Pains," *Wall Street Journal*, December 28, 1984, 34.

50. *Tax Notes*, November 19, 1984, 739. Although there are many examples of the president's intellectual aloofness, two of the most damning are Stockman, *The Triumph of Politics;* and *The Tower Commission Report* (New York: Bantam Books, 1987), 79−80. See also, *Wall Street Journal*, December 28, 1984.

51. Treasury Department, "Report to the President," 897.

52. Regan, *For the Record*, 219−20.

53. Ibid., 213.

54. Jane Seaberry, "James Baker an Enigma at Treasury," *Washington Post*, June 2, 1985, F1.

55. Center for the Study of American Business, "The President's Tax Proposal: Implications for Capital Formation," processed, St. Louis, Mo., June 1985, 5.

56. Quoted in Ronald Brownstein, "Wagering on Tax Reform," *National Journal*, February 2, 1985, 247.

57. Ibid.

58. Burt Solomon, "Oil and Gas Hit Paydirt in Reagan Tax Plan," *National Journal*, June 1, 1985, 1310.

59. Charles E. McLure Jr., "Where Tax Reform Went Astray," *Villanova Law Review* 31 (1986): 1657.

60. Blinder, *Hard Heads, Soft Hearts*, 171.

61. Ronald Reagan, "Tax Reform: Address to the Nation," May 28, 1985, *Weekly Compilation of Presidential Documents* 21 (June 3, 1985): 704, 707.

62. Charles E. McLure Jr., and George R. Zodrow, "Treasury I and the Tax Reform Act of 1986: The Economics and Politics of Tax Reform," *Economic Perspectives* 1 (Summer 1987), last page.

63. Dale Russakoff, "Experts Find Merit, Not Boldness," *Washington Post*, May 29, 1985, A1.

4   Strange Bedfellows: Tax Reform Meets Democratic Politics

Trying to tax people and businesses fairly. That's been the historic Democratic commitment. . . . But this time there's a difference in the push for tax reform. This time it's a Republican president who's bucking his party's tradition as protector of big business and the wealthy. . . . If the president's plan is everything he says it is, he'll have a great deal of Democratic support.
—Dan Rostenkowski, May 28, 1985

With those words to a nationwide television audience, Ways and Means Committee chairman Dan Rostenkowski, D-Ill., shouldered the mantle of tax reform and launched the painstaking process of translating a presidential proposal into statutory reality. Many knowledgeable observers—and virtually all of his committee colleagues—believe that Rostenkowski's support was the single most important factor contributing to congressional passage of the Tax Reform Act of 1986. "It was the personal ambition of one man, the chairman, that carried us through on this bill," maintained Rep. Ray McGrath, R-N.Y. "He was the driving force." A top administration official agreed, saying, "If it hadn't been for Rostenkowski, there would have been no tax bill. He was the star of this whole process."

Although the highly personalized character of legislative politics makes it easy to exaggerate the role of a few individuals, Rostenkowski's decision to embrace tax reform marked a critical juncture in the process of enacting the TRA. Constitutionally, tax legislation must originate in the House of Representatives, where it is the province of the Ways and Means Committee. As chairman, Rostenkowski had an arsenal of weapons with which to slow or even block reform had he so desired.

Yet Rostenkowski did far more than stand aside for a popular president. Though no reformer by background or temperament, he came to view tax reform as good policy and good politics—a historic opportunity to secure his reputation and protect his party's interests. To this end, he compelled his reluctant committee to go where it preferred not to tread, crafting legislation uniquely designed to pass the House. By doing so, Rostenkowski stoked the partisan engine of tax reform, placing enormous pressure on the Republican-controlled Senate to respond in kind or face the political fallout.

Success was hardly preordained. Most committee members had made careers out of enacting the very tax preferences that reformers now sought to eliminate. Moreover, groups representing virtually every segment of society—from nonprofit hospitals and charities to bankers and bond underwriters—were poised to attack. Many had already organized political action committees (PACs) to funnel campaign contributions to Ways and Means members, for an average of $168,224 per member in the 1983−1984 election cycle.[1] This average was the second highest for all House committees and some $40,000 more than the House average, all of which gave rise to confident predictions that tax reform would fail before it could begin. As one "public interest" lobbyist argued in 1984: "The tax bill is likely going no place, and the reason is that all the groups that benefit from the current system are all big contributors."[2]

He was nearly proved correct. When the Ways and Means Committee finally began to write a tax bill in September 1985, after months of monotonously negative hearings and lobbying, the odds on tax reform quickly went from bad to worse. After days of procedural wrangling and a series of often narrow victories on issues of modest controversy, Rostenkowski failed to turn back a revenue-busting amendment involving banks. The chairman was forced to suspend committee deliberations, and the process threatened to unravel. But, as was seen many times in the tax-reform saga, deft leadership turned the situation around through the combination of old-fashioned coalition-building techniques and media-oriented, entrepreneurial tactics.

H.R. 3838 stumbled badly again when it reached the House floor, where a coalition of angry Republicans and disgruntled Democrats voted down the procedural motion necessary to consider it. Almost left for dead, the legislation was revived once more, this time by direct, high-stakes presidential lobbying and by less dramatic but equally effective Democratic muscling. Because leaders on each side had staked their reputations on victory, tax reform slipped through the House—though barely—without so much as a final roll-call vote. Thus did a combination of leadership, cajolery, calculation, idealism, and luck first lend H.R. 3838 the unofficial title it would earn again and again throughout the legislative process: "the bill that wouldn't die."

The Inauspicious Context of Reform

From the beginning, smart money in Washington held that a tax-reform bill would never emerge from the Ways and Means Committee, at least in a guise that constituted serious reform. Many of these bets were laid by committee members, who had seen such efforts fail in the past and who recognized a multitude of familiar trouble signs. As one remarked:

> Initially, there were only three people in Washington who wanted tax reform—Ronald Reagan, Jim Baker, and Dan Rostenkowski—and only

one of them had a vote on the committee. It was a heartburn issue for members. We saw it as just dusting off all the esoteric ideas of tax professionals and putting them in one package.

This was an exaggeration, but only a slight one. Just a handful of reformers sat among the thirty-six Ways and Means Committee members, most notably Richard Gephardt, D-Mo., Bill Gradison, R-Ohio, Donald Pease, D-Ohio, and Fortney "Pete" Stark, D-Calif. Certain others were potential supporters, especially more liberal Democrats who took a dim view of tax loopholes for the rich. As Charles Rangel, D-N.Y., commented: "I thought it was terrific. It took the working poor off the tax rolls, closed the loopholes. I told Tip, 'This is what we've been fighting for. I don't care whose name is on it.'" But even he had serious problems with other features of the president's plan. Like many other liberals—on and off the committee—he was especially troubled by the plan's drastic diminution of statutory progressivity.[3]

Others parted company with the administration on strategy. For example, Marty Russo, D-Ill., preferred strengthening the alternative minimum tax (AMT) to assuage popular indignation about wealthy corporations and individuals who escaped or sharply reduced their tax liability. The AMT was a politician's dream, for it allowed hanging on to provisions that contributed to tax avoidance while at the same time sidestepping charges of collusion with special interests. Gradison, in contrast, wanted to continue slogging down the TEFRA-DEFRA trail by closing loopholes in a piecemeal fashion.

The small and divided contingent of reformers was surrounded by a larger, hostile army of opponents, including most of the committee's senior Democrats. Sam Gibbons, D-Fla., could be counted on to vigorously defend provisions favoring capital formation and overseas investment, just as J. J. Pickle, D-Texas, and James Jones, D-Okla., were certain to champion shelters for the oil and gas industry. Indeed, from banking and insurance to agriculture and labor, members' constituency and policy interests, up and down the ladder of seniority, ran counter to the goals of tax reform.

In addition, these members understood that tax reform threatened the committee's institutional power and electoral benefits. Tax expenditures were the revenue equivalent of public works projects: they allowed members to curry electoral favor by "bringing home the bacon."[4] This command over the tax code was an important commodity within the House, making the Ways and Means Committee one of the most prestigious in Congress. Yet tax reform required members to erode this source of power while they eliminated preferences they may have struggled years to achieve.[5]

All the President's Men

From the beginning, Republicans were even more hostile than senior Democrats. "We were livid over Treasury I," acknowledged one Republican staff member. While the restoration of some corporate preferences in Treasury II softened the opinions of some, others remained intransigent. How, they wondered, could a conservative president propose legislation whose greatest benefit went to low-income Democrats at enormous expense to core Republican constituencies? To them, party realignment based on tax reform seemed improbable at best.

Republicans' political concerns were reinforced by philosophical considerations. When it came to implementing policies, most preferred tax expenditures to more direct government intervention.[6] Direct federal grants, subsidies, and regulations required bureaucratic execution, but tax expenditures did not. Republicans liked the fact that individual taxpayers retained the freedom to discover and make use of appropriate tax preferences on their own. All in all, it seemed to them a cheaper, simpler, and less intrusive option, which had the added benefit of lessening tax liabilities.

Finally, House Republicans perceived tax reform to be dangerous economics. Most believed that weaknesses in the U.S. economy could be traced to inadequate savings and investment. They supported tax incentives intended to stimulate economic productivity and to enable U.S. firms to compete with heavily subsidized overseas competitors. ERTA had brought a cornucopia of such instruments into use—notably the investment tax credit (ITC) and accelerated depreciation. But these and other cherished provisions were threatened by the president's single-minded pursuit of lower tax rates. "Very dangerous," warned Rep. Philip Crane, R-Ill., during the House hearings.[7] "An economic disaster," agreed Rep. Bill Frenzel, R-Minn.

The Deficit Dilemma

Finally, Democrats and Republicans alike fretted because "revenue-neutral" tax reform did nothing about the looming federal deficit. In September 1984, Rostenkowski warned that his members had returned from a committee retreat, not with enthusiasm for tax reform, but with "a greater sense of fear of deficits." Two months later, after Treasury I had been unveiled, he reiterated the point. "Tax reform is a noble cause," Rostenkowski said, but "deficit reduction is a demand."[8]

Even after the president's plan was made public, congressional sentiment for linking tax reform to deficit reduction remained strong. Liberals in particular sought to use reform as leverage for raising revenues. But the leverage evaporated when the president gleefully announced that his "veto pen was ready" for any reform bill that hiked taxes. His stubbornness did not deter reform opponent and Majority Leader Jim Wright who "pleaded with the Speaker" not to support a revenue-neutral approach. "I argued as feverishly as I could, because I knew it would make our job [on the budget] so much more difficult." But Tip O'Neill was determined to avoid the partisan consequences of a tax-raising bill, and he backed Rostenkowski's ultimate decision to write a revenue-neutral reform bill. As the Speaker put it: "That Mondale statement [promising to raise taxes if elected] was the number one issue against us in 1984, and I just made up my mind that we would not raise taxes until Reagan asked us to." [9] Still, throughout the process, many tax writers remained dissatisfied. "We are literally fiddling while the nation burns," declared Tom Downey, D-N.Y., "trying to reform taxes [when] the fact is that we need to raise taxes, not reform them."

An Unlikely Ally of Reform

All this hostility was counterbalanced by Rostenkowski's unexpectedly enthusiastic embrace of tax reform. In this, the chairman surprised the oddsmakers. Having counted up the pluses and minuses, few of them expected Rostenkowski to take the president's bait. To begin with, reconsidering fifty years of accumulated tax law in a single session of Congress seemed nearly impossible. The U.S. tax code is 2,000 pages long, and length does not begin to convey its complexity and vexing detail. Revising just a fraction of the code could easily have occupied the committee for months. Rostenkowski later reflected: "If I had looked at the code—the challenge, just the *size* of it—I think I would have had second thoughts."

Nor was Rostenkowski a reformer by upbringing or temperament. On the contrary, the representative from northwest Chicago's "Polish corridor" was a protégé of mayor Richard Daley and a rough-and-tumble product of the last great political machine in the country. Back-room compromises—not idealistic crusades—were his forte, and he had little patience with political do-gooders. Rep. Don Pease, D-Ohio, "never got to first base" in his previous attempts to interest Rostenkowski in reform.

In the past, the chairman had never been reluctant to accept contributions, honoraria, and trips from organizations with a stake in tax policy. And his record for placing politics over principle was formidable. As David Stockman jibed, "the hogs were really feeding" at Rosty's trough during the struggle over ERTA back in 1981, when he and the president took turns playing Santa Claus in a bitter battle for House votes. [10]

Rostenkowski lost his bidding war with Reagan over ERTA, but the experience gave him ample reason to avoid working with the White House again. The administration's 1981 legislative strategy was based on a "bait and switch" with southern Democrats, designed to "put the squeeze on Rosty" and pry him loose from an otherwise hostile House leadership.[11] After going out on a limb to negotiate with the White House, Rostenkowski saw these talks collapse when the president refused to bargain. The whole experience left a bitter taste on Capitol Hill. As Tip O'Neill recalled his counsel upon seeing Treasury II: "I called Danny in and I said to him: 'Let's not get ourselves into that position again. If you want to work with Baker, fine, but never let go of the fact this is our baby.'"

Explaining the Chairman's Support

Notwithstanding all of these factors, Rostenkowski leaped at the chance to enact tax reform. It was, he said, his "easiest" decision "because it was a challenge." In truth, however, reform offered him much more than that. For one thing, it gave him a chance to win one for the Democrats, or at least keep them in the game. As chairman of the Ways and Means Committee, Rostenkowski had close ties to the Democratic leadership and institutional responsibilities to his party. The administration's argument that reform might be the key to electoral realignment could not be summarily dismissed. At the very least, senior Democrats knew the issue required cautious handling in the wake of Mondale's disastrous 1984 presidential campaign. After the election, Republicans had drawn almost even in partisan loyalties among the voters.[12] What if tax reform allowed them to cement those new ties? As one committee Democrat described the situation:

> This whole tax reform measure was not driven by economics, it's driven by politics. President Reagan and the Republicans would like to be the majority party and they are going after a class of voters who vote a lot and they want to give them tax cuts. And Democrats have traditionally been for tax reform, and they obviously want to remain a majority party, so they're defensively protecting tax reform.[13]

Democratic leaders perceived this as a battle for ideas as well as votes. They believed they had proprietary claims on tax reform, dating back to Stanley Surrey's efforts in the Kennedy and Johnson years. More recent reform proposals had been advanced by President Carter and by Sen. Bill Bradley and Rep. Richard Gephardt. Thus, Rostenkowski had powerful incentives to protect his party's heritage. As he expressed it: "I'm a Democrat. Reform, fairness—they've all been in the Democratic platform for as long as I've been a Democrat. And I'm not going to let Ronald Reagan get to my left, I'll tell you that much."[14] In this, he was strongly backed by House Speaker Tip O'Neill, who recalled that when the administration began seriously developing a tax-reform initiative: "I said: Danny, this is *our* issue. You know, Gephardt and Bradley started this, and whatever you do, don't let [the White House] steal the issue on us."

Moreover, eliminating loopholes for the rich, raising taxes on corporations, and reducing tax burdens on poor and middle-class Americans had powerful visceral appeal to traditional Democrats like O'Neill and Rostenkowski and their constituents. As Rosty later asked Americans in his reply to Reagan's tax-reform address, "Why should a bank teller pay a higher tax rate than the bank? Why should a gas station attendant pay a greater share than the oil company he works for? "

Invisible Allies

In the new game of tax reform, Rostenkowski found plenty of willing players among his staff. This was certainly the case at the Joint Committee on Taxation (commonly called the Joint Tax Committee or the JTC), a highly professional nonpartisan staff of economists and tax attorneys that serves both revenue committees of Congress. Among other things, the JTC advises and gives technical support to the chairman and members of the Ways and Means Committee, helps draft tax legislation and committee reports, and estimates the budgetary and revenue effects of proposed changes in the tax code. Its determinations of the revenues lost or gained by proposed legislative changes are authoritative.

Its monopoly over revenue estimates, along with its professional expertise, combine to give the JTC staff enormous influence over the congressional tax-writing process. Like the professionals at Treasury, they shared a professional commitment to the merits of tax reform. They, too, saw themselves as guardians of the federal revenue system and were committed to defending its purity from the "distortions" advocated by more parochial interests. Also like their counterparts at Treasury, they had a plethora of concrete reform proposals ready and waiting. As JTC chief economist Randall Weiss put it: "We had a series of lists of potential base broadeners prepared as soon as the president's bill came up. We had published pamphlets on tax expenditures and kept lists of possible reforms over the years. In 1982, for example, we had developed a series of base broadeners that looked a lot like the '86 bill."

As it turned out, JTC support was important politically as well as logistically, for it gave Rostenkowski's work the patina of legitimacy that comes from making "good public policy." [15] Indeed, in one proposal, Rostenkowski could advance legislation that: had the experts' stamp of approval; carried a Democratic logo of fairness; was touted by the press for promoting the public interest over special interests; and advanced his committee's reputation for effectiveness and upheld its tradition as guardian of the federal revenue system. For these reasons, the chance to enact tax reform was prized not only by the JTC but by Rostenkowski's personal staff on the Ways and Means Committee. By his own recollection, they played an important part in his decision to proceed: "I would have had second thoughts. But the Rob Leonards of this world [the chief tax counsel on Ways and Means] and the Joe Dowleys of this world [the committee's chief counsel] and the Ken Bowlers of this world [the deputy chief of staff] kept on the wave of, 'We can do it; it's big but we can do it.' "

The Voices of History

The political and policy concerns propelling Rostenkowski's leadership were reinforced by personal considerations as well. Comprehensive tax reform would be a historic legislative accomplishment that would redound to Rostenkowski's benefit for years to come. It is not uncommon for those who have acquired considerable power and position to refocus their energies with an eye toward history's larger constituency. Tax reform could easily be his ticket into this most exclusive club.

Success would also assuage earlier disappointments. "Rostenkowski had spent years as the new chairman suffering failure," observed one Ways and Means Democrat. After being embarrassed by the administration in his first test of leadership back in 1981, he was subsequently "outmaneuvered" by the wily Senate Finance chairman, Bob Dole, R-Kan., who used a procedural ploy to bypass the House and originate TEFRA in 1982. The next year, Rostenkowski was ambushed in his own chamber. When he bottled up a bill repealing a controversial TEFRA provision to establish income-tax withholding on savings-account interest, rank-and-file House members wrested it from his committee with a "discharge" petition, using their majority to pass it over Rostenkowski's opposition.[16]

Such defeats were especially damaging because Ways and Means Committee members are traditionally success and power oriented, and former chairmen, notably Wilbur Mills in the 1960s and early 1970s, had reputations for strong and effective leadership.[17] Although the committee was stripped of some of its power in the 1970s, Rostenkowski badly wished to reverse the slide.[18] Thus, the Chicagoan was searching for a way to vindicate his chairmanship when Reagan placed tax reform on the agenda in 1985. As he admitted later: "I was looking for reform. You know, I've kind of lived in the shadow of Wilbur Mills."

Rout Wright?

A final personal factor that encouraged Rostenkowski to support tax reform was his half-hearted ambition to succeed Tip O'Neill as Speaker of the House. The seriousness with which he pursued that goal now seems open to question, but his interest in it was widely discussed by his colleagues and the press during the early months of 1985, especially after Tip O'Neill announced his pending retirement.

The most direct path to the Speaker's chair was through a succession of increasingly powerful leadership positions, beginning with chief Demo-

cratic whip, progressing to majority leader, and finally to Speaker. Carl
Albert and Tip O'Neill had followed that route, and Majority Leader Jim
Wright had deviated only slightly. Rostenkowski initially followed it as
well, having been a deputy whip in the 1960s and 1970s; but rather than
accept the majority whip position in 1981, he opted for Ways and Means
Committee chairman upon the electoral defeat of Al Ullman. Rostenkowski thus acquired a powerful policy position, but one decidedly off the
leadership track. To show up Wright, he would need a dramatic partisan
accomplishment; tax reform, which was opposed by the Texan, might just
be that issue.

Still, although they were close friends, O'Neill questioned Rostenkowski's suitability for and interest in the post:

> Danny never once, ever, mentioned to me that he wanted to be Speaker
> of the House. But when the newspapers picked it up, he liked it. It made
> him a bigger man in the Congress. But was he a serious candidate? Naw.
> [Otherwise,] you don't act like Danny. Danny comes and says, "I've got
> this bill on the floor and you voted against me, so don't ever ask for
> anything in my committee again." That's the way tough local politics
> works. But you don't operate like that in Washington. You've got to put
> your arm around a guy and tell him with a little bit of warmth, "I'd like
> to have you do this, and this is the merit of this, and this is why it's good
> for the party," and things like that.

Perhaps Rostenkowski, too, recognized that neither he nor tax reform
was right for the job, for in the end his pursuit was short lived and half-
hearted, easily pushed aside by the pressures and demands of tax reform
itself. By that point, however, the chairman's other motives for pursuing
reform proved sufficient to keep him involved and deepen his commitment to the goal.

The Summer of Discontent

While the Ways and Means Committee chairman decided to pursue tax
reform with increasing vigor and enthusiasm, the question remained: How
could good intentions be translated into legislative reality? In Congress, a
huge gulf exists between policy desires and tangible accomplishments,
especially where complex and controversial legislation is involved.

Recognizing this, James Baker arranged a private meeting in Rostenkowski's office overlooking the Capitol as soon as he assumed the reins at
Treasury. There he quietly urged the Chicagoan to adopt a blitzkrieg
strategy, catching tax reform's opponents off guard. Ronald Reagan had
used a similar strategy in achieving his first major legislative success, the
Omnibus Budget Reconciliation Act of 1981, which eliminated and
restructured scores of federal programs and reduced spending by billions.
The Reconciliation Act passed because the normal legislative process was

short-circuited. Hundreds of program and spending decisions—which like tax reform affected nearly every segment of society—were subsumed into a single 300-page bill and rushed through Congress at breakneck speed. This tactic wrested decisions away from legislative specialists and interest groups and posed a single overriding question: "Do you support the economic recovery program of a highly popular president?" Baker hoped to do the same with tax reform, urging Rostenkowski to rush the bill through his committee without hearings and push it through the floor on the wave of momentum created by the president. Follow his advice, Baker boasted, and "hell, we can get this whole thing done and on the president's desk by July."

But it was not to be. Rostenkowski rejected this approach out of hand, recalling: "I sat in my rocker and said: 'Jesus, Jim, don't show me how imprudent you are! You are viewing this as though we are going to a conference. We're creating legislation, and this is the first step in the process. We're going to have hearings. I'm going to take testimony. This will take us at least a year—or two.'" "Those guys were just full of themselves," he continued. "There's no question that the president was on a roll. But I said, 'No way pal.'"

At the time, Rostenkowski knew that Baker was revising the Treasury tax-reform proposal to reflect Republican interests. He had thrown open the doors at Treasury to hear complaints and suggestions from affected industries and interest groups. The chairman was determined to do the same—to hold the president's proposal up for public scrutiny and to allow Democrats and his committee to shape a bill more to their liking. As he said in his televised response to the president's address on tax reform: "Democrats will not . . . give the president's reform plan a rubber stamp. . . . We will make some changes—correct some imbalances—seek to make it fairer." [19] He committed himself, in short, to protect the Congress's prerogatives and follow the ponderous path of conventional bill writing, despite the risk that doing so would give disgruntled interest groups time to mobilize and react.

Selling Reform

His success would thus depend on keeping tax reform in the arena of macropolitics, under the constant glare of the media spotlight, visible and relevant to the general public. This is quite unlike the micropolitics of typical tax policy making, where narrow and complex issues go unreported by the mass media and draw the attention and interest of only the few who are immediately affected. Taken separately, most of the issues involved in comprehensive tax reform would have fit this pattern of obscure and specialized "subsystem" politics. [20] The reformers' only hope was to group enough narrow issues together in one large package so that every taxpayer in America would be directly affected by, and have an interest in, seeing it enacted.

Initially, this strategy enjoyed considerable success. The president's decision to make tax reform his top domestic priority gave the issue high visibility. The president devoted a major portion of his 1985 State of the Union address to the subject. Months later, he delivered a special televised speech to accompany the release of Treasury II. Finally, during May and June 1985, Reagan stumped the country with a series of populist speeches, portraying tax reform as a tax cut for average Americans and the end of free rides for the "privileged few."

Reagan's populist message was picked up and seconded by Rostenkowski in his response to the president's address. He sought to reclaim the issue for the Democrats with homey appeals to the average taxpayer:

> [Tax fairness is] what Democrats are all about. . . . Our roots lie with working families all across the country—like the Polish neighborhood where I grew up. . . . Working families file their tax forms with the nagging feeling that they're the country's biggest chumps. Their taxes are withheld at work—while the elite have enormous freedom to move their income from one tax shelter to another.[21]

Rostenkowski ended this enormously effective speech with an appeal to the "silent majority [of] working men and women." He called on them to write letters and raise their voices in support of tax reform, drowning out the "legions of special interests . . . determined to stop reform." "If you can't spell Rostenkowski," he concluded, "just address it R-O-S-T-Y, Washington, D.C."

Tens of thousands did exactly that, as favorable mail poured in to Rostenkowski's office and to the White House in the wake of these two speeches. Reinforced by favorable media attention and saturating exposure, these populist appeals had an initial positive effect. Early public reaction to the general outlines of the president's plan was highly favorable. According to one poll, 49 percent approved of Reagan's proposal and only 23 percent opposed it. Similarly, initial readings of constituent reactions by members of Congress showed a favorable response.[22]

But as pundits had predicted, this early momentum waned. It is always difficult to keep the public spotlight on a single issue for long, especially once Congress gets down to detailed business. The president, too, has competing policy demands and interests. Absent dramatic new twists and turns, the media soon tires of the issue and turns its focus elsewhere. Thus, once the Ways and Means Committee began its lengthy hearings, attention shifted away from the public generalities of "reform" and toward its particular and often controversial components.

The shift in momentum occurred on two levels. A few aspects of tax reform posed problems for millions of people. Two-thirds of all itemizing taxpayers made use of the deduction for state and local taxes, and tens of millions more enjoyed some form of employer-paid fringe benefits or employed income averaging for the two-earner deduction. Such popular provisions were not viewed by the average taxpayer as special-interest loopholes. They were often incidental to where one worked or lived, and few used the provisions as a ploy to lower taxes.

Thus, as awareness grew that such items were slated for elimination or scaling back, public perceptions began to shift from widespread, superficial support for the reform concept to concern about the loss of specific preferences. Although a June 1985 poll had shown 49 percent in support of Reagan's proposal, another survey two weeks later showed support for the Reagan plan down to 26 percent. Although the White House insisted that most taxpayers would experience a net decrease in taxes because of lower rates (Treasury statistics estimated that 58 percent of households would pay less taxes, while 21 percent would pay more),[23] many taxpayers were reluctant to sacrifice an existing preference for politicians' promises of a better future.

Meanwhile, many other aspects of tax reform affected only a relative few. Indeed, hundreds of provisions on arcane subjects were now threatened: tax benefits for corporations in Puerto Rico, special capital-gains treatment of timber and mining, the completed-contract method of accounting used by defense contractors, and credits for taxes paid to other countries by international corporations. Ignored and often incomprehensible to the general public, these kinds of issues posed enormous stakes for some corporations and industries. By one estimate, the giant Du Pont chemical corporation stood to lose $1 billion of tax benefits under the president's plan, and the story was repeated nationwide. Thus, members of Congress began hearing detailed complaints about specialized components of tax reform, especially from industries and employers in their own states and congressional districts.

The Best Congress Money Can Buy? Lobbying the Tax Bill

During this period of committee hearings, congressional lobbying began in earnest. Over a two-month period, from May 30 to July 31, the committee held twenty-eight days of hearings, received statements from almost one thousand witnesses, and compiled over nine thousand pages of testimony. Putting the best face on tax reform, Rostenkowski devoted the first five days to proponents, beginning with Secretary Baker, and then turning to chief executives of the Tax Reform Action Coalition, former Treasury officials, IRS commissioners, public-interest groups, and economists.

A Loser:
The Investment Tax Credit

Many tax reform issues were obscured by complexity, but high visibility was no guarantee of success. Lobbyists and corporations working on behalf of the investment tax credit (ITC) quickly discovered that their issue was one of the fiscal linchpins of reform, costing over $30 billion in FY 1987 alone.

Because repeal would virtually pay for lower corporate tax rates all by itself, many believed it was a foregone conclusion.[1] "The Lord Himself could have come down and lobbied for the ITC and it wouldn't have made any difference," said one congressional tax aide. Repealing the ITC was also critical to the administration's efforts to "level the playing field" of investment.

The ITC contributed to sharply lower tax rates by manufacturers who invested heavily in new equipment, but it was of little benefit to service industries or to struggling manufacturers that did not make a profit. Many of these companies supported tax reform's lower rates, and they prevented powerful umbrella business groups like the Chamber of Commerce from lobbying on behalf of the ITC.

The companies that profited from the ITC were hardly prepared to accept repeal without a fight, however. Twenty-three large corporations, including Goodyear, Du Pont, and AT&T, contributed $800,000 to acquire the services of "superlobbyist" Charls Walker to argue their case before Congress and to purchase large newspaper ads blasting the reform bill.[2] Supporters also hired well-known economists like Martin Feldstein to prepare analyses of the negative effects of repeal on corporate investment and economic growth.

Making the best of a tough situation, defenders sought to piggyback concern about the country's foreign trade and budget deficits. They stressed that competing businesses were already more heavily subsidized in most other foreign countries and that Congress should solve the budget deficit before turning to tax reform.[3] Although these arguments enjoyed success among congressional Republicans, they were insufficient to save the credit.

[1] See Remarks of Assistant Treasury Secretary Ronald Pearlman, *Tax Notes*, June 10, 1085, 1197.
[2] Peter Kilborn, "Washington Watch," *New York Times*, December 16, 1985, D2.
[3] See statements before the Committee on Ways and Means by Ernest S. Christian, Jr., and Charls E. Walker, June 13, 1985, in House Committee on Ways and Means, *Comprehensive Tax Reform*, part 2, 1216−69, 1317−39.

A Winner:
The Research and Development Tax Credit

Advocates of the research and development (R&D) tax credit mounted a successful campaign to preserve the preference for high-tech investment. R&D enjoyed several advantages: the credit cost only 5 percent as much as the ITC—$7.9 billion over five years;[1] an R&D extension was already included in the president's tax plan, so supporters had only to preserve existing gains from revenue-hungry competitors; and the R&D credit had strong appeal as an inexpensive way to promote technological innovation and economic growth. So many legislators embraced it that one opponent complained: "There's nothing more dangerous than the U.S. Congress with an idea." [2]

The credit was due to expire at the end of 1985, so supporters began their renewal campaign before tax reform was on Congress's agenda. When high-tech firms failed to win House support for a permanent R&D credit in 1984, the industry was "forced to get serious." [3] Eighty-five electronics firms, research universities, and trade associations established the Coalition for the Advancement of Industrial Technology (CAIT) to promote renewal.

They began by commissioning a study of the credit's economic effects. CAIT's press aide explained: "You had to make the economic case. It might not be enough, but you at least needed that. It formed the basis for our lobbying campaign." The study argued that the existing credit had contributed to "impressive increases in R&D spending" and economic growth, and that similar incentives were used in Japan and elsewhere.[4] Not all experts agreed, but the study "was persuasive because [the authors] believed it before we hired them," explained a coalition staffer.

The research was used to mount a nationwide press blitz. It also lined up 200 cosponsors for H.R. 1188, a stand-alone bill extending the credit, which sent a political message to Rostenkowski. And, the coalition coordinated grassroots lobbying by its member corporations with the efforts of former Carter aide Stuart Eisenstadt, who took the case directly to Congress.

[1] The White House, *The President's Tax Proposals to the Congress for Fairness, Growth, and Simplicity* (Washington: Government Printing Office, 1985), 459.
[2] E. Patrick McGuire, *Tax Notes*, October 28, 1985, 336.
[3] Interview with Stephanie Becker, Public Affairs Director, Coalition for the Advancement of Industrial Technology.
[4] Martin Neil Baily and Robert Z. Lawrence, "The Need for a Permanent Tax Credit for Industrial Research and Development" (Coalition for the Advancement of Industrial Technology, February 1985, mimeographed).

For the remaining twenty-three days members sat through endless predictions of disaster. "If you cut out the entertainment deduction, sports is finished in this country," argued one developer on behalf of write-offs for luxury sky-boxes and season tickets to professional sporting events. University representatives maintained that limiting the value of charitable contributions would "cripple the innovativeness of American universities [and] hurt the competitive position of the country." The National Realty Committee warned of pending economic "disaster" if the president's proposals were added to tax law changes adopted in 1984. Although committee members had long since learned to take such claims with a grain of salt, they were sufficient to convince one member that "from now on it's all downhill." [24]

Throughout this bleak process, only one glimmer of hope emerged from the reams of negative testimony. Nearly all the opponents of the plan had adopted a posture of "we support the concept of tax reform, *but*," and then proceeded to explain why a particular provision affecting them should not be included. Despite all the specific objections, the lobbying community, which is paid for its political expertise, perceived a danger in being blamed for opposing tax reform despite growing signs of weakness in the public's support for any concrete proposal.

Hearing Aids

Individuals, corporations, and trade associations did not limit themselves to testifying at hearings. Mobilizing a wide array of other resources, virtually every group with an interest in taxation joined in what was called "the crucial lobby fight of 1985." [25] Their efforts varied greatly, however, because of differing strategies and political assets.

Organization and Deep Pockets.   Depending on the size of a group's wallet, organizational and financial resources can be impressive sources of group influence. The National Association of Realtors and the National Association of Home Builders are among the most powerful interest groups in Washington, in part because each operates a PAC making over $2 million in contributions every election cycle and because each has a large, sophisticated, well-equipped staff. Tax reform brought out the most, if not the best, from such organizations. For example, at one point the U.S. Chamber of Commerce deployed twenty lobbyists to try to block H.R. 3838.[26] Ad hoc coalitions also entered the fray. Lobbying to preserve the deduction for state and local taxes originated in the spring of 1985 with a group of New York real estate and commercial interests which feared that elimination of the deduction would devalue their holdings in highly taxed New York City (to the tune of $1.6 billion in 1987 alone) and accelerate migration to nearby states. Over the next two years, this group raised $1.7 million dollars, hired two of its own lobbyists, and contributed almost $600,000 to establish a broader nationwide lobby in Washington called the

Coalition Against Double Taxation, which included public employee unions, educational organizations, and groups like the National League of Cities and the National Conference of State Legislatures.[27]

Active (and successful) lobbying was not confined to industrial and commercial giants, however. Although interest-group resources varied tremendously, thousands of diverse organizations entered the fray—from the Lutheran Brotherhood to the government of Puerto Rico—prompting one member to groan, "There are 33,000 lawyers in Washington, and they all get paid big bucks to save one word or sentence ... in the Internal Revenue Code." [28]

Many also made campaign contributions. During the first six months of 1985, PAC contributions to members of the House Ways and Means Committee virtually tripled compared with the same period in 1983. On average, committee members received $46,425 in early 1985 compared with $16,750 in early 1983. This far outpaced the average rate of increase in PAC contributions during this period, and it reflected not only organizations' eagerness to give but also committee members' ability to charge. With tax reform on the agenda, many raised the price of admission to their Washington fundraisers. Honoraria also flowed to members of Congress and their staffs for speaking at group conferences—often staged at vacation resorts that provided informal access to decision makers. Although the effects of such financial contributions on members' behavior are ambiguous and controversial (see Chapter 6 for a detailed discussion), they were not universally available. Corporations, trade and professional associations, and labor unions enjoyed an overwhelming edge in providing such resources.[29]

Similarly, the organizations with deep pockets often enjoyed an advantage when it came to mobilizing their grassroots supporters. The life insurance industry, for example, spent $5 million to help generate 1.6 million pieces of mail protesting proposed changes in the taxation of insurance benefits.[30]

Communications Tools. Successful lobbyists know the value of good communication. Timely facts, clear arguments, a belief in one's cause, and access to the mass media all enhance prospects for success. Of these four, providing factual information has long been considered the most important. The volumes of testimony on H.R. 3838 demonstrate that tax reform was no exception as groups from housing to charities spent tens and even hundreds of thousands of dollars on speeches and studies detailing tax reform's economic and geographic consequences.[31]

Effective communication takes more than information, however. Particularly in specialized fields like tax policy, getting one's point across depends on the clarity and character of one's argument. "Nuclear physics is much easier than tax law," moaned the lobbyist for a higher education association.[32] In fact, arcane or complicated issues sometimes were impossible to convey effectively to a group's own membership, much less to Congress.

Although Ways and Means members and their tax aides were knowledge-able about the tax code, the TRA stretched their expertise to its limits and placed severe constraints on the time available to hear from every lobbyist and group. Lobbyists who were unable to make an argument quickly and clearly were often ineffective.

Access to the mass media constitutes a last important communications resource. According to one study, gaining media attention ranked highest on a list of rapidly growing lobbying techniques.[33] And although media attention often costs little or nothing, it is also less manageable. Media coverage of an issue depends on many factors, including the number of viewers or readers likely to be affected by a given policy and the degree to which an issue arouses conflict, consternation, sympathy, or interest. Such factors have generally relegated tax policy to the back pages of the business section, but that changed dramatically during tax reform.

As with organization and finances, all interests do not have equal access to the media, and not all coverage is equally helpful. In many ways, reporters and editors carry on the progressive tradition in American politics. That is, they tend to view society as sharply divided between a vulnerable but virtuous public interest and powerful but narrowly selfish private interests.[34] Because many in the press consider it their responsibility to expose the hidden power of the special interests, some of those interests involved in tax reform found their media attention highly negative—as in the case of galvanizing stories about wealthy individuals and corporations that paid little or no taxes. In contrast, groups purporting to represent the general public, such as the labor-backed Citizens for Tax Justice, received more sympathetic treatment in the press, thus helping to redress somewhat the imbalance of material resources between such concerns.[35]

Perceived differences in the legitimacy of interest-group positions influ-enced the judgments of representatives and staffs as well as reporters and editors. To varying degrees, most members of Congress have an interest in pursuing some version of the "public good" and behave accordingly.[36] In the view of one high-ranking staff member, they are prone to discount weak arguments, even if backed up by financial resources:

> I've seen the people who throw a lot of money around Capitol Hill and how well they've done. Generally they either do worse or no better than others. If you're throwing money around, the immediate suspicion is that you've got a case that really stinks. And the same thing is true of hiring high-visibility lobbyists. The suspicion is that you've got a case you couldn't hope of selling on your own. The members know that.

Situational Assets. The geographic distribution of an interest, its importance to particular members of Congress, and the extent of intergroup rivalry also affect prospects for a successful lobbying effort. Geographic distribution contributes much to an interest's representational strength on the tax-writing committees. Large, geographically dispersed industries like agriculture, banking, and real estate recruited many soldiers (every member of Congress has bankers and real estate agents as constituents), while obscure and abstract interests such as bond underwriters enlisted few. Still others, such as oil and gas, though more regionally limited, have been unusually successful at placing members on the tax-writing committees.

Also important is the intensity with which an interest is represented by one or more friendly committee members and the staffs who assist them. As John Scheiner, tax counsel to Charles Rangel put it:

> I was a lobbyist for six and half years. The thing that impressed me about this job was that I didn't really change my profession. The only difference was that I was lobbying for Mr. Rangel's constituent interests and I had the power of Mr. Rangel. The chairman would say, "Look, what do you need to support the bill? Here's what the budget comes to. Can you live with that?" If Charlie said yeah, then I had to fight with the staff over how to structure it.

In the tax-reform debate, even a widely distributed interest could be vulnerable if every member viewed it as a second priority. This was because revenue neutrality altered the tax-writing process. Prior revenue bills were often constructed through political logrolling, whereby special interest provisions were added, one to the next, until a winning coalition was achieved. As intended, revenue neutrality converted this process into a "zero-sum game: " each interest was in competition with all others, because "spending" limited tax expenditure revenues to benefit one interest precluded using them to aid another. The fierce competition for available revenues in the tax-reform debate jeopardized any interest that lacked an aggressive inside spokesman for its cause. In contrast, industries and interests comprising members' core constituencies generally fared better because they were tenaciously defended.

The new competition was most evident when corporate powerhouses, such as banks and insurance companies, went toe-to-toe. Entire sectors joined the fray, as many high-tax industries aggressively supported reform in exchange for lower corporate rates, while low-tax, capital-intensive industries actively opposed it. The new fiscal discipline even led to situations in which "you had companies split, with one division pressuring us one way and another division the other." [37]

The Ways and Means Committee Writes a Bill

By the time Rostenkowski concluded his committee's hearings on July 31, 1985, thousands of lobbyists had spent as many hours and far more dollars in an unprecedented attempt to derail tax reform. Indeed, as Ways and Means members returned from their August recess and prepared to "mark up," or

write, their bill, it seemed that those efforts had paid handsome dividends.
Lobbyists in the members' home districts had nurtured the grassroots well.
"There are legions of organizations that have concocted . . . let's-bite-him-in-
the-ankle-when-he's-home routines," observed one Washington tax lobbyist.[38] Yet ordinary taxpayers also raised objections, having heard or read
about popular deductions that would be discontinued by reform.

What, then, was Rostenkowski to do? First and foremost, he needed
nineteen votes to report, or send, a bill out of his committee to the full
House. While the chairman hoped for something with the imprimatur of
good policy, his overriding concern had to be building a coalition. His initial
strategy was a double-barreled calculus: working directly with individual
members to gauge their positions and alleviate their concerns, while
fashioning an overall plan with more popular (and especially middle-class)
appeal than the president's.

As he talked to his members, the consummate vote counter mentally
tallied heads. Would they support reform legislation, either as the president
proposed it or with modifications? If the answer was "yes . . . but only with
specific changes," Rosty cautioned flexibility. Intransigence, he warned,
would be returned in spades: "Because if you're against me, I might as well
screw you up real good." [39]

With responses in hand, the chairman returned to his staff. Sift through
the ideas, he instructed, incorporating as many as possible into a professionally respectable comprehensive proposal.

To further judge collective sentiment as well as to engender camaraderie,
the chairman staged a second committee retreat before the markup. A
prestigious group of economists was invited to attend, and most endorsed a
reform bill along the lines the president had proposed. One member
suggested that this retreat marked a turning point in committee attitudes:

> After we kicked out the experts and the staff—it was just the members—
> Danny spoke very emotionally about his sick daughter and how she paid
> more taxes than the airline she worked for. He's rough and tough, but I
> thought there were tears in his eyes. And the general feeling was: OK, let's
> give it a try. We may not be able to do it, but if he wants it that much, we
> ought to try.

During the next weeks, Rob Leonard and committee aides, together
with JTC director David Brockway and his staff, created a package that
met the president's basic criteria but was more generous to the middle
class. Rostenkowski's package not only gave a slightly bigger tax cut to
more individuals than the president had wanted, it also softened Treasury
II's restrictions on popular deductions for state and local taxes, employee
fringe benefits, and the so-called marriage penalty. These provisions were
paid for by further increasing taxes on corporations. Wary of opposition,
Rostenkowski floated the proposal before the public as a "staff option."

Beyond that, he asked the White House to hold its fire so as not to undermine the fragile coalitions he hoped to build: "I just wanted the White House to be still," he said. "That was the deal I had with Ronald Reagan, [to] withhold comments until he saw the final bill."

Reagan agreed, but at the same time he sought to play a more active role in the Congress at large. Beginning in September, the president launched another six-week, cross-country speaking tour to raise the visibility of tax reform and to rebuild its eroding base of popular support in the nation. Attempting to portray the issue in its starkest terms, the president called it: "A drama with heroes and villains and a damsel in distress. The heroes are citizens . . . asking for tax justice. The villains are the special interests. . . . And the damsel in distress? A lass named Endless Economic Growth."[40]

To further bolster the president's populist case for reform, Treasury released a study showing that 5,000 millionaires and 50,000 individuals with incomes above $50,000 paid less in taxes in 1983 than the average middle-income family. Weeks later, on the day before the Ways and Means Committee began its markup, the White House released another glowing report predicting that substantial long-term economic growth would stem from tax reform. "Gains will occur in consumption, job creation, savings, investment, capital formation, and reduced tax evasion," bragged the chairman of the president's Council of Economic Advisers.[41]

Growing Doubts

But tax reform faced nothing but trouble in the House. In their visits home during the August recess, members discovered that tax reform had aroused a deadly combination of public apathy and interest-group hostility. Any lingering dreams of making it a realigning issue, capable of mobilizing public sentiment behind the party that most firmly embraced tax fairness, had totally evaporated. "It's not catching on," reported one Republican. "The people in the street, they never even mention it," agreed Tip O'Neill. Worse still, when they did mention the issue, it was to complain about losing their credits or deductions. Opinion polls confirmed what politicians sensed. Compared with surveys conducted immediately after the president's May address in support of Treasury II, September polls showed that the initial favorable pluralities had vanished or turned negative.[42]

The demise of tax reform as a net positive had particularly damaging effects on House Republicans. Most already had grave doubts. They grew even more disillusioned as the thin promise of partisan advantage disappeared. Even staunch supporters like Jack Kemp began to focus on tax-reform negatives as conservatives took issue with individual provisions of the Ways and Means staff proposal.[43]

Democrats of all stripes reinforced Republican misgivings, as when the liberal Democratic Study Group (DSG) demanded and received a meeting of the House Democratic caucus to restate their qualms about progressivity and the deficit. More conservative Democrats were concerned too. They preferred the minimum tax route proposed earlier by Russo to thoroughgoing tax reform, for like him they saw it as the perfect mix of politics and policy. One member remarked: "When the public talked about tax reform, they were not talking about giving up their IRAs. They wanted to make it impossible for rich people to zero out their taxes."

Rostenkowski and the Democratic leadership pleaded patience and successfully resisted efforts to sidetrack reform. But gone was the talk of wresting a popular Democratic issue away from the president. For Democrats, tax reform boiled down to blame avoidance, pure and simple. As Tip O'Neill reportedly told the closed-door meeting: "I'm supporting Dan Rostenkowski to the fullest. Ronald Reagan will clobber us if we don't go forward." [44]

With restless Democrats assuaged, Rostenkowski turned back to his committee, only to encounter renewed resistance, especially once the "staff" proposal was unveiled. As many lobbyists and insiders had expected all along, the proposal threatened to be torn apart by competing policy and constituent interests. "It's disastrous," declared Rep. Tom Downey upon seeing the proposal. "I don't see who it helps." [45] As one of three committee members from New York, Downey was especially upset about the plan's continued limitations on the state and local tax deduction. Like Treasury II, Rostenkowski's proposal completely disallowed deductions for state sales and personal property taxes and restricted deductions for income and real property taxes to $500 or the amount greater than 5 percent of adjusted gross income, whichever was larger. This complex formula was completely unacceptable to the defenders of deductibility, who believed that any restriction would pave the way for eventual elimination. Already under great political pressure to resist any compromise, supporters (rightly) believed that they could win it all.

Other committee Democrats were equally dissatisfied. "I liked the Reagan plan better," declared Arkansas Democrat Beryl Anthony, who opposed the stiffer taxes on timber contained in the committee markup. Likewise, Rep. Frank Guarini, a Democrat from coastal New Jersey, observed, "There [are] more objections to it than the administration's proposal, especially on how it will affect trade. We have many industries that are in a very delicate posture now." [46] Such sentiments by junior Democrats simply reinforced those by more senior party members.

Making up the Rules

The difficulties of constructing committee majorities on key issues of tax reform became apparent as soon as the committee took up its first item of business: establishing a set of rules to govern the markup process. In accord with the political maxim that "he who writes the rules, rules," these procedural guidelines would determine the ease or difficulty of amending the staff proposal. In the end, four issues proved significant: whether the markup would be "open" to the press and interest groups or held behind closed doors; whether the committee would use current tax law or the staff proposal as its working document; whether amendments had to be revenue-neutral; and the order in which issues would be considered by the committee.

In its easiest votes, the committee decided to write the tax bill in closed session to permit free deliberations and limit the influence of interest groups, the press, and constituents. After experimenting with open markups during the 1970s and early 1980s, the committee had routinely turned to closed markups since 1983. It was a "dilemma for liberal reformers" who believed in open government, but they were forced to admit that "the best [tax] bills have come out of closed sessions." [47] The committee also voted to begin with the easier issues, leaving costly and divisive topics like deductibility and fringe benefits until later. By this approach, Rostenkowski hoped to build enough momentum to propel H.R. 3838 through more difficult times to come.

The remaining issues were resolved less amicably. Acceding to the chairman's wishes and to the president's demand that the package be revenue-neutral, the committee initially adopted a rule that required all amendments to be revenue-neutral as well. This decision meant that revenue-losing amendments must be accompanied by a companion plan raising comparable, offsetting revenue. Although the committee had earlier agreed to this approach, it now backtracked. For one thing, such amendments required assistance from staff experts, and this meant forewarning Rostenkowski. For another, revenue neutrality threatened to ignite open warfare: amendment sponsors could not merely extol the virtues of their own proposal but would have to suggest shrinking or eliminating provisions favored by their colleagues. So instead they endorsed a proposal by Sam Gibbons that only the final package, not individual amendments, need be revenue-neutral.

A second major rule change produced better results for Rostenkowski. Gibbons proposed to use current law rather than the staff document as the starting point for markup, and the chairman initially agreed. It was a lapse of good judgment that shocked his staff. Such a procedure would mean voting affirmatively on every single tough reform provision; in addition, current law rather than the staff proposal would prevail on tie votes. After heated discussions, Rostenkowski reversed this potentially disastrous decision the next day.

This struggle over rules, together with members' constant and vociferous attacks on the "staff" document also prompted Rostenkowski to embrace the sinking trial balloon as his own, attempting to raise the costs to members opposing it. In Rostenkowski's words: "They were just kicking the heck out of the staff. It came to me that if we're going to buckle down and write a tax bill, then we're going to fight, and I would have to put out a mark and let them take *me* on."

An Easy Mark?

Already off to a shaky start, the Ways and Means Committee found no firmer footing when it began the markup in earnest on October 3, 1985. Although Rostenkowski began with what were considered the "easiest" issues, in fact there was almost nothing easy about tax reform. So although the committee managed to defeat appealing amendments to exempt unemployment benefits from taxable income; to retain income averaging; to restore the existing 100 percent deduction for business meals and entertainment; and even to increase the earned-income tax credit for the working poor, it suffered increasing numbers of costly setbacks. The committee adopted amendments granting businesses more leeway when estimating their tax liabilities in advance and partially compensating for the loss of the two-earner deduction. It also restored several tax benefits in existing law, including tax credits for child care, the elderly, and disabled taxpayers along with exclusions for workmen's compensation and federal black-lung and disability payments.

Restoring the exclusion for workmen's compensation and disability payments alone created a $3.4 billion revenue loss in the committee's bill over five years. Yet, even more serious than the monetary loss was the pervasive sense that H.R. 3838 hovered on the brink of deep political trouble. Indeed, when liberal Democrats reported they had the votes to add a fourth, higher individual tax rate, raising the specter that the committee would reject one of the president's nonnegotiable demands, tax-reform advocates feared the worst.

Partisan pressures were also building. Even before the committee markup began, Rostenkowski's decision to hold the personal exemption to below the Treasury II level spurred an angry response from Jack Kemp and thirty-six of his colleagues. GOP conservatives urged the president to reject Rosty's $1,500 proposal, or any bill that failed their "family policy" and business promotion tests. Other insurrectionists on the Republican National Committee (RNC) joined in with a direct-mail campaign to Ways and Means Republicans' districts, urging voters to demand that the president's plan be adopted intact.[48] Committee Republicans shot back with a letter of their own, appealing for presidential intervention before this simmering feud came to a destructive boil. Observing such events, one columnist wrote in early October that tax reform appeared to be "lurching toward election year oblivion."[49]

Banking on Defeat

When the chairman suffered a trio of costly defeats on October 15, reform appeared to be flying rather than lurching toward oblivion. By a vote of 22 — 13, members endorsed an amendment by Harold Ford, D-Tenn., preserving the charitable deduction for nonitemizing taxpayers. Salvaging this preference was a great victory for charities and an even greater defeat for Rostenkowski, Reagan, and reformers who sought to eliminate it. Before adopting Ford's proposal, a tentative committee reduced its cost from $10 billion to $3 billion, by cutting further into the standard deduction. But tax professionals abhorred any such deductions for nonitemizers because the standard deduction was specifically designed to replace them all.

Already reeling, Rostenkowski was next blindsided by two quick but potentially lethal punches delivered by the junior Alabama Democrat, Ronnie Flippo. First, the committee voted 17 — 13 to permit banks to deduct a percentage of funds they hold as reserves against unpaid loans. Not only did members reject the chairman's own "bad debt reserve" proposal (limiting such deductions to actual losses), they adopted an amendment that was even more generous than current law, for an industry widely believed to be substantially undertaxed.[50] Having just played Santa to the fattest of cats, the committee decided to do a little something for the runts of the litter and voted a partial restoration of the loan-loss reserve deduction for thrift institutions as well. As the last votes were cast, even Flippo sat back in shock as Rostenkowski scowled at his rebellious committee. To be sure, Flippo's case was not devoid of merit. At the time, the banking industry was in deep trouble. While many large banks were on the verge of losing billions in bad loans to debt-ridden third-world countries, smaller banks in America's agricultural and oil-producing heartland were going out of business in record numbers. Moreover, as a certified public accountant, Flippo had his own professional standards for arguing the merits of his amendment as a bookkeeping matter.

But the vote was more than a sign of support for a troubled industry. It was a clear vote of no confidence in tax reform and, by implication, in the chairman. Realizing this, Rostenkowski stormed from the chamber. As he beat his retreat, boastful lobbyists celebrated their triumph. "We won! We won!" shouted bank lobbyist David Rosenauer as word filtered out of the closed committee room.[51]

"Can it be done?" wondered glum staff members as they trailed after their fuming boss. Having tested the strength of their support and found it wanting, they headed back to the drawing boards. With this string of revenue losers, the committee had dug itself a $13.6 billion hole compared with current law, and billions more compared with Rostenkowski's plan. Rather than picking up billions of dollars to lower tax rates, the committee was falling further and further behind. It was "the bottom of the valley," a deeply depressed Rosty later recalled.[52]

Notes

1. "Pac-ing the Deck," *Common Cause News*, June 13, 1985, 1.
2. Quoted in Brooks Jackson, *Wall Street Journal*, December 24, 1984, 26.
3. See Democratic Study Group, "Special Report: Reagan's Tax Reform Plan . . . An Evaluation," Rpt. No. 99-13, June 10, 1985.
4. For an analysis of the importance of such "particularized benefits" in the contemporary Congress, see David Mayhew, *Congress: The Electoral Connection* (New Haven, Conn.: Yale University Press, 1975).
5. Some have suggested that tax reform may have enhanced this committee resource by clearing the decks and thus increasing the value of new tax expenditures. As one committee member whispered when the tax-exempt bond provisions he favored were being eliminated, "I don't mind this. We'll just get it back next year." He did not win them back, and few members underestimated the difficulty of restoring terminated tax preferences. Indeed, had the political benefits of cleansing the code been evident to them, rational vote-maximizing legislators would not have waged the bitter battles they did to save favored provisions.
6. See remarks of former representative Barber Conable, R-N.Y., *Extensions* (Spring 1986): 8.
7. Statement of Rep. Philip Crane, *Hearings on Comprehensive Tax Reform*, Part 1, U.S. Cong., House, Committee on Ways and Means, 99th Cong., 1st sess. 781.
8. Dan Rostenkowski quoted in *Tax Notes*, October 8, 1984, 181; and December 3, 1984, 831.
9. Jim Wright quoted in David Broder, "Democrats Find Taxes Treacherous Territory," *Washington Post*, March 15, 1987, A4; Tip O'Neill quoted in ibid.; Tom Downey quoted in *Frontline* #411, "Taxes behind Closed Doors" (Boston: WGBH TV Transcripts, 1986), 3.
10. David Stockman quoted in William Greider, *The Education of David Stockman and Other Americans* (New York: Dutton, 1982), 58.
11. David A. Stockman, *The Triumph of Politics: Why the Reagan Revolution Failed* (New York: Harper and Row, 1986), 237−39.
12. See April 1985 Gallup poll results cited in Rhodes Cook, "Reagan Nurtures His Adopted Party to Strength," *Congressional Quarterly Weekly Report*, September 28, 1985, 1929.
13. Rep. James Jones quoted in "Taxes behind Closed Doors," 4.
14. Quoted in ibid, 3.
15. On the political value that stems from advancing legislation deemed to be in the public interest, see Steven Kelman, *Making Public Policy* (New York: Basic Books, 1987).
16. See Catherine Rudder, "Fiscal Responsibility and the Revenue Committees," in *Congress Reconsidered*, ed. Lawrence Dodd and Bruce Oppenheimer (Washington: CQ Press, 1985), 217, 218.
17. See Richard F. Fenno, Jr., *Congressmen in Committees* (Boston: Little, Brown, 1973), 2−5; and Steven S. Smith and Christopher J. Deering, *Committees in Congress* (Washington: CQ Press, 1984), 95−98.

18. See Catherine Rudder, "Tax Policy: Structure and Choice," in *Making Economic Policy in Congress*, ed. Allen Schick (Washington: American Enterprise Institute, 1983); and Randall Strahan, "Committee Politics and Tax Reform" (Paper prepared for the 1987 Annual Meeting of the American Political Science Association, Chicago, September 3–6, 1987).
19. "Democratic Response to the President," in House Committee on Ways and Means, *Comprehensive Tax Reform*, part 1, 99th Cong., 1st sess., 1985, 42–43.
20. J. Leiper Freeman, *The Political Process*, 2d ed. (New York: Random House, 1965); and Douglass Cater, *Power in Washington* (New York: Random House, 1964).
21. Ibid. Democratic Response to the President, 42.
22. See Pamela Fessler, "Legislators Begin Sifting through Tax Proposal," *Congressional Quarterly Weekly Report*, June 8, 1985, 1096.
23. The White House, *The President's Tax Proposals to the Congress for Fairness, Growth, and Simplicity* (Washington: Government Printing Office, 1985), 21.
24. See Steven Pressman, "Lobbyists Begin to Make a Case against Passage of Tax Overhaul," *Congressional Quarterly Weekly Report*, June 22, 1985, 1211; Testimony of Dr. Jean Mayer, President of Tufts University, *Hearings on Comprehensive Tax Reform*, part 4, 99th Cong., 1st sess., 3561; "Statement of the National Realty Committee," in ibid., part 5, 3891; and Rep. Robert Matsui, D-Calif., quoted in Pressman, "Lobbyists Make Case," 1209.
25. Pamela Fessler, "Tax Overhaul: The Crucial Lobby Fight of 1985," *Congressional Quarterly Weekly Report*, March 9, 1985, 449.
26. Peter Kilborn, "Washington Watch: Lobbying Cost of Tax Battle," *New York Times*, December 16, 1985, D2.
27. Bill Sternberg, "Developers Fund Tax Deduction Lobbying," *Crane's New York Business*, June 15, 1987, 7.
28. Sen. Alan Simpson, R-Wyo., quoted in Fessler, "The Crucial Lobbying Fight," 449.
29. For discussions of interest-group contributions to members of Congress, see "PACs Give Congressional Tax Writers Three Times More Money in 1985," *Common Cause News*, August 11, 1985, 4; Dale Russakoff, "Tax Writers Up the Ante," *Washington Post*, May 20, 1985, A7; and Kay Lehman Schlozman and John T. Tierney, *Organized Interests and American Democracy* (New York: Harper and Row, 1986), 249.
30. Dale Russakoff and Anne Swardson, "Tax Overhaul Battle Follows Lawmakers Home," *Washington Post*, August 7, 1985, A4.
31. Kilborn, "Washington Watch," D2.
32. Steven Pressman, "Groups New to Tax Lobbying Seek to Modify Reagan's Plan," *Congressional Quarterly Weekly Report*, August 17, 1985, 1641.
33. Schlozman and Tierney, *Organized Interests and American Democracy*, 155.
34. See Austin Ranney, *Channels of Power* (New York: Basic Books, 1983); and Frank Sorauf, "Campaign Money and the Press," *Political Science Quarterly* (Spring 1987): 25–42.
35. Citizens for Tax Justice, "Corporate Income Taxes in the Reagan Years: A Study of Three Years of Legalized Corporate Tax Avoidance," *Tax Notes*, October 15, 1984, 202–3; and Dale Russakoff, "U.S. Economy Is User and Abuser of Tax Breaks," *Washington Post*, March 17, 1985, A16.
36. See Fenno, *Congressmen in Committees;* and Kelman, *Making Public Policy.*

37. Interview with Rep. John Duncan.
38. Quoted in *Washington Post*, August 8, 1985, A4.
39. Quoted in *Congressional Quarterly Weekly Report*, July 6, 1985, 1318. According to one tax legislative assistant, "After that CQ interview with Rosty, members first heard about it on the floor, and they all came running back, asking for their copies. Because he means it! "
40. Ronald Reagan, quoted in Lou Cannon and Helen Dewar, "Tax Overhaul Hit in Poll, GOP Caucus," *Washington Post*, September 25, 1985.
41. David Rossenbaum, "Treasury Study Cites Tax Disparity," *New York Times*, August 2, 1985, D2; and David Rosenbaum, "Economic Growth Seen by Sprinkel in Tax Plan," *New York Times*, September 25, 1985, D1.
42. Quotations from Cannon and Dewar, "Tax Overhaul Hit," A3; and *Congressional Quarterly Weekly Report*, September 7, 1985, 1744. See also Lou Cannon, "President's Tour Ends Quietly," *Washington Post*, October 15, 1985, A3.
43. See *Tax Notes*, October 7, 1985; and Rowland Evans and Robert Novak, "Getting Blamed for Tax Reform," *Washington Post*, October 23, 1985, A23.
44. *Tax Notes*, October 7, 1985, 7.
45. Tom Downey quoted in Pamela Fessler, "Panel Begins Review of Comprehensive Tax Plan," *Congressional Quarterly Weekly Report*, September 25, 1985, 1912.
46. Beryl Anthony quoted in Anne Swardson, "Rostenkowski Reveals His Tax-Overhaul Proposal," *Washington Post*, September 27, 1985, A3; Frank Guarini quoted in Fessler, "Panel Begins Review," 1912.
47. Pamela Fessler, "Panel Expects to Rewrite Tax Code in Private," *Congressional Quarterly Weekly Report*, August 31, 1985, 1706.
48. Pamela Fessler, "Partisan Pressure Building as Tax Bill Markups Continue," *Congressional Quarterly Weekly Report*, October 12, 1985.
49. Cannon, "President's Tour."
50. At that time, large banks paid as little as 3.8 percent of their income in taxes, way below the top corporate rate of 46 percent. See House, Committee on Ways and Means, *Comprehensive Tax Reform*, part 8, 7468.
51. Jeffrey H. Birnbaum and Alan S. Murray, *Showdown at Gucci Gulch: Lawmakers, Lobbyists, and the Unlikely Triumph of Tax Reform* (New York: Random House, 1987), 125.
52. See *Tax Notes*, October 21, 1985, 229; and Hedrick Smith, *The Power Game* (New York: Random House, 1988), 559.

5   Back from the Brink: Tax Reform Passes the House

I wanted the press to kick us around for a week, and they did. It was almost at a point where my colleagues would come in and say, "Danny, let's do somethin'. I can't take the heat anymore."

—Dan Rostenkowski

In the aftermath of the October 15 vote, the members of the Ways and Means Committee were left to ponder a single question: Would H.R. 3838 survive? Three quick votes had transformed failure from an abstract possibility into looming reality. In restaurants across Washington, champagne glasses clinked as the foes of tax reform toasted its demise. On Capitol Hill, opponents gloated openly while their more ambivalent colleagues let out secret sighs of relief.

Fortunately for tax reform, such celebrations were premature. While the majority of committee members had sought to use their votes to send Rostenkowski a message, few had intended to issue a death threat. When it came to killing tax reform, Democrats in particular recognized the dangers of getting caught with the knife. If the bank vote was to be tax reform's last gasp, they would have no alibis.

Thus, one by one the reluctant committee members were forced to grapple with why they had gone along with Rostenkowski in the first place: to respond to the challenge of a popular president; to restore a measure of integrity to a sullied system; to prove their committee could meet its responsibilities and produce a bill; and, for Democrats, to avoid partisan blame.

As might be expected among experienced legislators, it took almost no time for many to realize they had gone too far. Representative Flippo's unexpected victory had been a giant misstep. "We could have changed it that afternoon," recalled Rostenkowski. "Enough members came to me and said they would switch." But the experienced chairman realized that the bank vote was only symptomatic of deeper distress. So he stepped back and called time out.

This break gave Rostenkowski a chance to rethink strategy and plan his next moves while he let his committee "stew" over what it had done. Eight days later, Rostenkowski returned to the field. Although this unlikely quarterback remained saddled with the same basic team of tax-reform misfits, he came back with a new and better game plan. He made three critical changes in his legislative strategy—tactical, substantive, and procedural—all of which would need to be implemented successfully if he were to win. Even then, H.R. 3838 nearly failed to cross the goal line when the president himself fumbled the ball.

The Press Goes to Work

On a tactical level, Rostenkowski decided to make better use of blame avoidance to motivate members. Weeks earlier Speaker Tip O'Neill had used the same strategy with the House Democratic Caucus. At that time, however, Rostenkowski had still hoped to emphasize committee esprit de corps. As he said:

> When we started to write the bill, there was a feeling that the Ways and Means Committee is somebody and we're going to do our job. I don't believe the members ever felt we were going to see the final product— that it would go anywhere on the House floor. It was just that we've got to get it out of the Ways and Means Committee and show that if the president suggests reform, we're willing to accept the challenge and come up with a bill.

But when the bank vote and mounting revenue losses demonstrated that collective responsibility alone would not hold the committee together, Rostenkowski, too, fell back on negative pressure. Indeed, on the afternoon of "Bank Tuesday," when Dowley informed him that they had enough votes to reverse the damage, the chairman had refused. "Naw, let it stew a while," he had said. "Let the press go to work."

And the press did indeed go to work, just as he intended. "Tax Committee Votes to Open New Loopholes," proclaimed the *Washington Post*. The following day, it published a longer article revealing that bank-affiliated PACs had contributed $33,000 to Ways and Means Committee members during the first half of 1985—a 79 percent increase over the comparable period in the previous election cycle![1] The implication was posed in black and white: all such votes would be cast as "selling out" to special interests. The effect was precisely what Rostenkowski had hoped for. "Is this what we want?" he asked his members. "Is this the image the Ways and Means Committee is going to have?"[2] They "were just blown out by the fact that the press started to criticize us," he recalled. "And it impressed on them that we *did* have to come up with a bill."

Deductibility: The Fulcrum of Reform

But more than psychological warfare was needed to put H.R. 3838 back on track. So, for the next eight days, while senior members were conferring with the Senate on a final FY 1986 budget resolution, Rostenkowski met privately with Baker and key committee members. One by one he sounded them out, searching for a magic combination of substantive changes. His first offering—the so-called staff proposal—clearly hadn't netted him a winning coalition. The core group of committee reformers was small and unpersuasive. Nor had he picked up many more Democrats by giving their constituents a better deal than Treasury II. Finally, the administration had failed to deliver enough Republicans. "The problem was," concluded David Brockway, the JTC staff director, "we just couldn't find a working majority on the committee. We had maybe twelve or thirteen, but on the harder votes we could never count on eighteen."

Rostenkowski knew that the deductibility of state and local taxes was the issue on which to build a new coalition. Despite administration attempts to divide high- and low-tax states, the issue had broad and intense support. The chairman knew that liberal members from high-tax states like New York would likely support the other elements of tax reform once the deductibility issue was resolved. Indeed, until he was persuaded to close ranks with his colleagues, New Yorker Charles Rangel had backed the more extreme proposals of Treasury I because of the benefits for his Harlem constituency. An accommodation on deductibility promised votes from other states, as well. Rep. Marty Russo, a protégé of Rostenkowski's from Chicago, worked hard to change his mind:

> My chief concern was that we put together a bill that would pass the floor that Democrats could be proud of. The state and local deduction was critical for Democrats. The bill was going down until he gave [in] on deductibility. But Danny was very dug in on it, so it was tough to take him on in a way that didn't make him dig in his heels even more.
>
> We had intense discussions about it. I could say things to him that no one else could. "This bill is going down," I told him. "And it's not an abuse. You never heard of anybody [sheltering] taxes because of this. And why hit Democratic states?" But he didn't want to lose all that money—$150 billion.
>
> So we worked hard to get enough votes to save it. When we got them, I went to Danny and said we had it. "I was always going to do something about this," he said. "It was just a matter of timing." "Well," I said, "the time is now."

Tip O'Neill also laid on the pressure, telling Rostenkowski, "Dan, the power of the Speaker comes down to whether a bill gets on the floor or it doesn't get on the floor. Two things I'm interested in: state and local taxes. You don't have those in the bill, you don't get a day in the court. Remember that."

Surprisingly, many southern Democrats from low-tax states were equally concerned about the issue. Most were lobbied by governors and local officials who already had difficulties raising taxes in their conservative states and who vigorously opposed changes that would make that task even more difficult.

Politics thus decided the question of *whether* to restore the state and local tax deduction, but it could not decide the technical question of *how*. Given

Rostenkowski's commitment to revenue and distributional neutrality, where would the JTC's numerical wizards find the billions needed to make up the loss? Indeed, one staff member quipped that it seemed like "mission impossible," not only because of the sums involved but because "most of its direct benefits went to upper-income itemizers." Because Rostenkowski had promised to produce a bill that was less generous to upper-bracket taxpayers than the president's proposal, preserving the deduction necessitated elaborate fiscal gymnastics to prevent its having the opposite effect.

Looking back at the JTC's successful completion of this difficult mission, Brockway recalled: "It was a real eye-opener. Previously I didn't think that you could [put together a bill] without touching the state and local deduction." In part, Brockway's solution to this arithmetical conundrum was to add a fourth, higher tax rate applied to upper-income individuals. The new rate collected additional revenues and counteracted the regressive effects of restoring the deduction.

Political Fallout. The decision to restore deductibility was not risk free. Above all, it severely strained the chairman's relationship with the president's men, since all factions within the Reagan administration adamantly opposed sparing the state and local deduction. Treasury experts believed it was "the right thing to do," while conservative ideologues endorsed it as a means of undercutting state government activism— "socialism" as one called it.[3] Finally, administration pragmatists joined up for the money. They needed the $150 billion to alleviate corporate grievances while protecting the president's chief goal: lower rates.

But the earlier bank vote showed that Treasury could not deliver Republican votes when it counted. Thus, while Rostenkowski still wanted bipartisan support, he opted for a solution that strengthened liberal and Democratic support for the bill. Paying for deductibility with higher taxes on the wealthy put an undeniable Democratic stamp on his legislation while alienating more Republicans. It thus reinforced the partisan competition that had propelled reform from the beginning.

The chairman met privately with deductibility supporters and assured them the provision would be retained in return for their loyalty. As state and local ringleader Tom Downey recalled:

> One day he called me into his office in the Capitol and he sat at the head of long table—the only thing missing was a candle which he could put out when the meeting was over—and he said, "I'm going to give you $65 billion and you better be with me on everything else." [4]

Although the issue was not formally raised until the end of the markup, and although there was no public announcement, it quickly became apparent what had happened. As soon as the markup resumed, the coterie of strong deductibility supporters switched sides and began voting routinely with the chairman.

Procedural Changes

But the markup did not resume, and the transformation of the coalition-building process was not complete, until one additional procedural change was made. Rostenkowski decided to alter the bill-drafting process by establishing ad hoc task forces to resolve especially divisive issues. A major problem throughout the markup had been the chairman's isolation—imposed by the need to fend off all challenges to the delicately balanced proposal his staff had proposed. "I would come into the room," he recalled, "and I would have to fight thirty-five other members. *I* would have to fight them. Even my allies were very quiet." Committee members found the markup equally frustrating, for to that point they had contributed little to the history-making bill. Until then, making one's mark on the bill had been portrayed as antireform, because virtually any change had negative effects on revenue or distribution. Frustrated by this fiscal and political straitjacket, members rebelled by opposing the chairman. As one complained: "All of a sudden, [support of] this 'staff' package has become a litmus test of our loyalty to the committee and to the chairman. We're supposed to have a role in writing this bill, too. " [5]

To rebuild a cooperative spirit, the chairman resurrected a technique that had worked during the DEFRA negotiations in 1984. This involved establishing first four and eventually twelve task forces to iron out differences on controversial provisions of the bill. Each had between five and seven members—normally four Democrats and two Republicans—and was chaired by a Democrat in favor of reform. These more "constructive" members were given considerable latitude to exercise their own judgment over policy issues. Moreover, task-force chairmen were allowed to fall short of the chairman's mark, as long as they raised an agreed-upon level of revenue over current law.

By all accounts it was a brilliant procedural stroke that accomplished its purposes. Rostenkowski said proudly, "They would work out a project, report back with some pride of creation, and then help me defend it." It was a result that surprised top committee staff, who originally questioned so much participation. "We had resisted working groups until then so the chair could control or influence the results," said committee staff director Joe Dowley. "But we had to have members spend their labor and ingenuity in this process to make it work, and the task forces helped tremendously." Marty Russo agreed, acknowledging, "Personally, I felt a great sense of accomplishment. I chaired the task force on the minimum tax, and we came up with $6 billion more than our target. So we got the [minimum tax] ball rolling." Although not all of the working groups did as well (many fell short of the chairman's targets), all allowed members to contribute more to the bill and to become a greater part of the legislative process.

From the Jaws of Defeat

From tactical and procedural changes to substantive alterations, Rostenkowski thus made a series of important moves to salvage tax reform and his own reputation for leadership. In his new-found role as reformer, the machine-bred Chicago "pol" picked his way along an unfamiliar path. He continued to meld the tried-and-true methods of inside politics—old-fashioned logrolling, heightened partisanship, and reliance on committee pride—with newer techniques that policy entrepreneurs had developed to advance difficult reform issues, especially exploitation of tax reform's powerful symbols and manipulation of the unrelenting press. With this double-barreled strategy, combining new and old style politics, the chairman began winning important votes instead of losing them.

As success fed upon itself—with members fearing to be caught on the wrong side of the issue—the bill-writing process went remarkably smoothly for the next month. The embarrassing gifts to large banks and thrift institutions were quickly taken back. In their place, the committee adopted an amendment by Pete Stark that favored small banks while still raising $2 billion over five years—$6.8 billion more than the Flippo amendment.

Moving quickly to consolidate his position, Rostenkowski accelerated the normally methodical process by stretching the committee's work into rare weekend and late-night sessions. Having already barred interest groups from the closed-door markups, he used speed to negate their indirect access via friendly members. By the time the interest groups realized what was happening and mobilized to alter it, an issue would already be decided.

The Ways and Means Committee worked even when the rest of Congress had left town. During a weekend markup in late October—in what the *Washington Post* called "the last chance for tax reform to overcome the special interests"—Rostenkowski won success after success. When members emerged from their weekend session on Monday, October 28, both reform supporters and opponents agreed: the committee was virtually certain to report a version of H.R. 3838 by the end of the year. Though there had been no announcements of any deals, staunch supporters of deductibility were voting in lockstep with the chairman, and they had ended their overtures to the diehard opponents of the bill.

As a result, substantive issues were being resolved in a manner generally consistent with tax-reform principles. In the space of three short days, the committee, among other actions: limited the tax advantages of corporate takeovers; reduced the attractiveness of employee stock ownership plans (ESOPs); toughened trust-fund rules for wealthy heirs; repealed the corporate dividend exclusion for individuals; and further tightened the president's proposal that was to allow corporate tax deductions for dividends paid to shareholders.

Both group dynamics and changing calculations fed the new momentum. Once the committee engaged itself in writing a bill, members expected to succeed. Ray McGrath, R-N.Y., observed that "once Danny got us through the awful beginnings on this bill, the issue got a life of its own within the committee. People started to get involved." Even reform opponents like Jim Jones admitted that "the committee developed a kind of camaraderie. No one wanted to be responsible for killing it on their watch, so, OK, we'll get it to the floor and let the House decide." During the markup, this sense of community was reinforced by the constant pressures of lobbyists locked outside the committee doors. As one staffer put it: "You were inside that room, and that made you different. And you would sometimes get this us-against-them attitude that we inside the room had to protect ourselves."

In addition, once it appeared that a bill would indeed be reported out of the committee, some recalcitrant members began to change their calculations about the merits of cooperation. When tax reform was going nowhere, members could afford to place greater weight on their immediate electoral and constituency interests. But once the issue began developing momentum, members had to weigh the costs of opposing it—and Rostenkowski—more heavily. Once success became likely, their constituency interests could be better served by cooperating with the chairman and salvaging what they could within the constraints imposed by tax reform.

Old Politics and New Reform

Thus, a great many provisions in the Ways and Means bill took care of the needs of supportive members and key constituencies. Those that won important favorable concessions included agriculture (favorable accounting rules retained for family farms), small business (favorable accounting and inventory procedures retained), organized labor (most fringe benefits retained exemption), and high-tax states and cities (state and local tax deduction continued). Specific industries that fared well included small banks (bad-debt reserves continued), life insurance ("inside buildup" not taxed as current income), and high-tech firms (research and development tax credit extended). Most of these victories were associated with specific committee members who became supporters of Rostenkowski's proreform coalition, including Dorgan, Downey, Russo, McGrath, Flippo, and Pickle. Other members won smaller favors in return for their support. Beryl Anthony, D-Ark., won favorable treatment for small timber growers; Ed Jenkins, D-Ga., won concessions for stone quarries, the fertilizer industry, tax-exempt bonds, and rural electric cooperatives; Cecil Heftel, D-Hawaii, won extension of a tax credit for geothermal energy; and Charles Rangel, D-N.Y., achieved an extension of the targeted-jobs tax credit.[6] Many more won additional favors in the form of transition rules.

Such victories should not be overstated. Unlike previous tax bills, virtually all of these costly victories involved the retention of existing tax benefits rather than the addition of new ones. Moreover, many of these groups and industries fared less well on other matters. Labor could not prevent the taxation of unemployment benefits. State and local governments lost billions on tax-exempt bonds. Income averaging and many tax shelters in agriculture were eliminated. High-tech firms received a higher, not a lower, tax on capital gains. Yet, compared with industries and sectors that faced substantial tax increases due to the reform legislation—capital-intensive industries, oil and gas producers, casualty insurance firms, defense contractors, large banks—the above groups were fortunate indeed.

Rostenkowski skillfully blended the old distributive politics of tax expenditures with the new politics of reform. By preserving tax provisions of greatest value to key members in the process of enacting reform legislation, the committee retained its all-important power to influence the tax code in beneficial ways. Charles Rangel observed that the committee was never even close to going out of business: "Even with all the reforms, members are responsive to their constituencies, and most people still enjoy some kind of preferential treatment—churches, education, nonprofits, pensions, home mortgages, low-income housing, state and local taxes. Just look at the tax code."

Once established, the committee's task forces helped continue the momentum by resolving specific tax issues in an array of sensitive fields (see Table 5−1). Politically, the task-force process worked very smoothly. When the groups recommended compromises, the full committee adopted them quickly and with little conflict, frequently by voice vote. As one reluctant tax reformer bemoaned: "The task force was constructed so that if you wanted to make changes, you lost on a tie vote. Once it went into committee, we felt we should support it."[7] Indeed, the task forces raised sufficient revenues and moved so quickly that interest groups were often left to sputter at a fait accompli. For example, in the area of tax-exempt bonds the task force raised $1.7 billion less than the chairman's mark but $4.2 billion more than current law, and this example was duplicated in areas from accounting to foreign tax issues. Indeed, the process moved so quickly that reformer Don Pease crowed, "The big issues we can handle rather easily. We [only] get bogged down on technicalities." "We've accelerated our pace a quantum leap," agreed reform opponent Bill Frenzel. "We're moving much too fast to produce anything good."[8]

Meanwhile, a hardened core of a dozen or so committee members— mainly conservative Republicans joined by a few maverick Democrats— grew increasingly disenchanted. The Republicans were the most unhappy. For them, the handwriting was on the wall. Discerning that a deal had been cut on deductibility (to be paid for by higher taxes on the wealthy), they suspected that there was little chance of putting back enough corporate tax

Table 5-1   Fiscal Resolution of Major Tax Issues
             by Ways and Means Task Forces, 1986-1990

| Date | Subject | Revenue effects[a] | |
		Rostenkowski I	Existing law
10/27/85	Small business	n.a.	n.a.
	Tax-exempt bonds	-1.7	4.2
	Low-income housing	-1.0	n.a.
	Agriculture	n.a.	n.a.
11/6/85	Pensions	-2.0	18.0
	Accounting	-2.9	60.5
11/15/85	Insurance	-2.1	10.3
11/19/85	Capital formation	-15-20	175.0
	Tax shelters		.5
11/20/85	Foreign tax provisions	-2.5	12.0
	Alternative minimum tax	+6.0	33.0

Source: Tax Notes, various issues.

Note: n.a. = not available

a. Over five-year period from 1986 to 1990, in billions of dollars.

preferences and investment incentives to satisfy their concerns. Given many Republicans' deep misgivings about tax reform and the often bitter relationships between the parties in the House during 1985, most committee Democrats (apart from Rostenkowski) had little interest in bipartisanship, believing that concessions to the minority were a wasted effort. As one Democrat put it: "My House Republican colleagues, with some exceptions, don't act responsibly. They're always against everything. They're going to do everything they can to make the bill palatable to them, and then they're not going to vote for it at the last minute."

The administration was also deeply disturbed. After a shouting match over the issue, Baker suspended his dealings with Rostenkowski until the bill was nearly completed, recalling:

> When the chairman gave away the state and local tax exemption, that made it almost impossible for us to get a bill out of the House that we could live with. There was a two-and-a-half week period there where I didn't go up for any markups and we basically were removed from the process.

Accordingly, for the first time, the president broke his commitment to Rostenkowski and publicly attacked the presumed decision to retain the state and local tax deduction.[9]

Putting the Pieces Together

Nonetheless, the markup progressed at an even faster pace, underscoring the strength of Rostenkowski's new coalition. As H.R. 3838's chances improved and more members concluded that cooperation with the chairman was their most profitable strategy, the committee began to move with lightning speed. Over $300 billion in tax expenditure savings poured in from accumulating reforms, including:

- accounting procedures ($60.5 billion over five years)
- capital investment and depreciation ($175 billion)
- alternative minimum tax liabilities ($33 billion)
- deferred taxation of pension benefits ($18 billion)
- foreign tax issues ($12 billion)
- insurance companies and benefits ($10.3 billion)

Fortunately, members were already familiar with many of the specific and often highly complex reform options, which had been considered earlier in the context of DEFRA and TEFRA. But such scope and breakneck speed would not have been possible without strong staff support. Indeed, the staff's traditional power was increased by Rostenkowski's nonsubstantive approach and by the extraordinary demands of comprehensive reform.

Although their ultimate responsibility was to the chairman and his broad policy goals, the staffs of the Ways and Means and Joint Tax Committees had a strong professional commitment to tax reform. Most believed that comprehensive base broadening was good public policy. Moreover, like experts in Treasury, they had an institutional responsibility to protect the integrity of the revenue system and to help in "resisting advocacy influences on tax legislation." [10] Their power was especially strong over the countless details that constituted tax reform. One embittered House Democrat who had lost a battle too many with the staff even complained: "If I really wanted to influence the way the law was written, I would have applied for a job on the Joint Tax or Ways and Means staff." Many members' legislative assistants shared these professional norms as well. "It was exhilarating," said one, "because you really felt like you were accomplishing something professionally."

Thus, the chairman's aides were delighted to be of service in this accelerating reform effort. JTC staff prepared long lists of "loophole closers" from existing bills and pulled dozens of others from their own files. They were equally adept at manipulating subtle (and sometimes not-so-subtle) changes in "break points" between tax rates, thresholds, and wording.

The Last Night

As November progressed, tax reform appeared to be racing along on a straight and surprisingly smooth track. Just to be sure that the wheels of committee progress were properly greased, Rostenkowski made one last of a series of visits to committee members, offering transition rules in exchange for clear commitments of support.[11]

As was so often true in tax reform, however, just as leaders rounded what seemed to be the last difficult corner, unforeseen difficulties cropped up. Euphoria had obscured underlying partisan tensions that erupted suddenly on what reformers had hoped would be a triumphant last day.

In retrospect, the stage had long been set for a climactic partisan drama. Although Rostenkowski had tried to maintain an air of bipartisanship, the administration was his principal conduit to committee Republicans. But, disapproving of Rostenkowski's decisions on deductibility, Baker and Darman had cut the communication link in early November.

Even when they were engaged in the process, Treasury officials lacked the trust of many Republicans on and off the committee, who felt they were "playing footsie" with the Democrats. This dissatisfaction was particularly strong with regard to Deputy Treasury Secretary Darman, who shouldered much of the responsibility for dealing with Congress on the legislation. As one senior Republican put it: "None of the Republicans liked Darman—I don't know of a one. Because he'd say one thing and do another. Of course he was smarter than all of us, but the problem was that he knew it."

At the same time, committee Republicans—who were reluctant supporters of tax reform to begin with—were being strongly cross-pressured by their House colleagues. Alarmed at the direction that tax reform appeared to be heading in the committee, thirty-eight highly conservative House members sent a public letter to the president on November 1, 1985, urging him to "abandon" the committee's bill and to begin the process anew.[12] Although initially less public in their opposition, Republican leaders in the House were little more supportive of the effort. As ranking Republican John Duncan, R-Tenn., observed, "Trent Lott (the House minority whip) and Dick Cheney (chairman of the Republican Conference) were opposed to it almost from the beginning."

Thus, although some committee Republicans shared in the sense of progress achieved during the last few weeks of markup, and while many still hoped that the remaining issues could be resolved, the underlying situation was highly unstable as the committee approached its final decisions. This underlying tension exploded into bitter partisan divisions on the final night of the committee markup—divisions that spilled over onto the House floor and threatened to bury tax reform yet again.

Meanwhile, an unsuspecting Rostenkowski began to savor the committee's upcoming achievement. Anticipating an uneventful conclusion the next day, on November 21 the chairman sent out a "Dear Colleague" letter to House members in which he outlined the principal features of what he termed a "fair" and "balanced" bill. Indeed, Rostenkowski had even invited Finn Casperson, a prominent member of the proreform business coalition, TRAC, to his office to await the successful conclusion of the markup, and to announce from there TRAC's endorsement of the bill in time for the evening news.[13] Finally, the president was expected to call ranking Republican John Duncan before the final vote was taken, urging Republicans to support what they believed was a tarnished bill in order to "keep the process moving."

Opening Old Wounds

But the president's call never came, and Casperson's announcement was never made. Nor did Rosty's hoped-for triumph ever make the evening news. His victory, such as it was, didn't occur until the next day, November 23, at 3:30 A.M!

Everything that could go wrong did go wrong, beginning with Republican reactions to the chairman's transition rule package. The JTC's professional commitment to write "generic" transition rules—which by their wording can apply to all similarly situated taxpayers—unexpectedly combined with Rostenkowski's earlier threats to remember his enemies created panic in the Republican ranks. Anxious representatives were unable to tell whether their favored constituents had been accorded special recognition in the bill. Instead, they encountered provisions like this:

> In the case of any health club facility, with respect to the amendment made by section 627(c)—
> (A) paragraph (1) shall be applied by substituting "April 12, 1984" for "December 31, 1983", and
> (B) paragraph (3) shall be applied by substituting "April 13, 1984" for "October 19, 1983" each place it occurs. [14]

As minority counsel Ken Kies recalled:

> [Rostenkowski] elected on his own to put together the transition package and then threw it on the table at markup without having given our members a chance to look at it, so none of them could tell if their projects were taken care of. He commenced the markup, which was the equivalent of total chaos for about an hour and a half because members were looking at me saying, "is this plant covered? . . . is that one in?" What ensued was like a massive trading session on the stock exchange.

Once the transition rule panic had subsided and the provisions were adopted, a catastrophic series of problems arose involving the final revenue estimates and tax-rate calculations for H.R. 3838. What began as a fairly routine process turned into a political and professional nightmare. Ever since he had agreed to retain the full state and local tax deduction, Rostenkowski had hinted that a fourth, higher tax rate would be necessary to pay for it. Yet when the JTC estimators installed a top rate of 38 percent, they fell unexpectedly short of revenues, triggering a mad scramble for funds that touched off political dynamite. In the end, the staff produced a bill with higher tax rates at lower income levels than Reagan had wanted, while also reducing the size of the personal exemption—the touchstone of conservatives' family policy. Even worse, the JTC had been forced to introduce an ugly and politically unwelcome "stagger" by which tax reform's pleasures (lower rates and revenue losers) came into effect later than its (revenue-gaining) pains. Rather than capturing for Democrats the banner of "tax fairness" for the middle class, Rostenkowski was on the verge of creating a bill that was less generous to this crucial voting block than the president's!

It had become supremely apparent that tax reform's cardinal rule of revenue neutrality cut two ways politically. On the positive side, it altered traditional tax-writing dynamics favoring particularized benefits for individual constituencies and interest groups in the revenue arena. This, in turn, transformed tax politics into a zero-sum game, leading one Ways and Means member to conclude:

> The overriding problem for lobbyists on this bill was dealing with revenue neutrality. They were accustomed, and so were we, to come in and say, "this will damage our economy, your district. You've got to do something about it." Nothing about the price tag of the issue or how you pay for that. They'd say, "That's your job, congressman." Well, that didn't wash here. You had to be able to go into the committee and make an amendment and say that you were going to give to Peter and had to take from Paul.

Such conflicts aided reform by dividing the business community and paralyzing opposition by their umbrella groups until very late in the game. Revenue neutrality also helped by increasing members' dependence on Rostenkowski's loyal staff as amendment sponsors were forced to seek their help.

On the negative side, however, this decision rule necessitated painful and even draconian measures to raise revenues, thus narrowing the ground on which a proreform coalition could be built. In this instance, the cause of middle-class fairness forced Rostenkowski to risk alienating proreform Republicans and high-tech businesses at the last minute by raising the capital-gains tax rate to 22 percent. This increase would affect the very highest income groups most significantly and provide revenues for middle-income rate adjustments, but it was higher than current law and higher still than the president's proposed capital-gains rate of 17.5 percent.

Still the agony of the estimating process had not ended. When JTC staff estimated the year-by-year effects on revenue, they discovered that the package would lose billions in its first three years and make it up with large surpluses in the end.[15] Both the yearly revenue fluctuations and the initial shortfall spelled political trouble. In particular, the tax bill's initial shortfall would exacerbate the deficit problem and provide a strong rationale for any member opposed to reform. Seeking ways to resolve this problem, the staff ground the markup to a halt. Though modern computers can perform thousands of calculations per second, the scope of the tax bill was so vast that each new revenue estimate took over fifteen minutes to generate. Eventually the JTC temporarily withheld data on the year-by-year effects of tax reform so that the committee markup could finally reconvene after a delay of several hours.

Fringe Issues

Not all delays were caused by estimating problems. Some represented unsettled political disputes. One such issue—the taxation of fringe benefits—belonged at the top of organized labor's list of tax-reform grievances. Retaining tax-free benefits had been labor's top priority since Treasury I, because improved employee fringe benefits were one of the most attractive features of union-negotiated collective-bargaining agreements.

Bowing to these pressures, Rostenkowski had agreed to retain the full tax-free status for employer-provided health insurance, the costliest fringe benefit. But encouraged by strong Senate support from Finance Committee chairman Bob Packwood, labor and many of its House Democratic allies sought to delete taxation of any fringe benefits from Rostenkowski's bill—including life insurance and legal benefits—at a cost of $10.5 billion. The unions found their champion in Charles Rangel, who promised labor to "at least ask for a roll-call vote" on the issue. A recorded vote was certain to be successful on an issue so important to Democrats' union allies, so a battle with the chairman was inevitable.

Rostenkowski's own support for AFL-CIO positions on key labor votes over the previous fifteen years averaged a healthy 85 percent.[16] Yet, the Chicago pol-turned-reformer needed to protect his shaky coalition. Scaling back tax-free benefits was economically "correct," and paying for their restoration meant increasing the top corporate tax rate from 35 percent to 36 percent—something he had promised TRAC he would not do. Thus far he had kept his word, believing that such promises were inviolate. Having climbed through the legislative ranks, Rostenkowski believed that dependability was critical to political effectiveness. Besides, at that very moment he had a prominent TRAC member waiting in his office, ready to proclaim that the committee's bill (with a 35 percent rate) was "good for business."

So, determined to keep his promise and to pass his endangered bill, Rostenkowski hustled Rangel and his coconspirators into the back room, to pressure them into submission. Unfortunately for the chairman, sentiment had swung decisively against him. Other Democrats had decided not to risk the wrath of labor on behalf of dwindling business and Republican support. Rostenkowski loyalist Marty Russo recalled:

> I talked to Baker that last night and saw we weren't going to have many Republican votes. We had to do a Democratic bill. Danny resisted this. He all along wanted a bipartisan bill, and he had given his word on this.

So we got into a big debate in the caucus. I told him Baker had said that we're not going to get more than 35 Republican votes on the floor. That meant we needed 183 Democrats to pass it. With labor against us, there was no way we could get more than 150. . . . Finally, Danny said, "If the Republicans insist on a roll call vote, we'll do it. I'll offer the amendment myself." Baker had said it was all lined up—that the Republicans had agreed to pass this by a voice vote. But something must have gone wrong.

Something had indeed gone wrong. Committee Republicans were already steaming over the transition rules, and the long delays let the pressure build higher. Although many of the delays had been caused by revenue estimates, when the Democrats emerged from their emotional caucus meeting, Republicans suspected the worst. When the final package was revealed, it included: (1) a top individual rate of 38 percent compared with the president's 35 percent; (2) a higher effective capital-gains rate of 22 percent compared with the president's 17.5 percent; (3) a lower personal exemption of $1,500 for itemizers, compared with the president's $2,000; and (4) the restoration of full deductibility for state and local taxes. Not a single major issue had been resolved to their liking. All in all, committee Republicans viewed the final package as an attack on them and a political affront to their president. In the view of many, H.R. 3838 was anti-investment, antisavings, and antifamily. Finally, it placed them in an untenable position with their Republican House brethren. "Such insults deserve to be returned" summed up the mood that produced a late-night Republican rebellion.

While the rest of Washington slept, Republicans began demanding roll-call votes on one contentious issue after another, greatly angering the chairman, who had sought to avoid recorded votes that placed members on the spot politically. As Rostenkowski had promised his Democrats in their secret caucus, he responded to the Republican maneuvering by offering his own amendment to raise the corporate tax rate to 36 percent, providing the funds to pay for Rangel's successful amendment restoring present-law treatment for all employee fringe benefits.

The bitter process dragged on until 3:30 A.M. Although the completed bill resembled the original version hewn by the staff and the Democratic caucus, it was a hollow victory for Rostenkowski. He had won the battle to report a bill, but he had lost his personal struggle to maintain enough bipartisan support to improve its chances on the floor. As Kies recalled:

When it was all over, the relationship between the chairman and the Republicans had deteriorated pretty markedly. At the beginning of the night on November 22, at least half the Republican members would have voted for the bill. I had their names. But by the end, because of the way they had been treated, they were so pissed off that none of them would have voted for it had the vote taken place that night—including Gradison.

So upsetting was the eighteen-hour marathon that Rostenkowski delayed the final vote until after the Thanksgiving recess, hoping that by then tempers would cool a bit and a few Republicans might climb back on board. It seemed unlikely, though. Bitterness and exhaustion replaced what should have been a committee celebration. Every Ways and Means member had endured months of hearings, months of markup sessions, and endless long days besieged by lobbyists and constituent complaints. When the "celebration" finally got under way at nearly 4:00 A.M., only one Republican joined in the party staged for members and committee staff. There was no satisfaction, or even relief, only the promise of more and bitter battles to come.

A Close Call

Future battles might have been averted had the president followed the original Treasury strategy and urged committee Republicans to support the committee bill "to keep the reform process moving." Using that rationale, committee Republicans would have no need to believe in the substantive merits of the bill. Their support would merely help keep it alive so it could be "improved" by the Republican-controlled Senate.

This strategy was agreed upon at a top-level White House meeting earlier on Friday, November 22, in anticipation that the committee would conclude its markup and report out a tax reform bill that afternoon.[17] As one senior Treasury official recalled:

> The president had just come back from some trip or summit and we had a meeting over in his office and got him to agree that he would basically say, "I don't like this bill but I want to keep the process alive. Therefore I urge Republicans to vote for it." He was supposed to call and write a letter to John Duncan.

Baker and Darman returned to Capitol Hill after the meeting, confident that a call would be made to the ranking committee Republican, John Duncan. In the meantime, however, the White House was getting counter pressure from party whip Trent Lott and other conservative House Republicans. Although "Darman had known for weeks what the final bill would look like," House opponents used the accumulation of "anti-investment" and "antifamily" provisions to convince Regan aide Dennis Thomas that the president should back off. Regan in turn persuaded the president to refrain from urging support for the bill until its impact on the economy could be studied.

"The president was turned around on it just before he went to bed," muttered a Treasury official. "It was not a smart decision. It permitted the Republican revolt to materialize." Deep partisan divisions on the floor are usually preceded by similar cleavages within committee. "The president might have called," agreed Rep. Duncan when asked whether anything might have kept partisan emotions from getting out of hand on the final night.

Reporting for Duty

After November's final-night fireworks, formal committee approval of H.R. 3838 two weeks later was anticlimactic. The vote was 28—8, indicating that the cool-down period had helped somewhat. In all, five Republicans— McGrath, Gradison, Daub (Neb.), Vander Jagt (Mich.), and Campbell (S.C.)—voted for the bill.

Publicly, the chairman seemed almost apologetic. "We have not written a perfect bill," admitted Rostenkowski. "Perhaps a faculty of scholars could do a better job. . . . But politics is an imperfect process." [18] H.R. 3838 was a political document, but one that largely accomplished what it set out to do. It protected House Democrats from charges they had thwarted legislation in the public interest. It placed a Democratic and slightly more populist stamp on the legislation. And it did so without, as Rostenkowski noted, "killing any powerful interests. We just sorta wounded 'em."

The chairman's strategy from the beginning had been to devise a Democratic bill with stronger appeal to middle-class voters than the president's proposal, while retaining large percentage tax cuts for the poor. Although H.R. 3838 contained percentage tax cuts for individuals slightly smaller than those contained in Treasury II (—9.0 percent compared with —10.5 percent), it contained larger average reductions for all income groups under $75,000. All income groups above that level received substantially smaller tax reductions in the Ways and Means bill (see Table 5—2). Moreover, the committee bill retained popular middle-class deductions that had been reduced or eliminated under the president's bill, including charitable deductions for nonitemizers, state and local taxes, and full fringe benefits. "There is something in there for everybody," proclaimed Rep. Pete Stark.

To help pay for these benefits, the committee bill raised more taxes from corporations than the president's bill. (See Appendix.) In particular, the plan called for a much stiffer minimum tax, slightly higher corporate rates, and substantial tax increases on large banks, heavy manufacturers, several natural-resource industries, certain tax-exempt bonds, and defense contractors. Yet corporate taxes were not broadened uniformly, and politically powerful and widely dispersed industries like real estate, agriculture, and small business emerged relatively unscathed.

The "Unruly" Floor

Keeping a promise made during the markup battle, House Republicans set to work developing a substitute for H.R. 3838. They knew from the hard lessons learned in committee that revenue neutrality would prevent doing all the things urged by House conservatives, but Ways and Means Republican leaders like John Duncan and Bill Frenzel believed they could construct a bill with lower rates and retain incentives for saving and

Table 5—2   Tax Liability by Income Class

Income class	Percentage change in income tax liability	
	Administration proposal	Committee bill
Less than $10,000	−72.4	−76.1
$10,000−20,000	−18.0	−23.4
$20,000−30,000	−9.3	−9.9
$30,000−40,000	−6.6	−8.9
$40,000−50,000	−7.3	−8.4
$50,000−75,000	−5.9	−7.2
$75,000−100,000	−8.9	−5.6
$100,000−200,000	−10.1	−7.2
$200,000 and over	−15.2	−5.8
Total	−10.5	−9.0

Source: Joint Committee on Taxation

investment. With advice from prominent noncommittee Republicans like Trent Lott and Jack Kemp, they directed the committee's minority staff to prepare a comprehensive alternative and released it to the public on December 6, 1985. In brief, the proposal substituted a lower corporate tax rate of 33 percent, retained a 5 percent investment tax credit, imposed a milder minimum tax, shortened the depreciation period on commercial real estate, and set the tax rate on capital gains at 20 percent. It retained present-law provisions relating to foreign taxes, oil and gas, and tax-exempt bonds. On the individual side, the substitute retained four tax rates but lowered the top rate 1 percent to 37 percent. Only 75 percent of all itemized deductions above $1,000 (except for home mortgage interest) were deductible, including state and local income and property taxes. The sales-tax deduction was eliminated.

All Quiet from the Western Wing

In the interim, there was no word from the president. "Deadly silence" emanated from the White House while aides hurriedly evaluated the economic effects of the Ways and Means tax bill and watched the progress of Duncan's alternative. Meanwhile, House Republicans lobbied the president to reject Rostenkowski's bill and support them. A worried Secretary Baker struggled to stop this destructive course of events, urging Reagan to accept political reality and endorse the committee's fragile compromise. The alternative was to risk a major political defeat. This confusion could only be settled by the president—something he finally did by issuing a statement on December 9. In it, Reagan noted his personal preference for the Republican alternative, but he also urged his party's members to vote for H.R. 3838 in the almost certain event that the alternative failed.

As weak as it was, this endorsement was enough to get tax reform back on a fast procedural track. With it, House leaders announced their intention to wrap up tax reform, and the legislative session, well before Christmas.

Given the normally well-oiled process by which the House of Representatives conducts its floor deliberations, it seemed a reasonable expectation. Unlike the Senate, the much larger House follows formal floor procedures that help it operate relatively efficiently. One such procedure involves adoption of a special "rule" defining permissible amendments and time limits before debating a major piece of legislation like H.R. 3838. Such rules of debate must be approved by a majority before the bill itself can be considered, but House leaders normally can count on such majorities from their members.

To the surprise of virtually all concerned, House Resolution 336—the rule permitting floor debate on H.R. 3838—was defeated on December 11 by a vote of 223 − 202. Only fourteen Republicans voted to allow consideration of the president's number-one legislative priority. One hundred sixty-four Republicans opposed the rule, as did fifty-nine disgruntled Democrats.

Once again, tax reform was poised on the brink of failure. Unless the vote could be reversed, the legislation could not even be debated, let alone passed by the House. Lacking a procedural go-ahead, it would die. "It caught us by complete surprise," admitted Speaker Tip O'Neill. "And I think it caught [House Republican Leader] Bob Michel by surprise too." "Shocked" was the word used by nearly all the staff and members of the Ways and Means Committee.

To be sure, there had been a few warning signs. The president's phone calls to Republican members asking them to support the bill reportedly made few converts.[19] Worse still, virtually no one worked to pass the rule itself. "I told Danny that no one was working the rule," recalled Ray McGrath. "Some members had committed to vote for the bill, but no one committed to work the rule." Moreover, the arguments being made for tax reform were strictly negative in tone. Joyless statements of pure blame avoidance were the best motivators that supporters could muster. Rep. David Bonior, the Democratic floor leader for the House rule, concluded his case for the resolution with a thinly veiled threat:

> Members of this body say the American people have lost interest; that they are not hearing from their constituents on tax reform. Yet, if this reform package fails, we will hear from the American people loud and clear. And they will want to know why their elected Representatives did not vote for a minimum tax [on] corporations or wealthy individuals . . . why we did not vote to provide tax relief for middle-income Ameri-

cans. . . . If we let this historic opportunity pass us by, the American people will not forget, nor will they be silent.[20]

A similar argument was delivered on the Republican side as Treasury officials sought to round up votes for the tax bill. According to the *Washington Post:*

> The administration's private message is political: The defeat of the Ways and Means bill would be victory for the Democrats and a black eye for the Republicans. . . . "The Democrats win either way; we win only if a bill emerges from the House," said a senior administration official.[21]

But negative suasion wasn't enough to stem the tide of Republican disaffection. "The Administration basically sold out to Rostenkowski," proclaimed an angry Richard Cheney, R-Wyo., chairman of the House Republican Policy Committee. "They cut out the Republicans in the House . . . and tried to jam it through." [22] Republican whip Trent Lott—whose job is normally to rally his troops on behalf of a Republican president—was even more graphic in his speech on the House floor: "How many of you in your secret heart of hearts wish that this issue would just go away? . . . We have an opportunity to defeat this rule, to kill this snake before it gets out of the hole." [23]

Republicans also rejected White House claims that the Republican-controlled Senate would redress the perceived deficiencies in the Ways and Means bill. Bob Packwood was already disabusing the president of that notion: the Senate traditionally accepts the basic structure of House-passed tax legislation. As Cheney put it: "They're going to end up with a bad bill out of the House, a bad bill out of the Senate, a bad bill out of the conference, and a bad bill on the President's desk." Putting the matter more colorfully, Frenzel quipped: "The phrase, 'The Senate will fix it up' is the moral equivalent of 'I'll respect you in the morning.' " [24]

From the Jaws, II

The resulting Republican insurrection was a crushing personal setback for Rostenkowski, who saw months of hard work under enormous pressure—which in his words had turned his stomach into "hamburger"—about to go down the drain. In political terms, however, it was primarily the president's problem. To many reluctant Democrats, who had been driven to support the rule and the bill simply to avoid the blame for blocking tax reform, the defeat of the rule by Republicans was a two-part gift. It killed the bill before they even had to vote on it, letting them off the hook with interest groups and constituents. It also changed the political calculus of tax reform, enabling Democrats to point the finger at Republicans.

> If [the Republican] party turns its back on tax reform and this loses . . . [it] will allow Democrats the opportunity to beat them about the head and shoulders saying, "Your own President wanted it, it was fair, and you

were too interested worrying about big corporations paying taxes to come forward and do anything to help the American people." [25]

According to Speaker O'Neill, the angry temptation to stick it to the minority even affected Rostenkowski: "Danny had worked so hard on the bill. He came steaming into my office [after the rule defeat] and said, 'To hell with them! If that's the way they want it, to hell with them.' "

The truth be told, O'Neill himself may have been tempted to let the bill die. He certainly allowed the White House to think so. When Reagan tried to ask him for a second floor vote, the Speaker toyed with him. Like Rostenkowski, O'Neill still smarted from a number of earlier, highly visible defeats at the hands of the administration. So, as he tells it:

> That night I went out to a meeting down at the Park Plaza hotel. My office called and said the White House was calling. I knew he was calling to give me the pitch. So I said, "Let's make 'em sweat!" And Christ, my office called back again. They said the president and the secret service and everybody else calling around and trying to locate me. And I said, "To hell with them, we're going to make them stew."
> The next spring, I'm at the opening game of the Red Sox, and Darman is there. And Darman says: "Geez, I remember that night. The president was so worried. Oh, boy was he upset, saying, 'He's pulling the rug on us! He's pulling the rug on us! He sees a political issue, that we're the ones who killed it. He's not going to give us another opportunity.' " But I told Darman, "No, I was only pulling his leg, making him sweat."

Happily for tax reform, the president eventually reached the Speaker, and O'Neill agreed to schedule another vote—but not until Reagan guaranteed fifty Republican votes.

By that time, Rostenkowski had suppressed his instinct for revenge. While the president's men set to work on the Republicans, Rostenkowski and the House leadership worked on the wavering Democrats. According to one account, while "lobbyists opposed to the bill worked feverishly all week to weaken Democratic support," the leadership mounted a many-channeled effort to sustain it. The regular whip organization had a regional network of deputy whips under the direction of the third-ranking member of the Democratic leadership, chief Democratic whip Thomas Foley, D-Wash. This group was supplemented by an ad hoc team of loyal Ways and Means Democrats who knew the detailed contents of the bill. When asked how this latter group contributed, Rep. Marty Russo replied: "The Ways and Means Committee has prestige. We go to other members with respect. We sometimes generate resentment, too, but we have respect. And we were proud of the bill. We had all invested too much time and effort in it to see it go down now."

The captain behind this committee whip operation was Rostenkowski. Russo, who acted as his first lieutenant, described Rosty's role after recovering from the rules defeat:

After we lost the vote, we were all physically and mentally drained. We could have said, "screw it—blame the Republicans." But the chairman said, "This is a good bill. This is our chance to do tax reform. Let's get going." Danny was an incredibly strong leader. He had presence. He had all that energy. He'd call one meeting after another. He kept us meeting the whole week. That was critical because the moment we gave up, that was the ballgame. His job was to keep us inspired. He was terrific.

Putting It Back Together Again

Rostenkowski's team was working well, but the Baker-Darman-Regan trio was having less success with the president's men. Although they picked up a few votes quickly from Republicans who had just wanted to "send a message" about being taken for granted, their effort was soon stymied. Even White House optimists could count no more than thirty-five agreeable Republicans. Moreover, virtually the entire party leadership in the House remained solidly opposed.

What could the president do? With congressional adjournment only days away, Reagan was courting failure, rejected not by unreasonable Democrats but by disloyal Republicans. Could lame-duck status be far behind?

To salvage his reputation, and perhaps his second term, Reagan opted for a high-stakes gamble. Hat in hand, he departed the safety of the Oval Office for the less familiar territory of the U.S. Capitol, where he hoped his presence and force of personality could persuade rebellious Republicans to vote yes on tax reform, if not for themselves, then for "the Gipper." Their refusal would become a personal rejection of their own president.

On Monday, December 16, Reagan met with about 160 House Republicans in an intimate, closed-door session. Looking "emotionally drained," the president urged them to "keep the process alive." [26] To provide political cover for switching votes, he promised to veto any bill that did not contain four specific changes desired by most House Republicans: (1) a top tax rate of 35 percent; (2) a full $2,000 personal exemption for every taxpayer; (3) a top capital-gains rate of 20 percent; and (4) a delay in the effective date for the elimination of many existing preferences. He further promised to put his commitments in writing to caucus president Jack Kemp.

Reagan's high-stakes gambit eventually paid off with fifty-six additional Republican votes for tax reform. Within hours, the White House had picked up enough commitments to meet O'Neill's quota. Observed Henry Hyde, R-Ill., who switched his vote, "You're confronted by the president and he's asking for something. It's hard to say no."

Out Like a Lamb

On December 17, a second rules vote was taken. This time it passed by a vote of 258−168, with twenty Republican votes to spare. Indeed, at the last moment, House Minority Leader Michel broke ranks with the rest of his party's leadership and voted to support the president on this all-important procedural test. Next the Republican alternative was defeated, 294−133. The last important vote came on a motion by conservative Rep. Philip Crane to recommit the bill to committee, which would effectively kill it. Crane's motion was handily defeated by a vote of 256−171, although nearly three-fourths of the still disgruntled Republicans supported the motion.

Astonishingly, no final recorded vote was ever taken to pass H.R. 3838. It was adopted on a simple voice vote. In the confusion, no one asked in time to put supporters on the record. While some suspected foul play, the Republican leadership staff admitted they had simply "dropped the ball." The most sweeping tax bill in thirty years passed the House with a whimper.

Lest anyone misinterpret this quiet conclusion, Tip O'Neill gave the media a chance to set the record straight. Speaking straight into the cameras, he declared: "Democrats tonight have rescued tax reform from the jaws of big business Republicans," he said. "Only the Republican Senate can stop tax reform now." [27] Dan Rostenkowski agreed, in his own inimitable and direct manner. "To an accomplishment of the House of Representatives," he said in a toast of champagne, "and to a bumpy ride in the Senate!"

Notes

1. Anne Swardson, *Washington Post*, October 18, 1985, A21.
2. Rostenkowski quoted in Hedrick Smith, *The Power Game* (New York: Random House, 1988), 559.
3. Keith Richburg, "Buchanan-Cuomo Feud Flares over Tax Plan," *Washington Post*, June 9, 1985, A1.
4. Downey quoted in Hedrick Smith, *The Power Game: The Congress*, PBS video, 1989.
5. Pamela Fessler, "Panel Votes Breaks for Banks, Charities," *Congressional Quarterly Weekly Report*, October 19, 1985, 2102.
6. Anne Swardson, "Late Trade-offs Produced Tax Agreement," *Washington Post*, November 25, 1985, A4.
7. Rep. Jim Jones, in Anne Swardson, *Washington Post*, November 17, 1985, A5.
8. Pease quoted in David Rosenbaum, "Rostenkowski Says Top Tax Rate Will Be Above 35% Reagan Goal," *New York Times*, November 18, 1985, D3; Frenzel quoted in *New York Times*, October 28, 1985, D5.
9. Anne Swardson, "Reagan Criticizes Changes in Tax Proposal," *Washington Post*, November 7, 1985, A7.
10. George Shultz and Kenneth Dam, *Economic Policy beyond the Headlines* (Palo Alto, Calif.: Stanford University), 63.
11. Transition rules are special provisions that delay or alter the application of new tax laws to particular situations or industries. Although they are intended to meet the legitimate concerns of taxpayers forced to adapt to a costly new tax environment, transition rules have traditionally been used as a coalition-building device. They can be used both to reward supportive legislators and to

reduce the number of members who might feel compelled to vote against a comprehensive tax bill because of a narrow but overriding constituency concern.

12. *Tax Notes*, November 11, 1985, 566.
13. Anne Swardson, "Late Tradeoffs Produced Tax Agreement," *Washington Post*, November 25, 1985, A4.
14. U.S. Congress, House, H.R. 3838, *A Bill to Reform the Internal Revenue Laws of the United States*, sec. 1572(b), 1282.
15. It was later determined that the year-by-year effects were not as negative as originally feared.
16. *Politics in America*, ed. Alan Ehrenhalt (Washington: CQ Press, 1986), 450.
17. Anne Swardson, "President Vacillated on Tax Bill," *Washington Post*, November 27, 1985, A1.
18. *Tax Notes*, December 2, 1985, 889.
19. Anne Swardson and Lou Cannon, "GOP Warned of Backlash If Tax Bill Dies," *Washington Post*, December 10, 1985, A1.
20. U.S. Congress, House, *Congressional Record*, daily ed., December 11, 1985, H11746.
21. Swardson and Cannon, "GOP Warned of Backlash," A14.
22. Pamela Fessler, "GOP Defeats Attempt to Consider Tax Bill," *Congressional Quarterly Weekly Report*, December 14, 1985, 2614.
23. *Congressional Record*, daily ed., December 11, 1985, H11748.
24. Cheney quoted in David Rosenbaum, "Reagan's Tax Effort Stalls," *New York Times*, December 13, 1985, D3; Frenzel quoted in *Tax Notes*, December 9, 1985, 991.
25. Rep. Tom Downey quoted in *Frontline* #411, "Taxes behind Closed Doors" (Boston: WGBH TV Transcripts, 1986), 22.
26. Pamela Fessler, "House Reverses Self, Passes Major Tax Overhaul," *Congressional Quarterly Weekly Report*, December 21, 1985, 2706.
27. Ibid., 2710.

6   The World's Most Distributive Body: The Senate Takes Up Tax Reform

I kind of like the tax code the way it is.
—Robert Packwood, November 1984

Dan Rostenkowski surprised many when he openly embraced the president's tax-reform goals in 1984. In contrast, Bob Packwood, Rostenkowski's counterpart in the Senate, surprised no one when he did not. Rosty had been the key to tax reform's success in the House, and everyone connected with the legislation knew that similar leadership would be needed in the Senate. But, beginning with Treasury I, Packwood had shown little interest in reform. When he succeeded to the chairmanship of the Finance Committee in 1985, he made it clear that the new responsibility had not altered his thinking. On several occasions Packwood was sharply critical of the president's proposal, even threatening to kill it.

The new Finance Committee chairman had many good reasons for avoiding the issue. Chief among them were the prospect of failure in his first important initiative, opposition to reform by an overwhelming majority of committee Republicans and Democrats, and the political pressure of a reelection campaign in Oregon in 1986. Moreover, Packwood found the promise of partisan advantage from tax reform unpersuasive. Finally, there was the problem of conflicting tax philosophies. Like many moderate Republicans, Packwood generally preferred tax incentives to government spending programs.

As Packwood was "first among equals" on the Senate tax-writing committee, his support was sorely needed. Yet the Senate more than any other institution had played a leading role in expanding tax expenditures over the past several decades. More than a few members of Packwood's committee had made careers out of enacting the very tax breaks that were now threatened. And, while tax reform was not quite as unwelcome on the Senate floor as in the Finance Committee, no one rushed to roll out the red carpet. All in all, as 1986 got under way, it looked as if tax-reform legislation had survived the House only to be buried in the Senate. Packwood, like most of his colleagues, had hoped that tax reform would die in the House. But when it did not, he and his Republican colleagues knew that they could not ignore the president's number-one domestic priority.

Initially, Packwood tried to finesse tax reform. His first attempt, the so-called Packwood I proposal, was an effort to have it both ways: to avoid the blame for killing tax reform, while giving up as few tax breaks as possible. Following the highly successful path that former chairman Russell Long had used to build up the tax code, Packwood tried to reform it in a similar but decremental fashion—extracting enough small concessions from members to lower the rates but not so much as to lose political support. In the process, he was careful to shelter his own concerns. Overall, putting politics on top meant paying more attention to the foes of tax reform than to its friends.

The strategy backfired. Packwood's proposal infuriated tax reform's strongest advocates. The press quickly dubbed it PAC-I: a sellout to political action committees and other special-interest constituencies. For their part, committee members eschewed all responsibility for tax reform. Angered by what they regarded as Packwood's own greediness, members found little in the proposal or its sponsor to stir their interest. Adopting one costly, self-serving amendment after another, the Finance Committee began a downhill revenue slide lasting until April 18, 1986, tax reform's so-called Black Friday. Then, deep in the hole financially and sorely beaten by scathing press coverage, Packwood abruptly suspended the committee markup, rather than confront almost total defeat.

The resurrection that followed was nothing short of miraculous. Overnight, the Oregonian became a persistent champion of tax reform, and his sudden catharsis breathed life back into the process. Having been brought to his knees by traditional tax politics, Packwood turned to a newer variety—an expert-dominated, media-fueled, and symbolic style of tax politics that Sen. Bill Bradley had honed earlier. In a remarkable turnaround, Packwood and a core group of six committee Republicans and Democrats, working entirely behind closed doors, developed and then sold a sweeping reform of the tax code to their colleagues.

From start to finish, this second phase of committee work took only twelve days! When it was done, the Finance panel had voted 20—0 to send a radical tax-reform proposal to the floor of the Senate. It had swept out many decades of tax-shelter buildup, slashing individual top rates almost in half and reducing the top corporate rate over 30 percent.

Thereafter, a powerful momentum developed for tax reform inside the tight-knit Capitol Hill community. The message was kept simple, if somewhat misleading. It pitted the "special interests" and the existing system against the "public interest" and the Finance Committee bill. Suddenly, opinion makers among the Washington press, who previously could say nothing positive about Packwood and the Finance Committee, found little to criticize and much to applaud. Once this message got out, tax reform became almost impossible to oppose even on the wide-open and unpredictable Senate floor. Swept along by a sense of history-in-the-making and a fear of being on the wrong side of it, Democrats abandoned their historical loyalty to progressivity and backed a bill that reduced tax rates to their lowest levels in fifty-five years. Republicans voted for a bill that eliminated taxes altogether for six and one-half million working poor people and backed a nearly $100 billion increase in corporate taxes, sweeping out some of their most cherished tax breaks favoring savings and investment. Even interest groups that once worked to kill the bill swallowed hard and supported it.

Looking back, tax reform in the Senate was a tale of old and new politics, about how forces for reform surmounted old legislative habits and political alliances to make a historic change in tax policy. Just as in the House, it came about partly from leadership and skillful politics and partly from luck and circumstances. Unlike in the House, however, once tax reform had won the battle for support in the Senate, its final victory seemed assured.

Dispatched for Burial in the Senate

The trip through the House was marred by much partisan and regional infighting, and many of the provisions of H.R. 3838 reflected those struggles. Still, if the bill didn't fulfill the dreams of the tax-reform purists, the "perfect worlders," the Ways and Means chairman was satisfied. House passage of tax reform was a tremendous personal victory for Rostenkowski, one that promised to boost the Chicagoan to an honored place among the historically powerful chairmen of his committee.

But Rostenkowski's and the Democrats' triumph became Packwood's and the Republicans' headache. All signs indicated the legislation was going nowhere. Its problems had to do with institutional norms and rules of the Senate as well as with Senate tax-writing traditions and the antitax reform climate prevailing among its members at the time.

Senate Folkways and Traditional Tax Politics

Of all the institutions in Washington that have a hand in tax policy making, the modern Senate is the least likely candidate for reform leadership. With the exception of the 1982−1984 period, in which tax- and task-master Bob Dole shepherded two tax increases through a reluctant Congress, the Senate has played a secondary role in tax policy, except when it came to complicating the tax code and narrowing the tax base, principally through the expansion of tax expenditures.

Republicans and Democrats alike have used the tax code as a way to jump-start the economy and specific industries, to reduce the cost of capital for business investment, and to advance a variety of other corporate and social causes. According to John Witte, between 1970 and 1981, 37 percent of all tax expenditure modifications originated either in the Finance Committee or on the Senate floor.[1] More important, while tax code modifications originating in the executive branch evenly balanced gainers and losers (by a 1:1.17 ratio), and House modifications were only slightly less balanced (1:1.34), the Senate ratio was a whopping 1:4.24, meaning that for every change made that increased federal tax revenues, the Senate advanced over four that lost money.

One reason tax expenditures are so often traced to the Senate is its relaxed rules of debate. Another is that senators show considerably less deference than their House counterparts to the proprietary claims of the standing committees. In addition, there is the order in which these two institutions act on tax legislation. Because all revenue legislation originates in the House, interest-group activity often is more intense in the Senate with members under continuing pressure to modify House-passed provisions on behalf of disappointed interest groups.

Indeed, in tax writing, the Finance Committee is the historical pressure point for clientele agitation, and it has been an unwavering supporter of tax incentives favoring myriad causes for as long as most can remember. Throughout the 1950s and 1960s, committee members regarded their task as fixing up "hot spots" in bills sent from the House.[2] During the 1970s Catherine Rudder concluded that, if anything, the situation was worse. "The process has become so manipulable that . . . it resembles an open caucus that can be taken over by virtually any group," she reported.[3]

If, as Rudder says, all groups are welcome at the Finance Committee, some seem to be more at home than others. Because the advantages of tax avoidance grow in proportion to tax liability, and because the complexity of the tax code favors those who have resources to fathom it, the Finance Committee is a special hunting ground for corporations, unions, and wealthy individuals. Political scientist David Price found that "No committee in the Senate is the target of more wealthy, powerful, and politically active interest groups than Finance." Most researchers conclude that this pattern persisted in the 1980s.[4] As Bill Bradley's tax counsel and reform advocate Gina Despres summed up:

> One of the things that strikes anyone who has worked in the Finance Committee is that when you go into a markup—except for the tourists— taxpayers are never present. It's all lobbyists and journalists. I used to fantasize about bringing in regular taxpayers from members' states by bus and having them sit up in the front row wearing t-shirts that said, for example, "Kansans for Tax Reform" or "Oklahomans for a Fair Shake."

From Activity to Influence

As discussed in Chapter 4, political scientists have long labored to understand the relationship between members of Congress and interest groups, paying special attention to patterns and mechanisms of group influence, especially the influence of campaign contributions on voting behavior.

There is no doubt that many groups hope to cement their connections to members with campaign contributions, honoraria, and other material gifts. It is equally clear that tax reform earned Finance Committee members a harvest of such rewards. For example, during 1985 PAC receipts by Finance Committee members nearly tripled their 1983 levels, well above the average rate of increase for the Senate. Energy, insurance, and labor PACs were especially generous, contributing a total of $3.1 million in 1985. In 1986 the average senator received $800,000 in PAC money, but a Finance Committee member could expect to do much better, topping $1 million on average, with Republicans doing even better than that.[5]

Of course, PAC contributions are not the only way interest groups make life easier for members of Congress. In 1986 Finance Committee members gave an average of twenty-three speeches to special-interest organizations and earned $39,146 in honoraria for doing it, nearly one-third more than the Senate average for that year. As muckrakers were quick to point out, many of those speeches were delivered in unusually pleasant surroundings, from Bermuda to Hawaii, all expenses paid, return tickets open.

Given the tax status and generosity of those who lobby the Finance Committee, many journalists and advocates of campaign finance reform equated PAC giving with special influence. The media routinely characterized the protection of parochial concerns as special-interest cave-ins, dwelling on the most crass examples they could find.[6] Their stories gave a largely accurate but incomplete picture of committee action, propelling the media into the role of would-be tax reformers.

In fact, groups do not gain influence just because they are large and important, because they contribute to congressional campaigns, or because they entice lawmakers with junkets. Indeed, decades of political science research has failed to establish strong or even consistent connections between campaign contributions and voting behavior.[7] Causality is difficult to prove because other factors intervene. Important controlling variables such as ideology and home-state connections are difficult to measure. Members may switch their committee and floor votes when they see that their own stands will not be decisive. A wide variety of pet concerns often can be packaged in a single amendment, masking self-interested voting patterns. Finally, members of Congress, like most people, are not entirely predictable over time or across settings and circumstances, making simple trends and patterns difficult to discern.

Adding it all up, it is not surprising that researchers come up decidedly short when they try to prove a connection using quantitative analysis. Our own examination of the relationship between key floor votes on the Finance

Committee bill, key House Ways and Means Committee votes during markup, and PAC contributions also failed to produce significant connections, even after taking account of important political and regional variables.[8]

Another reason for inconclusiveness is that voting analysis is not the only or perhaps even the best way to evaluate group influence. Indeed, members can do a great deal for interest groups besides vote in their behalf. For example, in tax reform, where the constraint of revenue neutrality severely limited the capacity of members to offer amendments, a record 682 transition rules (valued at nearly $11 billion) were second-best ways of rewarding special friends.

An equally well-recognized factor connecting interest groups to members of Congress is a member's ties to constituent businesses or industries at home. The tension between representing home states and districts and adhering to national interests (however defined) is a legitimate and enduring feature of American federalism. Tax reform was not unusual in this respect. Indeed, the single most consistent thread running through Finance Committee markup and back-room action was loyalty to one's own economic and other local concerns. It was thanks to the underlying premises such as revenue neutrality and base broadening that protecting home-state interests was always in painful confrontation with tax reform. As Packwood said:

> I understand that each of us have specific political problems. This is a federal structure and we all run from the same states all the time. This is not the British parliament where the party sends you out to run from someplace you've never lived in and that you're never going to live in. . . . We should defend our states because nobody else is going to watch out for our states. But, there are also issues that are generic. . . . The question is going to be, if we are going to have a meaningful tax reform bill . . . then it cannot be but for, but for, but for.[9]

Few involved in the tax-writing process apologized for standing up for constituent interests, even though it contradicted the goal of base broadening. As old-timer Russell Long asserted, "The committee should be an arena for interest aggregation and amendment." During tax reform, nowhere was this conflict more apparent than in the Finance Committee, and nowhere were accommodations more obvious. Even after members rejected the House version of H.R. 3838 as a starting point for markup, the familiar pattern of assisting aggrieved, sometimes quite narrow, regional and constituent interests persisted.

Looking for a Few Good Men

Because institutional structure and politics suggested that tax reform would be a dark horse if it ever reached the Senate, tax reformers put a

premium on leadership, starting in the Finance Committee. But trouble
was apparent as early as June 1985, when the committee began its
hearings. Altogether, over thirty tax-reform hearings were held on issues
ranging from economic effects to the constitutionality of taxing interest on
municipal bonds. Over a hundred witnesses appeared, submitting thousands of pages of written testimony. It took twenty-eight volumes to house
the record of these events.

As expected, complaints ran the ideological gamut and crossed party lines.
They swept over geographic boundaries and blanketed every sector of the
economy. The statements of Finance Committee members suggested that
nearly every organized group in the United States would be adversely
affected, as would average and not-so-average taxpayers. Even children
were pictured as under attack by tax reformers, at least insofar as they
might have their inheritances reduced!

Most of all, senators fretted about the loss of tax incentives to stimulate
and direct the economy. As JTC chief of staff David Brockway commented:

> Finance Committee members really believe that tax subsidies are
> necessary for business to raise money. That is contrary to what
> economists think unless they are supply-siders or being paid by industry.
> The committee had some really good sessions with Darman and
> Treasury specialists where we discussed the costs of capital and the
> component that tax subsidies make up of it, a component so small that it
> can be overshadowed in one day by a change in exchange rates. So when
> the members kept talking about the cost of capital and competitiveness,
> I thought they were blowing it way out of proportion. That shows you
> how politics works around here. Clearly the economists were right based
> on all the empirical evidence, but in the end the committee was
> influenced by the lobbyists who said, "We need heavy subsidies or
> western civilization will collapse."

A last thread running through committee thinking, but one that was
rarely brought up for public discussion, was skepticism about one of the
fundamental underpinnings of tax reform. Members did not accept the
reformers' assumption that the tax code should not be used for public
policy or (presumably) political pork barrel. Appropriately enough, it was
Long who finally voiced an objection. "The complexity of our code in the
main is not there because of some mischief," he lectured. "Most of it is
there in the effort to do more perfect justice." [10]

The Trouble with H.R. 3838

By late Fall 1985, it was abundantly clear that Finance Committee
members were even more opposed to H.R. 3838 than to tax reform in
general. Their grounds for disapproval were substantive and political.
Members firmly believed the House bill was far too hard on corporations.

142   Taxing Choices

Moreover, as one tax specialist observed: "By the end of the House bill they knew that the public was really skeptical. Tax reform was a dud. The administration couldn't go up to senators and say, 'This is really going to be a hot item.'" Politically minded Republicans in particular were bitter about their president's last-minute assist, enabling H.R. 3838 to pass the Democratic House. Said one insider:

> It was great politics for Kemp [who was running for president]. He got to say that he helped the president and saved tax reform, and he was guaranteed all this costly stuff at the same time. Then the bill gets thrown over on Dole's lap [who was also a candidate] as an impossible task. What is the likely result? The Senate would send back something that wasn't true tax reform, or they wouldn't be able to deliver a bill at all. There are some pretty cagey characters in this town.

Making matters worse for committee Republicans was the fact that the administration was publicly divided on reform. While Baker and Darman were talking up its merits to reluctant senators, Don Regan went on national television to criticize Rostenkowski's bill.

A Lack of Depth Perception

Thus, it came as no surprise that when the House labeled H.R. 3838 a Christmas present and sent it to the Senate in December, Finance Committee members quickly renamed it a belated Thanksgiving turkey.

In truth, such negative opinions were not formed through close inspection. Why were members so neglectful? By virtue of their multiple committee assignments, higher profiles, and associated scheduling problems, senators are more likely than representatives to rely on brief, secondhand interpretations of proposed legislation. A comparison of Ways and Means and Finance Committee assignments shows that while representatives relinquished other assignments to obtain their committee seats, senators rarely sat on fewer than three committees.[11] Moreover, so much tax law had been rewritten that the House bill was several inches thick and over 1,300 pages long. Although one Finance Committee member routinely displayed the four-and-a-half-pound document in order to ridicule its contents, he readily admitted that he hadn't wanted to look inside. One cynic declared, "We didn't start with the House bill because members would have to read it!" The tax bill that John Danforth, R-Mo., nicknamed "gorilla" found few members willing to get close. Instead, the broad contours of this unwelcome beast were enough for most, preferably packaged as memorandums or hearsay.

Backed into Leadership on Tax Reform

The only ranks thinner than those of prospective reform troopers were the ranks of reform captains. Likely candidates by virtue of their seniority and institutional status were Packwood, Dole, and Long. But each senator had his own reasons for resisting command—preferring to leave the cheerleading to the likes of junior Finance Committee member Bill Bradley.

Dean of the Tax Code.   Since arriving at the Senate in 1948, Russell Long had helped build the tax code into its present form. As Finance chairman he had wielded his powers to narrow the tax base and expand the public and not-so-public purposes of the federal tax code. Some of Long's service was to nationwide interests, but more went to his home state, Louisiana. Philosophically as well, he was committed to protecting the institutional prerogatives of his committee, of the Senate, and of Congress. For those reasons the ranking Democrat did not share the reformers' goal of eliminating the fruits of politicians' labors in the tax code.

The Artful Dodger.   Robert Dole shared Long's pragmatic approach to policy making and was a staunch supporter of his own state's economic concerns as well. Furthermore, after helping the president engineer the largest tax cut in modern history in 1981, Dole sorely regretted his dalliance with supply-side economics. The midwesterner was a budget balancer, not a tax reformer at heart, and he had his own fledgling presidential candidacy to worry about. Thus, when it came time to step out from the line, Dole looked conveniently at Packwood, pleading his own heavy load of responsibilities as majority leader and deference to chairmanship as reasons for not lending a hand.

Tax Reformer and Junior Statesman.   Meanwhile, Bill Bradley was hoping and working for tax reform. Like the president, Bradley had come to distrust the tax system through personal experience. As a young basketball professional, the twenty-three-year-old found that with careful counseling he could "decide how much to pay in taxes." [12] And to his surprise and disgust, the Princeton graduate and Rhodes scholar could consider himself to be a "depreciable corporate asset."

Fifteen years later Bradley had a second consciousness-raising encounter with tax policy, as a candidate for the U.S. Senate. Bradley's opponent in the race was New Jersey Republican Jeffrey Bell, one of the original supporters of the "10-10-10" tax-plan, progenitor of the Kemp-Roth tax-cut scheme. Bell lost the election, but his idea of financing low rates through a broadened tax base stuck, germinating during Bradley's early years on the prestigious Finance Committee. After Reagan's election, Bradley was the only committee member to vote against ERTA in 1981, correctly forecasting the deficit explosion that followed. Most of all, Bradley was appalled by the expansion of tax loopholes that accompanied partisan jockeying over this historic tax cut. Yet, as his aide Gina Despres said, "He decided that it wasn't enough to be against the president, you had to be for something." That something became the Bradley-Gephardt Fair Tax Act of 1982. It was Bradley the politician who first recognized that a potential, albeit unlikely, marriage between conservative supply-siders and loophole-closing liberals might generate enough support to enact revenue-neutral tax reform. By getting ahead of the wave and capturing credit, Despres remembered, "Bill believed that this was an opportunity for Democrats."

Politics notwithstanding, it was a more quixotic Bradley who gave Despres the go-ahead to do tax reform "right." Later, this duty-before-glory attitude served Bradley well, gaining him considerable credibility with Democrats and Republicans alike. In the early years, however, it freed Bradley to do what he liked best—digging into the details of public policy. Indeed, for a senator, Bradley spent inordinate amounts of time on the project, meeting nearly daily with Despres and his administrative assistant, Marcia Aronoff, and giving weekends and evenings over to its pursuit as well. His work habits led one phrasemaker to declare, "Not only was he going to *be* for it, he was going to *work* for it."

Nonetheless, considering the scope of the project, it was not Bradley, but his own mini—think tank of experts from inside and outside government that gave birth to the full-blown theory and details of the Fair Tax Act. In making a decision to proceed, Bradley had gathered a group of talented individuals including Despres; Aronoff; his press secretary, Dick Lerner; JTC chief economist Jim Wetzler and his colleague Ken Wertz; Jim Verdier, Cynthia Gensheimer, and Joe Minarik from the Congressional Budget Office (CBO); former assistant Treasury secretaries Dan Halperin and Don Lubick; and several lawyers from the Washington law firm of Caplin and Drysdale where Despres had once worked. Thereafter, when Bradley decided to proceed with his own bill, the group was trimmed to a select and willing few—the aforementioned Bradley aides, Wetzler, Randy Weiss (also from the JTC), and Minarik, who had moved from CBO to the Urban Institute (a private Washington think tank) and was by all accounts the most important theoretician for the Bradley plan.[13] This second group met weekly for nearly a year questing after corporate and individual base broadeners and trying at the same time, as Despres put it, to "make sure that, overall, the revenue and distributional estimates were as good as we could make them."

As early as 1982 Bradley began making a case for partisan action on tax reform, first in a speech before the Democratic miniconvention in Philadelphia, later one-on-one with party leaders. At that time, though, Bradley's framework was too comprehensive, his delivery too complex, and his politics too new for traditional Democrats. As one recalled, "He put us to sleep with his crazy notions and his endless examples." Later, in

1984 when Mondale was nominated as the Democratic candidate for president, Bradley attempted to sell Hubert Humphrey's protégé his bill as a plank in the Democratic platform. After a brief courtesy hearing, however, the young tax policy turk was shown the door. Mondale, a former Finance Committee member who appreciated Long's approach to taxation, feared for Democrats who crossed their constituencies, including himself. While Big Labor's opposition probably sealed the case, Mondale's mistaken idea that voters would see increased taxation as good for the soul was another important contributing factor.

Ironically, as described in detail in Chapter 3, it was the off-chance that Mondale might listen to Bradley that got tax reform rolling at the White House. Thereafter, when Rostenkowski took the president's bait, Bradley was also off and running. Of all places for a senator to be heading, however, this generally shy and unassuming tax reformer was making tracks toward the House of Representatives. In a rare show of institutional humility, Bradley worked actively to help tax reform pass the House, and he formed an unlikely alliance with Dan Rostenkowski that lasted throughout the tax-reform process. Indeed, although he promised himself he would never mix his old and new professions, Bradley even ventured onto the basketball court to lobby reluctant Ways and Means members on Rostenkowski's behalf. And, in a final act of charity, Bradley offered his own tax staff as circuit riders, helping fellow Democrats build their cases for tax reform to constituents. One Rostenkowski aide stated:

> Throughout 1985 he would ask us over on Saturday mornings—us and the Joint Tax Committee staff—and talk to us. He gave us ideas on how we could argue reform to our members. It wasn't just policy, although he was heavily into the policy, it was also *votes*. "Can I phone anyone? How can I help?"

As a result, Bradley earned Rostenkowski's respect and gratitude.

In short, Bradley devoted 1981 through 1984 to policy incubation and formulation and 1985 almost exclusively to political sales and service. And although his efforts bore fruit in the House, parallel attempts at moral suasion and entrepreneurship produced no important alliances in the Senate. Ironically, when tax reform got seriously under way in his own chamber in 1986, the New Jersey Democrat could do little more than lecture his colleagues because, unfortunately, he had nothing more tangible to offer.

Reluctant Reformer.   Although Packwood denies it, he demonstrated little love for and some irritation with Bradley during the period preceding his own conversion to tax reform. Later, Packwood changed his mind and heart when Bradley showed himself to be a willing and savvy helpmate. But early on, as journalist Dale Russakoff concluded, "[He] distrusted Bradley, believing he aimed to force the Republican Senate to kill the bill, giving Democrats an issue in 1986 and Bradley a chance to play saint in a chamber of sinners." [14]

But avoiding Bradley did not allow Packwood to eschew the revolution the junior senator had helped to launch. As chairman, Packwood was the only senior member of the Finance Committee who had to face up to tax reform. He would have to deal with it, like it or not. He did not like it. Always a maverick, the Oregonian rankled at being put on a political hot seat by the White House, especially in his first year as chairman. Indeed, when Treasury I was released, Packwood had urged the president to leave it on the shelf. "I hope you're not going to push simplification for simplification's sake," he urged, "[because] to go through the whole process and wind up without a dime's dent in the deficit just doesn't make sense." [15]

Revenue neutrality was not the only principle of tax reform Packwood questioned. He was supremely comfortable with using the tax code as a tool of government. On opening day of the Finance Committee hearings Packwood had said so explicitly:

> If for some reason we think something needs to be encouraged beyond the marketplace, whether it is for national security or other legitimate reasons, it seems to me we have two ways to do it. One way is to use the tax code, and the other is a straight-out government subsidy or government program. And for years at least, many of us have thought that the tax code was a more effective and efficient way to do it than a government-managed, government-run, government-loaned and on occasion government-owned program.[16]

Over time, the Oregonian had zealously promoted this philosophy on behalf of home-state interests and other causes he believed in. As the *Congressional Quarterly Weekly Report* observed:

> Packwood fought throughout his Senate career for tax cuts targeted to specific ends. He had pushed tax breaks for parents who send their children to private schools, for various energy conservation schemes, and for businesses that offer employees health care coverage. The sum total of Packwood's tax credit proposals over the years amounts to a full-scale Republican social agenda designed for enactment through the Internal Revenue Service code.[17]

The Cat's at the Doorstep

Negative feelings notwithstanding, the House had left an uninvited guest on the Senate's doorstep, and politics dictated that Packwood play the polite if unenthusiastic host. First, institutional competition demanded some hospitality. Then, too, during the Reagan years generally and in tax reform particularly this rivalry between chambers was strengthened by intense partisan competition between the Republican Senate and the Democratic House. In retrospect, however, personal ambition played the most visible part in picking up the challenge of tax reform. Faced with the biggest threat and opportunity of his political life, a kind of legislative "can do" took hold of Packwood, just as it had Rostenkowski. As aide Mary McAuliffe remembered, "It was Senator Packwood's first year as chairman. So, it was a leadership issue, a question of whether or not he could get his committee together."

Failure to move some form of tax legislation also might hurt Packwood's reelection chances. Political good sense advised pacifying Oregon economic interests by doing as little as possible, but it also required doing something. After all, lower- and middle-class voters, as well as more reform-minded Oregonians, might later blame Packwood for the specifics of the TRA, but seeming to oppose the symbol of tax reform before the election would be much worse. Thus, while Rostenkowski's hardest decision had been whether to accept the president's challenge, Packwood enjoyed no similar luxury. His dilemma was not whether to proceed, but how?

A Winter's Day for Tax Reform

Packwood got his answer when he packed the Finance Committee off on a retreat to Berkeley Springs, West Virginia, to make some preliminary decisions. Unlike the House retreats, it was for members only (with the exceptions of Baker, Darman, and a few top staff); no academics were invited. The weekend was cold by Washington standards, and when the first "temperature checks" were taken inside the lodge, they revealed that the climate for tax reform was also frigid. Not counting Packwood, sixteen of the nineteen senators present opposed it.

The tiny minority of would-be tax reformers included only two relatively junior Democrats and a single Republican: Bradley, George Mitchell, D-Maine, and John Chafee, R-R. I. As expected, naysayers included key power brokers such as Long, Lloyd Bentsen, D-Texas, and Bob Dole, although Dole was not present (he had pleaded a commitment in his home state). Long's opposition was a serious blow because as ranking member on the Finance Committee he would be needed to bring the Democrats in line. Bentsen's opposition was only slightly less discouraging since he stood second in seniority behind the soon-to-retire Long. And although Dole could not be accused of open opposition, the signals were hardly promising. He had a talent for sidestepping hopeless causes and had already sent signals about competing responsibilities as majority leader. Putting both things together, a staff member concluded:

> Dole stayed quiet, but he was absolutely prepared to let it die. Rich Belas [Dole's tax counsel] carried 5,000 amendments around with him at all times! They were all revenue losers [because] Dole had so many deals to do—all politically motivated. He is the Republican's main guy in the Senate and so has a crucial role to play that way.

For their part, the committee rank-and-file promised nothing but trouble. Building on a bloc of oil and gas votes that included Long, Dole, Bentsen, Max Baucus, D-Mont., and Malcom Wallop, R-Wyo., outspoken opponent David Boren, D-Okla., was actively soliciting conspirators for his "kill the bill" coalition. Moderates Dave Durenberger, R-Minn., and John Heinz, R-Penn., as well as conservatives such as Bill Armstrong, R-Colo., fumed openly about budget deficits. Others like flat-tax man Steve Symms, D-Idaho, professed that reform of the kind they could support was an idea whose time had not come.

Pack-I: Reform Meets Traditional Tax Politics

By the end of the retreat the committee had agreed to some ground rules and taken a few straw polls. Packwood was instructed to start fresh, crafting his own alternative from the ground up. Although historically the Senate has been content to let the House shape tax policy, making adjustments to reflect Senate thinking, during the 1980s the Finance Committee had shown far less deference.[18] By rejecting H.R. 3838 entirely, it showed the most muscle yet and continued its rise to equal partnership with the House in tax policy making.

Committee members might justifiably have prided themselves on being tough customers by standing up to H.R. 3838, but they were not much better than "weak sisters" when it came to facing up to tax reform in general. This was because the other important decision made at Berkeley Springs was to leave Packwood to his own devices. The rationale was obvious to those present, as one of them noted: "The members sent Bob Packwood off because they were not facing up to tax reform as a serious responsibility. They just weren't into it. It was the chairman's problem at that point, and they were seeing all sorts of political problems for themselves if they helped it along in any way."

I Did It My Way

Choosing the right procedural strategy was an important next step for Packwood. Following Dole's partisan style, Packwood could have attempted to hammer out a partisan consensus in private, hoping to win through bloc voting in open markup. But the near-total absence of Republican support precluded that alternative. He might try to form a bipartisan reform coalition. But that would mean bypassing his old friend and sometime mentor, Russell Long, something Packwood was not yet prepared to do. Or he could follow in Long's footsteps, buying votes one at a time with modest regard for philosophical, partisan, or ideological considerations.

Without guarantees that the finished product would be accepted, Packwood chose the method of his old friend, putting together a patchwork proposal, piece by political piece. The strategy was calculated to produce a majority of votes, and the process was painstaking, according to the Finance Committee general counsel and Packwood's top tax man, John Colvin:

> We looked at everything we could see. We looked at past positions. Every member was asked over and over again, "What is it that matters to you? " We would go out and have an hour with each member. After that Packwood had a meeting with each member, a different type of courting without staff. Then, there were group meetings. There were private meetings. And eventually you knew what they wanted.

Canvassing produced a list that even in summary stretched twenty-seven pages! Members wanted to preserve most of the better-known credits and deductions, including individual retirement accounts; the investment tax credit; the research and development tax credit; the rehabilitation and historic preservation credit; the energy credit; the targeted-jobs credit; and the deductions for charitable contributions, for state and local taxes, for second homes, and for business meals and entertainment. Also mentioned were House provisions related to foreign taxes, pensions, real estate, and banks and casualty companies. Finally members' wish lists gave high priority to home-state industries from timber to tourism.

Try as they might, Packwood's staff couldn't give everyone everything. The idea was to offer enough to buy support, but not so much as to unbalance revenues and expenditures. As one staff member admitted, this way Packwood would meet his leadership challenge without succumbing to thoroughgoing tax reform:

> We tried crafting it from a more traditional approach, looking at issues that were of particular concern to our members—timber for Packwood and Baucus, oil and gas for Long and Bentsen—saying we need to cut back, but helping them out. All the way around the committee we went, taking into account members' concerns, hoping we'd develop something that was tax reform.

Even reducing favors to a minimum, Packwood fell short of revenue neutrality. After tax rates were lowered to the president's liking, retained breaks exceeded revenues gained through base broadening by a large margin. This, in turn, propelled Colvin and his staff of lawyers into a revenue scramble from which they never emerged, leading the seasoned tax expert to note with a laugh and a wince: "On any given day we were at least $25 billion off! How do you get the thing to add up and also get votes? We asked questions and tried alternatives, but basically it was not working."

Revenues were needed, but to adhere to the president's rules they couldn't appear to be tax increases. Finally, Colvin eliminated the business expense deduction for excise taxes and tariffs that companies pay. That clever, if somewhat desperate, abdication of accepted tax policy principles gained Packwood a whopping $62 billion over five years. But when it was revealed to the public, nary an expert could be found to support the idea.

At the Federal Bar Association's March 1986 conference on tax law, former IRS commissioner Jerome Kurtz summed up the dominant professional view, stating that the excise tax proposal "violated a cardinal principle of the current tax system which has always held that such levies were deductible as part of the cost of goods sold." [19]

Overall, the content of Packwood I was a not-very-delicate balance of politics and policy. It contained just enough unconventional revenue raisers and reform to protect Packwood's own concerns as well as a long list of committee and White House demands.

As If Dollars Had Wings

With markup scheduled to begin four days later, Packwood unveiled his handiwork on March 13. He met with President Reagan first, then one-on-one with committee members, and finally with journalists and lobbyists who had assembled for the unveiling. Problems became apparent at every stop. After a brief audience with Reagan, Packwood emerged from the Oval Office claiming thumbs up, but later (much to Baker and Darman's surprise) White House Chief of Staff Don Regan stated on network television that the president wanted some things changed. Such signs of presidential waffling inadvertently opened the exit door for many Republicans who were already eager to take their places among tax reform's refugees.

Nor did Packwood get warm receptions from committee members. The chairman had given away a great deal, but apparently he was not generous enough. "It was a tactical mistake to try to buy off every member of the Finance Committee," one insider pointed out. "Nobody stays bought. They push and push and push." Colvin agreed. "We thought we had been responsive, but other interests just kept coming up."

Another reason for negativity was that so much was at stake. "This was the biggest thing to come down the pike in years," Brockway reminded the uninitiated. "Senators were not going to throw away their ability to shape this policy because Packwood gave them the equivalent of repairs on some two-lane highway in their state." Then, too, committee members were offended when they found that Packwood's own interests were spared tax reform's ax. Not only were fringe benefits preserved nearly in full, timber provisions were protected as well. Oregon and other natural-resource states received benefits totaling $1 billion more than present law, $11 billion more than H.R. 3838, and $7.4 billion more than Treasury II. A Packwood staff member openly acknowledged the expensive strategy:

> It is true that this area was tempered in the spread sheets. But Packwood was not alone. He had Symms and Baucus, Mitchell, Moynihan, Pryor, Boren, Long, and Bentsen, not to mention a few others who had an interest in mining and oil and gas. . . . He was building a coalition with

these interests. There was no question that he took care of Oregon, but it coincided with the interests of a lot of other senators.

The power play was too much for committee members, especially those whose states did not benefit. Editorial reaction to Packwood I was the worst of all. Major newspapers including the *Wall Street Journal*, the *Los Angeles Times*, the *Washington Post*, and the *Christian Science Monitor* were all negative. The *New York Times* summed up press reaction best, concluding that the "backward" plan demonstrated that Packwood "still opposes tax reform." The proof, editorialized the *Times*, was that he "perpetuates loopholes even Reagan feels pressure to close." [20] Meanwhile, Citizens for Tax Justice released a (perhaps questionable) poll showing that 77 percent of Americans opposed the plan.

Adding Interest and Subtracting Deductions

Two features of Packwood I in particular produced immediate hostile reaction: (1) the $62 billion proposal to eliminate the deduction for excise taxes and (2) the decision to include tax-exempt bond interest in the alternative minimum tax (AMT). As the Joint Tax Committee had predicted, the excise-tax proposal drew fire from business and consumer groups, as well as from tax professionals and tax-reform advocates. Consumer interests decried the idea as regressive, while Tax Reform Action Coalition members, led by the American Trucking Association, claimed it would be bad for business. Within days, the opposition rolled into high gear, gathering so much sympathy on the committee that Packwood was forced to schedule a hearing to listen to complaints. Throughout the first phase of markup, furor over this revenue linchpin rumbled like thunder in the background of committee action because everyone recognized that the monies it gained would ultimately be lost. This, of course, left a crucial, but unanswered question: "If not here, where?" [21]

A last-minute decision to include municipal bond interest in the AMT also brought angry cries of rage from governors, mayors, and the middlemen who profit from the sale of these public securities. Placing interest earned on newly purchased tax-exempt bonds under the AMT was certain to drive up interest rates that state and local governments pay when they market bonds, while the inclusion of interest on already-purchased securities, in effect, broke a promise of good faith to millions of bondholders.

Ironically, the provision was added more for political than for revenue reasons. Tax reformers had been making considerable political hay with tales of wealthy individuals and profitable companies that paid no taxes. The AMT answered politicians' prayers by allowing Congress to beat its chest on tax avoidance without eliminating tax expenditures that cause the problem. Under the AMT, when taxpayers invest in enough tax-shelter schemes to reduce their tax liabilities to zero, they must instead calculate an alternative minimum tax to pay. An airtight AMT law, of course, ensures that no corporation or individual can avoid paying taxes altogether. But that, in turn, depends on putting together a leakproof package of taxable preferences. Zealous staff and their reform-minded compatriots at Treasury argued that taxing previously tax-exempt interest was one way of doing that. Packwood bought the idea.

When word reached financial markets that Packwood had made a move on bonds, traders panicked, and the bond market collapsed.[22] Amid the clamor Packwood backtracked, hurriedly acquiescing to a Long-sponsored amendment to exclude interest earned on existing bonds. The March 24 vote (19−0), the first of markup, included even Packwood's "aye." Whatever the substantive merit, symbolically it was a very bad beginning.

Scoring Amendments and Getting Off the Mark

Off to a terrible start, Packwood's troubles worsened each day of markup. During the first week of serious voting, dozens of amendments were offered, and very few were turned back. Even Packwood's generous ($4.3 billion) treatment of depreciation compensating for the loss of the ITC wasn't enough for Finance Committee members. By creating an entirely new class of "productive property," Dole, Roth, Heinz, Wallop, and Baucus convinced fellow members to spend billions more on manufacturing assets. Nor did committee members stop there. The game next turned to getting other capital assets defined as "productive," making them also eligible for improved depreciation benefits. In short order, the committee approved a Dole automobile amendment and one for Heinz on real estate. The spending spree stopped only when Heinz proposed to reduce the useful life of a tuxedo from five to three years! Despite substantial kidding back and forth and an admonition from Packwood that "some things make us look really foolish," the amendment lost by a single vote.

And so markup went through corporate, accounting, pensions, trusts and estates, as well as foreign titles of the Packwood I proposal. Members offered amendments for themselves and for others. For example, Bentsen advanced an amendment for himself and for fellow southerner Lawton Chiles, D-Fla., to improve life for citrus growers plagued by bad weather and Brazilian competition. Farm-state Republicans Charles Grassley and Dole (both in the midst of reelection campaigns) obtained agriculture amendments that helped others with similar constituencies who were also facing electoral competition, including James Abnor, R-S.D., Mark Andrews, R-N.D., and Slade Gorton, R-Wash. Durenberger negotiated privately with Packwood for improvements on H.R. 3838's treatment of municipal bonds, increasing spending by $5 billion over the House bill and $1 billion over existing law. Even this wasn't enough for Danforth and Moynihan, who successfully championed the right of large nonprofit research institutions, notably Harvard, Yale, and Columbia, to issue tax-exempt debt without limit. By Friday, April 18, the committee was $29 billion above the mark of revenue neutrality, excluding the obvious problem of finding a $62 billion replacement for the excise-tax gambit.

To his credit, Packwood opposed nearly all of these amendments. To his greater credit, so did Bradley. Indeed, for Bradley, the markup was an unpleasant but not unexpected trial. Throughout those days he lectured to the walls on the finer points of achieving lower rates through a broadened base and on the regressive effects of amendments being offered. For his part, Packwood sometimes appeared irritated, especially when Bradley requested itemizations for the cost and distributional consequences of various provisions and amendments. At one point Packwood snapped, "If you are going to persist in these demands for new and different figures, we might as well shut down shop right now." [23]

Bradley was undeterred by his critics. Indeed, the highlight of his lonely war on traditional tax politics was a kamikaze-like attack on tax breaks for natural resource industries during which Bradley laid out the economic rationale for denying producer subsidies and offered amendments to do just that. For example, he tried unsuccessfully to phase out percentage depletion for oil and gas. "Even the White House Texans had allowed $2 billion in savings there," he chided. By Bradley's count, this preference gave $1.5 billion in benefits to fewer than 100,000 taxpayers with average incomes in excess of $75,000. Next, a Bradley amendment to cut back preferences for drilling-cost amortization, which would have produced a net gain of $1.2 billion, failed, despite the fact that 50 percent of these benefits went into the pockets of fewer than 31,000 taxpayers with adjusted gross incomes in excess of $100,000. But neither vote was close. Indeed, it was not until Bradley's attempt to repeal energy credits also failed that the obvious was finally admitted. Having lost by a whopping eighteen votes (which was, in fact, everyone present besides himself), Bradley winced, "It's getting lonely in here."

All in all, the second week of markup ended with a depressing box score for tax reform. The committee had taken dozens of votes, and the news for reformers was the worst it could be. Danforth remarked to his tax aide, "As I sat there in those weeks, it was like watching dollar bills with wings on them, flying out the window, taking tax reform with them."

Tax Reformers Take Aim

Gloom was everywhere except among lobbyists circling for the kill. The atmosphere was, as one tax-reform advocate summed it up, plain awful:

> The Senate Finance Committee was the laughing stock of Washington.
> Things had gone exactly as the most cynical lobbyists said they would.
> They were down at the bottom of the trough, and the people who were
> supposed to be leading the tax reform effort were pigging out the most.
> It was depressing and miserable and plain awful.

For Packwood in particular the problem was a great deal more than one of policy making gone awry. Tax reform had become a personal liability. If critics were calling the Finance Committee "a laughing stock," Packwood had to be regarded as the chief clown. In a scathing attack, the *New Republic* nicknamed him "Senator Hackwood" and dubbed his efforts PAC-I, a sellout to special interests. All over Washington and in newspapers across the country, Packwood's leadership abilities were called into question. The *New York Times* called his work "worse than no bill at all," an effort that "reeks of privilege" and "gleams like a Christmas tree." More ominous still, Packwood had become the butt of painful editorial jokes in newspapers back home.[24]

By the end of the second week of April, consensus said that things were going to get worse before they got better, if indeed they ever did. Many predicted that the coming week—when American taxpayers would send almost $500 billion to the IRS but would avoid sending over $400 billion more thanks to existing credits, deductions, exemptions and loopholes— would be the darkest yet.[25]

The End of the Beginning for Tax Reform

The week leading up to April 18 might accurately be called the end of the beginning. At the time, however, it looked more like the beginning of the end. On Wednesday, pension amendments lost another $10.6 billion with Heinz, Chafee, Grassley, and Pryor leading the way. Furthermore, two votes on two major amendments were scheduled for Friday, one on individual tax provisions affecting state and local taxes (sponsored by Moynihan and Durenberger), the other on business meals and entertainment (sponsored by Armstrong). If they succeeded, those amendments would add a whopping $32 billion to the existing $30 billion markup deficit. Yet, Armstrong was optimistic, and things looked so good for Moynihan that he and his tax counsel, Joe Gale, had already counted their winnings. Even Bradley would oppose Packwood on this one.

What were Packwood's priorities that Friday morning? At the heart of the problem was his own political survival. Old hands in Washington know that few altruists are present in the corridors of power where legislative majorities are built. As Chafee noted wryly, the Senate Finance Committee "is not an arena where high value is placed on chastity."[26] In this arena, nothing undermines influence as rapidly or thoroughly as failure.

Thus, on that Black Friday, Packwood's thoughts and those of his top staff centered on political stakes far higher than the purity of tax reform. Had the situation been reversed—with the committee approving enough of the plan to see it through—Packwood would not have changed course. When they did not, he faced a crisis of his political leadership. "The biggest problem for Senator Packwood," one aide remembered, "was that he was a new chairman. The question was, can this man lead?"

By 9:30 A.M., committee members had filtered into the Finance Committee hearing room, prepared for business as usual. Hundreds of lobbyists, journalists, and staff had waited in line for hours for a chance to bear witness to what everyone expected to be the best evidence yet that the Finance Committee was intent on burying tax reform in the Senate.

Instead, Packwood canceled markup, commenting that he was taking some time to think things over. Apart from the stony expressions of his own staff, shock registered on every face in the room and on those still in line outside. Despite Packwood's brave words, the whispers up and down the corridors of the Dirksen office building echoed words politicians hate most: Tax reform was Packwood's most important test, and he had *failed* it.

Political Miscalculations

By that point in tax reform Packwood had become an object lesson in the power of the press and the opposition to define political troubles on Capitol Hill in the most personal terms. The irony of Packwood's strategy for taking credit for tax reform while avoiding blame for changing the tax code was that it garnered him very little credit and a great deal of blame. Critics tied failure primarily to the Oregonian's cowardice in the face of special-interest pressure. And, as is almost always the case, the criticism carried some validity.

In hindsight, the plan was vulnerable on a number of counts. First, Packwood began his work without a theme, even while his assignment was one part of a policy process driven by great themes. He had plunged immediately into political bargaining. A single story epitomizes the extreme cynicism that at times pervaded the effort. Upon seeing proposals to protect small timber tax credits, Despres asked his staff, "Why had Packwood put the credit at 5 percent?" The response she got was, "Because we didn't think we could get 10." The unfortunate quip circulated throughout the Senate, becoming an ugly metaphor for Packwood's plan and a rallying cry for those he offended by it.

Second, Packwood failed to build member support throughout the preparation process, in part because he was left on his own and in part because he decided to act in secret. Recollecting the unusual way Packwood I was put together, one JTC staff member said:

> The Senate side operated entirely differently [from the House]. It was
> much more secretive. The Finance Committee staff itself wasn't privy to
> some of it, which was a very strange situation. We would get phone calls
> on one issue or another, and we were developing spread sheets in
> response to those phone calls. We were not to discuss our work with
> lower-level staff. The only person with whom we could share the spread
> sheets was John Colvin, and I assume he with Bill Diefenderfer.

Although Packwood's staff insisted that the dangers from too much
attention were greater than those from too little, and that Finance
Committee staff lawyers were fully involved in the preparation process,
the disadvantage of any such secret strategy is that outsiders are unlikely to
have anything vested in the results.

Third, by worrying so much about the reaction of tax reform's
opponents, Packwood and his staff paid too little attention to tax reform's
supporters, on or off Capitol Hill. Packwood had little time for do-gooders
in general, and reformers like Bradley had not converted a single Finance
Committee member to their position. For similar reasons, Packwood
ignored professionals on the Joint Tax Committee. Historically, JTC staff
are distrusted in the Senate, reflecting a suspicion that Ways and Means
chairmen have treated them as their own staff. Rostenkowski certainly did,
so much so that the JTC was nearly synonymous with H.R. 3838.

For the same reasons, tax-reform activists outside government were also
excluded. One of them recalled, "The corporate 'big boys' could get
through the door, but the Finance Committee had almost no time for
public-interest groups that supported tax reform." Another lamented, "We
were treated like lepers. The attitude was one of scorn for the basic tax
reform groups, while trying to make a deal with all the antitax reform
groups."

Old Strategies in New Circumstances

Packwood's approach to tax reform and his handling of the markup cost
him a significant measure of political capital. Yet, what made the situation
ironic was that he had adhered to longstanding tax-writing conventions in
the Senate. Even more ironic was that this highly publicized and
resounding failure paved the way for his ultimate success and for the
eventual passage of the TRA.

Finance panel chairmen seek near-universal support in committee
because they must keep an eye on the perils their tax bills face from hostile
floor amendments. This puts a premium on keeping committee members
happy. Thanks to strict limitations on the amendment process in House
debate, Ways and Means chairmen rarely face this problem. A JTC staff
member said, "Any chairman has the problem of the Senate floor. He is
going to need those members supporting him. I don't think people realize

the enormous advantage the House has with its closed rule."

In other areas, the changes Packwood made amounted to a battle plan for the upcoming House-Senate conference. Although many of the differences between H.R. 3838 and the Finance Committee plan reflected differences in the constituencies of the two houses of Congress, like good negotiators, both chairmen left room to maneuver in conference. For example, Rostenkowski's plan took a big swipe at capital-intensive industries, while Packwood's went in the opposite direction. And, knowing he would have to give ground later, Rostenkowski took a tough line with oil, gas, timber, and other extractive industries. Recognizing his ploy, Packwood more than made up for it.

Most important, Packwood followed a long tradition of incrementalism, eliminating tax expenditures the same way they had been added: bit by bit. Rather than, say, getting rid of the state and local tax deduction altogether, Packwood decided to scale it back. Likewise, he chose to do away with only 20 percent of the deduction for business meals and entertainment. Unfortunately for the Oregonian, the proposals were by no means the radical departure being demanded by increasingly vocal tax reformers. Equally unacceptable were the favors Packwood had bestowed in exchange for support.

Packwood's principal miscalculation was failing to accurately gauge changes in the political arena in which he operated. Instead, the Finance Committee chairman played according to the tried-and-true rules of tax politics—including trading tax preferences for votes and emphasizing special-interest considerations over larger considerations of tax philosophy. Packwood persisted with his strategy in part because the lessons learned over decades die hard, even though the circumstances that sustained them had changed.

What were these changes? Historically, the back-scratching, nonpartisan, distributive strategy had worked because it garnered very little public attention. The tax code itself lacks the ingredients of the kind of front-page saga that seizes public attention and holds it. But, thanks to the entrepreneurism of a combination of unlikely champions—including a conservative president, a machine politician, and a smattering of ideologically disparate young turks and potential presidential contenders—tax politics was suddenly grabbing headlines. It had moved from the quiet luxury of boardrooms, resorts, and restaurants and the private recesses of congressional offices into the broad daylight of public attention that is nearly always reserved only for momentous political struggles.

Those themes intertwined with the strong and colorful personalities involved to allow the press and opinion makers to mine every corner of the tax-reform conflict. With careful crafting, it became a struggle for grand ideas such as fairness and economic growth as well as a battle for the allegiance of middle America's voters. Most important, the struggle was portrayed as one between the public interest and special interests, between everyman who pays his fair share of taxes and a few Americans who are able to shelter their income. Once this populist theme caught on, it was played and replayed, in the press, among old friends and new converts to tax reform, and finally under the bright lights of television cameras that monitored the Finance Committee.

Interestingly, despite the populist rhetoric, few, if any, of these struggles were viewed with intensity outside Washington. And, as is more and more true in American politics, the political struggle—this time over tax reform—had a life of its own on the banks of the Potomac. Thanks to intense coverage by the congressional and economic press, as well as their own natural curiosity, politicians, their staffs, political insiders, tax experts, and a few interested bystanders were riveted to the action, unwilling to let go of the best political story in town. As a result, representatives of public interest groups could be seen on public affairs talk shows or in news interviews on the steps of the Capitol opposite invariably better clad special-interest lobbyists and paid experts. In those debates, tax reform protagonists conjured up images of sordid tax shelters, while business and industry antagonists were reduced to quibbling about complex and mostly unbelievable rationales for enhancing "savings" and "investment."

Making matters especially difficult for Republicans, as the majority party in charge of the Senate, was the fact that all this coverage provided good opportunities for partisan blame throwers. For example, in the Democrats' response to the president's weekly radio address (April 19), Ways and Means Committee member Robert Matsui blasted away, "Tax reform is a sinking ship, and the Senate Republicans are the ones with torpedoes."

Partisan potshots were not a welcome addition to Packwood's troubles. But since this kind of criticism is expected, it could be discounted to some extent. Then again, underestimating the growing power of tax reformers aligned with the pro-tax reform media was far more dangerous. Bradley first sensed the importance of changing the nature of the political game. And Despres correctly pointed out:

> One of the things we did was to make the question of who benefits central to the debate. We were conscious of the need to make the general interest a palpable force [so that] members became conscious that there was a cost to being for special interests. Even if the public wasn't a positive force you had to raise, psychologically, the costs to the politician. For all he knows, the next election challenger could run a T.V. spot zeroing in on some deal he had done. . . . This was a new discipline for people.

The "tar baby" psychology had always been part of the reformers' equation, but its potential force was underestimated in the Senate until Packwood fell victim. Later, Packwood recalled:

> Of course, what really drove us was that the wealthy paid no taxes. So you would go home and get the question from a logger in a coffee shed, "You know, I'm making $18,000 a year, and I pay my share in taxes. I don't mind, but why aren't they [the rich] paying something?" It's an unanswerable question. You say, "Well, it's because they bought municipal bonds or they invested in low-income housing." But, those answers don't work.

Hindsight, including Packwood's, is perfect. But, he *had* ignored the new dynamics of reform, playing instead into the hands of tax reform's opponents—his former soulmates—until the price of friendship became too high. In both political and policy terms, Packwood had built himself a house of cards; ironically, given important changes in the political arena, it was brought down by the same narrow political forces that had built it.

Notes

1. John Witte, *The Politics and Development of The Federal Income Tax* (Madison: University of Wisconsin Press, 1985), 283.
2. Richard Fenno, *Congressmen in Committees* (Boston: Little, Brown, 1973), 157.
3. Catherine Rudder, "Tax Policy: Structure and Choice," in *Making Economic Policy in Congress*, ed. Allen Schick (Washington: American Enterprise Institute, 1983), 211.
4. David B. Price, *Who Makes the Laws? Creativity and Power in Senate Committees* (Cambridge, Mass.: Schenkman Publishing Co., 1972), Chap. 4. For examples of interest-group influence see Alan J. Ciglar and Burdett A. Loomis, *Interest Group Politics* (Washington: CQ Press, 1983); Larry J. Sabato, *PAC Power* (New York: W. W. Norton, 1984); Stephen Miller, *Special Interest Groups in American Politics* (New Brunswick, N.J.: Transaction Books, 1983); and Michael Malbin, ed. *Parties, Interest Groups, and Campaign Finance Laws* (Washington: American Enterprise Institute, 1980).
5. See *Financing the Finance Committee* (Washington: Common Cause, 1986), 3—4; and "Gimme A Break," *Common Cause News*, February 11, 1986.
6. See, for example, Anne Swardson, "Packwood Proposal Seeks Wide Appeal," *Washington Post*, April 7, 1986, A1; Alan Murray and Jeffrey Birnbaum, "Senate Panel's Overhaul Effort Is Betraying Reform Impetus by Preserving Many Tax Breaks," *Wall Street Journal*, April 7, 1986, 54; Jeffrey Birnbaum, "How Tax Overhaul Bill's Scope Is Pared: A Maine Senator Hears His Constituents," *Wall Street Journal*, April 7, 1986, 54.
7. Recent research that has found no relationship between PAC contributions and voting behavior includes W. P. Welch, "Campaign Contributions and Legislative Voting: Milk Money and Dairy Price Supports," *Western Political Quarterly* 32 (Winter 1982): 478—95; Henry W. Chappell, Jr., "Campaign Contributions and Congressional Voting: A Simultaneous Probit-Tobit Model," *Review of Economics and Statistics* 18 (Spring 1982): 77—83; P. J. Feldstein and G. Melnick, "Congressional Voting Behavior on Hospital Legislation: An

Exploratory Study," *Journal of Health Politics, Policy, and Law* 8 (Winter
1984): 686–701; and K. J. Mueller, "An Analysis of Congressional Health
Policy Voting in the 1970s," *Journal of Health Politics, Policy, and Law* 11
(Spring 1986): 117–35. Research that has found at least some relationship
between PAC spending and voting behavior includes Kirk Brown, "Campaign
Contributions and Congressional Voting" (Paper delivered at the annual
meeting of the American Political Science Association, Washington, D.C.,
1983); John Frendeis and Richard Waterman, "PAC Contributions and
Legislative Behavior: Senate Voting on Trucking Deregulation" (Paper delivered at the annual meeting of the Midwest Political Science Association,
Chicago, 1983); James B. Kau and Paul H. Rubin, *Congressmen, Constituents,
and Contributors* (Hingham, Mass.: Martinus Wijhoff, 1982); Diana Yiannakis,
"PAC Contributions and House Voting on Conflictual and Consensual Issues:
The Windfall Profits Tax and the Chrysler Loan Guarantee" (Paper delivered
at the annual meeting of the American Political Science Association, Washington, D.C., 1983); and Laura Langbein, "Money and Access: Some Empirical
Evidence," *Journal of Politics* 48 (November 1986): 1052–62.

8. In order to assess the extent to which PAC contributions predicted congressional support for tax reform we analyzed key votes in both chambers. In the
House we selected nine Ways and Means Committee votes (numbers 20, 29,
31, 38, 45, 49, 53, 55, and 73 out of a sequence of seventy-three recorded votes)
on issues ranging from municipal bonds to banking preferences. Those nine
votes were selected for methodological and theoretical reasons, notably that:
(1) votes were recorded; (2) variation in the dependent variable was sufficiently large that it could be analyzed; (3) amendments were such that votes
could be defined clearly as "for" or "against" tax reform (many other votes
dealt with nonsubstantive issues such as closing the markup). Operationally,
this meant examining each of the nine votes and assigning "for" or "against"
values to cases according to whether or not members were aligned with
Rostenkowski's position. (In the votes used for this analysis his position was
consistently proreform.) These data were then converted into a ten-point scale,
indicating how many proreform votes members cast out of nine chances, with
a score of nine being the most proreform and a score of zero being the least.
Thereafter, Probit and Logit were used to ascertain equations relating PAC
receipts from the previous three election cycles, as independent variables, and
members' proreform scores as the dependent variable. The analysis considered
donations from all three cycles together, in combinations of two, and
individually. Even controlling for party, and the fact that some House
members were involved in high-visibility statewide races, no relationship could
be found. "Liberalness" as measured by Americans for Democratic Action
(ADA) scores was somewhat predictive (.10), but these results were also
statistically insignificant.

The Senate Finance Committee refused to release its recorded committee
votes, but we were able to analyze key Senate floor votes. Given the freedom
of senators to offer floor amendments and the variation observed on several
key votes, Probit/Logit analysis seemed appropriate. We analyzed floor votes
on three key issues: (1) restoring the IRA deduction; (2) raising the top
individual tax rate; (3) preserving the sales-tax deduction (*Congressional
Quarterly Weekly Report* numbers 125, 129, 131). The dependent variable
was operationalized as in the House analysis. Also as in the House analysis,
despite controlling for political party and liberalness, no significant correla-

tions were detected using any combination of independent variables or method of analysis.

9. Sen. Robert Packwood, Finance Committee Remarks, C-Span, Washington, D.C., April 18, 1986.

10. Russell Long quoted from U.S. Senate, Finance Committee Hearings, *Tax Reform Proposals*, Vol. 3, 99th Cong., 2d sess., 53.

11. For example, Senator Dole was majority leader and Senators Durenberger, Roth, Danforth, and Heinz chaired the Intelligence, Governmental Affairs, Commerce, and Aging Committees, respectively. Heinz also headed the Senate Republican Campaign Committee.

12. Bill Bradley, *The Fair Tax* (New York: Pocket Books, 1984), 17.

13. When Rep. Richard Gephardt became Bradley's House sponsor for the legislation, his aide, Jim Jaffe, joined this group. Indeed, Gephardt himself attended occasional meetings.

14. Dale Russakoff, "Bill Bradley Takes His Shot," *Washington Post Magazine*, Feb. 1, 1987, 34.

15. Packwood quoted in Jeffrey H. Birnbaum and Alan S. Murray, *Showdown at Gucci Gulch: Lawmakers, Lobbyists, and the Unlikely Triumph of Tax Reform* (New York: Random House, 1987), 189.

16. Senate Finance Committee, *Tax Reform Proposals—III*, S. Hrg. 99−246, 99th Cong., 2d sess., 1985, 58.

17. *Congressional Quarterly Weekly Report*, April 1, 1986, 1280.

18. In ERTA in 1981, the Republican-led Finance Committee engaged in a partisan bidding war with the House, thereby putting its own stamp on this already expensive legislation. Moreover, in 1982 Finance Committee chairman Bob Dole rolled over the less-skilled Rostenkowski, taking full credit for the historic TEFRA deficit-reduction bill, legislation that was ultimately enacted without a single hearing in the Ways and Means Committee. Finally, in DEFRA (1984), Rostenkowski got back in the game with Dole. Nonetheless, while some say Rosty gave the Kansan as good as he got from Dole, DEFRA reflected at least as many Senate as House provisions.

19. Kurtz quoted in *Tax Notes*, March 25, 1986, 1203.

20. "Moving Backward on Tax Reform," *New York Times*, March 9, 1986, A24.

21. Throughout tax reform a number of senators raised red flags like this one as often for their value as roadblocks as for their merit. The most obvious example was the drive by Sen. Rudy Boschwitz, R-Minn., to put solving the seemingly unsolvable deficit problem ahead of tax reform on the congressional agenda. Even before Packwood I was released, Boschwitz enlisted seven Finance Committee senators along with forty-two others, persuading them to sign a letter urging an explicit change in priorities. When that failed, coconspirator Max Baucus offered a similarly directed nonbinding "sense of the Senate" resolution. The vote (which occurred on April 10) was a successful 74−24, and it included thirteen of twenty Finance Committee members. Looking back, it is clear that at least some member opposition to curtailing excise-tax deductions was equally calculated. As Symms gloated, "This excise tax is ingenious. It will just about gut any support for the bill."

22. James Rowe, "Municipal Bond Market Sinks," *Washington Post*, March 20, 1986, E1, 6.

23. Packwood quoted in *Tax Notes*, March 25, 1986, 1313.

24. See, for example, Rowland Evans and Robert Novak, "Tax Reform or Sausage," *Washington Post*, April 18, 1986, A21; David Rosenbaum, "Tax

Revision in the Senate: A Question of Leadership," *New York Times*, April 24, 1986, D1, 2; and Jeffrey Birnbaum, "Packwood Finds His Leading Role on Tax Bill Provides a Boost in Senate Reelection Campaign," *Wall Street Journal*, July 7, 1986, 34.

25. Tax expenditures estimated in "Joint Tax Committee Estimates FY '86—'90 Tax Expenditures," quoted in *Tax Notes*, April 22, 1985, 401—11.

26. Sen. John Chafee, C-Span, Washington, D.C., April 18, 1986.

7   From Goat to Gloat: The Triumph
of Tax Reform in the Senate

If you don't believe in miracles, you're not a realist.
—Robert Packwood, May 7, 1986

Was Packwood I, as Pryor had said, too lame to ride? "Definitely," observed witnesses to the events of April 18. While Monday-morning quarterbacks blamed Bob Packwood for being too self-serving and inexperienced, the bottom line was that Packwood was too alone. "The fact of the matter is," David Brockway observed, "tax reform was failing—not because Packwood decided to oppose reform—but because the committee wasn't ready to vote for it." Indeed, looking around at his colleagues and self-interested bystanders, Packwood easily could rationalize that he had not failed at political consensus building—it had failed him. Thus isolated from friends and foes, he left the hearing room for a private lunch at the Irish Times bar with his top committee aide, Bill Diefenderfer. Speculation that this might finally be the end of tax reform was rampant.

The independent westerner didn't think so. After all, mavericks are used to being alone. Certainly Packwood had been during the Reagan presidency on issues ranging from military weapons sales to abortion. Thus, while a few of his staff were quietly contemplating the prospect of inglorious defeat over nouvelle cuisine at the nearby American Cafe, Packwood was on another side of the Capitol, planning his comeback over hamburgers and beer.

Realistically, Packwood had two options. He could push a stripped-down version of tax reform. Alternatively, he could fall back on "Bradley basics." That afternoon Packwood decided to try the latter—tax reform by the book. He called it "the radical approach," offering a top individual tax rate of 25 percent paid for by the elimination of nearly all existing exemptions, credits, and deductions. By his own admission, Packwood selected 25 percent for its symbolic value. "It was magic," he later said, "a quarter of one hundred." If the strategy worked, it would be a tremendous victory, greater than Rostenkowski's. If Packwood failed, he would go down trying to do the right thing. As he reasoned, the finger of blame for killing tax reform would be redirected toward his colleagues and their special-interest allies. He recalled:

> Bill [Diefenderfer] and I said to each other, "[The committee members] said they wanted a tax reform bill. Let's go back and—sort of like strapping on your guns at the O.K. Corral—let's go back and give them a tax reform bill." I don't know if it was because we wanted to see if their offer was a bluff or whether it was because about the only way we were going to succeed was to start with a bill that was real tax reform and fight to keep it [rather than] start with one that wasn't and attempt to transform it.

Yet, the idea was not just coy politics dreamed up over a few pitchers of beer. Throughout the previous summer's hearings Packwood had listened to elaborate defenses and overstated claims in support of hundreds of well-known and obscure tax breaks. And, he had not *always* liked what he heard. When a New Jersey official argued that there would always be a public purpose served when tax-exempt bonds are used by businesses in distressed urban areas, Packwood countered in frustration, "Would a massage parlor serve a public purpose?" The answer brought outright laughter from the audience: "Yes, I guess you could say that. So long as it was in a distressed area." By mid-August 1985, growing skepticism had already led Packwood to reconsider publicly the need for most tax incentives *if* rates could be radically reduced. Before fleeing the hearing room that Friday, Packwood once again publicly told the remaining onlookers:

> Basically, I think Bradley's concept is right. The lower we can get those rates, the better off we are going to be. And, if we can get it down to 25 percent, there will be a sea change in the debate over the political implications of deductions. . . . People will say, "At that rate, I don't mind giving a quarter of my income to the federal government so long as I can keep the other three-quarters." [1]

Packwood's switch in time to rescue tax reform was both a political and an intellectual catharsis. As committee member Mitchell observed, politicians are capable of intertwining career interests, politics, and philosophy in any decision they make:

> I think probably it was both politics and policy and a lot more. He's a man who is chairman of a major committee and Rostenkowski's just produced a bill for which people are saying, "Now, there's a chairman." This was a test of Packwood's leadership, wholly independent of the merits of the issue. Sure he wanted to get a bill, just as anybody in those shoes would.

Ultimately, the chairman's intellectual conversion deepened as he invested himself in the process of crafting, then selling the Packwood II proposal. The powerful ideas behind tax reform seduced Packwood in increments, and his attachment intensified as his experience deepened. Such psychological co-optation is common along Washington's power corridors where institutional demands and the responsibilities of high office force officials to carry messages that are not initially their own. As Buck Chapoton concluded, "Sure, Packwood became a convert. Remember, he had to produce a package. Then, it became his work product. We all become imbued with our babies."

Tax Reform by the Book

Ploy or brave deed, Packwood's decision made him the unexpected father of tax-reform in the Senate. He chose a "zero-based" tax-reform strategy where, in exchange for the lowest possible rates, previously undiscriminating members were challenged to set priorities. Slashing rates also increased the political salience of distributional considerations. "Who benefits" became politically more explosive because retaining tax breaks used by wealthier taxpayers *and* halving the top rate would have rendered the bill an embarrassing windfall for the rich. Altogether, Packwood's strategy was a high-stakes yet brilliant tactical maneuver, one that simultaneously enticed and threatened members. A tax-reform opponent on the committee commented, "As soon as we saw that top rate, we knew we were in trouble with conservatives and liberals." In the process, Packwood found a phalanx of ready support from Bradley, his allies, and the JTC staff. Indeed, the distribution of power among interest groups, staffs, and junior and senior committee members shifted almost 180 degrees as Packwood rejected the established practices of committee scions and turned for help to those he had until now rejected.

Joint Tax Committee to the Rescue

Packwood's first steps toward "real reform" took him to David Brockway's door. Packwood instructed the JTC to prepare a proposal with top rates of 25 percent for individuals and 33 percent for corporations. Beyond that, the professionals had a virtual blank check to fill in the details on the individual side of the tax code. However (proving that traditional politics was never entirely abandoned), the politically touchy area of corporate taxation remained in John Colvin's province and thus was virtually unchanged from the first round to the second round of Finance Committee action. Naturally, the plan was to be revenue-neutral.

The swap of staff responsibilities amounted to a near reversal of tax-writing roles from the Packwood I period. JTC's newly acquired clout came from its expertise and its capacity to offer Packwood political cover. Of chief importance, Brockway's troops were well suited to pursue serious tax reform. "Staff here had been working on this our entire careers," Brockway asserted. "We knew all the issues. We had the talent. So, we were ready when the opportunity came up." In its most basic elements the resulting plan was a textbook model of tax reform driven by a few simple ideas and values with conforming details filled in. As shaped by the JTC, a "fair" plan translated into one in which (within the constraints imposed by a low-rate system) tax reductions favored as much as possible the lowest-income taxpayers and in which income from all sources was treated uniformly. A "simple" plan was one that reduced the number of tax brackets and encouraged taxpayers not to itemize. Economic efficiency was to flow from a level playing field, an assumption that provided ample justification for discouraging investments in money-losing over money-making enterprises.

On April 24 Packwood called his committee together to consider the JTC's handiwork. Seventeen members were present in the "exec room," a small meeting area adjacent to the Finance Committee hearing room. Only Dole, who kept an appointment with the president, Spark Matsunaga, D-Hawaii, and Symms were absent. Around the small conference table faces showed a mixture of curiosity and tension. What would be Packwood's next step?

The chairman's bold plan was soon obvious. "Bill Bradley was right," he began in a matter-of-fact way, handing out a brief, one-page description of the Bradley-Gephardt Fair Tax plan. As Packwood resumed his enthusiastic primer on the virtues of rate reduction through base broadening, members sat in surprised silence. Even Bradley was taken aback, for he had not been contacted since the canceled markup. A few other Democrats appeared confused, and disgruntled Republicans wondered whether this meant that Packwood was substituting Bradley's plan, in effect raising the white flag of partisan surrender to the Democrats.

All such speculation ended as the next two sheets of paper were handed out. Packwood's answer was a plan in many ways bolder than anything yet seen in the arena of tax reform. As Packwood had ordered, the main features included an individual top tax rate slashed by half to 25 percent and a top corporate rate dropped by one-third to 33 percent. Insofar as preferences for individual taxpayers were concerned, the cupboard was bare. Even the sacrosanct deduction for home mortgage interest was gone. At the same time, in the area of corporate taxation, the plan was a deft combination of retained sweeteners from the earlier amendment spree and a single "plug number," signifying that $75 billion would be raised from further, unspecified changes. Twenty-five billion dollars in undetermined excise taxes filled in the remaining gap. With the top corporate rate slashed from 46 to 33 percent, $75 billion represented a modest contribution to tax reform from interests so closely tied to the Finance Committee. Even Treasury II had raised $120 billion. All in all, the proposal was an inventive combination of sweeping reform and politics-as-usual.

The meeting lasted two hours. There were those who liked the idea. Indeed, Packwood counted six who told him he was heading in the right direction. There were more who did not, though, and skeptics formed the largest group of all. The most eloquent among them was Russell Long. Like master to apprentice, he admonished his colleagues' "mild euphoria" because "it would evaporate under the harsh light of reality." Of course, the senior Democrat's speech held an important, but unspoken subtext of opposition, indicating that Packwood would have to reach deeper into Democratic ranks to find bipartisan support. In fact, however, the chairman already had bypassed Long by anchoring his proposal with Bradley's principles.

Naturally, the senator from New Jersey was elated. Despite the beating Bradley had taken from Packwood during markup and the fact that Packwood had rather quickly and, perhaps, too conveniently backed into Bradley's corner, the Democrat welcomed his new-found ally with no questions asked. Successful legislators have long recognized the value of sharing credit to achieve their goals. Bradley had done it with Gephardt, with the White House, and later with Rostenkowski, so he was more than willing to support Republican Packwood—in direction if not detail—for the larger cause of tax reform. Thus, he was the first to stand up for Packwood at the meeting.

By the end of the session when hands were finally raised, Packwood counted eleven members in favor of reporting a bill and five adamantly opposed. With this weak go-ahead and an admonition to put back preferences Bradley later described as "the truly sacred cows," Packwood adjourned the meeting.

Outside in the hallways of the Dirksen office building, interpretations were mixed. Bradley reported that the committee had received the proposal "politely" but that he "didn't see any bushes burning." Still, he urged reporters to see that the important thing was *direction*, not *specifics*. Best of all, Bradley lectured, "There was a turn toward putting everything on the loophole side on the table." Others gave the press a more skeptical reading, one chiding that middle-class taxpayers would surely resent being placed in the same marginal bracket as millionaires.[2] Indeed, later, Dole went so far as to claim that tax reform itself was "on the ropes."

Tax Reformers to the Rescue (Again)

Understandably worried about press coverage, Packwood had hoped to prevent premature leaks. But when committee member Bill Roth tipped journalists by sharing his work sheets with them, Packwood's staff scurried to control potential damage by contriving to name Brockway, not Packwood, as author of the plan and by scheduling a JTC-led press conference to field reporters' questions. The decisions were amateurish and unprecedented, and they reflected more than a little desperation. According to Packwood's aide Mary McAuliffe: "We were wrecks, so worried that the press would call Packwood a desperate or crazy man that we had David [Brockway] announce it. We gave him about three hours' notice, and he was great about it. We stood him out there so the press would push David, not Packwood."

However justified, the strategy failed miserably as a ploy to deflect responsibility. Seemingly undeterrable reporters kept calling questions to Packwood who, in turn, tried lamely to redirect them to a shell-shocked Brockway. Making matters worse, years of tax politics experience made it nearly impossible for reporters to take the bare-bones proposal as serious policy. So, they stuck mostly to politics in next-day coverage, casting doubt on Packwood's sincerity and aspersions on his character.[3]

Rebounding on Sunday, a surprisingly upbeat chairman appeared on a nationally televised public-affairs program. Almost immediately it was apparent to insiders that the mercurial Packwood had discarded the earlier subterfuge and become born again on the matter of tax reform. McAuliffe recalled: "I watched 'Meet the Press' on Sunday. We wanted Packwood to stay away [from it]. But, he went on, and he talked like [the 25 percent proposal] was the greatest thing he had heard of in his life. We were less comfortable. But staff's job is to be nervous for the boss."

Staff fears notwithstanding, Packwood had plenty of political incentive to forge ahead. And he also had his own characteristic single-minded determination pushing him along.

Meanwhile, Brockway had gone back to the computers to put together a proposal that would both qualify as real reform *and* secure majority support. Both he and Packwood knew that the plan could not be a cornucopia for the rich. They also knew that the only way to lower rates without such a windfall was to follow Bradley, devaluing or eliminating tax preferences that principally benefited this top group of taxpayers.

Which loopholes should be put back, and which should be closed? The least likely candidates for closing were those that benefited middle-income taxpayers, including charitable contributions, state and local property and income taxes, and medical expenses. The most likely were those that were the exclusive domain of wealthy taxpayers, especially those that couldn't be defended on grounds of economic growth. Following this logic, Brockway made surgical strikes on a few lucrative pockets of individual tax avoidance by disallowing so-called passive losses against other taxable income, repealing capital gains exclusions, and phasing out some deductions for certain higher-income taxpayers. By Tuesday, April 29, the plan was ready.

Passive loss reform contributed the lion's share of monies Brockway needed to keep the plan revenue-neutral. Historically, this was a key means by which the very rich protected their income from taxation. The trick lies in making investments that generate paper losses in excess of contributions, taking care not to risk more money than is ventured. Common examples are shares in limited real estate partnerships and oil wells. Investors are simply money partners in operations that, given the way tax laws are set up, are guaranteed to produce large paper losses that can be used to offset real income and so to reduce taxes.

Brockway proposed to bar taxpayers from using passive losses in this way. Actually, it was an old idea whose time he hoped had come.[4] Indeed, insofar as passive loss restrictions are concerned, scholarly credit goes to Stanley Surrey. A narrower version had actually passed the House a decade earlier, and in 1984 Moynihan and Chafee proposed barring passive losses when calculating an AMT. Finally, as recently as March 1986, Treasury had proposed the idea to Packwood. Ultimately, however, credit goes to Brockway for, like all successful entrepreneurs, his talent lay in creative timing.

A Core Group of Support

Armed with what he believed was a workable plan, Packwood called the committee together on Tuesday, April 29, for a second members-only meeting. During these back-room sessions Packwood's prospects brightened considerably with the emergence of what was known as his "core group" of tax-reform supporters: Bradley, Chafee, Danforth, Mitchell, Moynihan, and Wallop. The group met with Packwood each morning and on a critical weekend, crafting and successfully selling reform to balky colleagues. The TRA owes much to the quick enlistment of these members, whose ideologically broad, bipartisan coalition put substantial pressure on the remaining thirteen Finance Committee members, who feared being left at the station when and if the tax-reform train pulled out.

In the beginning, though, few core group members believed that such a plan would succeed. Why, then, did they participate? The answer seems to be that, as in all legislative coalitions, more than altruism or statesmanship united them. Their reasons for joining also included short-term political benefits, personal relationships, and individual interests and policy proclivities. For example, a phone call from Bradley lured reform-minded Mitchell to the first meeting, and friendship helped bring Chafee to Packwood's side. Wallop and Moynihan were drawn less by partisanship or past camaraderie than by pent-up personal exasperation. Moynihan, the urbane ex-Harvard professor, seems also to have heard the siren song of an intellectually intriguing exercise, one that promised to strengthen Americans' faith in the tax system. Wallop's decision was less intellectual; by all accounts, the Wyoming conservative was driven nearly exclusively by a belief that simplicity and low rates would be good for the economy and for Americans.

As for political payoffs, only a few core group members such as Bradley guaranteed their votes without attaching a price tag. Most wanted something. Moynihan hoped to limit damage to the deduction for state and local taxes, and Danforth contrived to protect a very expensive provision important to a big defense contractor in his state. Oil and gas was Wallop's achilles heel. Indeed, later, in the heat of battling over these breaks he left the core group, joining those intent on securing even more generous treatment for the industry.

Good intentions, intellectual whims, political self-interest, and personal and partisan loyalties are all common motives for joining legislative coalitions. In ways crucial for tax reform, however, the alliance was also unprecedented. Most important, the group was an unusually wide mix of conservatives and liberals. As reformers had hoped from the start, the combination of supply-side economics and populist politics began to form a powerful alliance carrying tax reform to the president's desk.

A second feature of the core group that was unique in recent committee experience was its bipartisan group decision making. As a Democratic senator recalled, centralized control and partisan coalitions had been the hallmarks of Dole's tenure.

> When Dole was chairman, the Republicans would hold a private conference on the day before markups. They had an internal decision rule that once they voted something in caucus, all would be for it. So on a twenty-member committee with eleven Republicans on the committee, six votes could carry an issue.

In contrast, throughout his chairmanship Long operated on a nonpartisan, quid-pro-quo basis. As one Long critic said, "Russell didn't work from a group, he sold indulgences."

Packwood's new approach focused on policy, and it was bipartisan and collegial. A staff member explained:

> Packwood met every day at 8:30 with the core group members in his office. We had assignments for them every day, working through the individual deduction issues and how they affected the distribution. That was the way it went, every day the core group meeting, looking at the options, comparing old alternatives against the distribution, and thinking up new ones.

Throughout this brief yet critical period when policy making was dominated by the core group, the chances of ultimate success were enhanced immeasurably by the powerful and convincing alliance of Republican Packwood and Democrat Bradley—the latter having eclipsed Long as the major Democratic voice on tax policy. These two dogged reformers worked long hours with the core group and the committee members, cajoling, compromising, even conniving, and, as a result, snowballing ever faster toward their shared goal.

Among the many meetings of the core group of tax-reform supporters, the most important occurred on May 3 when—unknown to lobbyists or reporters—they gathered to hammer out the final details of the Packwood II proposal. Richard Darman, who had sat in on a number of the meetings, attended, as did Roger Mentz, Ronald Pearlman's replacement as assistant secretary for tax policy. James Baker, an irregular participant in Senate action, was again absent, this time traveling to Tokyo with President Reagan for a long-scheduled economic summit. The personal staff of core group members rounded out the unlikely assemblage.

Significantly, that weekend was one of a handful of times when the administration was clearly visible in the Senate tax-reform process. And, as was always true on such occasions, Darman, not Mentz, called the shots. Among the president's aides the witty and arrogant Darman was the important administration player in the Senate, encouraging the process along, contributing his own ideas, and securing administration acquiescence (if not enthusiastic support). So dominant was he that Mentz, the nation's lanky and somewhat down-faced chief expert on tax policy, often appeared to serve as assistant to the quicker and more lively Darman. A staff member present at the meeting described their relationship:

> Darman was clearly in charge over Mentz. He was a big-picture guy, there to represent the secretary and the president. Mentz was the expert. Darman is a talker. He is a very confident person who dealt on the same level as senators. He and Moynihan go way back, for example. He was the kind of guy that took a lot of ribbing, which helps. Both Mentz and Treasury's legislative counsel viewed him negatively because of it. It was very unusual for a deputy secretary to take over tax policy like that.

Apart from finding $25 billion in revenues in the politically sensitive area of corporate taxation that continued to be Colvin's domain, the greatest difficulty the eclectic mix of personalities and philosophies faced that weekend was weighing retained preferences against distributional consequences. Popular but expensive deductions not generally thought of as loopholes were nearly sacrificed, notably the ones for state and local income and property taxes. With the sales-tax deduction already lost, Moynihan aide Joe Gale recalled how the other deductions were saved:

> Try as they might, they kept coming back with the tax cut too large for upper-income groups. One way to get the distribution back in line surgically was to put a ceiling cap or a percentage limit on what was left of our deduction. Mitchell was pushing that and Bradley too. That's where Moynihan said, "Look we've already tithed with the sales tax. Any further hit and I walk."

Catching the Tax Train

Unprecedented intensity and around-the-clock staff work paid off. Only six days after its first meeting and just four full committee meetings later, the small core group presented the Packwood II proposal in open markup, standing fast behind it during heated closed-door sessions that followed. With few substantive changes, the proposal passed the Finance Committee less than forty-eight hours later by the astounding vote of 20−0!

Packwood and Bradley had won resoundingly, leaving the rest of Washington to sputter, "How could this happen?" There is no doubt that the progress of Packwood and the core group turned the tables on traditionally entrenched interest groups by threatening and seducing their spokesmen on the committee. Thanks to these stalwart seven, other committee members began feeling both the push of politics and the pull of a truly momentous event unfolding before them. Each worried that a sudden, unscheduled departure of the tax-reform train would leave them behind, subject to media criticism, and unable to cut any kind of deal on behalf of their constituents. In addition, more and more members became caught up in the sense that history was being written, that something altogether different was propelling the legislation.[5]

Keeping Members In and Keeping Others Out

Success in establishing a new sense of group purpose and in holding members' attention during long meetings depended on maintaining a climate conducive to "table talk." A seasoned staff member believed that simplicity was one key to engaging members' interests.

> They were obviously trying to build emotion behind the idea. And it certainly built over time. The whole atmosphere was a dramatic change, and, in part, I'm convinced that the one-page description and a couple of backups made it understandable in plain English. It was not some thick document with a lot of specific rules about which interest got what.

Even so, it was history in progress that made this togetherness unusually potent. As Brockway observed:

> It's not simply a bunch of guys sitting in a room. It was feeling that you were doing something for your country. Members were susceptible to this feeling. It's rare that this happens, but it sometimes does. It was just a wonderful atmosphere. . . . Now we weren't the bad guys, putting the brakes on a proposal to help this interest or that, the kind of crap that usually goes on here in the Finance Committee.

Critical mass would not have been achieved without a new and higher level of secrecy as well. As in the House, secrecy meant closing the door to the "public," thus allowing members to say one thing in the hallway while doing another in the back room.

But from Packwood's viewpoint, it wasn't sufficient to sequester the members from outside interests. Fostering the right climate also meant "protecting" the committee from the members' own personal staff who normally hover behind them, whispering the pros, but more often the cons, of tax reform. In the minds of some realists, "Tax counsels are the liaison between members and special-interest groups." Their job typically is "to figure out how members can take care of their interests and constituents and then negotiate for them on their bosses' behalf."

Booting out personal staff not only limited members' access to troublesome details that are the undisputed forte of technically and constituency-minded tax counsels, it also helped prevent unwelcome leaks. As one such counsel acknowledged, it wasn't just what personal staff said *in* meetings that could hurt tax reform, it was also what they said *outside:*

> It was other members' staff that you were worried about. You protect your own senator, but you don't have to protect anybody else's. A legislative assistant might go to an interest group and say, "Hey, you told me that so and so was going to carry the water for you. Boy have I got news for you."

Of course, Packwood continued to enjoy the presence of his own small army of staff. On the question of who benefited from this imbalance of expertise, one tax counsel grumbled:

> They might have thought that members were happy not having their staffs nattering about special interests. But that is bullshit. The fact is, Packwood's people were there. Joint Tax was there, and they work for Bob Packwood. So he is briefed on the details, and other members are at a great disadvantage. We are not talking about simple stuff, so the cards were stacked in favor of Bob Packwood. It was almost like, "Let's leave the pros out because they are always raising issues."

Whether the participation of these professionals would have doomed tax reform will never be known. By the close of the first week of committee action, though, the political winds had shifted. Dole was the first to recognize the change. On Monday he reported, "Tax reform is hanging by a thread." By Tuesday he revised his comment to, "It's hanging by a rope." On Wednesday he convened a secret meeting of Finance Committee Republicans to endorse Packwood's plan.

By the following week, tax reform seemed destined to be reported, if not enacted. In part, this success was due to Packwood's skill at managing committee deliberations and a fortuitous combination of staff and committee membership. At the same time, a number of those closest to the process believed the unfolding drama had "an inevitability to it, almost like a Shakespearean play." Whether success ultimately owed more to individual efforts or to deterministic forces, four tide-turning factors made it possible.

The In-Crowd. Important as its substantive contribution was, the ultimate value of the core group was more the result of strategy than of policy because its presence posed a threat to those lagging behind. It was impossible for nonmembers to dismiss the numbers: the core group amounted to more than half of the eleven votes needed to report tax reform. Moreover, the group was a cohesive unit that mirrored the committee's partisan and ideological makeup. Last, the core group gained power by backing what Danforth called an "electrifying" idea. It is an old lesson of politics that "You can't beat something with nothing." Earlier, Sen. David Boren's killer coalition had milked feelings of apathy and agreed to stop Packwood. Now, caught off guard, they had nothing tantalizing enough to make a plausible substitute.

Caught with the Knife. There was universal agreement that the change owed much to the simple fear of being blamed for killing tax reform. During the amendment spree in early April, Packwood took most of the heat for failing. Burdens then shifted. The core group members began touting themselves as models of self-sacrifice. As Packwood later reported, "Each of us could stand before our colleagues and say that we had given up something as an indication of good faith." And they received press acclaim for doing so. *The Washington Post* applauded Packwood and the core group for promising more reform than any previous proposal. Going even further, the *New York Times* said, "What is now needed [is a] strong dose of fortitude." [6] Without a corresponding show of good faith, the committee members who opposed the core group would surely be blamed in the event of failure.

To be sure, directing blame or credit for tax reform was not at that time on the minds of average Americans. The members' fear was real but anticipatory, conjured up by media drumbeating and the threat of editorialists who sat with pens poised to criticize the faint-hearted. Thus, faced with Packwood's experience as an object lesson in what comes of dodging responsibility, fearing recriminations in upcoming elections or at other critical times, reluctant Finance Committee members found more reason to support than to oppose tax reform. Besides, it needn't be permanent. As Moynihan said, "It was a liberating experience to say 'our country' for six months. Later, there would be time to reconstruct old relationships."

Monetary Magic. Low rates posed a different kind of enticement, one that, an aide observed, pulled members in like a magnet:

> It was impossible to vote against rates that were that low because everyone had always said, "Well if the rates were only truly low, I wouldn't mind losing this or that." Then, too, low rates were something the American public could understand. It seemed dangerous to vote against something that was that understandable.

Members were equally candid about the allure of low rates. According to one: "We changed position because Packwood came up with two figures that were credible. All the negativism disappeared. We never thought as a group whether those two numbers were good or bad. There was never any discussion of that." And, according to a second:

> Senator Packwood did the boldest thing I have ever seen done in the Senate. He took that bill away from the Finance Committee and then several days later he came back to us and said, "What do you think about a proposal with two individual rates, 15 percent and 27 percent, and a 33 percent corporate rate?" That was a bold stroke that captured the imagination of the committee members. We were electrified by it.[7]

Having It Both Ways.   The final reason members hopped aboard the tax-reform train was that they could bring their corporate baggage along with them. In truth, on the business side of the tax code, Packwood's revolutionary reform bill was not very radical. With the exception of repealing the ITC (a foregone conclusion) and strengthening the AMT, Packwood left entire portions of the corporate tax code nearly untouched or weakened by earlier committee action. Colvin correctly pointed out:

> Most of the corporate side was never marked up in a detailed way. Depreciation was [making it more costly than under present law]. Natural resources was dealt with by preserving present law. Bonds was dealt with [loosened substantially over both House and administration proposals]. So, if it had been dealt with [before April 18] it was kept. Most corporate provisions had not, though, and they were kept as we had drafted them.

Last-Minute Deals

A close analysis of transition rules and amendments to the reported bill reveals how even the modest pain of corporate reform was eased through various deals on behalf of powerful clients of the Finance Committee. One individual who sat in on these negotiations on the final night described them as follows:

> We had a list of things we had to play with that we had to stick in the bill. We were short money, and Packwood was standing up there talking like an auctioneer: "I've got fifty [million] here. Can I take fifty [million] there?" Overall, that's what it came down to. He was holding up this paper and auctioning off provisions in order to pay for the last few special deals.

As would be expected, of all the last-minute maneuvers that took place on Tuesday, May 6, the oil and gas bloc's was the most successful. Throughout the twelve days between Black Friday and the final vote, the oil and gas coalition met often to gauge its position and plan its moves. In the end, oil and gas action came down to a back-room skirmish over partial exemptions from the AMT and from the passive investment rules for so-called working interests in these ventures. Boren was the most vocal proponent, but he spoke for more senior members, notably Long, Dole, and Bentsen. Behind the technical smokescreen, Boren's rationale was pure regional politics. Appropriately, it was Long who made the point clear when, responding to Mitchell's charge that exceptions were unjustified, he castigated the former judge for "blind justice."

> We fellas are lawmakers. We're supposed to know who we're helping and do it deliberately and know who we're hurting and do that deliberately. Now, the people in the oil and gas business are the most depressed industry in the United States. If you're sitting over there in court, I can understand your saying, "I'm blindfolded. I'm going to treat them all the same. This fella's broke, down and out. God knows he needs help. But, the hell with him. I can't do anything about that." If you're a judge, that's how you do it. If you're a lawmaker, you'd say, "That poor fella needs help. Let's help him." [8]

Rhetoric notwithstanding, the outcome was only a matter of who had the votes. In the end it was not Packwood, and so energy-state senators won their amendments to protect tax benefits enjoyed by "working interests" in oil and gas projects. Like others, Boren owed his committee assignment to Long, and all had profited handily from the alliance. It was a nonideological, nonpartisan marriage of convenience that no one, not even Wallop, was about to abandon, tax reform or no tax reform.

Energy's strong track record, in turn, was enough to convince the core group that, without an accommodation, the committee might be unable to report a bill. It shows that, even during a period of remarkable esprit de corps, traditional alliances never wholly broke down. Although other interest groups were less powerful and less successful, there is little doubt that many got substantially more from Finance than from Ways and Means.

With the oil and gas bloc satisfied, the committee returned to open session shortly after midnight. After a few unsuccessful Bradley amendments directed at oil and gas, the moment was at hand. At precisely 12:17 A.M., May 7, 1986, with a new-found voice of authority Packwood was able to say, "Will the clerk call the roll." One by one, rumpled-looking tax reform travelers voted "aye." For some on the dais, like Bradley, it was a well-deserved victory. For others, like Boren, it was a defeat. For the audience that had waited through the night it was unforgettable. By a vote of 20−0, Packwood had answered the question of whether he could lead. In so doing, the teary-eyed Finance Committee chairman sent H.R. 3838 to the full Senate, where its fate would be decided.

Taming the Senate Floor

After nearly forty years in Congress, Russell Long knew when it was time to cut his losses. Thus, it was no surprise that shortly before the core group's proposal was unveiled publicly on May 5, Long released his Democratic troops, urging them to support Packwood. Not that he had much to release. While Long easily enjoyed more respect than any member of the Finance Committee, in today's democratic Senate not even he could deliver the votes of his junior colleagues. Nor could Packwood guarantee his own troops, leaving him unsure of the final vote count as senators filed out of the exec room and into the camera lights.

For example, although Long had personally urged Sen. David Pryor to "be with Bob," the most junior committee member was determined to vote against the bill right up to the last minute. Pryor might have held to that decision had he not—by rank and party—been the last to vote. Waiting for his turn, Pryor listened as one after the other of his colleagues voted yes, including Boren. In the face of this momentum, like the last domino in line, Pryor fell under the weight of what everyone in the Dirksen hearing room now recognized was a truly historic occasion.

Experienced eyes saw the 20−0 vote as the Senate turning point: "You cannot underestimate the importance of not having anyone on the committee sniping at the bill on the floor," one asserted. Few Senate watchers would disagree. Historically, the freewheeling and unpredictable Senate floor has been the site of major modifications and amendment sprees in which billions of dollars of tax revenue have been lost to members' pet interests. Thanks to the disorderly conduct through which amendments are offered (they cannot be officially scheduled in the Senate), managers of tax bills do not always know what amendments are coming or in what form, though experience dictates they will eventually arrive. Senators, who are generalists by nature, regard most legislation as fair game, and they pay substantially less deference to committee expertise and proprietary claims than their House counterparts. Thus, whereas Rostenkowski's version of H.R. 3838 whisked across the House floor virtually untouched once its rule was approved, Packwood's prospects for escaping unscathed were dubious at best. Indeed, although the tax-reform train was rolling at full speed on June 4 when it reached the Senate floor, even minority leader Robert Byrd, D-W.Va., was unwilling to give up this chance to rearrange the box cars. As he warned in a floor speech:

> I do not believe that the Senate will be carrying out its responsibility under the Constitution and to the American people if we simply give the tax bill a slight look and say, "Let's not have any amendments here." That is not the way I see the responsibility of the Senate.[9]

Typically, Finance Committee chairmen have shown considerable willingness to accept such amendments. Long even defended the practice, saying, "A strong horse can carry a lot of riders." Indeed, despite Dole's considerable skills as a floor manager, debate over ERTA in 1981 lasted over one hundred hours, during which nearly as many amendments were agreed to. Even during periods of loophole closing in 1982 and 1984, Dole was forced to swallow a combined total of over 130 amendments during 150 hours of debate.

Given this history, it was smart for Packwood and his staff to resist counting their chickens yet. Indeed, Packwood's trepidation was complicated by the delicate fiscal balance of the legislation reported. Before budgetary red ink and revenue neutrality, amendments could ride on bills more or less free of charge. However, the ground rules had changed. Thanks to the fiscal vise of the new Gramm-Rudman budget process and to tax reform's obedience to the principle of revenue neutrality, floor amendments to H.R. 3838 were expected to be self-financing, taking from one part of the tax code to pay for changing another.

Once again, the standard of revenue neutrality worked like a double-edged sword. On one hand, it made possible the alliance between a president who refused to raise taxes and a Congress that, locked in partisan combat, feared being blamed for increasing the deficit. Revenue neutrality also helped forge the coalition between those on the ideological right who wanted lower tax rates and those on the left who wanted to eliminate loopholes for the wealthy.

On the other hand, the sacrosanct standard also left Packwood in a tight spot. Acquiescing to many amendments not only would endanger the fiscal integrity of the legislation and add to the mountainous deficit, changes in the after-tax distribution of benefits might also force a cascade of further changes in the bill, unraveling its delicate support. Running through the list of expected amendments—restoration of all or part of the IRA deduction, a reprieve or stay of execution for those who itemize their state and local sales taxes, a rate reduction for capital gains, and perhaps even an amendment to loosen passive loss restrictions—it was obvious that the lion's share of benefits from alterations would go to high-income taxpayers. If passed, these changes would almost certainly draw fire from liberal supporters, perhaps triggering a second round of amendments to increase progressivity. Higher rates, in turn, would lose Packwood businesses and corporations that were counting on rate reductions to offset the loss of tax incentives as well as conservatives who believed that low rates were compensation for repealing savings and investment incentives.

A final, revenue-related problem Packwood faced was that the Finance-passed bill had no cash reserve with which to acquire votes with transition rules or minor changes. (Rostenkowski had reserved such a rainy-day fund of $5 billion.)

Packwood's Strategy for Controlling the Floor

Recognizing the dangers and advantages of revenue neutrality and the delicate nature of his support, Packwood could not follow time-tested strategies for managing the unruly Senate floor. Looking for something different, he turned to Dole, Bradley, his core group, and tax reform's allies outside government for help. Together they devised and carried out a strategy for disciplining the floor consideration.

Along with some ordinary as well as some unusual parliamentary subterfuge, Packwood's tactics included: (1) the application of revenue neutrality rules to all amendments; (2) the use of an ideologically wide, bipartisan, and expanded core group of nearly thirty-five senators agreeing to oppose all amendments; and, (3) the forceful lobbying of an equally wide coalition of seven hundred business, social, and consumer groups. In addition, live television coverage of the Senate floor worked to his advantage.

In the end, this combination of good fortune, spade work, and clever management carried the Finance Committee's handiwork safely past the usual gauntlet of would-be tax artists and craftsmen lying in wait on the Senate floor. When tax reform finally passed the Senate on June 24 by a lopsided margin of 97−3, those who had hoped to change the bill had offered far fewer amendments than usual. Only twenty-four amendments were voted on over the course of twenty calendar days. Most of the amendments failed, including all of the "killer amendments" that had been portrayed (in one or two cases correctly) as middle-class issues. Thus, as policy makers steered their revenue-neutral course, for the first time in recent memory, a tax bill exited the floor in virtually the same fiscal state as it had entered.

In retrospect, there were only four important tests of Packwood's floor strategy, two of them (amendments on IRAs and on state and local tax deductions) coming early in the process and a third (proposals to add a third top individual rate) coming quite late. In addition, the strategy was tested against a flurry of high-minded amendments to repeal some of the most grievous transition rules that Packwood had used to buy support both on and off the Finance Committee.

Testing the Calculus

Once the Finance Committee reported tax reform, it happily adjourned for the two-week Memorial Day holiday. For JTC and committee staff, the holiday never began. Their recess was spent in legislative drafting and report writing because, as usual, it was up to the staff to finally say what the members had actually done. With a task so large and time so short, the legislation and accompanying language were not actually available until very shortly before the legislation was to be considered. The late release and JTC delays in responding to requests for revenue estimates (to be used with possible amendments) contributed to a nearly deserted floor for days after the bill was officially taken up. Senators and their staffs, still struggling to understand 1,300-plus pages of statutory and report language, had yet to decide if they liked what they were reading. Thus, few were willing or able to venture to the floor to suggest changes.

Delays in producing revenue estimates never did improve. Indeed the situation was so bad that on June 19, Dole's original target date for wrapping up the tax bill, Byrd took to the floor to complain that some Democratic senators had never received the revenue estimates they had requested. No doubt there was method in the madness, because as a Packwood aide recalled, under the revenue neutrality rules governing amendments, what members didn't know couldn't hurt Packwood.

While most members preferred to defer their evaluations of the Finance-reported bill, the media were immediately positive. Editorialists who couldn't find anything good to say about Packwood's first version of tax reform didn't need to see details to decide that they liked the second. On the usual amount of direct and hearsay evidence, a *Washington Post* editorialist reported that the Finance Committee bill could be the realization of "Stanley Surrey's dream." Choosing to ignore the staying power of the committee's corporate handiwork, the *Los Angeles Times* suggested that this hard-won victory over lobbyists demonstrated that "when there is an overriding sense of purpose and a fair sharing of costs, Congress is capable of acting in the public interest." [10]

Meanwhile, the ranks of pro—tax reform interest groups swelled daily, and the range expanded. This group of activists had always included good-government, consumer, low-income, and service-industry groups. Now, and for the only time during tax reform, the coalition encompassed special interests that had successfully loitered around the receiving end of the tax subsidy pipeline since 1981 but under tax reform stood to move to the fueling end. As a result, the coalition included virtually every kind of industry and organization as well as hundreds of individual corporations and businesses. It was such an unlikely mixture that some who attended the coalition meetings thought they had found the wrong room. Gina Despres marveled:

> Marcia Aronoff [Bradley's top administrative assistant] and I had been working with the Fair Tax Foundation, trying to meet with groups to foster support. At one meeting we had invited a real range—from Bread for the World to corporate lobbyist-lawyers in pinstriped suits. One fellow had dreadlocks and a fringe shirt, and across from him sat a top lobbyist in a T.V.-red tie. The corporate types would come in and say, "This must be the wrong room." And vice versa. It was a remarkable combination.

As expected, opponents-turned-supporters did little, if any, real work. Indeed, their most important contribution was that they remained quiet during floor debate. Yet even their silence was out of self-interest: organizations like the independent Petroleum Institute figured that complaining might backfire if Packwood decided to get even in conference.

Not all groups called it quits, though. Heavy lobbying continued on issues from incentives for capital formation to the retention of IRA benefits. Thus, as was true throughout the TRA process, the only outside-government, positive forces truly working for tax reform were organizations representing the nontaxpaying poor, good-government groups, and service industries that had borne the brunt of corporate taxes in the post-ERTA era. Those groups conducted telephone campaigns and stalked corridors, gathering commitments and making the all-important vote counts that enabled Packwood to determine when to hold and when to release senators from their commitments to oppose amendments.[11]

Two Quick Wins

Downing IRAs. On June 10, the first and most important test of Packwood's floor strategy came in the form of three successive IRA amendments. Since 1981, widely popular IRA provisions had allowed taxpayers to reduce their own adjusted gross incomes as much as $2,000 by contributing to individual retirement accounts. For Americans earning as much as $30,000 the benefit was small, amounting to less than $75 per return. Still, few letter writers considered IRAs an abused loophole, giving the effort to retain this deduction a populist veneer.

The most widely supported IRA amendment was sponsored by Alfonse D'Amato, R-N.Y. The amendment by D'Amato created a 15 percent tax credit for IRA contributions (to a maximum of $300), offsetting the resulting revenue loss with an increase in the corporate and individual minimum tax from 20 to 22.6 percent. When finally voted on, a motion to table the amendment passed by only the slimmest margin of three votes: 51—48. Shortly thereafter, the Senate dispensed with two other IRA amendments by much wider margins.[12]

The IRA amendments fell victim to a number of elements of Packwood's floor strategy. Perhaps most important, Bill Roth, a loud committee voice for IRAs, failed to offer any amendment because he couldn't come up with a satisfactory source of compensating revenue. Those who did offer amendments suffered from divided support. Parliamentary maneuvering contributed as well. When it appeared that D'Amato and Christopher Dodd, D-Conn., were prepared to strike, Dole spearheaded a leadership-sponsored drive in support of IRAs. Instead of offering an amendment to restore all or part of IRA benefits, fall-guy Roth was convinced to offer a gratuitous resolution of hope that IRA grievances would be redressed in conference, without (of course) altering the existing distribution of benefits. Because it salved guilty consciences and provided a facade of positive action, Roth's "sense of the Senate" amendment passed 96−4.

During the IRA deliberations and throughout the floor debate, would-be winners had to contend with Bill Bradley, Packwood's not-so-secret weapon against amendments. In this instance, Bradley came to the floor to dispute D'Amato and Dodd's claim that IRAs served middle-class interests. Looking straight into the newly installed Senate television cameras, using chart and pointer, Bradley launched his attack. Pointing to a corpulent figure of a taxpayer standing at the top of a hill looking down on another much leaner one, Bradley said:

> So what does this chart say? It says that . . . seventy-five percent of all taxpayers earning between $20,000 and $30,000 do not take an IRA. Ninety-five percent of all taxpayers earning between $10,000 and $20,000 do not take an IRA. [A] family making $20,000 a year . . . not having much entertainment other than the playground and the public park, not having any spare money [or] itemized deductions, that family is much less likely to take an IRA than is the family with a sizable portfolio of stocks and bonds. What about the $75,000 taxpayer? [He] takes a deduction which, on average is worth $2,000 and saves roughly $318.[13]

Bradley's play to the cameras was hardly prime-time fare, but neither was it only "average" as floor speeches go. Moreover, his scathing critique of D'Amato and Dodd was only the first of many similar attacks. The prospect of future televised ridicule was enough to deter other senators from getting in tax reform's way. As Despres exulted:

> Television was just fortuitous and terrific, providing an opportunity to make the general interest real. The general interest could be portrayed as the little man trying to crawl out of a hole. For each amendment, we could point to this little guy and show that he would get zip while the guy making $200,000 would make out like a bandit. This was show biz.

Another factor working against those who offered IRA and other amendments was the core of public interest and corporate lobbyists among the seven-hundred-member coalition that was hard at work scaring up "no" votes. As McAuliffe recalled, "The coalition met every day. We put television sets in so they could watch the floor. We had phones installed so they could call offices and make appointments to see staff."

But despite all those efforts, as the moment of voting on the D'Amato amendment approached, Packwood's tally turned up too few votes. The danger of a spree of budget-busting amendments sent Packwood running. He located Washington Republicans Dan Evans and Slade Gorton, hoping to trade an accommodation on the sales-tax deduction, which (coming from a sales-tax-only state) they desperately needed, for IRA votes, which he needed. Operating on the understanding that Packwood would support a sales-tax fix later, the senators reluctantly agreed, supplying Packwood a slim but winning margin.

Sinking the Sales Tax.   The next major issue raised on the Senate floor was another potential budget breaker: state and local sales-tax deductions. Yet, although the average taxpayer would be affected more by the proposed elimination of these deductions than by the changes in the IRA regulations, sales-tax forces never had the punching power of the IRA bloc—not in the Senate and certainly not in the Finance Committee. Although Durenberger and Moynihan, like senators from most high-tax states, publicly supported the restoration, few others did, including Long who represented a poor state certain to be hard hit. Overall, states represented on the Finance Committee depended less on the sales tax than the Senate average. Nor did anyone feel serious pressure from the National Governors' Association, which had supported tax reform in principle. Indeed, Gov. Richard Thornburgh of Pennsylvania was openly supporting the administration position.

Having thus lost in committee earlier, the Coalition against Double Taxation (CADT) turned to the wider Senate for help. Unfortunately for the interests CADT represented, Packwood's strategy of divide and conquer took hold with a monetary vengeance. The Finance Committee had raised $17.5 billion by repealing the sales-tax deduction, a substantial amount by any standard. And thanks to the self-financing requirement, those seeking to restore the deduction would have to locate counterbalancing revenues. Neither Moynihan (a core group member) nor Durenberger (who wished to preserve his municipal bond agreement) was even willing to try. This so infuriated the coalition that it threatened to run local spot commercials featuring the two as sellouts.

Two amendments were eventually advanced anyway. First, Dan Evans, Slade Gorton, and Phil Gramm, R-Texas, proposed allowing taxpayers to deduct *either* their state sales *or* their income taxes, but not both. This $3.3 billion amendment was to be paid for by prohibiting the deduction for interest paid on home equity loans. Second, speaking only for himself, Sen. Alan Dixon, D-Ill., proposed a partial restoration by placing a 1 percent floor under all itemized deductions. Neither amendment succeeded. After hours of debate and back-room arguing, a furious Evans was forced to withdraw his amendment, while Dixon acquiesced to defeat by voice vote.[14]

Afterward, Evans and Gorton could only shake their heads in disbelief: their earlier IRA votes gone for naught. Initially, everything seemed in order, but, unknown to Evans and Gorton, Packwood had not committed his troops; he had promised only that *he* would not vote against their amendment. Thus unprepared, the two senators were flattened by a ferocious core group attack. Bradley delivered the first punch, returning to his charts to point out that most taxpayers received little reward for deducting the already-regressive tax, while the least needy reaped a harvest. Thereafter, other group members came to do the really dirty work, defending the indefensible home equity tax break, a loophole so wide that homeowners (and only homeowners) would almost certainly use it to offset the costs of all manner of consumer debt. Finally, just to be safe, students of federalism came down to lecture them, arguing that the method they had chosen to pay for restoring the sales tax deduction was bad intergovernmental relations because it jeopardized the income tax. By putting income taxes into the equation with sales taxes, Evans had opened the door to further tampering in conference. Since income taxes were the mainstay of the progressive, high-tax states that fought hardest on this issue, Evans's cure was worse than the disease. As Moynihan later said, "The sales tax was no big deal for New York. New Jersey and Connecticut had higher sales taxes than we did."

Packwood's strategy worked, just as it had a day earlier when IRA amendments were debated. It worked so well, in fact, that the Finance chairman was able to watch the floor action from the wings, safely out of reach of the amendment's sponsors. Ultimately, the spectacle proved too much for majority leader Dole. He later intervened, helping to negotiate a 60 percent deduction for any excess of state sales over income taxes.[15]

Creating a Third Top Rate. A late amendment that posed the last serious test of Packwood's strategy was Mitchell's proposal to increase the bill's progressivity by creating a new individual top rate of 35 percent. As a core group member, Mitchell was well acquainted with the arguments for and against tax reform, and the highly regarded, intelligent legislator was ready with rhetoric and charts and even credibility to match his friend Bradley's.

Moreover, unlike many others, Mitchell knew that clever politics as well as good policy would be needed. So, not only did he pick the same individual top rate that President Reagan had, he added several sweeteners that promised to redress bill features many regarded as particularly troublesome. In a move sure to please those fretting about savings and investment, he used some revenue gained by his rate hike to retain a capital gains rate differential. And he deleted gimmicky provisions phasing out personal exemptions for higher-income taxpayers.

With critical political problems thus fixed, Mitchell turned to his real purpose, which was to put middle-class tax relief into the Finance Committee bill. As he correctly pointed out, in some respects the legislation amounted to a twisted version of Robin Hood, taking from the rich with tax shelters, giving to the rich without them. In contrast, as Mitchell wrote in a "Dear Colleague" letter, his proposed amendment would: (1) reduce the maximum tax rate paid by nearly 80 percent of taxpayers; (2) provide greater average tax relief to taxpayers with incomes below $75,000; and (3) more than double the amount of relief going to the

$30,000 — $40,000 income class, the group doing worst under the Finance bill. In short, Mitchell hoisted the banner of middle-class fairness, and he hoped that enough of his Democratic colleagues would rally 'round.

Throughout the ensuing five-hour floor debate, Mitchell returned fire for fire against his fellow core group members, and he lured nearly all of the Senate's prominent, liberal Democrats back to their party's historical cause, except for Edward Kennedy of Massachusetts and Gary Hart of Colorado. In the end, however, despite help from a few strong conservatives such as Sam Nunn, D-Ga., and Fritz Hollings, D-S.C., as well as the defection of a few Republicans who were locked in tight reelection races, Mitchell's drive failed miserably by a vote of 71 — 29.

The trouncing of an amendment that was so cleverly designed signaled several important facts about tax-reform politics in general and the Packwood floor strategy in particular. First, the Mitchell amendment tinkered with something Packwood had correctly described as "magic" — the bill's rate structure. Although even the unheralded House bill gave middle-class taxpayers a better deal, the Finance Committee's 15-27-33 rates were a powerful symbol of fairness. Indeed, to many politically self-conscious senators they had become almost as inviolable as Washington's many monuments.

Thus, Mitchell's amendment was tax reform's best test of the no-amendments coalition. By tying lower capital-gains rates to middle-class tax relief, Mitchell hoped to tempt enough conservatives to join liberals in a winning coalition. Yet those individuals were also the strength behind the marriage of convenience between loophole closing and rate reduction. In the end, it was that partnership that seduced conservatives, while Mitchell was able to sign up mostly liberals. Thereafter, by adding moderates to the mixture, Bradley and Packwood carried the day.

There is no doubt that home-state and special-interest politics were also closely tied to their victory. Despite the flurry of populist rhetoric that attended the introduction of the bill, many members had made deals that bound them to support Packwood. Earlier, for instance, members had watched as Packwood marshalled his troops behind an amendment by Howard Metzenbaum, D.-Ohio, eliminating a transition rule for the Unocal Corporation added at the request of California's two senators, Republican Pete Wilson and Democrat Alan Cranston. Wilson and Cranston had deserted Packwood during the IRA skirmishing, and when Metzenbaum's amendment passed overwhelmingly, it sent a powerful signal to others.

Self-interest was at stake in more than transition rules. Some close observers went so far as to say that it was the most significant factor in voting. According to one:

> While members talk in righteous tones about how everybody was sacrificing for the greater good, what bound them all together is that

almost everyone had some special interest that they were trying to protect, whether it was timber, agriculture, oil or gas, or whatever. Each one had something they were vulnerable on.

Last, Mitchell's drive fell short because—after all was said and done—it was not entirely obvious which of the two plans gave more Americans a better deal. Whether from floor speeches or newspaper editorial pages, it was difficult to sift through the statistics and evidence being tossed around. Suggesting just how much such confusion may have contributed to the outcome, Mitchell's tax counsel, Robert Rozen, said, "A lot of members thought the Mitchell amendment was a vote for higher tax rates, although the truth was that the amendment hiked taxes only for the top one-half of 1 percent of the population."

The Triumph of Tax Reform

According to an official count, a total of sixty amendments and motions were agreed to during 106 hours of Senate debate on tax reform over the course of thirteen legislative days. In addition to the amendments mentioned, H.R. 3838 had also to survive intermittent strikes against the most questionable (of the total of 174) transition rules led by Howard Metzenbaum, Senate gadfly against waste, fraud, and abuse. But after a flurry of rather specific, last-minute deals and the passage of a large technical corrections amendment, a final vote was scheduled.

Senate roll calls are usually noisy events during which members wander down to the well of the Senate floor in no particular order to vote, often lingering afterward to talk with colleagues. As might be expected in the case of historic legislation like tax reform, however, voting was a more solemn occasion. Instead of the usual noise and milling around, at precisely 4:00 P.M. on June 24, one by one members voted from their desks for the benefit of television cameras. When it was done, Packwood had fallen just short of the unanimous vote a few optimists had predicted. Only Paul Simon, D-Ill., Carl Levin, D-Mich., and John Melcher, D-Mont., cast "no" votes, while ninety-seven others, many of whom had hoped this day would never come, voted "yes." To what seemed like a collective nod of respect and amazement, the once dark horse of tax reform passed triumphantly by.

Notes

1. Sen. Bob Packwood, C-Span, April 24, 1986.
2. Senators Bill Bradley and Dave Durenberger quoted in *Tax Notes*, April 24, 1986, 327–28.
3. Anne Swardson, "Packwood Denies Authoring Flat Tax," *Washington Post*, April 26, 1986, A3.

4. Writing about how recycled ideas find their way to the public agenda, John Kingdon notes, "An idea is floated, and it gets thrown in the wastebasket. Then it comes back. Somebody fishes it out of the wastebasket and floats it again." In John Kingdon, *Agendas, Alternatives, and Public Policies* (Boston: Little, Brown, 1984), 136.

5. In 1971 Irving Janis coined the term "groupthink" to characterize situations in which "consensus" displaces "rationality" in group decision processes. While Janis used the term pejoratively to explain misguided decision making, many of the psychological and social characteristics he identified, including the importance of consensus building, camaraderie, and morale in decision making, are equally characteristic of group choices having less invidious results. Indeed, in many ways the esprit de corps that pervaded the Finance Committee during this phase of tax reform resembles the environment described by Janis. A short version of his theory is presented in Irving L. Janis, "Groupthink," in *Classic Readings in Organizational Behavior*, J. Steven Ott (Belmont, Calif.: Brooks Cole, 1989), 223—32.

6. *Washington Post*, May 5, 1986, A18; *New York Times*, May 4, 1986, E24.

7. Sen. John Danforth, in U.S. Congress, Senate, *Congressional Record*, daily ed., 99th Cong., 2d sess., September 26, 1986, S13788.

8. Sen. Russell Long, C-Span, May 7, 1986.

9. Sen. Robert Byrd, in U.S. Congress, Senate, *Congressional Record*, daily ed., 99th Cong., 1st sess., June 4, 1986, S6443.

10. Hobart Rowen, "Stanley Surrey's Dream May Come True," *Washington Post*, May 15, 1986, A21; "Taking the Radical Way, Senate Tries Tax Reform," *Los Angeles Times*, May 11, 1986, 5—6.

11. According to McAuliffe, the sixteen most active groups in the coalition were: Acorn, Allied-Signal, American Association of Retired Persons, Center for Budget and Policy Priorities, Children's Defense Fund, Committee for Fairness to Families, Computer and Business Equipment Manufacturers Association, CEO Tax Group, Tax Reform Action Coalition, 3M, Fair Tax Foundation, National American Wholesale Grocers' Association, National Taxpayers' Union, League of Women Voters, National Women's Law Center, and RJR Nabisco, Inc.

12. The other two were an amendment by Max Baucus, D-Mont., reducing the personal exemption by $310 to pay for a 15 percent IRA tax credit up to a maximum of $300 (failed by fifty-five votes) and an amendment by Alan Dixon, D-Ill., to finance present-law treatment of IRAs by placing a 1 percent floor on all itemized deductions (failed by sixty votes).

13. Sen. Bill Bradley, U.S. Congress, Senate, *Congressional Record*, daily ed., 99th Cong., 1st sess. June 11, 1985, S7246.

14. Reinforced by the awesome power of revenue neutrality, Packwood and his core group paid almost no attention to Dixon's amendment, which by virtue of its payment plan alienated nearly every member of the Senate.

15. As the amendment was constructed, it affected only a very few states, most of which were served by electorally vulnerable Republicans from high-tax states. Even this modest proposal was ultimately deleted in conference, though. Moreover, both Gorton and James Abnor, R-S.D., who had been swept in on Reagan's coattails in 1980, were defeated in 1986. Interestingly, this convoluted solution was paid for by a requirement that taxpayers identify all dependents by social security number. While the sales-tax solution was later deleted in conference, the paperwork requirement was kept.

8   Tax Bills Take Two: The Closed World of House-Senate Conference Politics

We all know that important laws are drafted [in conference], but I don't think one person in a million has any appreciation of their importance and the process by which they work.

Member of Congress, 1963

On July 17, 1986, the twenty-two recently selected conferees gathered to reconcile the House and Senate versions of tax reform. Nearly five years had elapsed since first-term senator Bill Bradley set to work with a few talented aides and experts on the Fair Tax Act of 1982. Over two years had passed since Don Regan dispatched a small band of Treasury Department professionals to work on Treasury I. After numerous bouts with partisan, interest-group, and institutional politics, these early starters were eclipsed by less immaculate conceptions of tax reform, reflecting the sometimes small, sometimes large differences in constituencies and coalitions that dominated the policy process.

In July 1986 bicameralism brought House and Senate together to do what neither the executive nor the legislative branch had yet accomplished: produce a common statement of law. It was historic work. Despite telltale traces of politics, the conference had before it two remarkable tax-reform documents, thanks to politicians' fears about being blamed for killing tax reform and their leaders' desires to capture personal, partisan, and institutional credit.

With the month-long summer recess set to begin August 15, those in favor of tax reform agreed that Congress should act quickly, producing a final tax reform bill before conferees returned home to their states and districts. Otherwise, they would again be besieged by tax reform's many opponents, re-armed with new charts, reports, and other evidence showing which among hundreds of provisions would damage home-state constituencies. In conference, as was true at other times, fast action favored reform.

This ambitious timetable left less than one month to reconcile over a thousand pages of tax law! In addition to conflicting rate structures and tax-cut benefit distributions, hundreds of miscellaneous technical differences and dozens of serious, substantive trouble spots remained to be dealt with. Notable discrepancies were the treatment of depreciation and natural resources such as timber, farming, and oil and gas (where the Senate version was more generous than the House version) and provisions affecting individual retirement accounts and state and local taxes (where the House was more benevolent). Indeed, the House and Senate versions of tax reform represented two different philosophies of taxation, with the Senate continuing to play hero to low rates and American corporations and the House to its own presumably middle-class constituency.

Could it be done? The task was formidable, but smart money was taking long odds on success. Many were virtually certain that the traditional politics of group pressure and logrolling would again be crushed by the counterforces of tax-reform politics. The dangers of not compromising loomed larger than those of reconciling differences.

Some participants had more to lose than others, however. In the event of failure, the buck would stop with chairmen Rostenkowski and Packwood. As a result, these two unlikely allies shared political and personal objectives that overshadowed the policy differences dividing their two houses and their respective political parties. As the conference proceeded, their determination to produce a historic bill proved more than a match for all the traditional and not-so-traditional troubles that befell the conference. Neither partisan wrangling, nor conferee gridlock, nor even a final-hour $17 billion shortfall swayed them from their course. Indeed, when the conference broke into a shouting match that both characterized and symbolized the clash of old interests and new forces in tax reform politics, it was Rostenkowski and Packwood who rescued it, shouldering full responsibility for completing the committee's work. Thus, it is fair to say that the most sweeping reform of the federal income tax in over fifty years was ultimately settled by centralizing decision-making power in the hands of two men.

In the last leg of tax reform's unlikely journey, Rostenkowski and Packwood forged the Tax Reform Act of 1986 and then sold the package to their colleagues. In the process, the political dynamics of avoiding the tag of taxer, spender, or friend of special interests forced conferees to swallow the most bitter medicine from each bill and strengthened the reformist character of the 1986 Act.

The story of the House-Senate tax-reform conference is no simple saga pitting individuals, institutions, or political parties against one another. Nor should its results be viewed as a scorecard of who won and who lost the battle between the House and the Senate. Instead, the last chapter of tax reform is very much the story of a three-legged race wherein the tying together of two men's political fates enabled tax reform to wend its way through the conference obstacle course. In this way, Rostenkowski and Packwood's political entwinement served as a catalyst for making history.

Conferencing in the 1980s: The Setting for Tax Reform

Although the version of H.R. 3838 that emerged from conference looked very different from the bills that had earlier passed the House and Senate, such a result was hardly unique to tax reform. Conference committees have been called "the third house" of Congress because of the enormous effect they often have on important pieces of legislation.[1]

Indeed, some scholars argue that the power of *all* congressional committees can be attributed not to their expertise or specialization but to the "ex post veto" they exercise in conference, which allows them to have the last effective word on most major bills and floor amendments.[2] To be sure, conference reports (the final compromise bills reported from conference committees) are not technically the last word, but they must be accepted or rejected by the House and Senate without amendments. This "take it or leave it" position can give conferees enormous latitude in shaping the provisions of important legislation, often resulting in bills that are vastly weaker or stronger than those passed by either house. The TRA of 1986 proved to be an extreme example of such leverage because the partisan and institutional stakes had become so high that rejection of the conference report became almost inconceivable.

For all their power, conference committees are remarkably unregulated by formal rules and strict conventions. Internally, there are no standard rules governing quorum, amendment, or voting procedures within conference committees. Externally, rules and procedures have been developed to provide some accountability between conference delegations and their respective chambers—governing conferee selection, germaneness, and public accountability—but such rules tend to be flexible and evolving. In the case of tax reform, they were often stretched to the breaking point.

For example, in the process of selecting conferees, committee or subcommittee seniority is generally the most important consideration. But in choosing the House delegation, Rostenkowski and Speaker Tip O'Neill bruised powerful egos by passing over the second-, sixth-, seventh-, eighth-, and ninth-ranking committee Democrats—and reached all the way down to the sixteenth—in order to assemble a band of reliable reform supporters. Even Packwood, who is known for observing institutional niceties and for nurturing committee collegiality, jumped over more than one committee member to reach others he wanted to take to conference.

Similarly, when it came to public openness, the TRA conference converted the sunshine reforms of the mid-1970s, which were intended to open up conference proceedings to press and public scrutiny for the first time, into one of the blackest legislative boxes ever seen on Capitol Hill. Only the two chairmen and their top staffs were present when most of the critical decisions were finally reached. Until they were called upon to ratify the agreements, most conferees seemed as far removed from the process as any Senate page.

While extreme, this gravitation toward "shun-shine" was not unique to tax reform. Over time, the openness experiment had led to all sorts of tricks to avoid it. Small rooms in hard-to-reach places, informal private discussions and caucuses, and extensive preconference staff work have all worked to limit the effects of the open-door policy. Perhaps because tax legislation is so heavily lobbied, tax conferences have been especially likely to adopt these strategies. Offers and counteroffers, staff work to iron out points of technical as well as substantive disagreement, and VIP "walks in the woods" are all typical of "tax conferencing gone treaty making" in its style of operation.

There is a general governance lesson in this dynamic—that a statesman's course is sometimes more easily steered through secret channels. But as Packwood explained, it is hardly textbook civics:

> John Gardner [the founder of Common Cause] has it exactly backwards. Statesmanship happens more often in the back room than out in front. The members really want to do what is right, and they can when they are not pressured by parochial interests. So long as it can be done in the back room, and they can say to these interests, "I fought hard, but the chairman was adamant, but I fought for it." I saw that time and time again in the back room throughout tax reform. Special interests have their lobbyists at the session but the public doesn't. They've got a phone system that puts out an alert—an all-points bulletin [saying] "Send in your telegram today." By the time you've gotten back to your office from the session, your secretary is saying, "What have you done? I've got ten phone calls."

Two Institutions, Two Versions of Tax Reform

After the 97−3 Senate victory on June 28, with just nineteen days until the start of conference, it is doubtful whether the aforementioned history lessons were on the minds of tax reform participants as technical preparations and preconference positioning got into full swing. More likely they were thinking about the immediate problem of reconciling the differences between the two bills. (For a detailed comparison of the major features of the House and Senate tax-reform bills see the Appendix.) Although staff members on both sides of the Capitol and on the JTC had already begun to explore possible compromises, the legislated differences were deeply rooted, reflecting the distinctive makeup of the Ways and Means and Finance Committees and the contrasting politics in the Democratic House and Republican Senate.

The most important conflicts lay in the areas of corporate taxation, the treatment of individual provisions not commonly regarded as loopholes, and overall rate and benefit structures. The Senate bill raised less than $100 billion in new taxes on corporations. Almost all of it was to come from a few big-money reforms, leaving many areas of corporate taxation nearly untouched. In contrast, the House bill raised in excess of $140 billion, more or less spread across industries. Although the Senate corporate reform strategy had made it possible to enlist much-needed committee support, during the waiting period, the House made clear its intention to even out the pain of base broadening.

A second area of difference lay in individual income taxation. In order to pay for its centerpiece low rates, the Senate bill made staggering changes in provisions affecting individuals. It eliminated many deductions and exemptions commonly regarded as legitimate, middle-class benefits. Notable among them were two big-ticket items, sales-tax deductions and tax-exempt IRA contributions. The House version of H.R. 3838 had been much kinder to this set of interests. Thus, Ways and Means Democrats set their conference sights on protecting a number of these provisions and, in so doing, taking credit for replanting the flag of middle-class fairness.

Finally, there was the matter of resolving differences in tax rates and after-tax distributions. The Senate bill had two individual rates of 15 and 27 percent, compared with the apparently more progressive House individual rates of 15, 25, 35, and 38 percent. In the Senate bill the top corporate rate was 33 percent, three points below the House number. The Finance Committee bill had passed the Senate almost entirely by the force of those exceptionally low tax rates, which worked as a linchpin holding together conservative and liberal support. Institutionally and intellectually, Senate conferees were absolutely committed to protecting the low rates.

No similar bipartisan support for a modified flat income tax ever emerged in the House. Indeed, the rates described as "magic" by Packwood were quickly decried as Republican witchcraft by House majority leader Jim Wright, who pictured them as yet another GOP-sponsored windfall for the rich. As an open opponent of tax reform, Wright's motives may have been less than pure, but there is no question that he voiced the sentiments of nearly all of the Democrats on the Ways and Means Committee. At a minimum they hoped to settle on a three-tier system, ideally with a top rate of 35 percent as the president had proposed. Nor could the practical demands of revenue neutrality be put aside. It was impossible for anyone with a calculator to see how such rates could be sustained in the face of efforts to preserve provisions important *either* to the House *or* to the Senate. In fact, within the limits of a 27 percent top rate, Packwood had always been favorably disposed toward evening out the benefits from tax reform, and Rostenkowski now seemed inclined to accept a flatter tax structure than conventional Democratic wisdom dictated. The most dangerous problem facing conference was the threat of a pitched battle between a few senators who were determined to keep this monetary magic alive *without* surrendering corporate provisions near and dear to them and House partisans who (with Rostenkowski's permission) were equally determined to use tax reform as an opportunity to make political hay in an election year by putting a visible, Democratic stamp on the president's number-one domestic priority.

No Leading Edge

In maneuvering for position during this interim period, Rostenkowski enjoyed a number of institutional advantages, but Packwood had the edge when it came to popular support for his version of tax reform.

Rostenkowski's Hand. Both chairmen faced reelection, but their situations were far from similar. While Rostenkowski was assured an easy victory in the fall, the Oregonian had escaped defeat in a hard-fought Republican primary in which his political fortunes fluctuated with the tides of tax reform. Thus, during the break between Senate floor consideration and conference, Packwood was naturally eager to return home to his constituents while his tax triumph was fresh news. Unfortunately, the trip left him less time to prepare for conference.[3]

Moreover, this was Packwood's first important tax conference in a leadership role. Not so for Rostenkowski, who had been Ways and Means chairman for six years. Although the Chicagoan had been outmaneuvered by Bob Dole in the past,[4] he could count on his seasoned and experienced aides Joe Dowley and Rob Leonard. With the exception of John Colvin, none of Packwood's top staff had participated in a tax conference, and not even veteran Colvin had done so in his present capacity.

Rostenkowski had the added advantage of serving as conference chairman, allowing him to control the time and place of meetings, the sequence in which issues would be taken up, who could speak and when, and the order of voting. Used skillfully, these parliamentary tools might be parlayed into substantive influence. It has long been the practice of the Finance and Ways and Means committees to alternate this position, but crafty maneuvering can sometimes pave the way to chairing a conference, in effect, out of turn.[5] Dole had made such an attempt just before the DEFRA conference in 1984 when he arbitrarily changed the date on House-passed legislation raising the national debt ceiling, thereby necessitating a conference to reconcile dates. Rostenkowski, who ultimately chaired the DEFRA conference, got the last laugh in this game of preconference strategy when he persuaded the House to accept the Senate date, thus negating the need for a meeting to reconcile differences.[6] The passage of a mundane piece of waterways legislation handed Rostenkowski another such chance in 1986, and he took it by calling for a conference just before the scheduled tax reform match-up. When Packwood bluntly declined the honor of chairing this orchestrated meeting, his refusal prompted the following Rostenkowski response: "I think I understand what the situation here is. The roll of the dice is affecting who will be chairman of a conference in the future. I am willing to play by the roll of the dice. Evidently, the Senate isn't." [7] In the end, Packwood backed down, agreeing to let Rostenkowski run the conference. Yet another Rostenkowski advantage lay in differences between institutional expectations about conferencing. As congressional expert David Vogler has reported:

> One consequence of . . . institutional distinctions is the fact that each chamber delegation approaches conference deliberations with different expectations. House conferees come to the bargaining table to uphold bills fashioned in committee workshops. Senate conferees come to make sure that individual senators' provisions to help certain segments of the public are not dropped from the final bill. [8]

Or, in the plainer terms of a Ways and Means member:

> All Senators are interested in is getting their amendments into these tax bills when we come to conference. They make no bones about it. They'll sit down for God's sake and say, "Now let's see, whose amendment is this? Oh yes it's [so and so's]. I told him I would support it. We are going to stand firm on that." [9]

In tax reform, this pattern held true in some respects. While both sets of conferees had pet provisions and strongly supported their institutional positions on particular issues, a determined minority of senators was especially obstinate about relatively narrow constituent and policy interests.

Historically, such special-interest, constituency, and personal attachments have been little more than conference irritants. In tax reform, however, thanks to adherence to strict standards of revenue neutrality, their price tags could easily upset the balance between overall policy goals and political compromises. From an institutional perspective, self-interest had made it harder to get things done; consequently, Packwood was never able to command the undivided attention of his conferees, while Rostenkowski had essential if not complete control of his. Although much was made of this at the time, it is not unusual between House and Senate. After all, while Finance chairmen are considered by their committee members to be "first among equals," Ways and Means chairmen are simply considered "first."

Packwood's Ace.   Against this institutionally stacked hand, Packwood had a single card, but tax-reform politics seemingly made it an ace. From the viewpoint of the all-important press, Packwood's bill was a winner and Rostenkowski's was not. Whereas the House version of H.R. 3838 was saddled with the label of political compromise, Packwood's version was hailed as true reform. Finally, while Rostenkowski's bill was met with lukewarm support from Democrats and opposition from Republicans, Packwood's bill received rave reviews from both sides of the political aisle.

Different Men, Different Strategies

Going into conference, Rostenkowski seemed to have the greatest number of advantages, but Packwood seemed to have the most important one.

Careful Attention to Politics. Rostenkowski approached the tax-reform conference much as he had approached tax reform in general: with a careful eye to politics. In order to maximize his chances for success, the Ways and Means chairman made two difficult but politically astute choices. The first was his already-mentioned decision to break seniority precedent in the selection of conferees. Had he adhered to normal rules, the list of House participants would have matched the committee roster running from the most to the least senior members on each side of the political aisle. But in order to create a firm cadre of Democratic followers, Rostenkowski passed over five senior Democrats including Sam Gibbons, the second-ranking Democrat on the Ways and Means Committee, Jim Jones, Andrew Jacobs, Harold Ford, and Ed Jenkins.[10] As Rostenkowski recalled:

> I did a very unusual thing in putting members on that conference. It's still a sore spot. But it was the only way to do it. I wasn't going to sit there after I'd gone through having my stomach feel as though it was hamburger for eighteen months and then go into the final phases of tax reform, me leading the conference, and have to worry about whether or not I was going to have votes.

Even GOP Ways and Means tax counsel Ken Kies saw the logic:

> [Rostenkowski] didn't want to fight a two-front war, one with his members, both Republican and Democrat, and another one with Packwood. So he made the decision to avoid that two-front war, [by] going over some Democrats [and] getting the guys that he knew he could depend on. This gave him enough people to outvote the Republicans if he had to.

Rostenkowski's second strategic decision was to accept the Senate tax rates as a starting point for negotiations. In truth, the move was a ploy to avoid direct blame for tinkering with the popular Senate rate structure. As a close observer said, Rostenkowski hoped to put pressure on the Senate to accept House corporate reforms *and* raise the top rates. He admitted as much later: "I didn't think we'd stay at 27 percent. I thought we'd go up to about 30 or more. . . . I would have liked to have gone to 35. . . . You know, you get more money, you take care of more middle-income people."

Given the lack of on-paper progressivity in the Senate rate structure,

Rostenkowski had a tough time convincing his conferees of the wisdom of this step, although he was helped along a great deal by wise appointments. Democrat Charles Rangel recalled that he agreed only because he was convinced that the rates would not last once conference got rolling. "I didn't think it would [stay there]," he lamented. "I thought 38 percent was too low."

Unfortunately for Rangel and other liberals, the ploy worked masterfully as a means of pressuring the Senate to accept more corporate reform, but it backfired as a catalyst for progressivity. Rostenkowski had badly underestimated the Senate's commitment to low rates. Perhaps he should have taken more seriously Packwood's frequent claim that "if there was a Holy Grail in tax reform, it was the rates." A Ways and Means staff member commented on the misstep with chagrin:

> My personal recollection . . . of one of the early conference meetings with the Democrats, just Democrats, was Rostenkowski saying, "We'll sit here and force them to dig themselves out of their hole—the 27 percent rate, the state sales tax, and some of those crazy minimum tax provisions, and the passive loss provisions." Well, some hole they dug themselves out of. We ended up jumping in with them.

A Preoccupation with Policy. Packwood had a less political approach to conferencing. After first trying unsuccessfully to appoint all twenty members to conference as a way of finessing seniority, he, too, made some exceptions to the norm in selecting conferees. Packwood bypassed tax-reform foe John Heinz, choosing core group member Malcom Wallop instead. At the same time, Long, in one of his few public shows of support, skipped over antitax reformers Max Baucus and David Boren to name Bill Bradley.

But despite these moves, Packwood's appointments yielded less satisfactory results than Rostenkowski's. The first problem was that Republicans defined tax reform as the Senate version, and only the Senate version. Second, while there were tax-reform supporters on the Finance Committee, few were willing, in effect, to give proxies to Packwood. Third, loyalty to tax reform was always tempered by commitments to other policy and constituent concerns. Fourth, thanks principally to Long, Packwood was forced to dilute his strength by balancing loyalty against ample representation for the oil and gas bloc. Consequently, although Packwood took virtually all of the core group members to conference, he did not enjoy the kind of support Rostenkowski did.

Other than attending to unavoidable details such as conferee selection and jockeying over who would serve as chairman, it is apparent that Packwood spent far less time than Rostenkowski plotting out procedural scenarios. Instead, when it came to strategy, Packwood was all substance. Whereas Rostenkowski often seemed to reduce policy making to politics,

Packwood had come to see traditional politics as secondary to tax reform. The transition was eased, certainly, by the fact that swaying to the reformers' beat had boosted his electoral prospects, whereas dancing with special interests had sent them plummeting. Even so, as the *Washington Post* drew the contrast, "Rostenkowski is a crafty vote-getter, schooled in machine politics; Packwood is an eclectic philosopher with a streak of independence." [11]

Agreement on the Outlines of Tax Reform

Marrying political and policy-focused strategies brought forth an apparently broad preconference agreement about the direction and content of the final tax-reform bill. The deal amounted to a trade-off in which the most reformist elements of each bill would be combined, producing a final version with corporate provisions looking more like the House effort and individual provisions reflecting the Senate's handiwork. The rate structure was to be a Senate contribution, while the tax-cut benefit structure was to match as closely as possible that of the House. Money gleaned from this effort would be used to repair the so-called stagger by which tax deductions, credits, and exemptions were "phased out" before tax rate cuts were "phased in," and to restore, if possible, certain tax deductions thought to benefit middle-class taxpayers. As Rostenkowski figured at the time:

> The logical compromise is to have the House move toward the Senate rates, and the Senate move toward the House after-tax distribution. [The bill would] take on the best of their individual reforms and our corporate reforms in payment. It's a formula that would give the new law the most fairness and economic force.

Packwood was quick to agree. Unlike most of his Senate colleagues, he was always willing to accept more corporate reform as the price for protecting his passive loss rules, AMT changes, capital-gains reforms, and the all-important Senate rates. Indeed, soon thereafter Packwood began floating the idea of raising corporate taxes $120 billion over five years, rather than the $100 billion called for in the Senate bill. A few days later, he upped the Senate corporate ante to as much as $125 billion. Moreover, Packwood assured listeners, "If the House can live with our effort to close down shelters and [strengthen] the minimum tax, I'm sure we can increase the tax cut for the middle class." [12]

This preconference shadow boxing was carried out almost entirely through newspaper and television instead of in traditional preconference staff meetings. Major newspapers and public-affairs television programs reported and also translated the meaning of public and private utterances by Rostenkowski, Packwood, and their staffs.[13] Thus, in an important sense, reporters contributed to the crucial building of a consensus.

Meanwhile, the press also detected that the White House and the

Treasury Department were at odds. When Don Regan stated publicly that the president was prepared to make corporate concessions to hold rates down, Jim Baker struck back, publicly warning tax writers not "to fall into this trap of playing to the audience to such a degree that we hurt economic growth. We don't want to kill the goose that laid the golden egg." [14] To be sure, these remarks reflected Baker's misgivings about the effects of corporate taxation on the economy, but they also served as a warning to the chief of staff to stay off Baker's turf. After brief skirmishing, Baker succeeded. The resulting White House silence allowed him and Darman to continue their low-profile style of participation and to hew to a farsighted kind of partisanship. By emphasizing winning above all, this left them free to deal exclusively with the institutionally strongest legislators, be they Democrat or Republican, from House or Senate.

Despite the momentary White House brushfire, by the time the conference officially opened, an agreement between major players seemed all but ensured. Rostenkowski even promised a conference in which tedium rather than tension would prevail. Packwood also exuded optimism, predicting in an interview with the Portland *Oregonian* that with agreement on the broad points, "The pieces will fall into place pretty easily." [15]

Covering Up Past Differences

In fact, the camaraderie was carefully orchestrated to mask difficulties that both men knew lay before them and to smooth over earlier conflicts. The short record of Rostenkowski and Packwood's stormy relationship before tax reform is well documented. Once, in a 1984 tax conference when Rostenkowski attacked fringe benefits, Packwood stated publicly that the Ways and Means chairman "didn't know what he was talking about." The two had also traded insults during the Superfund conference of 1985 in which Packwood made an open power play to Rostenkowski's own conferees. Most recently, they had skirmished publicly over who would chair the tax-reform conference. [16]

But tax-reform politics brought Rostenkowski and Packwood together to accomplish a feat neither could accomplish alone. Quite apart from the fact that both men had come to believe in the overall value of tax reform, the burdensome "cat" of responsibility was back, this time at the steps of the Capitol itself. The principal political pressures the chairmen faced included: (1) completing a bill by recess under pain of losing a once-in-a-political-career opportunity; (2) keeping the bill revenue-neutral to avoid blame for raising taxes or adding to the budget deficit; (3) improving things for the middle class so as not to be viewed as selling out to the wealthy; and (4) sidestepping responsibility for raising significantly the popular top individual tax rate of 27 percent. The *Washington Post* summed up their situation:

> [Although] they had nothing in common . . . as politicians, the chairmen are locked together whether they like it or not. Rostenkowski and Packwood share the goal of sending a bill to President Reagan's desk by Labor Day—and the knowledge that their reputations will suffer should they fail.[17]

For all these reasons, a casual survey of the public record during the weeks preceding conference revealed broad agreement and a great deal of collegiality. But those were the chairmen's words. Many conferees, especially senators, had quite different ideas, and so, to some extent, did Treasury Secretary Baker. It is both a vice and virtue of democracy that it slows the wheels of "progress." In legislatures, votes are the ultimate dividing line between success and failure, and tax reform was no exception. Rostenkowski and especially Packwood relearned that lesson over the next few weeks of conference.

Beginning to Get Nowhere

July 17 started out in an atmosphere that appeared almost routine as tax reform's cast and crew gathered in the chamber of the mighty Ways and Means Committee hearing room in the Longworth House Office Building for the final act of this unlikely drama. While the politicians had on their expressionless conference faces, nervous energy lit up the eyes of staff as they scurried about, attending to last-minute details. The heavy black briefing books they carried, describing not one but two tax bills, were signs of how many of them had spent their July recess. Beyond the dais, reporters settled into reserved places at long tables to the side and in front of the seats provided for lobbyists and ordinary onlookers. After nearly two years on the tax-reform beat, most sat impassively, organizing notes or reading newspapers. However, expressions grown dull from overexposure are likely to be deceptive in the case of the Capitol Hill press corps. In tax reform, certainly, neutral countenances belied the inner thoughts of men and women who had often unleashed their pens to advance tax reform in the past and would do so again. At the back of the room and outside in the halls special-interest lobbyists milled about. In some way or another they had all been losers to tax reform. Few had much hope of improving things for their clients in conference, and fewer still believed tax reform would falter at the final gate. Their only hope was that the clash of so many conflicting egos and agendas might produce a last-minute logjam that no one could untangle. Thus, as conference began, they clustered together to commiserate or plot strategy for improving their positions at the margins. With few exceptions, they would have little influence in the tax conference, settling for winning a transition rule here, a promise of a language change there. Indeed, this group of stalwart tax-reform antagonists had been reduced to playing the role of audience.

Such were the faces that Dan Rostenkowski saw as he walked casually to his place at the center of the dais. Having won responsibility for chairing this historic conference, Rostenkowski raised the wooden gavel that is the symbol of a chairman's authority and called the members to order. The last act of the tax-reform drama had officially begun.

Rhetoric Makes Rough Going

From the beginning it was apparent that predictions of an easy passage through conference had been premature.[18] The House took a particularly strong stand, considering that it had received so little applause for H.R. 3838. Unpopularity left House conferees undeterred, however, for they had been toughened by a full year of tax-reform pain. They also knew about the Senate bill's ugly little secrets, which the admiring media had thus far glossed over. As a result, for them, "conference amounted to little more than opening a new theater in an old war." Like battle-scarred veterans, Rosty's troops came to play it tough on vulnerable elements of the Senate bill, notably the retroactivity of some provisions, the heavy-handed treatment of real estate, the elimination of a number of middle-class tax preferences, the overly generous depreciation provisions, and the free ride given to defense, oil and gas, and other natural-resource industries.

Most important, House Democratic conferees honestly opposed the Senate rates which, after all, were substantially below those proposed by Ronald Reagan himself. They wanted the rich to pay more, not less, something that could only be achieved by closing loopholes exploited by wealthy individuals *and* by reducing top individual tax rates less drastically. Conferees recognized, however, that direct confrontation could be political suicide because large *rate cuts* were equated with significant *tax cuts*. Thus, while tax-reform politics made the Senate's low rates impossible to be publicly against, deeply held Democratic beliefs made them impossible to be for.

Recognizing this, committee Democrats put their faith in Rostenkowski's strategy for splitting the difference between the top House and Senate rates. Besides, each Democratic conferee had given his pledge to help the chairman secure tax reform. And, Rostenkowski's reputation for punishing ne'er-do-wells could not be ignored. One observer put it in terms that seem to fit Rostenkowski's roughshod Chicago persona: "If you don't go along with Rostenkowski when it counts, you are going straight to the shithouse. What's worse, Danny is going to come by every once in a while to urinate all over you. And, remember, his visits could go on for years." By the same token, supporting Rostenkowski in this, his most important endeavor, would not be forgotten. As top Rostenkowski aide Joe Dowley concluded, "His is an old-fashioned, John Wayne view of the world that really isn't so old-fashioned. After all, to make it work on the Hill you reward loyalty with loyalty." As a result, despite strong reservations about the Senate bill and a determination to win as many as they lost, these six Democratic conferees were willing to let their man trade for what he needed.[19]

In comparison, thanks in part to the false security that sometimes follows a big win, some senators gave early indications that they expected to prevail outright. Moreover, the stylistic contrast between this patrician group and their plain-talking House counterparts couldn't have been broader, and it only added to the difficult psychological dynamics. Putting these points together, one prominent JTC staffer commented:

> The Senate came in patting themselves on the back, saying how great they were. They thought they had invented something new, and they had visible scorn for their opposition. That's where the problem was. You're making a mistake when you scorn someone with power who has already staked out the substantive groundwork. They thought the House should be pushovers. To this day some of them think that Rostenkowski, this thug, had beaten them up! Watching, it was like somebody from prep school going downtown and getting in a fight, realizing too late that people don't always fight just with their hands.

When it became apparent that the Senate bill would not prevail on its (to them) obvious merits, Senate conferees became excessively frustrated, taking each new corporate contribution to tax reform as a defeat for them and for the American economy. To be sure, one reason so much corporate reform was demanded was that so little had been undertaken in the Senate. But from the perspective of these members, conference was a kind of purgatory in which the Senate suffered mightily, first for committing small sins that had provided easy solutions to base broadening but were later exposed as unacceptable short cuts, and second for relying so heavily on the vagaries of revenue estimating.

For three days members met in open session, alternately badgering and balking. The only real result, according to a Senate staff member, was increasing discomfort:

> Our guys did not want to give. Wallop stated that in one of the sessions. Then, too, the other side spent its time beating up on our "outrageous" rate system by implying that we didn't want the wealthy to pay. Our members were outraged at the public attack. If these meetings continued, the credibility of our bill would be lost. When they were suspended, I said, "Thank God."

Between Fact and Rhetoric

While the rhetoric subsided, ill will lingered on. House attacks had led some senators to dig in early, but self-righteousness brought the Senate only a peevish House delegation. Senators might have made more headway had they been able to provide acceptable support for their claims that the House bill overtaxed corporations. They could not because, among other things, economists differed sharply on the matter. Academic confusion was especially evident on the economic worth of leveling the playing field versus preserving incentives for jobs and capital formation.

Far from generating convincing statistics, Senate conferees confronted the opposite. On the day the conference opened, Citizens for Tax Justice released an updated report listing forty-two major companies that had paid no federal income taxes during the 1982—1985 period. Some of the companies had even collected refunds. That report and another conducted by Tax Analysts were widely circulated in House and Senate offices. To the chagrin of Senate conferees, there were many well-known names on that list, including AT&T, Du Pont, Boeing, and General Dynamics.[20] Such horror stories established a hostile tone toward corporations in most early press coverage of the conference.[21] For the most part, reporters cast this historic bout as one between corporate America (assigned the role of *the* special interest) in the Senate corner of the ring and taxpayers in the below $60,000 income category (assigned the role of *the* middle class) in the corner of the ring occupied by the House. Although there was substantial truth to this simple analogy and it spiced up an otherwise dull subject, media spin had the untoward effect of transforming activities in the rather gray world of tax policy into a morality play in black and white.

In the absence of countervailing academic evidence or discrepant opinion polls, print and television stories reported studies of corporate tax avoidance, speculation about which corporate provisions were most likely to go, and editorials favoring a tougher stand on business and industry. Journalists who had praised the Finance bill only a few weeks earlier wanted the Senate to take the logical next step, doing for corporations what it had just done for individual taxpayers.[22]

The Demise of Middle-Class Differences.   House Democratic rhetoric fared no better during the early days of conference and for many of the same reasons. Claims by House members that their bill was better for the middle class faded for lack of proof. Indeed, some evidence suggested that they were simply wrong. It was hard for Democrats to sell the notion that families earning as much as $60,000 per year—nearly three times the national average—deserved to be called middle class. Then, too, new JTC data revealed that differences between the House and Senate in the individual tax cuts going to taxpayers earning less than $50,000 had substantially lessened, so much so that the price tag for bringing the Senate distribution in line with the House had dropped from $20 billion to a mere $5 billion.

JTC analysis of 1984 returns also showed that House claims that IRAs amounted to a pension plan for the middle class were incorrect. As *Congressional Quarterly Weekly Report* reported at the time, taxpayers earning $20,000 to $50,000 received less than one-third of all IRA benefits in 1984: "The new arithmetic made it much more attractive to target the deduction to the under-$50,000 group," something the House had earlier resisted.[23]

Conference Gridlock

By July 24, when conferees gathered for their fourth meeting, preliminary waves of political rhetoric had washed over the conference and more or less disappeared from public attention. During the previous two days when meetings were sidelined so that the House could turn to budget reconciliation problems, conferees had time to reflect on where they were and where they would go next. Rethinking brought the enormous difficulties ahead fully into perspective. It seemed clear that if the conference committee were to complete its work by the August recess, something would have to be done to speed up negotiations.

Most participants saw two reasons for shifting procedural gears: (1) the amount of paper that had to be sifted in order to reconcile the two bills and (2) the lack of privacy in conducting their business. The stunning range and complexity of issues under debate confounded the conferees as well. With the entire tax code up for grabs, it was hopeless to expect conferees to negotiate their differences across the table. Instead, delegation of authority and a move to replace direct bargaining with a system of offers and counteroffers seemed an appropriate response to the dawdling pace.

The TRA was not unique in this respect. The rapid increase in complex "mega-bills" and omnibus legislation in recent years has reduced members' abilities to take a hands-on approach to conferencing. As a seasoned Ways and Means staffer pointed out, this has increased the role of staff specialists in legislative policy making because they are needed more than ever to define problems, prepare alternatives, and iron out technical differences:

> Conference epitomized the new role of staff in Congress in that members could not be expected to master or even grasp all of the areas under consideration. [It is important to] remember that even during the Rostenkowski-Packwood negotiations we relied on teams of staff experts. At most we could expect members to be familiar with and grasp what they were concerned about.

With regard to privacy, the first three days of posturing contained some familiar, unpleasant lessons about doing business under the bright lights of public and press scrutiny. Generally speaking, the need for back-room sessions to surmount heavy political pressure has increased in the Gramm-Rudman era. Conferees find ways to escape the sunshine in a painful, nearly year-round quest after spending cuts, tax hikes, or both.

Such fiscal pressure also affects conferences by limiting options that participants have for resolving conflicts. Historically, conferees have been able to settle their differences in two ways: by choosing between stronger or weaker provisions or by staking out an agreeable middle ground. This latter strategy of "splitting differences" has often been favored in tax conferences.[24] Especially in the heyday of easy money before tax indexation and large deficits, political support could readily be bought in this fashion. But it was obvious to everyone at the TRA conference that such a strategy would not work given the stricture of revenue neutrality. Instead, large doses of strong medicine would be needed, forcing members to make numerous politically painful sacrifices.

Because demand for such fiscal sacrifices put a premium on privacy in the deliberative process, beginning July 24 conferees suspended their public meetings until the final night of conference. Moreover, in recognition of their own incapacity to handle substantive table talk, conferees held only three additional closed-door, face-to-face sessions.[25]

Win Some, Lose Some

Despite its obvious problems, the conference might have struggled along meeting face to face in the back room had it not been for the aforementioned JTC-revised estimates of the Senate and House tax-reform bills. Although revenue estimators willingly admit that cost estimation is an inexact science, professionalism puts a high price on accuracy. Thus, when complete data on 1984 tax payments became available, JTC chief estimator Bernie Schmidt returned to work to fine tune his models. The results were both good and bad, and there could be no picking and choosing among them. Indeed, JTC's findings demonstrated yet again the remarkable power of professional revenue estimators to give to and take away from politicians in a revenue-neutral environment and, in so doing, to direct the policy debate.

So sensitive were the results that Rostenkowski called a private meeting of all conferees on July 24 to hear them. Dabblers in philosophy would have nodded their heads at the JTC work product for it was a perfect example of yin and yang. Analysts had bestowed $15 billion on Senate conferees by revealing that $5 billion rather than $20 billion was needed to match the House after-tax distribution. "So much for the claim that our bill was worse for the middle class! " thought senators.

With the good news came the bad. According to projections, the Senate bill fell short by $21.2 billion. In contrast, the House bill seemed to have picked up a whopping $38.3 billion. "We may have lost the middle-class fight," House conferees comforted themselves, "but, there's corporate reform coming." And, to that end they rightly refused to begin bargaining until the Senate satisfied the revenue neutrality rule.

Bill Bradley's response to this turn of the numbers was to suggest that the situation was now "more fluid." Reporters for *Tax Notes* put it more bluntly: "This attempt at tax reform," they editorialized, "is being run by the numbers. Revenue neutrality and the practical necessity of dimming the legislative urge to spend requires that tax policy decisions be made according to revenue estimates." [26] Both views were correct. Professionalism inadvertently succeeded where politics failed by getting the conference down to business. Moreover, JTC estimates brought heavy pressure on Packwood and his fellow conferees to face up to corporate reform. Consequently, when the closed-door session broke up, it was agreed that if Rostenkowski would accept the Senate bill and its rate structure as a tentative basis for decision making, Packwood would put together a package of changes rebalancing the Senate bill and making up the difference in after-tax cuts to the middle class.

To observers, it seemed that after nearly a week of political spear chucking the conference had finally begun. Indeed, this view proved correct, for during the next three weeks (July 24 to August 12) the Senate produced not one but two offers. The House responded with a sweeping counterproposal of its own. And, in a move that surprised everyone, Ways and Means Republicans countered Rostenkowski with their own offer in a failed attempt to end the disenfranchisement of House Republicans.

Congress watchers know that this kind of back-and-forth bicameral bargaining is largely conducted by staff members. As a result, by the time negotiations ended abruptly in stalemate on August 12, most conferees had become little more than part-time participants, coming to meetings only for progress reports and to review proposals and counterproposals prepared by the chairmen, their staffs, and the staff of the Joint Tax Committee. Their isolation increased to such an extent that after another week of "chairman summitry," one disgruntled tax counsel dubbed the conference the "Dan and Bob show," a perspective shared by many others. A conferee's tax counsel went so far as to say: "The only dynamic working there was Packwood and Rostenkowski. Nothing took place between the members of the full conference that was at all relevant to what was in the final report. Even the meetings of the Senate conferees were irrelevant to what was really going on."

This view understates the contributions of conferees to earlier versions of tax reform via the Ways and Means task forces and the Finance core group. That work, after all, set the parameters for later negotiations. Still, with the exception of Bill Bradley, who mediated between both parties and both chambers and who was a frequent visitor to Rostenkowski's office in the Capitol, many members felt left out of the uniquely centralized conference. Remarking that it was not only House Republicans who were out of touch, Ways and Means minority tax counsel Ken Kies recalled:

> The one thing I started to realize early was that the Democrats didn't have any more idea what was going on than the Republicans. Among others, for example, I'd be stopped in the House garage by Gephardt, and he'd say, "Hey, what's going on?" I'm thinking, if he doesn't know what's going on, who does?

A Run for the Money

Because the Senate bill fell short on money, the unpopular task of preparing initial offers fell to Senate conferees. It was a chore in which they had little interest and no enthusiasm. Thus, for some at least, the minuses of disengagement were counterbalanced by the pluses of a furlough from tough choices. This, of course, made resulting decisions harder to accept.

Packwood's First Try.   In an initial effort designed to please strong-minded conferees and to preserve as much of the Senate bill as possible, Packwood sought help from Treasury Department officials. Assistant Secretary Roger Mentz was happy to oblige with ideas from the exotic to the mundane. Thus, working in part from a Treasury list, Packwood offered a $26 billion proposal to the House on Saturday, July 26. It contained some legitimate consolidation of House and Senate bills, as well as suggestions that were nowhere to be found in either version of H.R. 3838.

House Response.   Like any first offer, this one was filled with tricks designed to finesse hard choices and also to test the resolve of House conferees. The response from the House was not the one the Senate had hoped for, nor was it comforting to Treasury's ghostwriters. In disdainfully rejecting the offer, Rostenkowski laid blame at more than Packwood's feet, reserving a portion of his stored-up ire for Baker, Darman, and Mentz. As if to make what was already plain transparent, he asked Packwood to tell Treasury officials to leave the room even before the July 24 meeting had begun.

With the administration's representatives thus dismissed, Rostenkowski turned his troops loose to criticize the proposal in frank terms. House Democrats accurately charged that Packwood's offer was more smoke and mirrors than genuine reform. Moreover they noted that over half of the sixteen items listed were nongermane, that is, they were not included in either the House- or the Senate-passed bill. Although the Ways and Means chairman was not above transgressing such legislative boundaries on occasion himself, it was not in Rostenkowski's interest to do so here, and the rules governing conferencing allowed him to reject such ventures. Applying those standards, House members vetoed the following items:

1. limiting mortgage interest deductions to no more than the purchase price of a home, plus the cost of any improvements ($3.9 billion)

2. including tax-exempt income when calculating taxes for certain high-income individuals ($1.5 billion)

3. reworking sales-tax tables (less than $50 million)

4. reducing the maximum amount employees may contribute to 401(k) retirement plans ($1.5 billion)

5. making state and local governments subject to the same rules as private employers in paying payroll taxes ($1.1 billion)

6. taxing credit unions with assets of more than $10 million ($.9 billion)

7. collecting federal excise taxes from refiners or importers rather than from wholesalers to prevent tax evasion ($1.0 billion)

8. requiring that prepaid income be accounted for when it is received ($1.5 billion)

House conferees grudgingly agreed to eight other Senate proposals, while warning Packwood to extract even more revenue from them in the next round of revisions. Suggestions given a tentative nod of approval were:

1. curtailing tax-exempt bonds in unspecified ways by $2 billion over five years

2. compromising on the House repeal of the General Utilities rule (which gives corporations a way to avoid being taxed at both the corporate and shareholder levels during mergers)

3. increasing taxation on foreign income

4. agreeing to tax payments to utilities earmarked for capital improvements

5. cutting from 50 to 25 percent the Senate bill deduction for health-insurance premiums paid by self-employed individuals

6. maintaining the present-law threshold for payroll tax payments to the federal government rather than easing this requirement as provided in the Senate bill

7. reforming contributions in aid of construction

8. moving up the "sunset" on the research and development tax credit by one year[27]

Senate Reaction. The House response did not sit well with most Senate conferees, who remained skittish about the impact of reform on business. Indeed, the all-or-nothing position preferred by some demonstrated once again how thin support for tax reform was on the Finance Committee and how some members were unwilling to submit to the usual pattern of conference give-and-take as a result.

Rostenkowski was able to take a firm first-round stand because, as Don

Pease quipped, the Senate had inadvertently broken a cardinal rule of the tax-reform policy-making process: "It's realism time at the O.K. Corral. Our basic position is that the Senate came up short. [It] has to come up with ways to raise the revenue which are acceptable to us." [28] Colvin agreed:

> There was a lot of discussion in the early stages about the Senate "anteing up." But to the extent that the Senate was giving up items, it was because the Senate was $23 billion short and so was obligated to come in with a revenue-neutral bill. They weren't *giving* anything to the House. They were meeting their obligations.

Packwood's Second Try.   In meeting its obligations, the Senate reluctantly agreed to try again. Packwood promised to draw exclusively from the House bill and include $4 billion for a few benefits the Senate wished to restore—including an expansion of the tax credit for poor workers and a larger standard deduction for the elderly and the blind. Indeed, the proposal was offered the very next day, and it contained the eight previously mentioned acceptable provisions (totaling $11.5 billion) as well as some restrictions of corporate benefits. In terms of the latter, Senate conferees raised $17.4 billion by:

1. limiting depreciation deductions by corporations ($6.8 billion)
2. eliminating income averaging for farmers ($.3 billion)
3. repealing the corporate capital-gains differential ($4 billion)
4. repealing the bad-debt reserve allowance for nonfinancial institutions ($.5 billion)
5. limiting bad-debt reserves for banks and thrift institutions ($3.9 billion)[29]
6. disallowing deductions for debt incurred in purchasing or carrying tax-exempt bonds by banks and thrift institutions ($.5 billion)
7. extending capitalization rules to accelerated depreciation on all assets, not just those placed in service after March 1, 1986 ($1.7 billion)
8. accepting House provisions affecting the targeted-jobs tax credit ($.5 billion)[30]

The total contribution of this proposal was $29.7 billion over five years.

The dollars attached to these sacrifices were predictably hard-won. Danforth told reporters that he had "choked and gagged and gasped" before swallowing them. He and other Senate conferees believed that this second offer was sufficiently generous that no further discussion ought to be necessary. "This," they asserted, "was the Senate's last offer." [31]

The House Comes Back

It was not enough for the House. In Rostenkowski's view, Packwood and his troops had only begun to march toward a point of agreement. Having first signaled that the offer was a "good start," Rostenkowski quickly turned to the Ways and Means and Joint Tax committee staffs for a strong counteroffer. At that point the staffs' preconference work devising possible merging of House and Senate bills came into play. Proving how much of tax reform was a reinvention of the wheel and how well Rostenkowski used staff resources to his advantage, he had a counteroffer within twenty-four hours, one that many thought looked like a third tax plan. Indeed, because it so threatened to transform the conference universe with a single bold and unexpected stroke, this tough, partisan-inspired counteroffer was nicknamed the "Big Bang."

In comparison with the short and vague Senate revenue-raising proposals, the Big Bang was a fairly complete balance sheet for the finished tax-reform product, with nine pages devoted to detailed revenue estimates and five more to an accounting of which chamber would accommodate on which provisions to achieve this result. Press headlines captured the real message behind the details, however: "Democrats Try to Put Party's Stamp on Tax Bill." Indeed, the House stuck to its positions curtailing tax benefits for extractive industries, taking a bite out of such politically sensitive, industry-specific tax breaks as those for oil and gas drillers, timber concerns, and miners.[32] Equally important, the House proposal sought $28 billion in reduced depreciation benefits. That amount represented a $10 billion-plus reduction from original House depreciation provisions in H.R. 3838, but it was still more than $21 billion higher than the Senate's most recent offer. Finally, after considerable internal wrangling, House conferees retained the entire deduction for state and local taxes.

By way of concessions, these would-be traders agreed to reduce by 5 percent the House plan's stiffer corporate minimum tax. They also compromised in areas where the Senate had been tougher on individuals, notably by disallowing charitable deductions for taxpayers who do not itemize and agreeing to phase out consumer-interest deductions.

These were important concessions. Yet many others were substantially less painful. For example, despite their expected negative effect on real estate—an industry dear to many Ways and Means members—the Senate's passive-loss rules read like a page from the classics of populistic tax reform. Thus, in consenting to this and other "democratic" elements of the Senate bill, House protests were only mild.

Ways and Means Republicans' Counter-Counteroffer

Meanwhile, details of the Big Bang leaked to the Senate before the ranking minority member of Ways and Means, John Duncan, and his fellow Republican conferees had even been briefed! In haste, on August 4 the disgusted minority floated a Ways and Means Republican alternative to Rostenkowski. The proposal exactly split the difference between chambers on corporate base broadening, raising $20 billion less than the

Big Bang, but $20 billion more than the most recent Senate proposal. Predictably, Rostenkowski rejected the entire list.[33]

Meanwhile, Packwood was campaigning in Oregon when news of the Big Bang leaked on July 31. Without many substantive details, he stayed quiet, clearly preferring to withhold judgment until returning to Washington; his colleagues, however, exploded with frustration. At least one impolite Republican conferee spoke out of turn, publicly rejecting the House counteroffer before Chairman Packwood had officially even received it. With the barn door thus already opened, Packwood broke his silence with half-hearted criticism on August 4, telling reporters that he was disappointed and that no Senate counteroffer would be forthcoming.

The Senate's Final, Final Offer

The rejection was made official on Tuesday, August 5, at the first conference session held since July 28. The closed and unofficial meeting was held halfway between the Senate and the House, in a Ways and Means hearing room below the House chamber in the Capitol. Despite earlier threats to the contrary and some very tough talk, by the end of the meeting Packwood had agreed to prepare yet another final list of proposals to narrow differences on business taxes. After nearly three weeks of painful work, Senate acquiescence was not hard to figure out. Moynihan may have put his finger on the explanation when he told reporters, "The feeling is how do we get this over with?"[34]

For the next week Packwood struggled to do just that. It was not an easy task. Finding enough money to return the Senate bill to revenue neutrality had been hard, and it had used up every bit of Packwood's wiggle room. Thus, although Rostenkowski's ploy of accepting the Senate's tax-rate structure never produced the rate increases he had hoped for (individual and corporate top rates were ultimately raised only a single percentage point each, from 27 to 28 and from 33 to 34 percent), it was very effective in forcing the Senate to close more corporate loopholes.

Senate Independence

Packwood's troubles were largely a reflection of senators' reluctance to give up policy say-so in the name of tax reform. Time and again, Packwood returned to the table to put new twists on old ideas for broad-based corporate reform in an effort to gain needed votes. Time and again, the result was outright refusal or grudging acceptance.

Not only did conferees despair over changes affecting most corporations, they also dug in on narrow policy and constituent concerns. For example, Bill Roth—an advocate of savings incentives and a consumption tax to discourage spending—made IRAs his line in the sand. When Packwood went back on his promise (made earlier during Senate floor debate) to help Roth out in conference, the Republican from Delaware withheld his support.

Similarly, Danforth was determined to preserve the so-called completed-contract method of accounting for defense contractors. When he couldn't, this much-respected Presbyterian minister voted against the conference agreement and, later, against the TRA. To be sure, Danforth's rationale was not entirely predicated on the future effects of tax reform on Missouri defense contractors. Yet, as one staffer recalled: "Danforth decided that there were two things he really wanted. [One was] the completed-contract method of accounting. His high-risk strategy was to give his unswerving support in exchange for a promise to save [it]. But, it was expensive, and he lost."

Danforth and Roth were not the only victims. But, as is generally the case in legislative politics, in conference losers tended to be loners. Thus, for example, while Danforth was the only supporter of defense contractors and so ultimately lost, Russell Long successfully limited the damage to oil and gas by seeing to it that his interests were well represented on the list of conferees. In this world of zero-sum politics, failure might be delayed by loyalty to Packwood, but, as Brockway noted, it was unlikely to be avoided entirely:

> It was like one of these caribou herds going through Alaska, with the wolves circling it. As soon as predators separated out one of the weaker ones, it was dead. It might take an hour before it was caught. The wolves are patient. But, eventually they separate one out, nip it in the leg, and the rest is inevitable. Danforth's problem played out that way. There was absolutely no way you were going to come out of conference retaining $8 billion for defense contractors that hadn't been paying taxes for years and years and years. With the Senate constantly being squeezed, the House could wait for Danforth.[35]

House Loyalty

In the process of hard bargaining, disparities between chamber loyalties became uncomfortably obvious. Rostenkowski's institutional advantages and approach to naming conferees began to pay large dividends as the conference got down to brass tacks. He secured support for a number of difficult decisions that might not have been accepted by a more senior list of conferees. For example, in the politically explosive matter of the state and local tax deduction, nonconferee Tom Downey had played a strong hand in committee. The prospect of further disloyalty had been enough to strike him from the list of potential conferees. At the same time, Rostenkowski's decision to count on the greater tractability of another New Yorker, conferee Charles Rangel, gave him needed breathing room. As Rangel pointed out:

I remember one meeting with the governor [Cuomo] ... and he wanted
[me] to agree to vote against the bill if the whole deduction wasn't
retained. And I asked, "Let me get this straight. You want me, a
conferee, the third-ranking Democrat on the committee, to give that all
up. ..." I had to be concerned with the poor, with labor, with charity,
and education.

When asked how he felt when sales taxes were omitted from the final
House proposal, Rangel winked twice and replied, "I guess it was a tactical
thing that they didn't have time to tell me about."

Yet Another House Rejection

Packwood's struggle to minimize defections and still raise contributions
showed in the package he previewed privately for Rostenkowski on August
11. Altogether, he was able to produce only an additional $3.5 billion,
raising the Senate corporate offer to $118.5, $27 billion short of Rostenkowski's latest. Most money came from yet another finesse. In a transparent attempt to hang onto remaining corporate provisions *and* to the Senate
rate structure, Packwood and his colleagues had jumped at a suggestion by
John Chafee to suspend inflation indexing for one year, raising $21.5
billion in not-so-funny money. Another decision which suggested that
common sense and basic fairness were sometimes lost in the race for
revenue was one to *retroactively* rescind the "three-year recovery rule,"
which allowed nontaxation for the first thirty-six months of federal pension
benefits.[36]

Even while Packwood worked to put his final offer to rest, another
conference trouble sign was rising: the Senate's attempt to raise $17 billion
by increasing IRS collections, to be achieved by beefing up the agency's
budget (at a cost of $150 million). Back in late April, with a finger to the
political winds, the JTC had set the revenue estimate for this at a
whopping $17.6 billion. The ploy fooled few. Even Reagan's budget
director, James Miller III, publicly questioned whether one dollar of
increased IRS budget authority could generate ten dollars in collections.[37]

Packwood was not about to give up the badly needed revenue. He tried
to sidestep the president's chief budget officer by directing the IRS to shift
existing resources to revenue-generating activities. But this tack did not
please IRS Commissioner Lawrence Gibbs. In a move that underscores the
diverse and competing interests within the executive branch—even on the
president's number-one legislative priority—Gibbs stormed up to Rostenkowski's office to protest. Although he was later forced to recant publicly
by an embarrassed Secretary Baker, the deed was done.

Thus alerted by bureaucratic infighting, Rostenkowski went on the
march against the trust-fund proposal. And, when he convened a conference meeting on August 12 to discuss Packwood's latest ideas for corporate

base broadening, Rosty demanded that the Senate find another $17 billion to replace it. Packwood's distress was visible, and rage registered on the faces of other Senate conferees.

Adding further pain to an already painful situation, House conferees next objected to most of what had been dreamed up, especially the idea of delaying indexing. Having thus rejected the major revenue raiser in the proposal, House members turned toward favorite areas of corporate fat. With this onslaught, the meeting disintegrated into angry charges and countercharges. Indeed, relations had sunk so low that it appeared the conference might deadlock. In this moment of peril observers pondered the unspoken question, "Which way now?"

One-on-One on Tax Reform

With all his years of experience, Russell Long had anticipated such a stalemate. In hopes of salvaging the bill, he had privately discussed turning things over to the chairmen in the event of committee gridlock. Not surprisingly, Packwood and Rostenkowski liked the idea.

Given his role as one of the principal architects of the existing tax code, it seemed unusual that Long should volunteer to reduce his own influence. Yet, while he was no admirer of either bill, forty years in Congress had impressed on Long the value of political realism. The Louisianan figured that one way or another Congress had to pass a sweeping tax-reform bill in the 99th Congress, and he fretted about what further delay might mean for Louisiana industries. If the economy worsened in the coming months, JTC estimators would need even more corporate base broadening to produce the same amount of money, and this, of course, spelled trouble for the oil and gas preferences Long had thus far been able to protect.

But more than money was at stake. Long believed that Congress ought to be a full partner with the president in democratic governance and that institutional integrity depended on protecting legislative traditions. Earlier, one such rule of conduct, that Senators ought to protect their states, had led Long away from tax reform and down the trail of support for oil and gas. In August 1986, though, other important traditions moved him back toward tax reform: "Senators ought to support the Senate," Long believed, and "Finance Committee members should support their chairman." Indeed, back in April Long promised as much to Packwood: "Mr. Chairman," he had said, "Do it your way and I'll do the best I can to go along with you." [38]

Finally, Long was due to retire, raising the question of how he hoped to be remembered. With Rostenkowski's private pledge to minimize the negative effects of tax reform on the oil and gas industry, Long had no wish to go down in history as a champion of special interests who had

obstructed the most sweeping tax-reform proposal in over a half-century.
"Elder statesman" suited him better. With all these motives in mind, the
quiet, plain-spoken Long urged his colleagues:

> Well, it doesn't seem to me there's much progress being made here. We
> senators have a lot of confidence in Mr. Packwood, and I suspect you
> folks do in Mr. Rostenkowski. So I don't see why those chairmen don't
> get together by themselves and come up with a proposal that we all can
> then consider.[39]

Coming when so little had been accomplished by the conference
committee, it was a remarkable suggestion disguised in ordinary language.
At first, the delegation of responsibility seemed only one example of a
trend already evident in the Reagan era. Arguably, in this period of
legislative "shun-shine" and increased partisanship, conferences already
looked more like diplomatic summitry than legislative markup. As chief
diplomats and spokesmen for their respective delegations and institutions,
the chairmen hold death, if not life, power over policy in conference. Yet
the delegation of responsibility in H.R. 3838 was especially notable
because it came at a time when so many of the difficult questions, large
and small, remained unanswered. Although conferees had narrowed their
differences, they had settled on almost nothing and, as Kies recalled, many
areas of significant dispute were still untouched:

> In terms of the way most conferences have been done, this one was
> unusual. At some point, members usually sit down and talk through the
> issues. That never happened in this conference. Conferee discussions
> never got above what I would call Tax Reform 101. So there are a lot of
> things that got included in the bill which you are going to hear about
> over the next few years. Members will say, "Oh, I didn't know that they
> did that."

In retrospect, it is not overstatement to say that on August 12, the
conferees turned over their most troublesome problems to the only two
members who couldn't avoid them. Strict standards of democratic representation may or may not judge their action harshly, but there is no doubt
that this abdication was a last-gasp effort to forestall total stalemate.

The Room without Windows or Doors

In the week leading up to August 16, Rostenkowski and Packwood held
more than thirty meetings in the Chicagoan's prestigious office in the
Capitol, laboring nearly around the clock across a small table in what one
senator called "the room without windows or doors." For those meetings
each had his men: Diefenderfer and Colvin for Packwood, Dowley and
Leonard for Rostenkowski. And of course, seated at the end of the table in
a position an equal distance from each side were the ever-present David
Brockway and his deputy, economist Randy Weiss. Yet, even this expert
cadre of staff was not enough to satisfy the information demands of so

sweeping a rewrite of the federal tax code. So, teams of experts from House, Senate, and the JTC were shuttled in and out to define problems, lay out options, and make recommendations. By mid-week, Colvin and Leonard had been dispatched to other meeting rooms for parallel negotiations as a way of further expediting decision making.

Near the meeting table was a small bank of phones, strung like a life-line to the JTC offices and to a Univac computer that hummed day and night, grinding out hundreds of iterations of revenue projections. Despite well-known flaws in the estimating process, JTC numbers on costs and benefits remained the litmus tests for tax reform.

Very little of what was discussed in those sessions reached the public, at least not directly. What did leaked out as howls of pain from upset conferees. Indeed, legislators on both sides of the Capitol developed good reasons to regret their abdication of responsibility as the chairmen bowed to the rigid regime of revenue neutrality. They made decisions few would think sensible (for example, taxing college students' scholarships and fellowships) as well as others that seemed long overdue (eliminating a modest $600 million worth of oil and gas tax breaks).[40] Yet, while some constituencies suffered more than others in the last-minute wheeling and dealing, neither partisan loyalty nor personal relationships predicted who got hurt. Instead, money forecast all. So much revenue was needed that Rangel not only lost his beachhead on the sales-tax deduction, he saw it wash away entirely.

Thanks to the centralization of responsibility, by August 14 Packwood and Rostenkowski were putting the finishing touches on a final agreement. The way for the settlement was paved by three important Packwood concessions. The first raised the top corporate tax rate by one point to 34 percent. The second added another $4.2 billion in corporate base broadening, half from depreciation subsidies and half from miscellaneous business provisions. The third finally allowed the individual top tax rate to slip up one notch to 28 percent. At last, it seemed, the Senate had tithed enough.

Unfortunately, it was not to be. Throughout tax reform, the revenue estimators had haunted the process. In what were to be its final hours, those harbingers of statistical trouble were working on yet a final re-estimation of the agreement between the Finance and Ways and Means chairmen. In fairness, revenue estimators had few options. JTC is bound by law to re-estimate pending legislation whenever the Congressional Budget Office revises its economic forecast. New CBO forecasts were due in August, and given the weak state of the economy, Brockway had warned everyone to be prepared for trouble.

Late in the evening on August 14, JTC's unwelcome messengers arrived at Rostenkowski's office where the two chairmen and their aides were working out final details. Ugly numbers jumped off the page: another $17 billion shortfall, $10 billion of it on the corporate side! The most recent Senate proposal added $124 billion in new corporate taxes that afternoon. Now, as a result of incorporating new economic assumptions, it retained only $114 billion by nightfall. The rest had become lost in a thicket of economic assumptions.

What was Packwood to do? He had been struggling for modest millions in concessions from Senate conferees, and the new revenue estimates meant he would have to get agreement on billions. Out of frustration, the Finance chief sought to ignore the problem, phoning Baker for approval, which he easily got. A year earlier, Baker had stated that 1 percent of total tax revenues was an adequate definition of revenue neutrality,[41] so, he and Packwood reasoned, "In a trillion dollar economy, what difference did $17 billion make?"

Rostenkowski, however, would not let the problem be reduced to fiscal semantics. He was well aware that the static re-estimates were no more than a rough, snapshot guide to tax reform's actual price tag. But there would be no hidden tax cuts on the Illinois Democrat's watch. If Reagan and the Republicans wanted a tax cut, let them ask for one.

Despite a midnight stroll around the statuary in the historic and inspiring Capitol rotunda, the two chairmen could not find a way to bridge the large gap that lay between them and tax reform. The night shift of news reporters who had already written tax reform's victorious headline was not sure what to believe anymore. As John Colvin remembered, "The press reported it as a last-minute snag. It was more than that. It was absolutely dead!" In fact, while Rostenkowski and Packwood did not wish it and while some Capitol Hill night owls could not believe it, the two physically and emotionally exhausted tax-reform warriors had finally hit a wall.

Thus, Diefenderfer interrupted a late-night Colvin-Leonard review session with pension specialists to report, "It's over. We're short and we are going to break up until after the August recess." Like worn-out travelers finally halted, they were relieved and ready to head home (or in some cases to nearby pubs for a chance to relax and unwind). As Colvin told it:

> There's not much in the way of tax reform humor, but this evening was my personal favorite. We were meeting in the conference room of the Joint Committee—maybe twenty of us sitting around. Everyone had the House bill, which was so many inches thick, the Senate bill, which was so many more inches thick, the tax code, which was *really* thick, and a pile of other materials. If you multiplied that amount by twenty you had a lot of paper on the table. When I made the announcement that we were breaking up, I'll bet every piece of paper was interred in a briefcase in about sixty seconds! It was a unanimous "Thank God." We left almost as though we didn't have a care in the world.

Stumbling over the Finish Line

Not a care, that is, until 7:00 A.M when Colvin was awakened by a phone call from Packwood. It was Friday, August 15, the date set for congressional adjournment, and the Finance chairman wanted a press conference to clear the air. He also wanted to get together with top staff to review the prior evening's events and plot the next steps. Rostenkowski, too, was heading toward the Capitol to meet with trusted aides. Even so, neither believed the process could be resurrected immediately, and both wanted to be on the next plane home.

An already-scheduled Rostenkowski-Packwood photo session with *Time* magazine at 7:30 A.M. brought the men no closer together even as they obligingly joined hands in a V-sign for victory. The picture would later provide the cover for *Time* magazine, but that morning it was a painful and public reminder of what seemed out of reach.

Rostenkowski returned to his office to wrap up unfinished business, while Packwood vented his frustration with the Joint Tax Committee at an impromptu press conference in the Senate gallery. "There's no point in talking about what we're going to do now," Packwood said. "We've been intentionally misled." [42] It was the second time Packwood had abused or otherwise misused David Brockway. This time, however, the sometimes hot-tempered legislator had clearly crossed the line of fair play between members of Congress and their staffs in his search for a scapegoat. As a top Republican aide asserted: "Whipping boys are one thing, this was another. I have never seen a chairman attack staff like that in public. I've seen them dressed down in private. That's done all the time. But, you don't go on national television and say, 'This guy lied to me.'"

Packwood's angry attack later made Brockway a folk hero in the eyes of Senate insiders, but the moment was painful for the hard-working veteran and his team. It also reflected how far their relationship had regressed from the enjoyable days in which Brockway and his staff had helped Packwood prepare the "27 percent solution."

Having publicly vented his frustration with legislating-by-number, Packwood headed for what he presumed was a last meeting with Senate conferees. The session was held in Long's hideaway office in the Capitol. Upon arriving, he got an unexpected pep talk. "Go back and try again," senators urged. Cheerleaders included more than tax-reform advocates Bill Bradley, Pat Moynihan, and John Chafee. Long pushed Packwood on for the same reasons he had suggested shifting tax-reform responsibilities earlier. Other oil-and-gas-state senators shared Long's fears if not his view of Congress, and they, too, joined in a chorus of support.

Newly encouraged that he would ultimately get acceptance of future compromises, Packwood did what he wanted to do all along. He telephoned Rostenkowski; and Rostenkowski greeted the phone call warmly. He had long ago abandoned hope of attaining the House Speakership and had grown fearful that tax reform, too, might slip from his grasp. So they agreed to pick up where they had left off the night before. At 11:30 A.M. Colvin began rounding up his staff, while Brockway and Dowley did the same.

By late afternoon, the entire cast had reassembled. Tension-filled yet disciplined meetings continued throughout the day, evening, and into the night. As if some psychological dam had been broken, Rostenkowski made an important concession by agreeing to adjust the so-called break points between tax brackets (and in so doing reduce the total individual tax cut). Packwood surrendered his share as well, or to be more accurate, the remaining shares of colleagues like Danforth. As a result of surprisingly amicable give-and-take, by 11:00 P.M. all that was left was to mechanically combine the two bills. The chairmen went home to sleep while the bleary-eyed staff stayed behind to prepare the briefing papers the conferees would need the next morning.

Last-Minute Adjustments

Unprecedented summitry had produced a single tax-reform statement affecting every economic interest and taxpayer in America. In the process, two men and a handful of staff had made many minor as well as the most important decisions of tax reform, including the following:

1. holding very close to the original rates in the Senate bill
2. abandoning hope of wiping out the so-called stagger by which tax preferences were eliminated before rates were reduced
3. making only a modest adjustment in the after-tax individual benefits distribution called for in the Senate bill
4. accepting nearly all the Senate reforms affecting individuals and the concept of passive losses
5. compromising on IRAs
6. eliminating the deduction for sales-tax payments altogether (and thereby stiffening the law beyond what was contained in either bill)
7. cutting back substantially the Senate bill's generous depreciation provisions
8. injecting reform into highly contentious industry-specific areas of the tax code
9. holding the damage to oil, gas, timber, and mining to a modest level.

Although there was no doubt that centralization got the job done, there was considerable doubt whether so isolated a policy process could also produce the necessary signatures on the conference agreement in time to beat the August recess. Proving skeptics right, the next day the two chairmen were forced to endure a final lesson in legislative politics when meetings on both sides of the Capitol failed to produce majority support.

Senate Lessons.   After a phone call from Packwood, Baker and Darman arrived at a Saturday morning Finance Committee meeting designed to produce a Senate stamp of approval. Packwood was concerned about the reaction of his conferees, and he wanted the administration there to apply extra pressure. With conferees once again seated around the table in the Finance exec room, Packwood handed out an eighty-three-page "summary." Since no one had time to read it, what few final insights conferees gained into the details of this historic agreement came from an oral primer delivered by Packwood.

As they were described, highlights of provisions changed in last-minute negotiations would:

1. raise corporate taxes by $120 billion and cut individual taxes the same amount

2. partially fix the stagger by putting top rates at 38.5 percent in the first year, but provide that all but 20 percent of taxpayers get a tax cut in 1987. Thereafter, rates would drop to 15 percent and 28 percent for individuals and 34 percent for corporations

3. increase the personal exemption to $1,900 in 1987, $1,950 in 1988, and $2,000 in 1989

4. eliminate the deduction for state and local sales taxes

5. cut back the completed-contract method of accounting by an additional $3.5 billion

6. reduce depreciation benefits by $13 billion

7. subtract $850 million in oil and gas benefits

The medicine was strong enough that despite eloquent pitches from tax-reform advocates Packwood counted only three yes votes—Bradley, Moynihan, and himself. When he recessed the meeting without agreement, lobbyists outside enjoyed a momentary delusion. Could it be that the senators were going to turn Packwood down?

The conferees convened two more times that Saturday. At the first session, most were distracted by the surprising news that the House members weren't happy with Rostenkowski's last-minute negotiating. "If that is true," a jaded observer thought, "perhaps Packwood had done as well as could be expected." Then, too, Bob Dole made a stirring pitch for Packwood, saying that as majority leader he supported the chairman.

For reasons that will never be entirely clear, but that included a few last-minute promises for favorable transition rules, by the second meeting majority sentiment had swung back to support. Indeed, when votes were counted, Packwood lost only two of those present (Wallop and Danforth). (In the end, he would lose another Republican, the skeptical Bill Roth, but for now he did not because Roth had left for Delaware without leaving a proxy. And, Packwood had the good sense not to ask for one.)

House Lessons. Meanwhile, Rostenkowski was having his own troubles. Despite a tough take-it-or-leave-it stance and a blunt promise to remember quislings during transition-rule writing, Rostenkowski encountered opposition. On the one hand, House conferees had even less time and help than senators in understanding the language they were being asked to agree to, and as representatives, most believed in doing their homework. On the other hand, distributional tables made easy reading, and Democratic conferees didn't like what they saw. Percentage tax cuts were supposed to decline smoothly as income rose, but the slope of the line had become erratic. Specifically, Rostenkowski's agreement to bracket changes had inadvertently reduced to nearly zero the aggregate tax cut for the $50,000 to $100,000 income class. Upon discovering it, the conferees so often described as "rubber stamps" showed some surprising steel. "Go back," they told Rostenkowski, "and tell Packwood we want the distribution made right."

With time running out, solving the problem required a sophisticated understanding of tax-code dynamics. What solution would not also cause new dislocations in the delicately balanced bill? In this last crisis, Bill Bradley came forth with an answer that carried the day. "Why not," he said, "put back a 5 rather than 4 percent surtax on the wealthiest taxpayers?" The resulting revenue could be used to improve the distribution of benefits (something House conferees wanted) without raising the top rate to 29 percent (something Senate conferees refused to do). Coming from Bradley, the advice carried weight on both sides of the Capitol and across party lines. At last, House and Senate were satisfied.

Looking back, it seems fitting that junior senator Bradley, the legislator who conceived tax reform, also delivered it, with an answer devised by his own pair of experts, tax counsel Gina Despres and economist Joe Minarik. It seems equally appropriate that more senior congressional and executive branch leaders, Packwood, Rostenkowski, and Baker, then met in secret session to give their blessing to his idea. Though not natural reformers, those three men, representing Congress and the president, were essential to legislative success.

With the committee's work finished, conferees gathered at 9:30 P.M. in the Ways and Means hearing room, inviting the "public" back to observe and so to legitimate the final pro-forma voice vote. The display was more for the record than for those who were physically present. There was nary an average American to be found that Saturday night. Instead, the audience for the benediction was composed almost entirely of the tax-reform faithful: Hill staff, lobbyists, and journalists. As a result, to those who had watched tax reform's highs and lows, the moment seemed anticlimactic and out of touch. Having correctly proclaimed, "They said it couldn't be done. Well, we've done it," Rostenkowski could only have been speaking to the history books when he summed up the tax-reform story with words mythologists might use as signposts of participatory democracy. They were rarely true during tax reform: "We've had a lot of help around Washington . . . and [we] appreciate it. But, we would have never come even halfway without the steady, often silent, faith of the millions of average taxpayers who freely comply and expect to do better."

In fact, the public remained more than a little skeptical, and conference, like nearly every hurdle in tax reform, was not surmounted by popular outcry. Indeed, even the president (who spent all the crucial weeks of conference on his California ranch) and his men who stayed behind were little to be found during the last phase of legislative consideration. Instead, conference was driven by a congressional elite of senior members and junior activists. It was an act of the very few on behalf of the many. Whether citizens would appreciate it, or for that matter whether the two chambers would approve it, remained a question mark that late night of August 16, 1986.[43]

From Conference to Congress

After the vote Rostenkowski was ebullient, and he exercised a chairman's right to capture most of the final conference headlines with a glowing victory speech unusual for a back-room politician. In contrast a rumpled and exhausted Packwood had surprisingly little to say. Instead, he leaned over to his comrade-in-arms Bradley, admitting honestly, "I didn't believe it would happen." That said, with a conference agreement finally in his hands, Packwood then forecast its final passage after what he predicted would be "spirited debate." [44]

The conference report did pass—first in the House on September 25, then in the Senate on September 27. And debate *was* spirited. Even so, despite fears that special-interest groups would mount a last-ditch attack and that weak grassroots support would give them an opening, neither vote was even close. The lobbyists were absent, as many of them had already turned to planning return engagements in 1987: most expected Congress to confront inevitable problems by making "technical" (and perhaps even substantive) legislative corrections to the TRA.

House Debate

In keeping with its constitutional prerogatives, the House was the first chamber to take up the conference report. It was a privilege few members appreciated.[45] All along, tax reform had been propelled by a strange combination of positive and negative energies. It succeeded because a few dogged and well-placed individuals made heroic, if not always purely motivated attempts to save it and because their efforts were grudgingly approved by the optionless majority.

This joyless dynamic continued to the very end. Having first delayed floor consideration because legislative counsel and committee staff (deluged by thousands of transition-rule requests) required an extension to complete their drafting, Rostenkowski next stumbled onto a shaky vote count. Revisiting the GOP insurrection of 1985, House Republican leaders were unable to get a majority of followers to support the conference report. Considering the weak state of the economy, House Republicans wished Packwood had been more successful fending off corporate reform, and they were still troubled by the loss of incentives for capital formation. Democrats wavered too, but for different reasons. They had trouble accepting the unprogressive rates and the loss of middle-class benefits in exchange for tax cuts for the working poor and fewer loopholes.[46] Finally, members of all ideological stripes and geographic regions had complaints about provisions that affected their own districts and states.

Against all the pent-up anxiety about supporting tax reform were fears about opposing it: worries about voting against a perceived tax cut, about losing important transition rules, and about future electoral consequences of opposing "reform" per se. As in the past, these recurring concerns plus another letter from the president to Republicans restored members' shaky resolve. Thus, after an extra week allocated to legislative drafting and another to building member support, the report was scheduled for a vote.

Although the conclusion was foregone, House floor debate lasted for almost four hours, combining "for the record statements" of anguish about district and constituency losses as well as rhetorical praise and condemnation. Bill Archer, R-Texas, took on the role of opposition leader because John Duncan, the ranking minority member on Ways and Means, and a TRA supporter, would not. By that point, Archer was joined on the floor by very few Ways and Means or other Republicans. When he raised the now familiar specter of doom and gloom—"Why should we gamble [with the economy] when we don't have to?"—he was drowned out by a chorus of Republicans claiming credit. As Guy Vander Jagt, chairman of the National Republican Congressional Committee and fellow conferee warned, "I personally would give my right arm to run against an incumbent who voted against this bill."

Democrats, too, went through the rhetorical motions of praise and credit claiming. Clearly overpowered, critics like Jim Wright stayed quiet while Rostenkowski, Gephardt, and retiring House Speaker Tip O'Neill used their final speeches to sound traditional Democratic themes. As Speaker, O'Neill had the last word of the afternoon, and he used his time to remind everyone that by taking six million working poor off the tax rolls, H.R.

3838 "was the best antipoverty bill in this House for at least a half a dozen years."

Thus, as tax-reform notables Baker and Darman looked on from the gallery, and as Bradley watched from the rear of the floor, the House passed tax reform by a vote of 292−136.[47]

Senate Passage

The Senate began debate the next day, passing H.R. 3838 twenty-four hours later by an even larger margin, but with the same kinds of reservations. Most important, in the days leading up to floor consideration members fretted about the absence of public support to counter interest-group complaints. Regrets added up to little more than that, however. Submitting to the same political dynamic as the House, three out of four senators swallowed their reservations and reported to Packwood and Bradley's head-counters that they would be supporting the conference committee report.

With so large a cushion of commitments in his pocket, Packwood appeared relaxed during the period scheduled for Senate debate. He filled proponents' time by replaying his chronology of tax reform, a history lesson he had first delivered in June. More interesting commentary came from the opposition minority, Republican and Democrat.

The most noteworthy Republican testimony came from John Danforth who, having decided not to filibuster the bill as he had once threatened, settled instead for recounting a less complimentary version of the TRA's legislative history as well as offering a spirited critique of the bill itself. Danforth's commentary filled twelve pages in the *Congressional Record* and made a compelling case that while the TRA "has some very good things in it," on balance, the legislation was neither "simple," nor "economically productive," nor "fair," as reformers had promised. Gesturing to a nearly empty chamber, Danforth asked, "Why vote for something that you don't like . . . that you think is bad?" As the Missourian answered his own question, the rationale was not that members truly "liked the bill." Hardly. As he editorialized, the real reasons amounted to little more than individual "inertia" confronting massive legislation or fear of "crossing one's party, one's president, or one's chairman." Then, too, Danforth asserted, members acquiesced to avoid some future "30-second, negative campaign commercial" or because they might lose a special break or transition rule. Although Danforth's speech contained obvious truth, his statement was more for "the show" than "the game" since even he admitted, "I do not expect to win."[48]

On the Democratic side, Carl Levin captured the most attention with his stand for greater progressivity. Indeed, in the hours that intervened between the conference report's introduction and the Senate vote of passage, Levin, along with Paul Simon, seemed to be the only Democrats willing to stand up for this heretofore-liberal commandment. Finally Howard Metzenbaum also returned to the floor to pick up where he had left off in June, castigating tax writers for newly added special-interest transition rules.[49]

But in the end, lively debate swayed few votes. The only real surprise was that the unruly Senate for once acted at the appointed time and easily passed the conference report by a vote of 73−24 on September 27, 1986.[50]

Home to the White House

After two years, tax reform was on its way back home to 1600 Pennsylvania Avenue. The initial send-off had been filled with pomp and promise, and although the return trip through Congress had taken its political toll, the president wanted to exploit the occasion of signing H.R. 3838 to cement this fiscal jewel in the crown of his second presidential term.

As a marine band played "Hail to the Chief," Reagan stepped briskly out to a waiting audience of hundreds, including famous and not-so-famous faces of tax reform and a contingent of ordinary citizens from Bourbon County, Kentucky. The setting that bright fall day on the south lawn of the White House was picture-perfect.

The mood was somewhat less so. Try as Reagan's public-relations team might, by October 22 when the president sat down to sign the Tax Reform Act of 1986, it was impossible to inject further drama into the proceedings. After a month of more careful attention and a not-insubstantial amount of criticism, the superlatives that are frequently used at such moments did not seem to fit the occasion.

Once victory was ensured and details about the official changes it would bring began surfacing, talk turned to more substantive aspects of the legislation. On every front of tax reform's battle—for simplicity, for fairness, and for economic growth—overly optimistic expectations were belatedly called into question. The continued slowing of the economy fueled concerns about whether the TRA might contribute to a recession and larger deficits. Skeptics mocked tax reform's "fairness," arguing that it would make little difference on taxpayers' bottom lines. Such critics now publicized what was already known to careful observers: the lowest income individuals earning $10,000 and below would receive the biggest *percentage* benefit, but that would mean an average of only $37 more in their pockets. The opposite was true for taxpayers earning more than $200,000, whose benefit from the reform would average $2,900.[51] Finally, simplicity—lost early in accommodations between politics and policy—could not now be found in the 900-page law. Indeed, according to expert accountants, in many ways the tax code was more complicated, not less. As a result, the wiliest among them were already able to advise clients on how to modify their behavior, blunting the negative and exploiting the positive aspects of tax reform.

Congressional tax action over the previous month also returned business to its usual course. As if to prove the skeptics' point that tax-writing practices would not be changed by tax reform, Congress sent an *unfinished*—but still official—tax-reform bill to the president. After weeks of bicameral, partisan, and member-to-member wrangling, the chambers still could not agree on a single resolution for officially enrolling the bill as required by congressional procedures.

Missing players also dampened the mood. While Democrat Rostenkowski was at the president's right hand, Republican Packwood was missing from his left. The Oregonian could not spare time from his reelection campaign. Although Packwood's strenuous efforts were rewarded at the polls two weeks later, his success was the exception. Packwood's party went down to a stunning defeat in the November election, losing control of the Senate and mocking the early White House hopes of a party realignment based on the success of tax reform.

Bill Bradley was absent too, though not by choice, having been grounded by fog in Portland, Oregon. Bradley had already gained well-deserved political mileage out of tax reform despite eschewing the limelight throughout. And the rising Democratic star earned a final unsought headline, this time for his conspicuous absence.

Reagan himself seemed to misstep in the final minutes. Although the "Great Communicator" filled the historic moment with stirring words delivered in flawless Reagan fashion, he inadvertently signed the historic legislation incorrectly, by writing his last name first.

And so the last page of the story was officially turned. That the standing ovation the president and his tax-reform partners in Congress and the executive establishment received was marred by small failures and momentary setbacks should do little to diminish the remarkable nature of their political accomplishment.

Notes

1. David J. Vogler, *The Third House* (Evanston, Ill.: Northwestern University Press, 1971). Only about 15 percent of all bills enacted must go to conference in order to reconcile differences, but this fraction includes virtually all major pieces of legislation.
2. Kenneth A. Shepsle and Barry R. Weingast, "The Institutional Foundations of Committee Power," *American Political Science Review* 81, no. 1 (March 1987): 85–104.

3. "Packwood Finds His Leading Role on Tax Bill Provides a Boost in Senate Reelection Campaign," *Wall Street Journal*, July 7, 1986, 34.
4. On this point see Catherine Rudder, "Tax Policy: Structure and Choice," in *Making Economic Policy in Congress*, ed. Allen Schick (Washington: American Enterprise Institute, 1983), 196−220.
5. Because revenue legislation begins in the House, there is a historic bias in this procedure favoring the House. By virtue of its power to schedule legislation, the House can control the order in which money bills are put before the Senate, thereby dictating whose turn it is to chair particular conferences.
6. Lawrence D. Longley and Walter J. Oleszek, *Bicameral Politics: Conference Committees in Congress* (New Haven, Conn.: Yale University Press, 1989), ch. 8.
7. "Dispute over Who Will Chair the Tax Conference," *New York Times*, July 8, 1986, A14.
8. David J. Vogler, *The Politics of Congress*, 3d ed. (Boston: Allyn and Bacon, 1980), 249.
9. John Manley, *The Politics of Finance: The House Committee on Ways and Means*. (Boston: Little, Brown, 1970), 269. See also Charles Clapp, *The Congressman: His Work as He Sees It* (Washington: Brookings Institution, 1963), 285.
10. *Congressional Quarterly Weekly Report*, "Tax Conferees Start Work, Highlight Problems," *Congressional Quarterly Weekly Report*, July 19, 1986, 1601.
11. *Washington Post*, July 12, 1986, A12.
12. See "Senators Who Pushed Low-Rate Plan Named to Panel to Draft Final Tax Bill," *Wall Street Journal*, July 16, 1986, 48; "Conferees Begin Work on Tax Overhaul Today," *Washington Post*, July 17, 1986, A7; and *Wall Street Journal*, July 16, 1986, 48.
13. "The MacNeil-Lehrer Newshour," July 16, 1986; and "House-Senate Conference: The Best of Both Worlds?" *Tax Notes*, July 7, 1986, 6−8.
14. "Regan Supports More IRA Deductions Than Senate's Tax Plan Would Permit," *Wall Street Journal*, July 9, 1986, 54. See also, "Consensus Emerges on Key Elements of Tax Bill; White House Signals Willingness to Compromise," *Tax Notes*, July 14, 1986, 93−94; and *Wall Street Journal*, July 14, 1986, 3.
15. See "Tax Reform Warmup: Harmony on Some Points," *Congressional Quarterly Weekly Report*, July 12, 1986, 1566−67.
16. See for example, "The Tax Reform Conference Gets Underway," *Tax Notes*, July 19, 1986, 190; *Washington Post*, July 12, 1986, A4; and Jeffrey Birnbaum and Alan Murray, *Showdown at Gucci Gulch*, 255−56.
17. *Washington Post*, July 12, 1986, A4.
18. See for example, "Taxing of Industries Splits Conferees Sharply," *New York Times*, July 21, 1986, A1; and "No Progress in Tax Bill Talks," *Washington Post*, July 22, 1986, A10.
19. House Democratic conferees were J.J. Pickle, Charles Rangel, Pete Stark, Richard Gephardt, Marty Russo, and Don Pease. Republican conferees were John Duncan, Bill Archer, Guy Vander Jagt, and Phil Crane. These four, who had never been influential in tax reform activities, were equally inconsequential in conference.
20. The study by the nonprofit organization Tax Analysts found that one-sixth of the Fortune 500 companies paid no taxes in 1985. According to this research,

the accelerated depreciation of equipment and plants was most at fault in helping to lower corporate taxes. Depreciation was a point of substantial disagreement between the House and the Senate, where the House had raised $30.2 billion over five years and the Senate had given away $.8 billion over present law. For more on these points see "Studies Show One in Six Corporations Pays No Tax," *Congressional Quarterly Weekly Report*, July 19, 1986, 1600; and "Joint Committee Revenue Comparisons of House and Senate Provisions," published in *Tax Notes*, August 4, 1986, 455–65. See also, "Reagan Urged Not to Comment as Conferees Work," *Washington Post*, July 18, 1986, A4.

21. See, for example, "Conferees Set to Study Higher Taxes on Business," *New York Times*, July 17, 1986, D6.

22. See, for example, "Why I Don't Like the Senate Tax Bill," *New York Times*, July 14, 1986, A17; "Tax Collecting on Commission," *Wall Street Journal*, July 11, 1986, 20; "Senate Would Save Foreign Golf Pros Some Long Green," *Washington Post*, July 10, 1986, A21; and, "Don't Tempt the IRS into Bounty Hunting," *New York Times*, July 8, 1986, 28.

23. "Tax Conferees Decide to Tackle Big Issues First," *Congressional Quarterly Weekly Report*, July 26, 1986, 1679.

24. Longley and Oleszek, *Bicameral Politics*, ch. 4.

25. Thanks to the rules governing open conferencing, these sessions were not billed as conference meetings. And, although as Bradley remarked, "temperatures were taken," no official votes were ever recorded, nor were official minutes kept.

26. "Paint by Numbers: Conferees Discuss New Revenue Estimates," *Tax Notes*, July 28, 1986, 295.

27. "Senators to Submit New Revenue Plan after House Conferees Spurn Eight Proposals," *Wall Street Journal*, July 29, 1986, 2. For revenue estimates, see *Tax Notes*, August 4, 1986, 462.

28. "Senate Tax Conferees to Offer New List of Revenue-Raising Ideas," *Washington Post*, July 29, 1986, A4.

29. Thanks to an intensive lobbying effort that included efforts by former assistant secretary for tax policy Buck Chapoton, former majority leader Sen. Howard Baker, and then Federal Reserve Board chairman Paul Volcker, this provision was later modified by Rostenkowski and Packwood, restoring some of the benefits banks enjoy in this regard. See, for example, "Bank on It," *Tax Notes*, August 18, 1986, 627.

30. *Tax Notes*, August 4, 1986, 464.

31. "Packwood Proposed Higher Business Taxes," *Washington Post*, July 30, 1986, A7.

32. See *Tax Notes*, "House Offer on Tax Reform," August 11, 1986, 566; *Washington Post*, July 31, 1986, A18; "Conferees from House Set Position," *New York Times*, July 31, 1986, D1; "House Conferees Shaping Tax Stand," *New York Times*, August 1, 1986, D1, 2; and "House Tax Conferees Agree to Delete Break in Treatment for Capital Gains," *Wall Street Journal*, July 31, 1986, 2.

33. A summary description of this proposal is contained in "Corporate Hit Could Sidetrack Tax Conference," *Congressional Quarterly Weekly Report*, August 2, 1986, 1728–29. See also "Rostenkowski Rebuffs GOP Bid to Raise Tax Rate," *Wall Street Journal*, August 5, 1986, 9.

34. "Conferees Remain Divided on Business Taxes," *New York Times*, August 6, 1986, D2.

35. Even so, conferees were generally better off than nonconferees. For example, having won a net expansion of tax-exempt bonds in committee, Durenberger sat helpless as a nonconferee while Senate bond provisions were quickly jettisoned in the struggle for revenue. The same could be said of House members. Robert Matsui and Ed Jenkins also worked to minimize the tax-exempt bond hit, but it was avid opponents like Pete Stark and J. J. Pickle who went to conference.

36. Under the Senate-passed tax-reform bill, the changes in federal pension plans would be phased in over two years, coming into full effect for those who retire in 1989. Under this proposal, the changes would be effective for workers retiring after January 1, 1987. The provision was estimated to raise $1.8 billion over five years, but it caught many soon-to-retire federal employees by surprise, as they planned for a situation in which pensions would be free of taxation for three years.

37. *Tax Notes*, August 18, 1986, 626.

38. Russell Long, C-Span, April 18, 1986.

39. Birnbaum and Murray, *Showdown at Gucci Gulch*, 268.

40. For a discussion of this decision see "Packwood and Rostenkowski at Odds over Shortfall," *Tax Notes*, August 18, 1986, 626.

41. U.S. Congress, Senate, Committee on Finance, *Testimony of James A. Baker: Hearing before the Committee on Finance*, 99th Cong., 2d sess., June 11, 1985. *Tax Reform Proposals, Vol. I*, 99th Congress, 1st sess., 47−48.

42. "Blaming the Messenger," *Tax Notes*, August 18, 1986, 623.

43. On these points generally, see Daniel Patrick Moynihan, "The Diary of A Senator," in *Newsweek*, August 25, 1986, 26−29.

44. "White House Urges Final Approval of Tax Act," *Washington Post*, August 18, 1986, A1, 6.

45. See, for example, "House Ambivalent about Final Tax Bill: Passage Likely Despite Lack of Enthusiasm," *Washington Post*, September 17, 1986, A8.

46. See "Reagan Pressures House to Approve Tax Revision," *Washington Post*, September 24, 1986, A6; "Tax Overhaul Vote Represents Moment of Truth for GOP as It Tries to Shed Big Business Image," *Wall Street Journal*, September 12, 1986, 64; and "House Majority Leader Hits Tax Plan," *Washington Post*, September 18, 1986, A17.

47. An earlier and more important vote, Archer's motion to recommit the bill to the conference committee, and thus attempt to kill it, was defeated 268−160.

48. Danforth's lengthy testimony, which provides a candid account of his view of Senate and conference deliberations as well as spirited critiques of the revenue estimation process and the final version of H.R. 3838, can be found in U.S. Congress, Senate, *Congressional Record*, daily ed., 99th Cong., 2d sess., September 26, 1986, S13787−99.

49. For a discussion of Levin's and Metzenbaum's speeches see "Senate Passes Tax Reform," *Tax Notes*, October 6, 1986, 5−8.

50. In the process, the Senate affirmed ten of twenty-three House colloquies. Colloquies are often used during legislative debate as a means of clarifying congressional intent. As a result, conference reports include many such bicameral conversations. During consideration of the tax-reform conference report forty-five colloquies covered such topics as the meaning of ITC

transition rules for self-constructed property, public approval requirements when state and local governments issue tax-exempt bonds, and the application of the new passive-loss rules. Demonstrating that House and Senate can disagree even while they agree, thirty-five colloquies were turned down altogether, either because one chamber or another rebutted them or because they remained silent.

51. "On Bottom Line, Not Much Difference," *Washington Post*, August 18, 1986, A1, 6.

9 Explaining the Riddle of Tax Reform: Three Perspectives

> *Models of the behavior of political institutions generally depend heavily on prevailing images of the policy process. This dependence is not altogether comfortable, for no sooner do institutional models become settled and widely accepted than new policy patterns emerge to call them into question.*
> —Lawrence D. Brown, *New Policies, New Politics*

Few notable legislative achievements were as improbable as the enactment of comprehensive income tax reform under the Tax Reform Act of 1986. So it seemed, from every perspective. Virtually all participants in the process, at every step along the way, believed that legislative success was highly unlikely. And their "insider" expectations were powerfully reinforced by outside experts. Yet all were proved wrong. The TRA passed the House of Representatives by a vote of 292—136 on September 25, 1986, and the Senate by a vote of 73—24 two days later. And on October 22 tax reform completed its two-year odyssey, returning to the White House where Ronald Reagan signed it into law.

Although the battle over tax reform is now history, its unexpected adoption challenges scholars to reconsider conventional theories of politics and policy making.[1] Further, the size and sweep of the TRA, bringing nearly every important institution and interest in national politics to the foreground, provides a good testing place for new theories. The story has implications, not only for students of tax policy, but for those concerned with other nonincremental or "breakthrough" policy changes as well, from consumer and environmental protection in the late 1960s to economic deregulation in the late 1970s. Individually, each of these victories also surprised seasoned political observers. Collectively, acceptance of these policies sheds light on the evolving character of the policy process itself.

Explaining the Adoption of Tax Reform: Two Traditional Models

Business as Usual: The Pluralist/Incrementalist Perspective

Standard interpretations of "business as usual" in Washington usually employ what may be termed the pluralist/incrementalist approach. These two concepts, linked by both logic and observation, account for most "normal politics," including much of the historical development of the tax code itself.

Pluralism, a variant of long-established interest group theory, interprets policy making principally as a process of adjustment among contending organized groups through bargaining, compromise, vote trading, and similar methods. Some theorists see government as little more than a mechanism for sanctioning accommodations reached by such interests. Earl Latham once declared that the legislature simply "referees the group struggle," ratifying the victories and defeats in statutory form. What is called public policy, he said, is the "equilibrium" among groups reached on a particular issue at a particular point in time.[2] Although pluralists do stress the multiplicity of political resources, they nonetheless ascribe special power to groups representing business or other easily organized economic interests. Unorganized, poorly represented interests—which may include much of the public at large—are expected to exert less influence.

The theory of incrementalism, to which pluralism is usually linked, emphasizes outcomes as much as processes. Incrementalists recognize that most new policies, most of the time, involve only small departures from their predecessors. In part, this is explained by human limitations. Analysts emphasize that no individual can fully evaluate all of the relevant policy options, as is required for truly rational decision making. Instead of "maximizing," real decision makers need simplifying shortcuts or rules of thumb. The incremental process is one of these.

Incrementalism has a political explanation as well. Incremental decisions are normally the path of least resistance where there is a pluralistic distribution of power. Because the existing allocation of benefits should conform closely to the allocation of political influence, any attempt to dramatically change current policy would be expected to spark heated opposition.

The Pluralist/Incrementalist Model and Tax Reform. The traditional pattern of tax politics has been a variant of the pluralist/incrementalist model. Though the income tax has grown dramatically in fiscal importance and complexity since 1913, it has not changed substantially in structure, and proposals to replace or greatly modify it have never advanced far. The political influence of organized interests is demonstrated by the steady growth of tax expenditure provisions, as well as by the shift of relative tax burdens onto personal taxation and away from the better-organized corporate sector. Indeed, to many observers, tax policy exemplifies pluralist/incrementalist politics.

Yet traditional interest-group politics, though long the dominant force in tax policy, can hardly explain the enactment of the TRA. Quite the opposite is true. Although individual interest groups won concessions during the tax-writing process, tax reform succeeded only because its advocates overcame staunch opposition by most organized groups.

Tax reform was heavily lobbied, from shortly after its origin in the

Treasury until the final vote on the Senate floor. Moreover, the members of the tax writing committees of Congress were clearly disproportionate beneficiaries of the financial contributions distributed by political action committees. This organized opposition threatened not only to divest tax-reform legislation of individual provisions but to undermine the entire effort. Many agreed with the "public interest" lobbyist who warned, "The tax bill is likely going no place [because] the groups that benefit from the current system are all big contributors." [3]

In the end, however, even the combined efforts of these well-organized, well-heeled opponents failed to block, slow, or even greatly alter this landmark legislation. The TRA resulted in a monumental rewrite of the entire personal and corporate income-tax code. Taken singly, perhaps, any one of its changes could be termed an incremental adjustment, but their sheer number, adopted simultaneously, belies any such description. Indeed, many of the specific provisions added or deleted would have been significant tax legislation in and of themselves. Further, those same actions stripped away numerous special preferences. Corporations lost tax benefits totaling $120 billion over five years, including such well-known ones as the investment tax credit, to the more obscure "completed contract" method of accounting. A huge number of noncorporate preferences were stripped or trimmed as well, including some that most taxpayers viewed as loopholes and others—such as the two-earner deduction and IRA savings benefits—that they did not.

This is not to say that interest groups had no effect on reform legislation. Certain provisions affecting large, organized constituencies, or those with strong support on the tax-writing committees, emerged relatively intact— from home mortgage deductions (defended by the realtors and home-builders) to most fringe benefits (a great concern to labor unions and insurance companies). So, too, did an array of provisions benefiting a mixed assortment of more specialized interests, from the research and development credit to most oil and gas provisions. Still others were granted favorable transition rules, limiting the effect of changes. Yet tax reform gave new meaning to the term "winning." Whereas past legislative victories earned expansions of tax benefits, winning on the TRA mostly meant reducing the anticipated damage. In tax reform, winners were those who retained some tax benefits instead of losing them altogether.

It also is true that at various points institutional leaders used a pluralist bargaining strategy. Indeed, Secretary of the Treasury Baker made the accommodation of interest groups the hallmark of Treasury II. Unlike his predecessor, Don Regan, Baker thought instinctively in terms of coalition building and opened the doors of the once-secret process to lobbyists of every stripe. In keeping with his own centrist and power-broker tendencies, Representative Rostenkowski also blended tax-reform ideas with interest-group demands to produce legislation that was uniquely structured to pass the House of Representatives. After a near brush with failure, he redefined his coalition during the Ways and Means Committee markup, granting concessions on provisions of greatest importance to House Democrats. To secure additional votes to report a bill within the revenue constraints imposed by reform, Rostenkowski turned to task forces within his committee, co-opting members into the process by allowing them to carve up portions of the pie to their own liking. And he used transition rules aggressively to keep his restless troops in line during subsequent floor and conference action. Similarly, Senator Packwood's first attempt at producing a reform bill was a testament to the power of committee members' alliances with various constituencies and interest groups. When this attempt at pandering to pluralistic politics collapsed in failure, Packwood successfully gambled on radical reform on the individual side of the tax code. Overshadowed at the time, however, were the far more modest incremental changes wrought by his committee on the corporate side.

In such instances, pluralist bargaining assuredly helped tax reform along. Without some accommodations, it is doubtful that Baker would have produced a proposal acceptable to the president and his Republican constituencies, that Rostenkowski would have gained essential Democratic support in the House, or that Packwood would have been able to send a bill to the Senate floor.

But this bargaining was quite different in scope and character from that observed in ordinary efforts to pass a tax bill or predicted by pluralist/incrementalist theory. It was not the motivational force behind reform, nor did it define the major contours of the TRA. Instead group bargaining and pluralist coalition building provided side adjustments designed to make congressionally unpopular legislation more palatable and passable. Furthermore, many of the short-term accommodations did not survive. Thanks to scathing press criticism, the excesses of group bargaining often led to their own undoing, as after the bank vote in the House and the failure of Pack I in the Senate. Similarly, the requirements of the conference process left little room for bowing to interest-group demands. The final legislation devised by the two chairmen was neither as kind to Democratic constituencies as the House bill, nor as beneficial to corporations as the Senate's.

In its overall character, then, the TRA is neither pluralist in tone nor modest in the scope of its departure from its predecessor, and interest-group bargaining was clearly not the dominant influence on the legislation. Indeed, losers constituted a virtual *Who's Who* among the U.S. economic interests that traditionally have shaped tax policy, including real estate, heavy industry, large banks, casualty insurance, defense contractors, and multinational corporations. "This tax bill is really a testament to the limitations of special interest groups," observed Ways and Means Committee member Tom Downey, expressing a view shared by virtually all those engaged in the process. "They were annihilated. They took a beating the likes of which I could not have imagined before it occurred." Economist Alvin Rabushka concurs, noting that because the general interest prevailed over the multitude of special interests, the adoption of the TRA actually contradicted the public choice paradigm.[4]

Ironically, the clearest "winners" in tax reform were the poor, six million of whom were removed from the tax rolls. Yet this group is much less active politically than the bulk of the population, and much less well represented by professional, paid advocates. Though the poor benefited from tax reform, they in no way produced it; like many of the losers, they were simply taken along for the ride.

What explains these unexpected outcomes? In part they must be attributed to unique characteristics of the tax-reform process. In particular, the constraints of producing a revenue-neutral bill forced the distributive politics of taxation into a redistributive mold. Under these conditions, gaining protection for a targeted tax preference meant robbing provisions that favored some other group or raising tax rates overall. This virtually guaranteed organized opposition—an implication understood by Treasury officials from the start. As then-assistant secretary Manuel Johnson said: "The key was to combine low rates with a reform package, making the whole thing revenue-neutral. The whole strategy was to create a zero-sum game between special interests and the average taxpayer. That was always the name of the game." Treasury's strategy worked. Given the comprehensive nature of the tax-reform legislation being considered, simply finding a remaining potentially vulnerable tax preference that could be tapped for additional revenue was a difficult task. There also was the problem of obtaining the revenue estimates required to offer an actual amendment. Because such technical expertise was controlled by proreform leaders in the Congress and administration, tax reform's complexity strengthened the hand of reformers.

At other key points, organized interests were completely shut out of the development of tax-reform legislation or were kept off balance by the degree of secrecy. This was most clearly true at the beginning and the end, at TRA's initiation in the Treasury Department and during the closed conference. Virtually no one outside of a small group of Treasury officials—including the White House, the cabinet, members of Congress, and most interest groups—was privy to the content of Treasury I as it was being developed. During conference, most conferees were often in the dark after responsibility for producing a report was delegated to the two chairmen. Secrecy also often prevailed in between these key events.

Finding it difficult to write tax legislation in the "sunshine," Ways and Means Committee members voted to close each markup session to the public. Key meetings of the Senate "core group" excluded not just the public, but committee members' staffs as well. Although most major interests still had a (more or less reliable) pipeline to the inside through some supportive committee or staff member, the scope of the legislation and the speed with which it proceeded often limited the utility of such connections. Rostenkowski's task forces typically prepared their recommendations overnight, giving groups little time to organize and respond to concrete proposals. In the Senate, the entire Pack II bill was composed in private in the astonishingly brief span of just twelve days.

Finally, reformers were assisted by the small coterie of groups that viewed tax reform in general as economically beneficial to their own interests. In addition to assorted public interest groups, this segment was composed primarily of highly taxed corporations and industries—such as wholesalers, retailers, and many electronics firms—that received few tax subsidies and would benefit disproportionately from lower corporate tax rates. Such groups and corporations organized a formal coalition, the Tax Reform Action Coalition (TRAC), to lobby for reform. The coalition was joined by some seven hundred groups representing consumer, business, and social interests, peaking in size and energy just before the Senate debate. These groups played an important role in helping Packwood manage the unruly Senate floor, sending a number of their best lobbyists to man the phones and pigeonhole members in a surprisingly successful attempt to round up needed votes. But most important, both in the House and Senate, TRAC's well-publicized efforts helped inoculate reformers against charges of being antibusiness or antigrowth.

Still, such lobbying can hardly be credited with initiating the legislation or providing more than an assist in its passage. Only a fraction of TRAC's members ever really labored for the cause; other interests offered less support than blessed silence. In no sense did this coalition equal the strength or multiplicity of groups opposing tax reform. Had Congress merely "refereed" the group struggle, TRA would not have been enacted.

Old-Style Reform: The Presidential/Majoritarian Perspective

The traditional process by which the system of American politics overcomes the structural obstacles and political inertia that block nonincremental policy changes occurs on those relatively rare occasions when it resembles the reform ideal of responsible party government.[5] In this presidential-majoritarian form of policy change, a strong president sweeps into office along with large, unified party majorities in both chambers of Congress. He mobilizes the substantial resources of his office to construct a coherent legislative program and rallies the public and his party followers behind it. Under such circumstances, the legislative backlog of an entire political generation may be disposed of in a few weeks or months. But such periods of activity are usually brief. The presidential party coalition typically succumbs to internal forces of disunity or to electoral losses, returning the nation to a period of political stalemate and policy consolidation.

The presidential/majoritarian model thus links great changes in policy to decisive shifts in the electorate. It accords nicely with the progressive reforms secured by Woodrow Wilson in 1913 and 1914, with the outpouring of New Deal legislation under Franklin Roosevelt in the 1930s, and with Johnson's Great Society program in the mid-1960s.[6] With some degree of stretching it can even be made to accommodate Ronald Reagan's legislative triumphs in 1981, when Republicans won control of the Senate and secured effective if not nominal control of the House of Representatives by dint of extraordinary levels of party unity on key votes.

The Presidential/Majoritarian Model and Tax Reform.   Historically, the formulation of tax policy has been consistent with this pattern, as Susan Hansen has shown. Viewed in the long sweep of history from 1790 forward, "major tax innovations show strong links to periods of political realignment and social crisis, in marked contrast to the incremental policies characteristic of "normal" politics." [7] Furthermore, the presidential/majoritarian model might seem to offer a ready explanation for the legislative acceptance of the TRA. Movement toward its adoption emerged from campaign politics during the 1984 presidential contest. It gained a prominent position on the national agenda because the issue was adopted by a popular president (after winning forty-nine states in an electoral college landslide victory) as the number-one item of his domestic program. Given Republican control of the Senate, and the size of the president's electoral "mandate," legislative success, even for a bill of this scope, might seem to have been ensured.

Presidential politics also fixed a number of key features of the final legislative package. From the beginning, Ronald Reagan made it clear that he would not accept a proposal that produced an overall increase in revenue. During legislative consideration, the White House gave frequent warnings that his "veto pen" was poised to bar any tax hike. And, as in prior years, the prospect of lower marginal rages was his own greatest attraction. His firm position on both matters established strictures that shaped tax reform throughout its consideration.

Considered more closely, however, this seemingly promising model does not adequately describe the TRA's enactment. Though right in a few key features, it is wrong in significant detail.

First, throughout the process, the role played by the president was somewhat less grand than the honorific "chief legislator" implies. There was a substantial commitment of executive-branch resources, with Treasury Secretaries Regan and Baker and Deputy Secretary Richard Darman spending the better part of three years crafting legislation and lobbying Congress in what many judged to be a "first class" effort. Nonetheless, neither the Democratic House nor the Republican Senate used Treasury I or the White House's official proposal, Treasury II, as the starting point for its own deliberations. And, although Reagan helped focus public attention on the issue for most of the two-year period, his personal involvement was episodic and only modestly influential compared with that of past master legislators.

Second, and more important, Reagan never mobilized a partisan majority in favor of reform. His party did not control the House of Representatives, and conservative control of that chamber was lost after the 1982 election. Moreover, congressional Republicans, as a group, were the least enthralled with tax reform. Their mass defection in the House nearly killed the legislation in 1985. In the Senate, too, Robert Packwood and many of his Republican colleagues initially viewed tax reform as a direct attack on their preferred style of government and their most supportive constituencies. Finally, few GOP partisans in either chamber ever accepted the administration's early argument that tax reform would shift voters from Democratic to Republican loyalties. Their own conversations back home indicated limited support and, indeed, growing doubts as the specifics of the proposal became understood.

Thus, had the president been forced to mobilize a tax-reform coalition primarily within his own party he would have almost surely failed—as Carter had before him. In fact, recognizing that tax reform needed Democratic aid, White House spokesmen were forced to downplay the prospect of potential partisan benefits, at least in their public statements.

What actually drove tax reform forward was not Republican pressure in the face of Democratic resistance, but a process of interparty competition in which leaders of both groups first sought to win credit with the public for enacting reform and later competed to avoid blame for killing it. Historically and theoretically, partisan divisions among the three institutions of government should obstruct action. As James Sundquist observes:

> When one party controls the executive branch and the opposing party has the majority in one or both houses of Congress, all of the normal difficulties of attaining harmonious and effective working relationships between the branches are multiplied manifold. . . . When the president sends a recommendation to the opposition-controlled Congress, the legislators are virtually compelled to reject or profoundly alter it.[8]

But in this instance, divided party control over the two chambers of Congress, and between the Democratic House and the Republican White House, helped advance the TRA. As on environmental issues previously, party competition forced Democrats in the House, and then Republicans in the Senate, to respond to the reform proposals of their partisan and institutional rivals in ways that would never have occurred if a single party had unified control.[9]

This process of party competition began very early in the tax-reform saga, contributing even to the Reagan administration's initial decision to propose tax legislation. For key advisers in the Reagan White House, concerns about the negative effects of tax reform on a host of Republican constituencies initially outweighed the positive but more theoretical economic arguments mustered by reform proponents in the Treasury Department. What convinced them to consent to the study that, in turn, produced the landmark Treasury I proposal was an even stronger political concern that Walter Mondale was about to claim tax reform, viewed as a potentially popular issue, for the Democrats. As former White House chief of staff James Baker frankly stated: "The true reason that we as an administration undertook an examination of this issue was because we were concerned that the other side would be embracing it and using it against us in the 1984 presidential election." This, of course, never actually occurred.

When Treasury's study was completed and its recommendations were released after the November election, there was still no assurance that Reagan would pursue tax reform as a primary goal. Baker and others in the White House were genuinely taken aback by the scope and political audacity of the Treasury plan. Several alternative issues (such as foreign trade and crime) were briefly considered as possible substitutes on the president's agenda for the second term. In the end, however, the continuing expectation of potential partisan advantage overcame these internal objections. With Mondale having pledged to raise taxes rather than reform them, some Republican activists in the White House, in Congress, and in the Republican National Committee began championing tax reform as a vehicle for a long-anticipated party realignment. Those political operatives hoped to secure a stronger political base for the next generation of GOP candidates by granting a measure of tax relief to lower- and especially middle-income voters and by ensuring that corporations and the wealthy did not escape their fair share of the tax burden. This argument of partisan advantage eventually made headway among previously skeptical White House advisers. In particular, Richard Darman, the administration's premier policy strategist and then deputy White House chief of staff, joined the chorus of realignment enthusiasts, convincing his own skeptical boss, James Baker, that tax reform was both legislatively "doable" and politically desirable.

The administration's ultimate decision to make tax reform the center-piece of its political and policy agenda posed two important challenges to

Democratic leaders in the House: retaining leadership on what had traditionally been a Democratic issue and neutralizing the effect of the Republicans' electoral gambit. Though many Democrats harbored doubts that tax reform could provide the basis for realignment, the party's vulnerability on taxes made some sort of response nearly inevitable.

Although tax reform began in the administration as a positive proposal to secure political credit and electoral gain, the politics of reform quickly degenerated. By the time the House Ways and Means Committee began marking up legislation in the fall of 1985, it was clear (from both opinion polls and congressional contacts with constituents) that base broadening lacked widespread political appeal. Although this realization dampened enthusiasm for reform in Congress, it failed to halt the partisan competition propelling it forward. "Blame avoidance" simply replaced credit claiming as a motive force.[10] Neither party, and neither chamber of Congress, wanted the proverbial dead cat on its doorstep.

This competition reflected a fear of potential voter reaction rather than anything more tangible. The public was skeptical of many specific reform proposals but also showed great dissatisfaction with the income-tax status quo and did favor the symbol of reform. Legislators in both parties therefore feared that a skillful political opponent might turn the issue against them at some later date. As Rep. Tom Downey observed:

> This was blame avoidance in part when we went into it.... If [the Republican] party turns its back on tax reform.... Democrats [will have] the opportunity to beat them about the head and shoulders saying, "Your own president wanted it, it was fair, and you were too interested in worrying about big corporations . . . to help the American people." So it is largely a process of dodging political bullets. The party that dodges them best can turn around and use some of those bullets against their adversaries.[11]

Such concerns sustained tax reform through both chambers on to the final signing ceremony, even though expectations that it would have great partisan benefits had evaporated. In fact, the cause never did become popular: a poll conducted in September found only 19 percent of those interviewed in favor of reform, with only 16 percent opposed. A poll the following April showed marginal improvement in the sense of tax fairness: 74 percent of respondents agreed that "many rich people pay hardly any taxes at all," a bit less than the 81 percent of two years previously.[12]

The New Politics of Reform: Ideas, Experts, and Entrepreneurs

The two foregoing models are quite familiar. Each has been carefully formulated and often applied in policy research. Yet, it is apparent that neither the pluralist/incrementalist nor the presidential/majoritarian model is able to adequately explain the enactment of the Tax Reform Act of 1986. Although each accounts for some elements of the legislation, neither captures the entire dynamic.

Instead, both the success of tax reform and specific features of the legislation are largely the result of a quite different set of conditions, political actors, and forms of behavior. Some of these have been described above: party competition, the constraint of revenue neutrality, and the enforcement of secrecy at key points in the process. Other significant factors include policy ideas and professionals, political entrepreneurs, and the news media.

If these were important only in the passage of tax reform, the TRA would constitute an interesting but isolated historical curiosity. But they are not. The same elements help to explain the enactment of other significant legislation that is difficult to account for on the basis of interest-group politics and presidential-party leadership. For example, many consumer and environmental regulations, as well as economic deregulation for air transportation and other fields, pitted the interests of broad unorganized publics against narrow, highly organized opponents. Given the seemingly unequal sides, "it may seem astonishing that regulatory legislation of this sort is ever passed," James Q. Wilson writes. Yet "it is, and with growing frequency in recent years." [13] In part, the TRA may be viewed as only the most recent, complex, and far-reaching instance of this "new politics of reform." [14]

The Role of Ideas

As described by Wilson and others, the new politics of reform begins with an emphasis on the significance of ideas in politics. Unlike traditional pluralism, this alternative orientation treats ideas as an independent creative force in the political process.

The origins of this perspective might well be traced to an often-quoted comment of the economist John Maynard Keynes. In his own masterwork, Keynes concluded with the observation that

> the ideas of economists and political philosophers, both when they are right and when they are wrong, are more powerful than is commonly understood. Indeed the world is ruled by little else. . . . I am sure that the power of vested interests is vastly exaggerated compared with the gradual encroachment of ideas.[15]

Such observations about the "power of ideas" generally had little influence on political science, however. Throughout the 1950s, 1960s, and 1970s, academic experts on government generally relied instead on the concepts of power, influence, and interests to account for the results of legislative struggles. Indeed, because American politics lacked the grand ideological passions and debates between the extremes of left and right that character- ized most European nations, it was widely regarded as purely pragmatic and interest-based, outside of the tradition of genuine intellectual discourse.

In recent years, however, a few political scientists have emphasized the role of beliefs and ideas as an independent and influential force in politics. For example, Wilson's study of regulation concluded:

> A complete theory of regulatory politics—indeed, a complete theory of politics generally—requires that attention be paid to beliefs as well as interests. Only by the most extraordinary theoretical contortions can one explain [recent regulatory actions] by reference to the economic stakes involved. And even when these stakes are important . . . the need for assembling a majority legislative coalition requires that arguments be made that appeal to the beliefs (as well as interests) of broader constituencies.[16]

Deborah Stone contends that "ideas are the very stuff of politics. People fight about ideas, fight for them, and fight against them. . . . Moreover, people fight *with* ideas as well as about them. The different sides in a conflict create different portrayals of the battle—who is affected, how they are affected, and what is at stake." [17] John Kingdon argues, "The contents of the ideas themselves, far from being mere smokescreens or rationalizations, are integral parts of decision making in and around government. Governmental officials often judge the merits of a case as well as its political costs and benefits." [18]

As these quotations suggest, the "politics of ideas" is distinguished from the more traditional "politics of interests" because it assumes no one-to-one correspondence between personal gain and political action. In an essay in a recent volume on the influence of ideas, Gary Orren emphasized:

> People [in politics] do not act solely on the basis of their perceived self- interest, without regard to the aggregate consequences of their actions. They are also motivated by values, purposes, goals, and commitments that transcend self-interest or group interest. . . . At times, in effect, people act as they feel they *should* act.[19]

Changes in politics, society, and the economy in recent years may have heightened the importance of such behavior and could explain the recent development of this ideational model. Party loyalties have diminished and increasing reliance is placed on mass communications. More Americans are highly educated than in the past, and the percentage of professionals in the work force has increased more than 50 percent since 1960.

This "professionalization" of the labor force is important because experts of various kinds are the natural generators and propagators of ideas. They leave their mark, in part, through scholarship, teaching, or writing—activities that often make an impression only slowly. When expert professionals are employed in and around government itself, however, they can influence policy much more directly. Daniel Patrick Moynihan, for example, traces much of the War on Poverty to what he called the "professionalization of reform." [20] He notes that sociologists, doctors, economists, lawyers, writers, and others helped to define the problem of poverty, which came to be viewed as the paramount issue of the mid-1960s. More generally, Samuel Beer says:

> In the fields of health, housing, urban renewal, transportation, welfare, education, poverty, and energy, it has been, in very great measure, people in government service, or closely associated with it, acting on the basis of their specialized knowledge, who first perceived the problem, conceived the program, initially urged it on the president and Congress, went on to help lobby it through to enactment, and then saw to its administration. [21]

Experts and Tax Reform.   The movement for tax reform rested above all else on the shared conviction of knowledgeable experts that the federal income-tax system had grown indefensible from the standpoint of professionally salient values. Furthermore, the ideas and activities of tax policy professionals—notably economists, but also reform-minded tax attorneys—strongly influenced the content of tax reform throughout the policy-making process. Professionals had come to agree on both the need for and, to a lesser but still very important extent, the proper design of tax-reform legislation. They worked both outside and inside the government for its inclusion on the policy agenda. They devised proposals conforming to professional standards, thus establishing the parameters of debate. Finally, through the uniquely professional status and orientation of the Joint Tax Committee, they exerted influence over many details of the legislation.

The concept of comprehensive tax reform was, of course, "invented" decades before the TRA began moving ahead on Capitol Hill. In earlier times, it had limited influence on congressional action. But the themes and principles of tax reform were able to flower in part because they were far removed from the hard realities of electoral, interest-group, and congressional politics. In the intervening years, when politicians and government officials seemed unwilling to address the growing problems of federal income taxation, there was a great deal of discussion among academics and practicing tax professionals about the proper character of a more desirable revenue system. Thus, by the mid-1980s, most experts—including those within government—were in agreement on basic principles.

According to the consensus, an ideal income tax should be horizontally equitable; it should be investment-neutral; and it should be administratively efficient. All three goals could be obtained by broadening the tax base and lowering rates. Beyond this point, economists differed as to the taxable base to broaden, whether it be income (yielding a flat or modified flat-rate income tax) or consumption (creating a tax based on consumed income). But these differences were balanced by a relatively new agreement marrying base-broadening principles, not with the traditional liberal goal of more progressive taxation, but with the supply-side goal of lower rates.

This professional consensus was especially important because Treasury's tax experts initially got virtually free rein. Once the president requested that Treasury produce a reform proposal, "outsiders" had virtually no further input. Consequently, the initial Treasury I plan was an astonishingly pure expression of expert views. Although never formally proposed as legislation, it—rather than the existing law—set the standard against which subsequent proposals were measured.

Furthermore, the basic contours of the TRA itself—base broadening, reduced rates, revenue and distributional neutrality—all were fixed at that early stage, solidifying the conceptual consensus laid out by the Bradley-Gephardt proposal. In fact, Treasury experts, not the president, completed the stricture of revenue neutrality. The president was unwilling to raise taxes; economists both inside and outside the administration thought it unwise to reduce revenues—a viewed shared by most other political figures. Expert consensus accounts, too, for the removal of the poor from the tax rolls, a costly feature of Treasury I adopted without instructions from the president and also without controversy. Treasury experts even made the choices that produced the sharp business tax hike. Responding to Don Regan's request for a lower, simpler personal rate structure than the one first proposed by departmental estimators, Treasury lawyers recommended an increase in the corporate tax rate from 28 percent to 33 percent. Though unplanned at the start, the individual tax cut that resulted was embraced by the president and, indeed, sold to the public as tax reform's main attraction.

Still, as one would expect, the ideas of tax professionals were less overtly dominant through the remainder of the legislative process. Beginning with what became the president's formal proposal, Treasury II, the work of tax professionals was reexamined and shaped "through the lens of pure politics." Whenever the product of experts, from Treasury or the JTC, directly clashed with the immediate needs of coalition building, professional purity consistently lost out—as in the treatment of fringe benefits and state and local taxes by the House and of corporate provisions by the Senate. Moreover, both Rostenkowski and Packwood elected to design their own tax bills de novo, rather than use either of the Treasury proposals as a markup document.

Nevertheless, to look solely at these politically motivated departures from the professionals' design is to greatly understate their influence. Most provisions did *not* engender overt conflicts between political demands and professional norms. Further, the vast scope and comprehensive structure of the reform plan overwhelmed legislators and left enormous numbers of issues to be decided by staff. These experts also made action possible in the face of the TRA's mind-boggling complexity. For example, in the waning hours of conference, teams of staff speeded the decision process by working out solutions in many areas of disagreement for the two chairmen's ultimate approval. Had it not been for their parallel effort, the clock would almost certainly have run out on Rostenkowski and Packwood.

Staff members also provided the encouragement and energy needed to keep the process going through its many dark hours. Rostenkowski was certainly swayed by the enthusiasm of key aides: "The Rob Leonards and Joe Dowleys and Ken Bowlers of this world kept on the wave," he said, "by [saying] we can do it; it's big but we can do it." Even at the point when Packwood and other leaders hoped to see tax reform buried in the House, the talented staff who served him were of two minds. Politically, they were aware of the dangers, but professionally, they were eager for a chance to work on a career-capping project.

Finally, by controlling the critical revenue estimates, the small band of professionals under JTC's David Brockway exercised life-and-death power over countless alternatives considered by decision makers. Revenue estimators and those who managed their work were the invisible hands in the legislative marketplace, directing choices and often controlling outcomes. One can therefore appreciate the attitude of one disillusioned member of the Ways and Means Committee who remarked, "If I had really wanted to influence the way the actual law was written, I would have applied for a job on the Joint Tax or Ways and Means staff."

Values and Symbols in Tax Reform. When it came to affecting policy outcomes, the ideas of experts were important throughout the legislative process. In a field as complex and arcane as tax policy, that may not be surprising. But that is only half the story. In the new politics of reform, ideas are an important force in a second and distinctive way.

Some have suggested that the power of ideas as a political dynamic stems mainly from the desire to make "good policy." Steven Kelman contends:

> The level of public spirit in the policy making process is reasonably high and . . . is important in understanding the results of policy making in the United States. By "public spirit," I mean the wish to choose good public policy, evaluating options against a standard of general ideas about right and wrong.[22]

Such a view suggests the interpretation that tax reform was enacted because a majority of participants wanted to do what was right, and they relied on the experts to define "right" for them.[23]

For some of the participants in the process, this "public interest" objective was paramount. Apart from the tax experts themselves, whose definition of good policy coincided nicely with their professional interests, some members of Congress devoutly believed that tax reform should be enacted because it was "right" and courageously chose to subordinate their own electoral interests to this pursuit. But for most, the attraction of the reform idea was less straightforward. Indeed, if a commitment to "doing right" were all that was required, tax reform should have been enacted many times before.

In fact, opinions varied sharply about what constituted "good policy." Even economists had real and sincere differences on many specific tax issues, like the need for special incentives to encourage investment and savings. Legislators, lobbyists, and citizens who lacked economists' faith in the supremacy of efficiency and neutrality could honestly grant a higher value to policies that benefited charitable giving, federalism, or economic competitiveness. Many in Congress and outside it who argued that tax reform should be tied to deficit reduction, or disagreed with the nature of certain features, did so because they believed that the better and more substantial arguments were inclined in those directions.

The power of the ideas that actually propelled the adoption of tax reform seemed to lie more in the realm of symbolism than of intellectual rigor.[24] They appealed to greed and fear, as well as to logic and reason. As the earlier references to fairness, blame avoidance, and the inoculating effects of TRAC's advocacy suggest, vague but powerful symbols, plus a concern for appearances—sometimes cynically manipulated—lent dynamic force to the reform campaign. Rostenkowski observed early in the process: "Those who are gathering to derail tax reform should recall [Reagan's] knack for dividing complex issues into two simple parts—good and bad, fair and unfair, givers and takers—and asking, 'which side are you on?'.... It's a devastating question that could unleash a potent backlash."[25] The desire to avoid this eventuality drove reform relentlessly through the political process, often overshadowing substantive content. Tax symbolism had a direct bearing on the character of specific reform proposals, with certain features being designed to suit the purposes of propagandists more than policy analysts. Public relations values, not economic ones, led Don Regan to develop a 15-25-35 rate structure for Treasury I, rather than the more awkward-sounding 16-28-37 devised by staff. Yet this slight change in enumeration had enormous fiscal consequences, forcing a sharp increase in business taxes and creating new tax cuts for many more individuals. The symbolic power of simple, low rates became even more important in the Senate, where a two-rate structure became the focus of reform. In conference, preserving the appearance (but not the reality) of that two-tier structure was judged so crucial that, when a third and higher rate had to be restored in order to maintain revenue neutrality, it was done covertly, with perverse distributional effects. Tax reform is not unique in these respects. As Mark Moore observes:

> Many ideas that become powerful lack the intellectual properties that policy analysts hold dear. Most such ideas are not very complex or differentiated. There is no clear separation of ends from means, of diagnosis from interventions, of assumptions from demonstrated facts, or of blame from causal effect.... Moreover, it is not clear reasoning or carefully developed and interpreted facts that make ideas convincing. Rather, ideas seem to become anchored in people's minds through illustrative anecdotes, simple diagrams and pictures, or connections with broad common sense ideologies that define human nature and social responsibilities.[26]

The case history of tax reform does offer striking illustrations of these propositions, however. For example, poll data suggest that the public was dissatisfied with income taxation, but its understanding of the tax's operation and relative burdens were a caricature of reality. Although both experts and the public agreed on the need for action, there were sharp contrasts in their views on appropriate remedies and their understanding of such key concepts as "fairness" and "simplicity." Sensational stories about wealthy corporations and individuals who had paid no taxes at all captured the imagination of the public. For them, the spirit of tax reform could be expressed by a tough minimum tax that would prevent the avoidance of tax liabilities. Experts, however, viewed such a minimum tax as anathema to true reform and even as an indication of failure. Their goal was a comprehensive definition of income and true horizontal equity, which threatened popular deductions and exemptions and raised the possibility of other actions that would surely have astonished the general public.

Although the emotional aspects of tax reform had more influence on the citizenry than experts did, some key figures also were won over to the cause by highly personalized representations of tax inequities. For Ronald Reagan, there was the memory of marginal rates so high that actors limited their movie roles—and thus incomes—during World War II. For Bill Bradley, there was lingering resentment at being considered a "depreciable asset" during his career in professional basketball. For Dan Rostenkowski, there was the shock of discovering that his daughter had paid more in income taxes than the airline she worked for. For these leaders, as for the public, interest in the cause was sparked as much by these archetypes of injustice as by more complex analytical claims.

In short, tax reform must be judged as a victory for the experts, since many of its provisions moved the code closer to their ideal of reform. The political process through which reform was enacted, however, encouraged and probably depended upon symbolic representations and misunderstandings of their concerns and proposals, as much as on reasoned analysis.

Entrepreneurs in the Policy Process. On many specialized policy issues, particularly those in which the executive branch assumes leadership, experts alone may formulate policy. But when it comes to nonincremental policy changes, where the manipulation of symbols is important, a second set of actors—who specialize in placing ideas into the political arena— often help shape the policy agenda. The term "policy entrepreneur" has become the accepted designation for these champions of ideas.

The concept of policy entrepreneur parallels that of the entrepreneur in the private sector. A business entrepreneur is a person who brings together land, labor, and capital and ideally is rewarded for his or her creativity by financial profit. Similarly, a policy entrepreneur is someone who assembles the key ingredients essential for government action. In Kingdon's description, policy entrepreneurs are people willing "to invest their resources— time, energy, reputation, and sometimes money—in return for future policies they favor. Their return might come to them in the form of policies of which they approve, satisfaction from participation, or even personal aggrandizement in the form of job security or career promotion." [27]

Entrepreneurs are not necessarily the originators of important policy ideas. More commonly, they act as middlemen between professional experts, who formulate and perfect policy solutions, and the broader political arena. Entrepreneurs simplify and distill those complex ideas and then link them to values that are accepted by and are familiar to the broader public. This is frequently a vital role. Wilson has traced the enactment of much recent regulatory legislation favoring dispersed over narrow organized interests directly to the efforts of such policy entrepreneurs. He writes:

> [Enacting such laws] requires the efforts of a skilled entrepreneur who can mobilize latent public sentiment (by revealing a scandal or capitalizing on a crisis), put the opponents of the plan publicly on the defensive (by accusing them of deforming babies or killing motorists), and associate the legislation with widely shared values (clean air, pure water, health, and safety). [28]

In such cases, Wilson says, the entrepreneur is a "vicarious representative" of groups not directly involved in the legislative process.

Such policy entrepreneurs occupy no fixed position in or outside of government. They can be members of Congress, independent advocates, civil servants, legislative staff members, think tank employees, lobbyists, or writers. It is noteworthy, however, that policy entrepreneurs do not rely on, and typically do not hold, positions of great formal power or visibility. Rather, they gain influence largely because of their expertise, persistence, and skill, plus an ability to develop "symbiotic relationships" with other political figures who are, as often as not, hungry for action proposals. [29]

Policy entrepreneurs also must rely heavily on what Wilson calls "third parties" such as the news media to build support. It is there that the second aspect of the politics of ideas comes to the fore. Unable to steer events by exercising formal power, entrepreneurs manipulate ideas and symbols to alter the behavior of others. When the opportunity arises, policy entrepreneurs often seek to "expand the scope of conflict" from narrow, anonymous centers of decision to much larger, more visible, and almost certainly more favorable political arenas.[30]

Policy Entrepreneurs and Tax Reform. In tax reform, experts worked hand in hand with politically junior middlemen who packaged more sophisticated concepts for mass merchandising and then marketed them to those who counted most. These entrepreneurs played a vital role in placing tax reform on the political agenda. Indeed, during the early 1980s, the cause itself was almost indistinguishable from the names of its most noted congressional proponents. It was through the Kemp-Kasten and particularly the Bradley-Gephardt plans that tax reform gained widespread recognition.

For such men, the cause was attractive because they could at once pursue their policy ideals and enhance their reputations. As Bradley's tax legislative assistant put it, "We had nothing to lose and everything to gain." In contrast, tax reform was not, and almost certainly would not have been, initiated by institutional leaders, who by virtue of their position and responsibilities had much to weigh against quixotic causes, however nobly defined. They acted on it only when circumstances dictated. Rostenkowski did not pursue tax reform until President Reagan did, and Packwood initially as much as told the president "no." Even the Reagan administration did not pursue reform seriously—until it looked as though Democratic presidential nominee Walter Mondale might endorse the concept, at Bill Bradley's urging.

The role of policy entrepreneurs, then, was quite different from that of the professionals. None of these energetic merchandisers developed as much expertise as the professionals possessed. Indeed, Charles McLure, who served as deputy assistant secretary for tax analysis at Treasury in 1984—85, later commented, "Having spent all my adult life—somewhat in excess of twenty years—studying tax reform, I did not need to be taught the subject by Bill Bradley and Jack Kemp." But in the arena of political ideas, they contributed something even more important—a politician's ability to seize a useful idea and tie it to a potentially compelling problem. They took technical concepts like horizontal equity and investment neutrality and converted them into powerful populist themes like fairness and economic growth. Their ability to link such themes to more complex professional standards helped move tax writing from C-Span to prime time. Groups such as Common Cause and Citizens for Tax Justice reinforced their efforts by establishing the notion that supporting tax reform (in whatever form) was a way to uphold the public's welfare, while any expression of opposition (even the most principled) was to be considered the product of excessive dependence on special interests.

Still, although these entrepreneurs played a vital role, it was also a limited one. They kicked the ball off but orchestrated little of what followed.[31] Kemp and Gephardt moved toward other pursuits, notably presidential politics. The most successful, Bill Bradley, was also the most single-minded. As Joe Dowley recalled, "He showed he was not only willing to be for tax reform, he was willing to work for it." Still, although Bradley devoted much of his time to the cause, he was often limited to making suggestions and taking directions. Indeed, Bradley would not have played a cornerstone role in the Senate's floor debate had Russell Long not decided to stand aside.

The Politics of the Media

Publicity is the entrepreneur's least costly and most effective resource. Because they usually lack the power of those in formal authority, entrepreneurs depend greatly on the media to help them realize their objectives. For example, consumer activist Ralph Nader first attracted attention to the issue of auto safety through a magazine article containing dramatic charges and revelations. Such stories, insider "leaks," and other information disseminated by the press provided much of the foundation for the development of consumer protection policies. The media thus served a representational as well reportorial function in the development of this legislation, as Mark V. Nadel notes: "Just as lobbyists inform their clients of what the government is doing and what they themselves are doing to further the clients' interest, the press informs the consumer constituency about government actions and the actions of private advocates of their interests." [32] Publicity provided through the press on consumer issues was "always favorable," Nadel adds. In part, media writers may simply reflect the values held by their readers, who are likely to favor safer cars, cleaner meat, and purer water. Reporters also regard consumer advocates as much more reliable sources of information than business groups or even government agencies. But it has been argued that the tendency of journalists to favor the "little guy" in such disputes has certain other attractions. Analysts Lichter, Rothman, and Lichter suggest:

> The media are increasingly . . . eager to unmask the hypocrisy and puffery of the [political] combatants. This more aggressive style of reporting provides several internal rewards. By deflating the claim of all sides that their own selfish interests represent the public interest, journalists . . . establish themselves as the final repository of the public interest, the only actor without an ax to grind. All this can produce a

gratifying self-image as guardian of the little guy against the establishment, the truth against flackery, the common good against partial
interests.[33]

The Media and Tax Reform. Without strong media support, tax
reform would not have been adopted. At every step of the way, the
legislation was prodded on by intensive, and mostly favorable, press
coverage. For example, the federal government's "hometown" paper, the
Washington Post, placed tax reform on its front page twelve times in
1984, fifty-four in 1985, and forty-six times in 1986. Similarly, the *New
York Times*, which has a large audience nationwide, ran fifteen front-page
stories in 1984, fifty-three in 1985, and forty-six in 1986. In contrast, not a
single front-page story on tax reform appeared in either publication
between 1978 and 1982.[34] This close press scrutiny made all involved
aware of each step toward enactment and fully alerted them to the
dangers of failing to meet reform objectives.

Only some of the credit for this coverage can go to the entrepreneurs'
efforts. Tax reformers had tried long and hard to enlist the media to their
cause, with only sporadic success. Historically, the subject had been viewed
as too arcane and complex to be worthy of prominent or extended
coverage. Few expected legislators, let alone journalists and citizens, to be
interested in its intricacies.

By the mid-1980s, however, a variety of external factors contributed to
tax reform's newsworthiness. Tax policy gained salience after the Califor-
nia-led property-tax revolt of the late 1970s. The supply-side theory, and
the dramatic rate cuts of 1981, also brought tax issues to center stage,
focusing attention on taxes and their relationship to U.S. economic growth.
"We never had the press interested in what we were doing in the '70s,"
David Brockway of the Joint Tax Committee recalls:

> It was only the cattlemen, or oil and gas, or low income housing—all
> those groups that inevitably the members would react to. It changed in
> the early '80s when the president began tapping that general resentment
> about taxes and saying, "Look, the message is very simple: taxes are too
> high." Then the members had to respond to the general public. Taxes
> had become large-scale politics like SALT or something. It was a
> different ballgame.

In particular, the release of Treasury's proposals gave the media a new
and sharper angle, a story in stark black and white that pitted special
interests and the status quo in tax policy against the public interest and tax
reform. This theme, which Bradley and others had been sounding for
years, was amplified first by the purity of Treasury I and later by the
president's endorsement. This prospect actually fed on itself: White House
misgivings about the political ramifications of tax reform were overwhelmed in part by the publicity favoring the plan, as Eugene Steuerle
later stressed.

Treasury I's uncompromising application of economic principles gave the study credibility among the press, while Reagan's subsequent emphasis on "fairness, simplicity, and economic growth" gave journalists the hooks needed to make front-page news. Using the time-tested tactics of early muckrakers, ambitious journalists normally consigned to cover the arcana of tax policy were drawn into the more visible but quite comfortable role of reformers. In the tradition of investigative reporters, they seized on the themes that had brought them into prominence and continued the story, translating it from technical economic and legal language into words that held their editors and—more important for tax reform—Washington itself spellbound.

This media attention turned tax reform into a "tar baby" in the political village that is bounded by Washington's Beltway. Thanks to it, tax policy was no longer interesting only to those who played the game. In media hands, the TRA battle became an epic struggle between good and evil— certainly the best political story in town. And, like all good stories, it was highly personalized. Overnight, one might find himself presented as a tax villain. As a Rostenkowski aide recalled, "The press did its share, running pictorials of many of those who voted against us." Later, Bob Packwood was singled out by the media as the Senate "bad boy" on tax reform. So, too, those who hoped to salvage things for powerful economic interests in conference were dealt a mighty blow by the press, who in editorials and articles speculated that the final price for tax reform must be further corporate sacrifice.

The lesson was not lost on wavering legislators. After the press began "kickin' the crap out of the committee," in Rostenkowski's colorful words, the bank vote was reversed and tax reform was again off and running in Ways and Means.[35] Similarly, the man unceremoniously dubbed "Senator Hackwood" by a merciless press became born-again in a matter of days when he altered his strategy. His Finance Committee colleagues reported a bill in less than two weeks as they shivered to think what price might be paid for standing in front of a rolling train—or worse, being tagged as the ones who derailed it. Packwood recalls, "It helped tremendously to almost immediately have editorials from the *Post* and the *Times* saying that's the way we ought to go. That gave members heart."

Reflecting back on these and other key junctures in the process, two journalists who covered the story concluded that the media's "message was obvious": [if legislators] allowed tax reform to die, they would take a beating in the press, and probably in public opinion." [36] In fact, it is clear that populist rhetoric, bright lights, and the casting of tax reform as something legislators could only be "for" or "against" converted many who would not have sympathized with the cause under other circumstances.

Leadership: The Missing Ingredient

Tax reform, Dan Rostenkowski once said, was "the bill no one wanted." He meant to suggest the lack of enthusiasm for the cause among both organized interests and the unorganized public, as well as among legislators themselves. And, it may fairly be said that, in the beginning, no one *important* wanted it. With the exception of President Reagan, who by most accounts never fully understood his own proposal or even the legislation he eventually signed, most institutional leaders came to tax reform belatedly and with reluctance.

Yet if *no one* wanted it, tax reform would not have passed. In fact, professional experts wanted it. Diligent but poorly positioned entrepreneurs promoted it. With help from good-government groups who put their research skills to work to snare sensation-hunting journalists, the media strongly encouraged it. Indeed, in many respects, the enactment of tax reform closely followed what might be termed the "ideational/entrepreneurial" model of reform. This explanation puts tax reform in a family, not with prior decisions in tax policy, but with a variety of other surprisingly successful efforts to enact new programs (or abolish existing ones) in the face of determined, well-organized opposition.

But to attribute the legislative success of tax reform to ideas, experts, policy entrepreneurs, and the press ignores at least one critical explanatory variable. If one asks participants in the reform process—from members of Congress to staff to lobbyists—what single factor was most responsible for the TRA, only a few say "the power of an idea whose time had come." Fewer still point to entrepreneurs like Bill Bradley. Instead, the vast majority credit those with leadership responsibilities. "Ronald Reagan, pure and simple," said one House Democrat. "If it hadn't been for Rostenkowski, there would have been no tax bill," maintained a high administration official. "We got it because the president of the United States, the Speaker of the House, the chairman of the Ways and Means Committee, and ultimately the chairman of the Senate Finance Committee decided they wanted the bill," according to a top congressional staff member.

Such answers could be taken as products of Washington myopia. Active participants may be so close to the process that they cannot see the intellectual forest through the institutional trees. But here, the truth does seem to be otherwise. By every indicator, the efforts of leaders were absolutely critical to the enactment of tax reform. It was they who put reform so firmly on the agenda that it could not be ignored: indeed, they escalated the partisan and institutional stakes at every turn. Having decided for personal and political reasons that they would take action on reform, they became converts to the cause and devoted themselves

completely to its success. In so doing, they virtually compelled their
followers to proceed down a path that most resisted.

Tax reform, then, did not just "happen." It was neither in the air nor in
the stars. Rather, this massive legislation was willed into action by men in
powerful positions who concluded that moving tax reform forward *at least
one more step* coincided with the best interests of their institution, their
party, themselves, or their country. Kingpins, not young turks, skillfully
blended new- and old-style reform politics, and it was they, rather than the
entrepreneurs, who ultimately rode the wave of tax reform into history.

Their decisions, while conscious, were not necessarily well considered.
President Reagan was poorly informed about many of the details of the
plan that he strongly endorsed. Dan Rostenkowski remarked that he might
not have undertaken the task if he had deliberated more thoroughly: "If I
had looked at the code, the challenge, just the size, I think I would have
had second thoughts." Nonetheless, the backing of such leaders was
fundamental to the legislative success of the cause. Before Ronald Reagan
put the issue on the policy agenda, tax reform was seen as "years ahead of
its time," as Tip O'Neill told Bradley and Gephardt. His presidential stamp
of approval alone made it worthy of serious consideration. Although
Reagan rarely fulfilled his expected leadership responsibilities once Rostenkowski picked up the legislation, his men continued to represent the
president—mostly working around the edges but on occasion in the very
center of congressional activity.

Once the president put tax reform on the government's action list, it
almost certainly would not have advanced had it not been for other skilled
leaders. To achieve success, they creatively used all the resources at their
disposal. They aggressively used the traditional tools of staff, timing, and
distributive benefits to meet their goals. Moreover, they brilliantly adapted
the newer techniques and strategies of entrepreneurial politics to serve
their ends, manipulating symbols and utilizing the press. The dynamics of
tax reform changed as reluctant legislators faced leaders who had put their
careers on the line for the cause and who were crafty enough to use every
means at their disposal to get it.

In the House, it was Dan Rostenkowski who "picked up the challenge
and did it," surprising many in the process. He had no reputation as a
reformer and no prior intention to act. But, faced with concerns about
partisan protection and personal reputation, as well as policy content, he
compelled a reluctant committee to move ahead. He negotiated with
committee members and sought to lessen their concerns. He closed the
markup to outside groups. He gave a brilliant public performance in
responding to the president's televised address on tax reform. He manipulated symbols, seeking to make the House bill "fairer to the middle class."
When the committee balked, he used media pressure as well as direct

appeals to committee pride, to bring it back into line. When necessary, he altered his coalitions to build a majority. And finally, by producing a Democratic bill, he compelled the Republican Senate to respond, in what had become a high stakes game of partisan one-upmanship.

Packwood accepted the challenge when only three committee members wanted to proceed. Failing first in his effort at using time-tested methods of political coalition building, he changed strategies. He joined forces with Bradley and the reformers and seized media attention with a startlingly pure reform bill on the individual side, while pacifying his committee members with old-fashioned constituency politics on the corporate side. Like Rostenkowski, he appealed to committee pride and team spirit—as well as electoral self-protection—and he masterfully used the symbols of reform and the vise of revenue neutrality to push a reform bill through the Senate floor with virtually no amendments.

In conference, the leaders were in complete control. When the demands of tax reform proved too much for conferees and the normal style of conferencing, Packwood and Rostenkowski assumed full responsibility. Meeting around the clock and in secret, while relying on teams of staff experts, those two men were able to do what the full conference committee could not: piece together a unified tax reform bill from the distinctive legislative handiwork of both chambers.

Leadership and the New Reform. This strong leadership role has implications that extend beyond tax policy to the new politics of reform in general. The risks involved in legislation that pits dispersed benefits against concentrated costs means that entrepreneurs are often critically important in placing such issues on the policy agenda. Moreover, on issues of limited scope or on individual provisions of omnibus bills, their efforts alone may be sufficient to win enactment. For example, passage of section 504 of the Rehabilitation Act of 1973, which prohibits discrimination against the handicapped in programs receiving federal funds, is generally credited to the initiative of a single legislator, Rep. Charles Vanik. This seemingly innocuous but ultimately very costly provision was not considered at all in congressional hearings, not mentioned in the Senate committee report, or spoken about on the floor. Similarly, the so-called Buckley amendment, which guarantees students access to their educational records, had its origins in a brief article in *Parade* magazine. It was adopted as a Senate floor amendment, without hearings or informed debate, upon the sole initiative of Sen. James Buckley. Such cases surely testify to the influence that can be wielded by individual legislative policy entrepreneurs.[37]

But on larger more controversial legislation, formal leaders are often central to the enactment of reforms, even though their role has not always been stressed in earlier studies. For example, activist Warren Magnuson was chairman of the Senate Commerce Committee when consumer protection regulations were enacted in the 1960s. Similarly, Edmund Muskie was chairman of the Senate Public Works Committee's Subcommittee on Air and Water Pollution, as well as a presidential contender, when he exerted leadership over the landmark environmental regulations of the late 1960s and early 1970s.[38] To attribute such legislation solely or principally to the work of policy entrepreneurs and supportive social movements is to ignore a factor of leadership that was central to the politics of adoption, if not to policy initiation.

The behavior of leaders on tax reform parallels that in airline, trucking, and telecommunications deregulation. Though deregulation, like tax reform, was built on an ideational consensus among experts and across parties, it was moved toward implementation and enactment by legislators in key committee assignments, as well as by President Ford and the institutional heads of the regulatory commissions. Sen. Edward M. Kennedy was an early deregulation advocate, but Sen. Howard Cannon (like Rostenkowski and Packwood) was a late and unlikely convert to the cause. Yet despite his initial skepticism, Cannon was moved to defend both the prerogatives of his committee and his own reputation for legislative effectiveness by helping to shape ambitious, far-reaching reform statutes.[39]

The remarkable willingness of such leaders to embrace innovative reform seems to reflect the pressures of publicity and responsibility that are focused on them. Martha Derthick and Paul Quirk suggest that, in contrast to other legislators:

> Leaders on an issue will be more prone to act on their conceptions of the public interest, because it is more irresponsible for those in a position of power to do otherwise. They will be more prone to use the issue to gain the respect of colleagues and other elites, because their behavior is more closely watched. And with regard to reelection, for the same reason, they will direct their appeals to broader, even though less attentive, audiences within their constituencies. Compared with other congressmen, leaders will have diminished regard for the wishes of organized interest groups and sometimes even for the economic interests of their states or districts.

Furthermore, in deregulation as in tax reform, competition among such leaders had a major effect on the scope and pace of legislative action. The authors add, "When numerous leaders in different parts of the government became involved and began competing with one another, policy change occurred very fast."[40]

Conclusion

The new style of reform politics to which tax reform owes its existence has appeared with growing frequency in recent years. Although it has become more common, the results of the process are no less surprising in each successful case. Careful analysts, shrewd legislators, and smart-money lobbyists repeatedly have failed to foresee the possible acceptance of these reforms.

"It can't happen here" has been the usual forecast and, in truth, the obstacles to legislation in such fields as civil rights, aid to education, antipoverty assistance, health insurance, consumer protection, environmental quality, occupational health and safety, sex discrimination, and the deregulation of airlines, trucking, telecommunications, and broadcasting were considerable. But in these and other cases, the political barriers dropped away. Some of these achievements can be at least partly explained by the "old" reform politics: presidential leadership, an aroused public, and strong partisan support. But others fit more closely the new politics of reform, emphasizing the role of ideas, experts, entrepreneurs, and the media. What certainly seems established, by tax reform and parallel cases, is that the advocates of far-reaching policy shifts now have not one but two roads to travel. This new political map doubles their chances of reaching a favored destination.

But why is the acceptance of such legislation still so surprising? In part, success remains unexpected because the pattern of legislative victories appears only across varied policy fields. Within any single realm, historic patterns of political behavior remain stacked against far-reaching change. But, when the aggregate of important nonincremental changes, often adopted in the face of determined interest-group resistance, is weighed, a revised appraisal of the American policy process is needed. Though still improbable, such reforms are increasingly possible. Lingering images of "deadlock and drift" seem dated and incomplete.[41]

Such outcomes also are surprising because they flow from a pattern of politics that is inherently less predictable. Traditional interest-based politics is stable because the underlying patterns of interest change only slowly over time, as society, government, and the economy evolve. Ideas, however, appear not only in the form of lasting ideologies but frantic fads. Public moods and intellectual commitments often come and go quickly. Entrepreneurs similarly may switch issues or fade from view.

To some extent, the unpredictability of the new politics reflects the increasing individualization of politics, the erosion of more stable political alliances, and the fragmentation of governing institutions. Highly atomized structures, as our political institutions are now thought to be, are often erratic: they can move quickly from stagnation to rapid change and back again. "An atomized politics," Anthony King observes, "may share one characteristic of a human crowd—a tendency to move either very sluggishly or with extreme speed."[42]

Finally, as this assessment shows, it is only through fairly complex and fortuitous combinations of actors, strategies, and circumstances that dramatic change can occur.[43] The case of tax reform underscores the observation of Rep. John Brademas that "any bill passed by Congress is a tapestry woven from strands of intellectual effort, political opportunity, institutional rivalry, and personal ambition"—a nice summary of this legislation.[44]

Tax reform also illuminates Brademas's cautionary observation that "the safest response to those who ask how policy is made in American government is, 'It all depends.' "[45] For the political analyst, the case history of tax reform is a warning against excessive reliance on any one model of the policy process. Applied like cookie cutters, standard models do not fit tax reform. Using models as a kind of compass makes the job of identifying essentials easier but also points up the fact that no single one explains everything. In fact, the TRA policy process has something to tempt every theoretical taste. Like themes in a larger symphony, three different patterns of policy making emerge, disappear, and sometimes return to featured places in the tax-reform story. The politics of pluralist bargaining, of presidential leadership, and of entrepreneurial mobilization may each contribute at different stages, or to different aspects, of the resolution of a complex issue.[46]

Indeed, the goal of analytical clarity is better served if the models are reconceptualized as distinctive "systems of power," rather then deterministic patterns of action. There is in contemporary American government one system of power revolving around organized and constituent interests, another around presidential elections and parties, and a third around ideas. To some degree, each constitutes a separate "game" with its own rules, resources, umpires, and plays. Yet, the nature of the dominant game can change in mid-play, with new players added or dropped. Unpredictability is inherent in such a dynamic contest. But this more flexible image corresponds better with the character of contemporary power relations. We now have, as journalist Hedrick Smith writes:

> . . . a more fluid system of power than ever before in our history. Quite literally, power floats. It does not reside in the White House, nor does it merely alternate from pole to pole, from president to opposition, from Republicans to Democrats. It floats. It shifts. It wriggles elusively, like mercury in the palm of one's hand, passing from one competing power center to another, with the driving leadership on major policies . . . gravitating to whoever is daring enough to grab it and smart enough to figure out the quickest way to make a political score.[47]

Because "normal" tax politics operates as a game among interests, involving few but the most attentive, tax reform seemed a certain failure. Here, the advantage lay with the best organized and most skilled—just as pluralist theory suggests. To this problem most advocates and analysts saw only one clear solution: a change in the game to presidential/party politics.

Success on these terms seemed to require a mobilized electorate, strong presidential leadership, and unified party control of the institutions of government. Such conditions seemed improbable, however, leading to more pessimistic forecasts.

Nonetheless, President Reagan embraced tax reform in the hope of gaining electoral advantages. In the end, though, tax reform was adopted because the dominant character of the game changed once again. Experts, entrepreneurs, and the media all played important roles, but when key legislative leaders put their own reputations and resources on the line, the highly publicized cause advanced from the apparently unmovable to the seemingly unstoppable.

This change in the game and its players is illustrated by the events that followed Packwood's conversion to reform. Having failed to produce a bill through normal bargaining strategies, and convinced of the need to do so, Packwood turned for assistance to the very "do-gooders" whose involvement he had previously disdained. Further, he adopted as his own the entrepreneurial techniques of symbolic manipulation, making sure that his proposal was emotionally appealing. While never abandoning the traditional tools of leadership, Packwood made it clear to recalcitrant members that if the legislation died, the fault would be theirs, not his. As Packwood himself put it, he "strapped on his guns" and entered the "O.K. Corral." If the committee really wanted true tax reform, as they had said, then "we'll give them tax reform. We'll call their bluff." Thus, Packwood shifted the uncomfortable weight of press and political attention from himself to committee members.

Just as the nature of the game changed throughout the tax-reform process, so did its goal. Initially, it may be said, good public policy was the prime objective for reform—the motivation of experts and entrepreneurs. But partisan credit-claiming came to the fore as the Republican administration seized leadership on the tax-reform issue and catapulted it into the headlines. When it later became apparent that tax reform lacked the popularity anticipated, blame avoidance became the chief aim, as congressional leaders struggled to protect their individual reputations and those of their party. This led the "impossible dream" of generations of reform proponents to its astonishing conclusion.

What next? First, there is no reason to expect that the tax-reform victory of 1986 will be succeeded by another drastic overhaul of the revenue system. Although all the experience cited here shows that skeptical forecasts should not be too easily advanced, the point to be emphasized is not that the "subsystem" of tax policy has changed, but that the *overall political context* in which *all* such subsystems are embedded is different. While, on the one hand, the 1986 experience shows that tax policy is more fluid than had been supposed, traditional forces will probably reassert themselves as tax issues recede to their more usual place toward the bottom of the policy agenda. Further, the logic of the new politics of reform suggests that policy entrepreneurs and political leaders are more likely to seek their fame in more novel territory. At least for the time being, the field of taxation has probably been drained of the opportunities for political credit and partisan gain that make such exhausting forays worthwhile.

Yet, the main lesson of the tax-reform process is clear: there are features of contemporary American politics that *do* facilitate far-reaching policy change. The influences of experts, policy entrepreneurs, and the media, coupled with the commitment and legislative skills of established leaders, can turn existing policy on its head. Further, this and other parallel observations suggest that what is here termed the "new politics of reform" increasingly prevails, while older, more rigid power systems resting on interest and party are declining in importance.

In part, then, we concur with Derthick and Quirk, whose analysis of economic deregulation concludes by suggesting that "a major virtue of the current American political system . . . lies in the resources and rewards it offers for overcoming particularism." The combination of advanced communications and institutionalized expert analysis now gives political leaders "a good chance" of defeating narrow interests.[48] But assertions about the system's responsiveness to popular sentiment should be made cautiously. It is tempting to characterize adoption of the TRA as a "testament to democracy's health" or a "triumph of the American democratic system."[49] Yet even though the actors who moved it forward might claim and believe that they spoke for the public's welfare, this study also demonstrates that they did so with limited public involvement and little public support.[50]

Furthermore, just as policy malleability should not be confused with political responsiveness, neither can it be equated with political responsibility. Murray Weidenbaum, who chaired President Reagan's Council of Economic Advisers in 1981—1982, sees the tax-reform effort as a "clever way of diverting attention from the tough problems involved in cutting the deficit." Other economists believe that further steps are necessary and have advanced revisions of earlier proposals. Joseph Pechman thinks the 1986 act has "greatly improved the fairness of the tax system" and has "removed major distortions from the economy," but also points to "mistakes and missed opportunities" where the law departs from a truly comprehensive definition of income. Similarly, Charles McLure describes the tax system as "more equitable and more neutral than it was a few years ago" but urges additional base broadening to remedy the "serious flaws" that remain. Robert Hall and Alvin Rabushka claim that the TRA "made a number of key improvements," but champion further reductions in the top marginal rate and a drastic simplification of tax forms. A few are even less sanguine, asking whether revenue shortfalls, administrative complexity, and harsh penalties mean that the U.S. income tax system has "outlived its usefulness." [51]

Thus the debate among tax experts continues. But a truly remarkable political event need not have produced a truly remarkable legislative document. More time, more analysis, and more debate are needed before the full impact of the Tax Reform Act of 1986 can be determined. What is plain now is its significance for students of policy making. As President Reagan observed at the TRA's signing ceremony, somewhere during the twenty-three months between initiation and adoption "the impossible became the inevitable." The TRA thus forces revisions in widely accepted portrayals of American politics, just as it did to the tax code itself. In particular, it suggests that—without alterations of its basic constitutional structure—our governmental system has acquired new potential for surmounting the political obstacles of organized interests and bridging the seemingly unbridgeable gaps between separated institutions and divided parties.

Notes

1. For this reason, it is not surprising that the adoption of the TRA has attracted the attention of a number of scholars. Some of these analysts, through independent research, have reached conclusions paralleling significant parts of the interpretation presented here. Perhaps the first assessment was James M. Verdier's "The Tax Reform Act of 1986: Some Lessons of Policy Change" (Paper delivered at the annual research conference of the Association for Public Policy Analysis and Management, Austin, Texas, October 30—November 1, 1986). See also his historical essay, "The President, Congress, and Tax Reform: Patterns over Three Decades," *Annals of the American Academy of Political and Social Science* 499 (September 1988): 114—23. A symposium on tax reform appeared in *The Journal of Economic Perspectives* 1 (Summer 1987). Another early interpretation, focusing on action in the House Ways and Means Committee, was Randall Strahan, "Committee Politics and Tax Reform" (Paper delivered at the annual meeting of the American Political Science Association, Chicago, September 3—6, 1987). An informed "insider's" account was presented by one of Senator Bradley's key advisers, Joseph J. Minarik, in "How Tax Reform Came About," *Tax Notes*, December 26, 1987, 1359—73. The passage of tax reform and failure of welfare reform are contrasted in Dennis Coyle and Aaron Wildavsky, "Requisites of Radical Reform: Income Maintenance versus Tax Preferences," *Journal of Policy Analysis and Management* 7 (Fall 1987): 1—16, and a cross-national analysis was presented in Swen Steinmo, "Shaping Policy Preferences: Political Institutions and Tax Policy in the United States, Sweden, and Britain" (Paper presented at the annual meeting of the American Political Science Association, Washington, D.C., September 1—4, 1988). Both past trends and recent changes in tax policy are explored in Gary Mucciaroni, "The Politics of

Comprehensive Tax Reform," unpublished ms., September 1988. The preliminary statement of our own findings was presented as Timothy J. Conlan, David R. Beam, and Margaret Wrightson, "Taxing Choices: Ideas, Interests, and the Politics of Tax Reform" (Paper presented at the annual meeting of the American Political Science Association, Washington, D.C., September 1–4, 1988).

2. Earl Latham, "The Group Basis of Politics," *American Political Science Review* 46 (June 1952): 390.

3. Quoted in *Tax Notes*, December 31, 1984, 1356.

4. Alvin Rabushka, "The Tax Reform Act of 1986: Concentrated Costs, Diffuse Benefits—An Inversion of Public Choice," *Contemporary Policy Issues* 9 (October 1988): 50–64.

5. James L. Sundquist notes, "By the 1960s, political science had developed a dominating theory as to how the American constitutional system should—and at its best did—work. The political party was the institution that unified the separated branches of the government and brought coherence to the policy-making process. And because the president was the leader of his party, he was the chief policy maker of the entire government. . . . This established theory presupposed one essential condition: there would . . . be a majority party in control of both branches of government." See "Needed: A Political Theory for the New Era of Coalition Government in the United States," *Political Science Quarterly* 103 (Winter 1988–89): 624–25.

6. The most useful study of the outpouring of Great Society legislation is James L. Sundquist, *Politics and Policy: The Eisenhower, Kennedy, and Johnson Years* (Washington: Brookings Institution, 1968).

7. Susan B. Hansen, *The Politics of Taxation: Revenue without Representation* (New York; Praeger Publishers, 1983), 62.

8. James L. Sundquist, *Constitutional Reform and Effective Government* (Washington: Brookings Institution, 1986), 75–76.

9. For an examination of this same form of interparty competition in environmental policy making, see E. Donald Elliott, Bruce A. Ackerman, and John C. Millian, "Toward a Theory of Statutory Evolution: The Federalization of Environmental Law," *Journal of Law, Economics, and Organization* 2 (Fall 1985): 313–40.

10. On the growing importance of blame avoidance in congressional behavior, see R. Kent Weaver, *Automatic Government: The Politics of Indexation* (Washington: Brookings Institution, 1988).

11. Quoted in "Taxes behind Closed Doors," *Frontline* #411 (Boston: WGBH-TV Transcripts, 1986), 22. On the importance of such future-oriented strategic calculations in congressional behavior, see Gary C. Jacobson and Samuel Kernell, *Strategy and Choice in Congressional Elections* (New Haven, Conn.: Yale University Press, 1981).

12. Polls cited in Barry Sussman, *What Americans Really Think and Why Our Politicians Pay No Attention* (New York: Pantheon Books, 1988), 153–54.

13. James Q. Wilson, ed., *The Politics of Regulation* (New York: Basic Books, 1980), 370.

14. What is here called the new politics of reform actually was quite influential during the Progressive era. On the role of experts and muckraking journalists in securing the passage of early food and drug legislation, see Mark V. Nadel, *The Politics of Consumer Protection* (Indianapolis, Ind.: Bobbs-Merrill, 1971), 7–19.

15. John Maynard Keynes, *The General Theory of Employment, Interest, and Money* (1936) (New York: Harcourt Brace Jovanovich, 1964,) 383—84.
16. Wilson, *Politics of Regulation*, 372.
17. Deborah A. Stone, *Policy Paradox and Political Reason* (Glenview, Ill.: Scott-Foresman, 1988), 25.
18. John W. Kingdon, *Agendas, Alternatives, and Public Policies* (Boston: Little, Brown, 1984), 131—32.
19. Gary R. Orren, "Beyond Self-Interest," in *The Power of Public Ideas*, ed. Robert B. Reich (Cambridge, Mass.: Ballinger, 1988), 13.
20. Daniel P. Moynihan, "The Professionalization of Reform," *The Public Interest* 1 (Fall 1965): 6—16.
21. Samuel H. Beer, "Federalism, Nationalism, and Democracy in America," *American Political Science Review* 72 (March 1978): 17.
22. Steven Kelman, "Why Public Ideas Matter," in *The Power of Public Ideas*, ed. Reich, 31.
23. Much of this argument is presented by Rabushka, who attributes the TRA to "the power of an idea—the political and economic appeal of a low top rate—[which] won over Packwood, his colleagues on the Senate Finance Committee, and ultimately the majority of Congress." See "The Tax Reform Act of 1986," 64. He believes that a presentation of his own flat-tax plan, heard by Bill Diefenderfer, led to the development of Packwood's proposal.
24. The importance of symbolism in politics is explored in Charles D. Elder and Roger W. Cobb, *The Political Uses of Symbols* (New York: Longman, 1983), as well as by Murray Edelman in *The Symbolic Uses of Politics* (Urbana: University of Illinois Press, 1964) and in other works.
25. Quoted in Strahan, "Committee Politics and Tax Reform," 25—26.
26. Mark Moore, "What Sort of Ideas Become Public Ideas?" in *The Power of Public Ideas*, ed. Reich, 79.
27. Kingdon, *Agendas, Alternatives, and Public Policies*, 129.
28. Wilson, *Politics of Regulation*, 370.
29. See Nelson W. Polsby, *Political Innovation in America: The Politics of Policy Initiation* (New Haven, Conn.: Yale University Press, 1984), 171—72.
30. See E. E. Schattschneider, *The Semi-Sovereign People: A Realist's View of Democracy in America* (New York: Holt, Rinehart, and Winston, 1960), 2.
31. In a televised interview in 1985, Bradley said that the thing that gave him the most satisfaction when he was a basketball player was "making the move that set up the pass that set up the screen that set up the shot, when I was the only person in the hall who knew what was happening." When the sports commentator followed up with "You must really miss that," Bradley laughed and replied, "Not at all, I am still doing it." Certainly he must be credited with making such a key move on tax reform. Joseph Minarik, personal correspondence, October 19, 1988.
32. Nadel, *The Politics of Consumer Protection*, 192.
33. S. Robert Lichter, Stanley Rothman, and Linda S. Lichter, *The Media Elite: America's New Power Brokers* (Bethesda, Md.: Adler & Adler, 1986), 57, 130. On the progressive-reformist tendencies of the press generally, see Austin Ranney, *Channels of Power* (New York: Basic Books, 1983) and Frank J. Sorauf, "Campaign Money and the Press," *Political Science Quarterly* 102 (Spring 1987): 25—42.
34. These figures are based on a content analysis of the *New York Times* and *Washington Post* indexes under the heading "tax reform." In addition, we

found a total of eleven 1984, non-A-1 front section *New York Times* stories, ninety-two in 1985, and eighty-one in 1986. The *Washington Post* published thirty-five such stories in 1984, eighty in 1985, and eighty-one in 1986. As would be expected, nearly all of these stories appeared on the front pages of the business sections of these papers.

35. Quoted in Hedrick Smith, *The Power Game: How Washington Works* (New York: Random House, 1988), 559.

36. Jeffrey H. Birnbaum and Alan S. Murray, "Tax Reform: The Bill Nobody Wanted," *Public Opinion*, March/April 1987, 43.

37. On Section 504 and the Buckley amendment, as well as other similar cases, see Timothy J. Conlan and Steven L. Abrams, "Federal Intergovernmental Regulation: Symbolic Politics in the New Congress," *Intergovernmental Perspective* 7 (Summer 1981): 19−26.

38. For a detailed account of the entrepreneurial reform activities of Magnuson and his committee staff, see David Price, *Who Makes the Laws: Creativity and Power in Senate Committees* (Cambridge, Mass.: Schenkman, 1972). For an account of Muskie's role, as well as a description of a case of partisan and institutional policy escalation that parallels tax reform, see Charles O. Jones, *Clean Air* (Pittsburgh: University of Pittsburgh Press, 1975).

39. Martha Derthick and Paul J. Quirk, *The Politics of Deregulation* (Washington: Brookings Institution, 1985), 66−67.

40. Ibid, 103, 241.

41. Noting the success of the deregulatory and tax reform efforts, James Q. Wilson also has argued that "it is increasingly implausible to use 'deadlock' as a word to describe economic policy making in America." See "Does the Separation of Powers Still Work? " *The Public Interest* 86 (Winter 1987), 47.

42. Anthony King, "The American Polity in the Late 1970s: Building Coalitions in the Sand," in Anthony King, ed., *The New American Political System* (Washington: American Enterprise Institute, 1978), 393.

43. Joseph Minarik suggests that "the passage of tax reform required the most incredible confluence of circumstances—almost like an alignment of the planets." "How Tax Reform Came About," 1372.

44. John Brademas, *The Politics of Education: Conflict and Consensus on Capitol Hill* (Norman: University of Oklahoma Press, 1987), 22.

45. Ibid, 52−53.

46. The value of examining a complex event through multiple models is a major point of Graham T. Allison's classic, *The Essence of Decision: Explaining the Cuban Missile Crisis* (Boston: Little, Brown, 1971).

47. Smith, *The Power Game*, 14−15.

48. Derthick and Quirk, *The Politics of Deregulation*, 257−58.

49. Stephen Chapman, "Tax Reform Is a Testament to Democracy's Health," *Chicago Tribune*, October 1, 1986, 15; Jeffrey H. Birnbaum and Alan S. Murray, *Showdown at Gucci Gulch: Lawmakers, Lobbyists, and the Unlikely Triumph of Tax Reform* (New York: Random House, 1987), 289.

50. Post-enactment opinion polls found majorities describing the reformed tax system as even more complicated and inequitable than the old one. See Kenneth E. John, "After All That Hype, the Taxpayers Aren't Any Happier," *Washington Post National Weekly Edition*, June 27−July 3, 1988, 37; Albert B. Crenshaw, "Most Find Tax Filing Is Overly Burdensome," *Washington Post*, April 5, 1989, F-1.

51. Joseph A. Pechman, "Tax Reform: Theory and Practice," *Economic Perspec-*

tives 1 (Summer 1987): 17, 21; Charles E. McLure, Jr., "Tax Policy for the 1990s: Tending to Unfinished Business," in *Thinking about America: The United States in the 1990s*, ed. Annelise Anderson and Dennis L. Bark (Stanford, Calif.: Hoover Institution Press, 1988), 289; Robert E. Hall and Alvin Rabushka, "An Efficient, Equitable Tax for the 1990s," in ibid., 301—10; Murray Weidenbaum, *Rendezvous with Reality: The American Economy after Reagan* (New York: Basic Books, 1988), 89; Albert B. Crenshaw, "Has Our Tax System Outlived Its Usefulness? " *Washington Post National Weekly Edition*, April 24—30, 1989, 20.

Appendix: *Evolution of Key Tax Reform Provisions*

Provision	Existing Law[a]	Bradley-Gephardt[b]	Treasury I[c]	Treasury II[d]	House Bill[e]	Senate Bill[f]	Tax Reform Act[g]
Individual tax rates	11–50% (14 brackets)	14, 26, and 30%	15, 25, and 35%	15, 25, and 35%	15, 25, 35, and 38%	15 and 27% (plus hidden 33%)	15 and 28% (plus hidden 33%)
Personal exemption	$1,080	$1,000 – $1,600	$2,000	$2,000	$1,500 – $2,000	$0 – 2,000	$0 – 2,000
State and local taxes	Deductible	Income and property deductible	Deduction eliminated	Deduction eliminated	Deductible	Sales tax restricted	No sales tax deduction
Charitable donations	Deductible	Deductible	Repealed deduction for nonitemizers; limited for itemizers	Repealed deduction for nonitemizers; retained for itemizers	Limited deduction for nonitemizers; full deduction retained for itemizers	Repealed deduction for nonitemizers; full deduction for itemizers	Repealed deduction for nonitemizers; full deduction for itemizers
Interest	Deductible	Unlimited deduction for mortgage interest at 14% rate; other interest deductions restricted	Indexed and limited nonmortgage interest deductions	Unlimited deduction for mortgage interest on primary homes; other interest capped at $5,000	Unlimited deduction for mortgage interest on first and second homes; other interest limited	Unlimited deduction for mortgage interest on first and second homes; no deduction for consumer interest	Unlimited deduction for mortgage interest on first and second homes; no deduction for consumer interest; other limits

(Appendix continues)

Appendix (continued)

Provision	Existing Law[a]	Bradley-Gephardt[b]	Treasury I[c]	Treasury II[d]	House Bill[e]	Senate Bill[f]	Tax Reform Act[g]
Fringe benefits	Employer-paid health and life insurance not taxed	Employer-paid health and life insurance taxed or limited	Tax-free health benefits capped; life insurance taxed	Basic health benefits taxed; life insurance taxed	Employer-paid health and life insurance not taxed	Employer-paid health and life insurance not taxed	Employer-paid health and life insurance not taxed
Capital gains	60% exclusion; 20% top effective rate	No exclusion; 30% top rate	No exclusion; 35% top rate	50% exclusion; 17.5% top rate	42% exclusion; 22% top rate	No exclusion; 27–33% top rate	No exclusion; 28–33% top rate
Alternative minimum tax	20% for individuals; 15% for corporations	No minimum tax	No minimum tax	Minimum tax revised and expanded	25% for corporations and individuals; expanded coverage	20% for corporations and individuals; expanded coverage	20% for corporations; 21% individuals; expanded coverage
Corporate tax rates	5 brackets; 46% above $100,000	30% tax rate	33% tax rate	15–25% up to $75,000; 33% above	15–30% up to $75,000; 36% above	15–30% up to $75,000; 33% above	15–30% up to $75,000; 34% above
Investment tax credit	Yes (6–10%)	Repealed	Repealed	Repealed	Repealed	Repealed retroactively	Repealed retroactively

	3–19 year recovery with accelerated writeoffs	Replaced ACRS with economic depreciation	Replaced ACRS with true economic depreciation; indexed	4–28 year recovery period; indexed for inflation	3–30 year recovery period; partially indexed	Accelerated depreciation; longer recovery for property	Accelerated depreciation; longer recovery for property
Depreciation	3–19 year recovery with accelerated writeoffs	Replaced ACRS with economic depreciation	Replaced ACRS with true economic depreciation; indexed	4–28 year recovery period; indexed for inflation	3–30 year recovery period; partially indexed	Accelerated depreciation; longer recovery for property	Accelerated depreciation; longer recovery for property
Business expenses	Deductible	Deductible	No entertainment deduction; limit on meals	No entertainment deduction; limit on meals	80% deduction for meals and entertainment	80% deduction for meals and entertainment; no miscellaneous deductions	80% for meals and entertainment; others limited
Tax exempt bonds	Most interest excluded	Private purpose bonds taxed	Private purpose bonds taxed	Private purpose bonds taxed	Private purpose bonds capped or taxed	Some private purpose bonds capped or taxed	Private purpose bonds capped and taxed

Sources: Tax Notes, December 10, 1984, 991–1000; and *1986 Congressional Quarterly Almanac* (Washington: Congressional Quarterly Inc., 1987), 492–93.

a As of 1986.

b First introduced August 5, 1982.

c Publicly released November 27, 1984.

d Proposed May 28, 1985.

e Passed December 17, 1985.

f Passed June 24, 1986.

g Signed October 22, 1986.

Index